Discovering Music

Discovering Music

FOURTH EDITION

HOWARD D. McKINNEY
Rutgers University

W. R. ANDERSON
London Musical Times

AMERICAN BOOK COMPANY *New York*

Acknowledgments

Grateful acknowledgment is made to the following publishers and individuals for permission to reprint material which is in copyright or of which they are the authorized publishers:

Ernest Newman and the London *Sunday Times* for quotations from Newman's critical articles.

New Yorker Magazine and Dr. Irwin Edman for quotations from "Varieties of Musical Experience."

G. Schirmer, Inc. for thirteen measures from Roy Harris' *Third Symphony* (copyright 1939).

Charles Scribner's Sons for selection from *Arabian Nights Entertainment* by William Ernest Henley.

Basil de Selincourt for extracts from his concert-program notes.

Prelude

This book has been written with a double purpose: (1) to guide the uninitiated traveler who would embark upon a journey into the complex land of music; and (2) to be a Good Companion to those who, having already set sail, have made some discoveries for themselves and are eager to shape their course towards wider worlds.

The ability to "listen" to music rather than merely to "hear" it is not, as such, a natural capacity, but one that has to be acquired and developed by active, continual, and highly pleasurable observation. The power to cultivate this listening skill varies as does any other human accomplishment, but no cultivation is possible without guidance.

The principles used in the preparation of this guidebook have been shaped out of extended experience rather than fashioned out of theories. We believe that the greatest incentive for embarking upon voyages of artistic discovery should be the pleasure that one can derive from them. Housman has said that the nature of such arts as poetry and music is more physical than intellectual; it is the sense of delight that can be obtained from reading a poem, or looking at a picture, or listening to good music that attracts and holds us. It is this yielding of delight that will lead us on in a search for other wonders. Art educates in the proportion that it gives pleasure. We have shaped our treatment along sound pedagogical lines, and have proceeded from the known to the unknown; it will be found that we have placed the points of departure in familiar and interesting territory.

Some books of this nature are based upon the traditional educational process of starting at the earliest times and working up to the present. Others begin at the present and work as faithfully backwards. In the course of the treatment, they too often give historical and technical information as to how music has been put together, and how it can best be listened to so as to recognize its formal structure, but pay insufficient attention to the actual cultivation of the reader's enjoyment and enthusiasm. Our method is to begin with the everyday musical experiences that are both real and satisfying, and use these as stimuli and points of departure for further artistic development. That is why we have not kept to strict chronological order. This arrangement of material has been found useful in giving students, in a year's work, a realization of their own capacity for participating in the world's heritage of musical experience. The authors believe it will prove equally useful in the hands of the general reader who has had no formal musical training.

We have felt that a book planned along these lines must be more than just a history of music or a dictionary, although it should contain much historical material and include a glossary of musical terms in common use. Impressed by the cultural value of music, still insufficiently recognized, we have constantly associated musical ideas with those of other arts. Though it is impossible, in a book of reasonable size, fully to develop these comprehensive ideas, enough has been given, it is hoped, to show how music can take its proper place in civilized life. As part of the life of its period, music, like everything that has contributed to growth, can be analyzed and reasoned about and its existence justified. Through such processes its nature and influence can be understood.

We think that most books try to do too much, and especially to tell too much. Telling does not go far in music — doing and discovering are so much more important. Talking about music is of very little value unless one hears it, too; so we have discussed musical works that are constantly to be listened to, these progressing from the easily understood compositions to the more abstract — a logical outcome of the emphasis on enjoyment as the chief end of listening. We have taken most of the illustrations from the repertoire of phonographically recorded music. Thus laymen, teachers, and students will have in their hands lists of the finest material upon which to build a good library of records.

In our discussions, we have used ordinary technical terms, as far as they were necessary; surprisingly few of them are needed. When they are necessary, however, it seems foolish to go out of the way to avoid them. If anyone is interested enough in a subject to study a book of this sort, he will learn its vocabulary quickly enough, and be pleased to call a thing by its right name. We have not tried to make this a critical book, though we hope that its readers will get out of it a great deal that will broaden and strengthen their critical judgment. If all of the music mentioned herein is not immediately liked, the student will find out why this is so, and thus gain valuable knowledge.

The subject matter has been arranged in a manner suitable for presentation in class form, and appropriate topics for further discussion along similar lines have been furnished at the end of each chapter. Suggestions for further reading have likewise been made, and the reader who follows these will find himself possessed of a great fund of information which will be of inestimable value in the development of his listening powers.

Acknowledgment must be made of the help that has been received from various sources, especially the members of the "music-appreciation" courses who have proved the value of this material in actual use over a period of years. F. Austin Walter has helped in preparing and copying different sections; Wilbert B. Hitchner and the teachers who co-operated with him have shown the effectiveness of this method of treatment for high-school pupils. A word of appreciation is also due those authors and publishers who have given permission to quote from their works.

Prelude to the Second Edition

The use of this book over a period of some years and in widely varying circumstances has suggested the changes and additions made in this new edition. A number of new chapters containing additional information and musical examples have been added; but the fundamental method of approach to the subject, a method that has proved itself time and time again in practice, has not been altered.

Owing to the exigencies of war, the cordial co-operation and constant consultation that made the first edition of *Discovering Music* so successful have not been possible in preparing this second edition. While I must be held responsible for most of the changes and additions that have been made, this new volume goes forth on its mission with the fond hopes of both authors for its continued usefulness in its important field.

HOWARD D. MCKINNEY

Prelude to the Third Edition

In this third edition the authors are happy to have resumed again full co-operation, incorporating the results of further experience through using the book in daily teaching.

A great deal of fresh matter has been added, and the contents have been re-arranged to make the work still more effective. The basic course material consists of the numbered chapters; from time to time will be found "Interchapters" containing supplementary information which will be valuable for study by those readers who wish for still further enlightenment.

HOWARD D. MCKINNEY
W. R. ANDERSON

Prelude to the Fourth Edition

The opportunity of further increasing the usefulness of this book in a fourth edition enables us to include a number of new features, besides enlarging and extending those which experience has proved valuable to a wide diversity of students. The order of some chapters has been altered, many more music-type examples have been included, and the whole book brought up-to-date. The only way a book of this kind can be kept alive is through experience gained in the classroom and many of its improvements have been suggested by colleagues actively engaged in teaching courses in music appreciation throughout the country. We gratefully acknowledge their help and inspiration.

HOWARD D. MCKINNEY
W. R. ANDERSON

Table of Contents

CHAPTER 1

The Place of Art

≼ફ ફ≽

BEAUTY AND THE LIFE OF TODAY

In an article which appeared recently on the feature page of an American newspaper, a thoughtful reporter, who had spent a good deal of time wandering about the Old World enjoying and admiring the beauty left behind by the genius of the past, asked the very practical question "Of what use is beauty in the world?" We can make this question more specific. In a period inclined to see beauty in the machinery that performs its daily work, in factories that provide its money, or in skyscrapers that house thousands of its workers, of what use is an understanding and appreciation of the beauty of paintings, statues, mosaics, churches, palaces, or the literature and the music of the past? A number of years ago, John Ruskin said that the most beautiful things in the world are the most useless. The modern reaction to this would probably be the ingenuous question asked by a modern factory manager: "Well, if beautiful things haven't any use, what good *are* they?"

Our newspaperman feels that the development of taste is the only use of beauty in this world. The more one learns to appreciate the beautiful, he says, the more he will avoid and despise the ugly. A man cannot learn really to like Shelley and Keats, Goethe and Shakespeare, and at the same time continue to read pulp-paper confession magazines. If a man becomes enthusiastic about the music of Beethoven or Brahms, he loses his taste for much of the music turned out by Tin Pan Alley. An understanding of and a liking for the works of Michelangelo, Rembrandt, Da Vinci, or El Greco are the best possible antidotes for the cheapness and vulgarity of many present-day examples of the representative arts.

"All right," you may say, "granted all this, what then?" Is the person who spends his time cultivating his taste more content than the one who is concerned only with the beautiful things of life? Does the man who can see beauty in a field of daffodils or in an Alpine sunrise or in "that loveliest of trees, the cherry hung with bloom along the bough" enjoy life more than the man who derives his pleasure from reading favorable reports of a company in which he has invested or from the financial pages of his newspaper during a rising market? The hard-headed newspaperman says that he does. The observant reporter wonders if the modern concern with usefulness is not thoroughly idiotic and suicidal, and if the world would not be better off if it cultivated a sense of abstract beauty and gave *usefulness* a good rest. If the admiration—he goes so far as to say the adoration—of beauty can develop our taste to the point where we can learn to appreciate it to the full, he is sure that the avenues of life's enjoyment will become wider—that we will find more joy in life, and without additional expense.

AN AMERICAN CULTURAL CRISIS

The development of taste would help meet the alarming crisis which we are facing today in American cultural life; a crisis that, because it is not so obvious, could be even more dangerous than those political or social crises with which we constantly live. Keen observers of our national scene have said that we are living in the midst of a society which has been developed, technically and ideologically, for the satisfaction of the practical demands of a rapidly swelling population—food, clothing, transportation, labor-saving devices, and, above all else, entertainment. We live in an environment in which a wide gap exists between the richness of our private life and the poverty of our public interests, between high physical-comfort standards within our homes and low spiritual standards outside them. Indeed, in the midst of a period whose unequalled wealth, technical improvements, and potentialities for leisure achievement have made the acquisition of decent taste possible, we seem to manifest on a massive scale, a tendency toward crass, ugly taste and in-artistic, vulgar expression.

As a nation we devote an enormous amount of time to the systems of mass communication developed in our radio, television, movies, and recordings. In fact, we spend more time with these than with any of our other activities, with the exception of sleep. Experts estimate that television alone consumes as much as a fifth of an average American's family life. At the midpoint of this century, comic books sold more than a billion copies a year at a cost of over a hundred million dollars—four times the budget for all our elementary and secondary schools. The movies and television reproduction of films reach an unbelievable number of people each week. Yet, with all this activity in the communications industry, there has been little increase in the regard of our people for the fruits of learning and art, in respect for those who produce them, or in understanding that these activities are of inestimable value in raising the cultural level of a great nation.

While this crisis in our culture may be obvious to only a few of our citizens, it is a crisis, nevertheless, and a serious one. As history shows clearly enough, no great nation can be said to be worth imitating or following if it has not achieved a high level of culture. If we continue along the path upon which we have embarked, it is at least questionable whether we as a nation will ever achieve this position.

THE LASTING QUALITY OF ART

What is to be done? If the peripatetic reporter had been more of a philosopher, he might have realized that what he called the cultivation of a sense of beauty is only one of a number of "useless" human pursuits which contribute to the development of taste and so to a better and more rewarding life. One of these pursuits is a study of philosophy—the attempt to comprehend reality through the consideration of the relationships between things and ideas, faith and reason, human nature and political power. Another is the cultivation of one's spiritual and imaginative powers through religion—the adoration and service of a higher power of some sort and an attempt to understand its commandments. A third, possibly inclined to be overdeveloped today, is the study of science—that is, the perception of accuracy, the investigation of physical laws, and the development of the practical apparatus necessary for living. All these are important in the education of a complete, social being, ready to undertake his responsibilities in life and equipped to get the most out of living it.

Not the least of the varied activities necessary for a complete life in a difficult world is an understanding of art, the activity by which man, in all the years he has lived in the world, has communicated his experiences and transformed the things he has used into what we call *beauty*, thus making the world a pleasanter place. Valid reasons have often been advanced for maintaining that the knowledge and experience to be gained from a study of the artistic activities of man is really superior to other kinds of historical knowledge. The German philosopher Schopenhauer said that only art essentially aims at showing us life and things as they are in truth; these, because of the mist of objective and subjective contingencies, cannot be directly discovered by everyone. As the age-old aphorism has it:

> *All passes; Art alone*
> *Enduring stays to us.*

In its widest and most significant conception, art has not been concerned merely with the skillful making of things or their creation for practical use. The artist—the man who creates these manifestations of beauty which have no seeming value—produces a building, a piece of furniture, a ceramic plate, a poem, or a symphony as a means of communicating to us something which concerns nature, man, or the truth about life and existence. What he tells us, if we but learn to understand it, may be as valuable as or, indeed, more valuable than what we learn from philosophy or science. Only when we begin to realize that art is a knowledge equal and parallel to the other means by which man learns to understand his place in the world, do we perceive its importance.

The saying that "art is long and time is fleeting" is simply a terse expression of the idea that art endures far beyond the confines of any single human being. Because it contains within itself the real meaning of human existence, it has endured beyond all the other accomplishments of mankind—systems of religion, social and economic societies, scientific theories and achievements. Thus art has a very special value, and its message is of particular and unusual significance. In the words of the French poet and novelist Théophile Gautier:

> All things return to dust
> Save beauties fashioned well.
> The bust
> Outlives the citadel.
>
> The gods, too, die, alas!
> But deathless and more strong
> Than brass
> Remains the sovereign song.
> —Translated by Santayana

CHAPTER 2

The Co-operating Beginner

᪻᪻

WHAT IS ART?

In a book on the interrelation of the various activities which we call the arts—music, literature, painting, as well as the more practical arts of wood carving or furniture designing—Thomas Monroe observes that it is possible to distinguish at least twenty-two different meanings of the term *art*.[1] Most of these are based on the concept of skill. For our purpose we will define by suggesting that art *is* a skilled way of making or doing something which results in the creation of beauty and order and, in addition, serves as a kind of language. This language is not of the ordinary variety, but one able to express feeling, sentiment, and emotion, as well as to communicate personal and social experience.

Since it is a language of intuition and perception, capable of being understood without having to be translated into terms of reason, art can express the inner nature of life and existence without providing statements which are permanent and "true" for all time. We do not learn the ordinary truths of everyday life from art. If we did, photography would be the greatest of the representative arts, displacing painting as a means of expressing what the artist wishes to communicate. The artist creates an image of the world out of his imagination, an image that does not seek to *approximate* truth, in the manner of the scientist but, rather, seeks to *exalt* truth. Every great work of art—a symphony, a poem, or a painting—creates the

[1] *The Arts and Their Interrelations.* New York: The Liberal Arts Press, 1949.

6

world's image through producing and organizing beauty rather than through reflecting on the phenomena of its existence or the behavior of its inhabitants. It transfigures humanity in a way that glorifies life rather than one which attempts to portray its reality. For this reason if for no other, a life which is able to apprehend art is not only a more beautiful but also a better life. This is the predominant motive for including the appreciation of art in any program for fully educating the young.

THE COMMUNICATION OF ART

When the creator produces what we call art, the results are not necessarily transcendent or surpassing. The experience which the artist undergoes or the truth which he has been able to apprehend may be of such universal stature that a Goethe's *Faust* or a Beethoven symphony is produced; or it may be so limited that the results are nothing more significant than a homespun quilt or a newspaper column. The only requirement is that they must do honor to life and afford a satisfactory image of what it can and should mean.

Through his technical powers the artist reports his experiences and expresses his ideas. The better the technique, the more orderly and beautiful is his expression and, usually, the clearer his communication. The greater the treasure of wisdom upon which he draws, the more universal his concept and the more important his utterance.

It is not always realized that those who would understand the communication of the artist must co-operate to make his message comprehensible. Everyone who reads a poem, looks at a picture, or listens to a symphony experiences only as much as his capacity and culture admits. The necessity for the co-operation of the beholder arises from the fundamental fact that a work of art produces its effect through the imagination. The effect will depend on the imagination of the beholder, as well as the imagination of the creator. If the beholder's power of imagery is poor, or lacking entirely, the work of art will have little or no consequence. If, through inherent capacity, experience, or education, imagination can animate or arouse the beholder, the communication becomes significant. Moreover, the best art is too spiritual to be given directly to the senses, as Schopenhauer says in his fine essay on *Art and the Art of Music*, it must be "born in the imagination of the beholder, although begotten by the work of art."[2] For this reason the preliminary sketches of a painter are often more revealing and communicative than the finished picture, and the well-sculptured figure of a great hero is more inspiring and effective than a real photograph or wax dummy.

There are many different forms which the created communication of the artist can take. Generally speaking, they may be classified into the *useful arts*, such as carpentry, cooking, or organ building, and the *fine arts*—architecture, sculpture, painting, literature, and music. The useful arts are the consequence of necessity and craftsmanship, the fine arts, of superabundance and imagination. Philosophers down through the ages have had a wonderful time attempting to classify the different kinds of art. Without trying to emulate them, we may say that, of all the arts, music is the most universally attractive and the most readily apprehensible to the average man. It speaks to us in a language entirely its own, a language in which the inner nature of all life and existence expresses itself. Unconcerned with specific thoughts and exact ideas, music can speak to us with a force and power readily understood by all who have learned to listen to it. Concerned so largely with emotion, it is the ideal means of transmitting the experiences of a sensitive artist directly to a responsive listener.

MUSIC FOR ITS OWN SAKE

We have become so accustomed to presuming that music is an essential part of our everyday lives that only in moments of reflection and introspection do we become fully conscious of its tremendous power. The average person seems to think of music always as a means to something else—to reading, to relaxation, perhaps to nothing more important than passing the time. Music is generally considered merely an amenity rather than something that is satisfying in its own right, something that can dominate our whole lives, possess our whole beings. There is nothing in listening to music,

[2] Arthur Schopenhauer, *The World as Will and Idea*. Bk. III, Supplement, Ch. 34 and Bk. III, Sec. 52 (1819). Reprinted in *Readings in Philosophy*, New York: Barnes & Noble, 1950.

according to popular conception, other than placing ourselves under its sway—sitting quietly and letting it flow through our consciousness. We may receive some vague sort of emotional thrill from it, or we may be interested in the mannerisms of the pianist as he forges his way through some intricately difficult passages. We may be entertained by this bit of music because it reminds us of an army on the march, or because it suggests a May morning in the country, the wind in the trees, a rippling brook, a crowded square in an Oriental city, or whatever our imagination may be able to suggest. We are not greatly concerned if we do not like what we have heard, for there is plenty of music with pleasing tunes and vigorous rhythms, without bothering about this difficult music of the classics.

There seems to be little need for considering music other than as something to be enjoyed—and by "enjoyed" the average person means something to be whistled, hummed, or danced to. It may be used as a means of spending time when there is nothing better to do, or as a background for some other activity. What could be better than some music on the radio as an accompaniment for luncheon, a bridge game, or for the quiet moments available to the businessman as he peruses his evening paper?

Perhaps our average hearer may be inveigled into going to a concert because some internationally known star is to sing or play, or (if he is honest enough to admit it) for no more serious reason than that it has become the fashionable thing to do. He rarely thinks of music as something to be listened to seriously and enjoyed for its own sake.

Certainly there is a type of music so light and "recreational" that we need have no compunction in talking or playing bridge through it, and concert-going may have certain pleasures other than purely musical ones. But the great music is of a different kind. Lawrence Gilman tells of a philosopher who, during the time he was occupied in reading his favorite subject, became white as a sheet. Are there listeners who feel as intensely about such music? We often make the statement that a person is "passionately fond of music." Is he really? As Gilman pointedly asks, what does such an individual do with his music, or for it? "Will he forgo leisure, forget his meals, face poverty? Will the blood leave his face after he has spent an hour with Beethoven's *Appassionata*?"

HOW LISTENERS DEVELOP

The reader of this book, by the very fact that he has enough interest in music to want to know how to get more out of it than he does at present, knows that there are people, plenty of them, who realize the tremendous potential powers of music. In their lives music is a factor far above that of mere social amenity, even though perhaps an hour with Beethoven does not make any great disturbance in their vasomotor system. These fortunate ones seem to have acquired a technic by which they are able to get something from music that is not perceived by the average person. They seem to have found some sort of touchstone that brings them closer to the infinite. What is this technic that enables the individual to train himself so that he can hear things others miss? Is there really a means by which the initiate into the mysterious art of listening gets more from music than the man in the street, who knows nothing about it except "what he likes"?

If there is any doubt in the reader's mind as to the answers to such questions, let him talk to someone to whom the art of music has become indispensable, overpowering, imperative—someone who has learned to enjoy intelligently such music as the Bach *Passacaglia*, Brahms' *First Symphony*, or Debussy's *Pelléas et Mélisande*. A music lover will tell the inquiring listener that his appreciation of such music is a treasure which he values the more because he has not always possessed it; that he has come through the gradual, cumulative process of learning to understand what the composer has put into music, a process of acquiring ears to hear. If the man who possesses these great treasures of music is honest, he will admit that the music of Bach and Brahms and Debussy has not always meant to him what it means to him now; that at one time in his listening career he preferred the romantic harmonies and colorful suggestiveness of Tchaikovsky's *1812 Overture* or Grieg's *Peer Gynt*.

Then he will go on to tell how, when this more obvious kind of music had yielded him everything it possessed, when he had learned to recognize the reasons for its popular appeal and to realize its weaknesses, he of necessity passed on to works of greater scope and more general significance. New composers were taken up, men whose music was somewhat more reticent in revealing the secrets of its beauty but possessed greater universality of content and emotion and was more skillfully constructed. This music was in turn enjoyed, its particular excellencies recognized, its shortcomings noted. The process was repeated, and the conquest was extended to type after type of music, until the music lover came into the realm of the immortal composers. Here, no matter how much he may hear of their music or how eagerly he may try to solve the riddle of their beauty of utterance, no matter how often he reacts to the intellectual and emotional stimuli of their music or how great is the satisfaction he obtains from it, there is always something in reserve. There is something beyond the reaches of his searching, an inexhaustible supply of beauty ready to satisfy any demands which may be made upon it. He has at last "arrived" and is ready to understand the finest things in music, fully equipped to share the spiritual contributions of its greatest composers.

All this is not to say that a process such as this has necessarily been consciously directed. Hearing a great deal of music, the student has subconsciously chosen what happened to be best suited to his particular stage of development, letting the rest go by. The process has of necessity been a slow one, and there have been many "blind spots"—things which have not been clear to him as he progressed. Some of these may always remain, for nobody can appreciate everything; it is not often worthwhile to try, though we can always enlarge our range of sympathy and understanding if we want to. Any man can improve his taste, and that, as we have said, is the important thing—the thing that will bring joy into our lives. We should lay ourselves open to *quality* in general and give all reputable composers a good trial. Frank Roscoe has a good saying: "Education is more a matter of infection than injection." If we expose ourselves to the infection of great music, we are bound to catch it.

Some may start with an enthusiasm for jazz or popular music. This is quite natural, since these types of music make an instant, immediate appeal by their obvious melodies and striking rhythms. A rather strait-laced educator has alleged that this kind of music is actually for adolescents—real or retarded—who use it not as art but as a sex stimulant. There is, of course, much more to it than that: such music has quite legitimate uses as a relaxation or, like tobacco, as a mild anodyne. We will have to agree, however, that this type of popular music is not a foundation on which to build a real sense of appreciation. Its rhythmic monotony (necessitated by its special purpose), its brief themes, its repetitiousness, its lack of what we will come to recognize as *development*, and its frequently poor structure—all mark this as "side-issue music," not very useful as a basis for developing the taste of the amateur.

With some native ability and a willingness to keep his ears open and his mind free, the ambitious listener might better start from the level of Chopin's melodious lyricism, Grieg's northern elegiacs, or Tchaikovsky's gorgeous colorfulness. The problems of his musical evolution will quickly solve themselves if he has the opportunity to hear many performances of fine music and receives some hints as to how he can co-operate in the process of listening to them.

LIST OF SUGGESTED MUSIC

Here are three examples, in order of complexity, which illustrate how simple it is to begin the adventure of listening. Listen to them carefully, noting the points made in the descriptions, and you will be on your way. Then listen to the Brahms movement, without trying to follow it too closely, to hear what the biggest music sounds like.

Peer Gynt Suite No. 1, "Morning Mood"[3]   GRIEG

Probably no single piece of music better illustrates what a talented, imaginative composer can do with the simplest material. This whole piece consists of a manipulation of one idea. Try to detect its repetitions, changes of pitch, and differing orchestrations.

Strings

The Nutcracker, "Waltz of the Flowers"   TCHAIKOVSKY

Here there is a more elaborate musical structure. After a section which, with its sweeping harp passages, is obviously introductory, a number of definite sections are heard, each of them built out of a separate musical idea. Then comes a conclusive passage, suggestive of all the sections, which rounds out and completes the structure as

[3] Excerpt reprinted by permission of G. Schirmer, Inc., New York. Copyright 1922.

a whole. The good tunes and attractive rhythms make this very easy to listen to.

Romeo and Juliet, Overture-Fantasia   TCHAIKOVSKY

This is much more complicated and is typical of the manner in which larger pieces are put together. Written when its composer was only twenty-nine, it tells one of the great love stories of all time. It should arouse in every listener all the creative imagination he possesses. Note that there are three sections, widely different in mood and emotional content. The first, which begins the piece, is quiet, sustained, of a definitely religious nature, and built upon this theme:

The second section, the body of the piece, agitated and calm by turns, is built of two contrasting themes. An energetic one with full orchestral tone suggests violence and may be thought of as representing the strife between the families of Shakespeare's young protagonists.

The second theme, introduced after a marked change in color and mood, is gracious, expressive, and suggestive of the lovers.

These themes of the second section are elaborated, developed, and interspersed with references to the introductory theme from the first. The composer builds up tremendous excitement and tension but never goes beyond material from the original musical ideas. At

the end of this section, the strife and love themes, a little more elaborately expressed, are heard again. At the very end of the piece, sustained and reflecting the moods of the beginning and the love theme, comes the third section, as a sort of Epilogue. Thus the composer rounds out his musical scheme to correspond to the poetic idea—the program—of his piece.

Symphony No. 1, in c minor, First Movement   BRAHMS

An ardent admirer of this symphony characterizes its composer as follows: "Brahms does not dazzle, but is true and lasting; he stands like a rock in the welter of strife, of problems and experiments, and holds out his hand to all those who strive toward what is great and noble, regardless of sensation."

TOPICS FOR DISCUSSION

Comment on your own experience as a music lover. At what level of experience did you begin, and where have you now arrived?

How much has music been an active influence in your own liberal education? Has the music been serious or light?

Is there any circumstance in which it is legitimate to have music without attending to it?

The famous novelist Sir Compton Mackenzie writes his books to the accompaniment of phonograph records of good music, using them as a kind of stimulus. What do you consider to be the effect of this use of music? How would you distinguish between this definitely productive effect and the influence of music on the performance of household tasks, for example?

Music has been used occasionally as a semi-anesthetic in operations. What would you suppose the process might be? How would it be done?

CHAPTER 3

Why We Like Music

ತ§ಿಲ

The best reason in the world for undertaking the study of a subject is the natural liking and aptitude we may have for it. Although we may not be able to explain why, most of us are conscious of the fact that we do have a liking and a certain amount of aptitude for music. Someone has well called it the most universal avocation, the thing we most naturally turn to for a hobby when we would have our attention diverted from our usual pursuits. Most people think of music in this way and are quite indifferent to the more significant role it might play in their lives, although they react instinctively and naturally to this art in ways that are different from their ordinary experiences.

In an attempt to account for our natural liking for music, a well-known psychologist, Carl E. Seashore, who spent the most fruitful years of his long professional career in the study of music and its action on the human consciousness, wrote a little book called *Why We Love Music*.[1] In it he gives a sort of natural history of the psychological origin and development of our love for music by examining its objects and motives. We can profitably study what Seashore says because he probably knew as much about the subject as anyone. In simple terms, the reasons for our liking music are these:

MORALE: PHYSICAL AND SPIRITUAL

We like music because it instills in us a sense of physical and

[1] Philadelphia: Oliver Ditson Co., Inc., 1941.

emotional well-being. We seem to be endowed with a mechanism that reacts and responds to *sounds* without any conscious effort on our part. This mechanism involves not only the central nervous system, which controls the actions of our muscles and our senses, but also the autonomic nervous system with its regulation of internal secretions which affect all our emotional reactions. Experiments have shown that sound can directly affect such physical functions as the circulation of the blood, digestion, hunger, and thirst, as well as the psychological experiences of pleasure and pain.

Thus do the scientists explain our natural physical and emotional response to such sounds as the blare of trumpets or the sweetness of violins. Other considerations quite aside, the purely physical effect of the hundred members of an orchestra playing in full accord and the stirring strains of a good military band as it leads a regiment in parade are important factors in our lives; we are aroused and enlivened by some sound combinations, quieted and dispirited by others. This natural reaction of our organism to sound underlies all our musical experience; we are not capable of controlling these responses, and without them music would lose a great deal of its natural appeal.

FROM ANOTHER WORLD

Another, and very important, reason for our liking music is the fact that its domain is so largely outside our ordinary world, its field of operation so entirely beyond sensory impressions and physical reactions. We may not be able to help reacting to music physically, but our greatest enjoyment comes from the fact that its world is so largely one of memory, imagination, and feeling. In the midst of a humdrum, practical, pressing world which badgers and confuses, music takes us outside ourselves, transports us, as nothing else can, into another existence. In listening to intricate and refined manipulation of tonal resources such as we find in Delius' *Over the Hills and Far Away*, we do respond, certainly, to physical sensuousness and tonal allure, but what haunts our minds and captures our spirits is this music's imaginative, otherworldly atmosphere, its peculiar blend of a reminder of things that exist best in the memory, and its suggestion of things that have never existed at all.

Thus music possesses us as does a dream; it lives within us as something entirely apart from material and tangible experiences; its appeal is heightened by the fortunate necessity of its indefiniteness. All the other arts are conditioned by the physical means which they employ. The writer is naturally limited by the meaning of the words he must use, the painter or sculptor by certain exterior associations of the objects he represents. Music, based as it is on sound, has no need for any exact connotation or literal significance outside itself, and so it exists as the ideal means for communicating subjective concepts—that is, our feelings.

MUSIC AS PLAY

We like music also because it is an ideal form of play. Seashore reminds us that we are all really of the same age—born millions of years ago—and that, in spite of inhibitions and restraints developed through the centuries, we delight in play. It is in play that we get a definite and liberating sense of freedom, of creative power, of doing things purely for the joy of achievement, without ulterior motive or designed effect. Moreover, play is a positive force, whose success, in strong contradistinction to the world about us, depends on our accepting its fictitious nature: "It rests upon make-believe; liberated from realities, it accepts the ideal and lives it as real."

All art is play, of course, but none of the other arts lends itself so ideally to fulfilling this psychological need as does music. The man singing lustily in his bath, somehow stimulated by the sound of running water to do his noisy best, a group of listeners under the sway of a great interpretation of a forceful piece of music, a dancer, stirred by the rhythmical excitement of the music, or perhaps lulled by its dreamy flow into an ecstasy of pleasure—all are playing in the ideal sense. Music furnishes them a medium for expressing themselves, for exhibiting their joy in living, their aspirations for the future, their nostalgia for the past, their desire for freedom, their love for action. This is one of the simplest and most direct of the charms which music possesses, and one of the reasons people turn "instinctively" to it for recreation.

THE ATTRACTION OF RHYTHM

We are strongly attracted to music because of its rhythm. By "rhythm" in music most of us mean but one thing—the regular pulse which we all feel in the flow of the music, the pulse that is marked by a regular recurrence of what we call a beat. Unless this is present we cannot sense music at all. All of us, even those barely able to distinguish one tune from another, seem to be able to learn to "hear with our feet"—to beat out the underlying rhythmic impulses of music.

Using the term in its wider sense, however, as meaning movement marked by a regular recurrence of certain features or elements, we find that there are many other rhythmic attributes of music to which we react. If you will turn to the picture of the arched doorway on page 95, you will find that certain features of this twelfth-century architecture are grouped to make maximum impression on the eye of the beholder. Note the alternation of the molding patterns over the arch, the balancing of the pillars on either side of the door (each with its own pattern of design), and the rhythmic effect of the huge hinge which supports the door. The human ear seems to demand some similar sense of grouping in what it hears. Thus, we find the composer grouping the musical ideas he uses—measures into phrases, phrases into sentences, sentences into still larger units—to make a unified yet varied rhythmic whole. We also demand certain dynamic rhythms (alternations of loud and soft) and timbre rhythms (alternations in the various tonal qualities) in the music we enjoy. All this gives us, without our being aware of it, perhaps, great listening pleasure and increases the satisfaction we derive from music.

The psychologist explains this by showing us what this rhythmic grouping does; it enables us to perceive more easily what we hear; it brings into relationship certain features that give a sense of balance and expanse to what we hear; it alternates stimulating and soothing influences which enrich and objectify our associations and tone up our whole organism. Seashore explains it well when he says that rhythm in music is a play within a play; the composer realizes the need for it, the performer makes us aware of it, and we react to it.

AN EXPRESSION OF EMOTION

Music has often been called the language of the emotions. While aestheticians may question the complete validity of such a statement, certainly a great deal of our pleasure and enjoyment in music comes from the fact that in its essence it expresses and embodies emotion.[2] In its truest sense, art is an "objectification or expression in a communicable form, of an artist's actual reaction to some stimulation or of his 'experience'."[3] In music, this stimulation or experience is likely to have been an emotional one, and thus one readily understood by us all. A great artist—Beethoven, for example—is moved by some profound personal experience; he reacts keenly to the sorrows and sufferings of humanity or to the personal awareness of a limitation of his physical powers. Through his ability, as a sensitive human being, to feel these emotions and as an artist to grasp their essence and objectify it in a medium by which it can be communicated to others, he produces great works of art—the *Eroica Symphony* and the *Symphony in c minor*.

It is a demonstrable fact that, of all the sensory mediums, tone is most closely associated with the emotions. Music thus becomes the ideal communicative medium for artists and the most purely emotional of all the arts. When we add to this the fact that music, to be intelligible to us, must be re-created by an interpreter—a third person who comes between us and the composer and, of necessity, adds his own emotional significance to what he plays—we realize the secret of music's great human appeal and its power in the lives of men.

In this sense we can say that music is a language of the emotions; it is at once both a message and a means of communication which puts creator, interpreter, and listener in the same world of experience.

MUSIC AND INTELLIGENCE

Intelligence also plays a strong role in music. We like music because we can learn to understand it as a thing in itself, can recognize how it is put together, how it proceeds from point to point, and how it reaches a climatic finish. Pride in such intellectual achievement is very human and lies directly at the base of all artistic interest. The ability to understand different art forms, to analyze the

[2] The psychologist defines an emotion as "any one of the states designated as fear, anger, disgust, joy, grief, surprise, yearning, etc."
[3] F. R. O'Neill, *The Relation of Art to Life*. London: Routledge.

ways by which the artist achieves his effects, to see the relationships between the different elements that make up the whole, to sense the affinity between the different arts—all these deepen our insight and increase our understanding of music, or painting, or architecture. Then too, there is the joy of acquiring interpretative skill in music, of learning to read those symbols left behind by the composers (the notes), of securing sufficient physical and mental agility to be able to play an instrument or to sing. These "glimpses into the vistas of unexplored resources" cannot but intensify our love, awe, and admiration for music as an art which, no matter how ardently we may try, can never be fully mastered.

THE POWERS OF SUGGESTION

A final reason we love music is that it tends to give some form of realization to our inmost dreams and longings, because it stands as a sort of symbolic suggestion of everything we desire, or believe in, or hope for. The listener tends, as Seashore says, "to live himself concretely into the feeling" suggested by the music. Most of us, as we listen, live realistically within the music insofar as the realm of interests allows. Such associations and suggestions may be enjoyed for their own sake; the listener is often inclined to forget the music entirely in the imaginative associations it stirs in his mind. The truest enjoyment, however, comes when these symbolic suggestions are somehow fused in their general meaning with the music which calls them to mind.

Let us take as a concrete example one of the most significant pieces of music ever written, a work that stands up magnificently through the years because of its quality as *music*, and yet which has probably as powerful, direct, and human an appeal as any other music in existence: Beethoven's *Fifth Symphony*. Anyone who is at all sensitive to music will come under the spell of this work, for there is evident in it a titanic struggle, a wrestling with some of life's greatest problems, and a decision as to some of life's deepest meanings. At once, without being aware of the mechanics of the process, we are apt to be diverted by all sorts of symbolic suggestions—the harshness and ruthlessness of life, the necessity for human struggle, the consolation beauty brings, the ominous precariousness of our existence, the exalted happiness that comes from surmounting difficulties. All these and many more may come to our minds as the music progresses. We realize that all the diverse forces of our lives are present in this music; it shows us as well as anything ever created by the mind of man that "we ourselves are our own Heaven and Hell." We can, and probably do, enjoy these associations for what they are themselves—a sort of work of art deserving of separate consideration—but not until they have become blended and fused in their general meaning with Beethoven's music do we realize their full impact. Not until we are conscious of how inextricably they are woven into the warp and woof of Beethoven's glowing fabric (a realization which comes only after considerable study; see Chapter 32) do we really enjoy this symphony.

So it is with all other types of music, whether they sound the note of joyous exaltation, religious fervor, or consuming passion. Sacred oratorios, dramatic operas, moving symphonies, even the small piano pieces—all make use of this fundamental power of music to "seize the individual for some form of dreamlike realization of the subjects of his longing." The professional musician tends to frown on this enjoyment of associations and images; to him music exists for its own meaning and beauty, and he hears it as a combination of note patterns, colors, rhythms, and so on. He consciously suppresses any of his own feelings, associations, and characterizations that the music might evoke and assumes a critical, analytical viewpoint, from which he surveys only its composition and structure. In so doing he may easily miss the real significance of the music, as does the untrained listener, for whom music's only appeal is through the associations it arouses.

The wise music lover avoids both extremes. But he must never forget, as Henri Bergson puts it, that "beneath the thousand rudimentary actions which are the outward and visible signs of an emotion, behind the commonplace conventional expression that both reveals and conceals our individual mental state," it is the emotion, the original mood, that composers attain and wish to communicate to us. "Beneath their joys and sorrows . . . they grasp something that has nothing in common with ordinary language, certain rhythms of life and breath that are closer to man than his inmost feelings, being the living law—varying with each individual—of his enthu-

siasm and despair, his hopes and regrets." To miss these aspects of
the reality of human experience revealed to us by a composer is to
miss the greatest significance of his music.

We will soon show that the fullest understanding of music depends on something more than natural tastes and aptitudes. One must
always remember that there are many degrees and levels of musical
understanding, and that we are not all capable of liking music to the
same extent and in the same way. The individual's attainments in
music depend not only on his innate capacity (which, of course,
differs greatly with different people), but also on his musical experience and training. This accounts for the wide divergences of opinion
that we hear expressed on every hand. Not many people are so
honest as Mark Twain:

> Huge crowd out tonight to hear the band play the *Fremersberg*! I
> suppose it is very low-grade music—I know it must be low-grade—
> because it so delighted me, moved me, stirred me, uplifted me, en-
> raptured me, that at times I could have cried, and at others split my
> throat with shouting. The great crowd was another evidence that it was
> low-grade music, for only the few are educated up to a point where
> high-class music gives pleasure. I have never heard enough classic music
> to be able to enjoy it, and the simple truth is I detest it. Not mildly, but
> with all my heart.
>
> What a poor lot we human beings are anyway! If base music gives me
> wings, why should I want any other? But I do. I want to like the higher
> music because the higher and better like it. But you see I want to like it
> without taking the necessary trouble, and giving the thing the necessary
> amount of time and attention. The natural suggestion is to get into that
> upper tier, that dress circle, by a lie—we will *pretend* we like it.

LIST OF SUGGESTED MUSIC

Listen to each of the following well-known compositions carefully. Referring to the reasons given in this chapter for our liking
music, try to decide why *you* like the music.

Gaîté Parisienne	OFFENBACH
España	CHABRIER
Symphony No. 6, in b minor (Pathétique), Last Movement	TCHAIKOVSKY
Water Music	HANDEL

Washington Post March   SOUSA

Fugue in g minor (Little)   J. S. BACH

Concerto in E flat Major, K. 482 (piano, orchestra)   MOZART

Swan of Tuonela   SIBELIUS

Music for Strings, Percussion, Celesta   BARTÓK

TOPICS FOR DISCUSSION

Imagine yourself at a gala concert of a world-famous orchestra. In looking over the festive and well-dressed audience, try to determine the percentage of those who came (a) because it was the thing to do; (b) to be included in the social and intellectual elite; (c) to satisfy their curiosity; (d) to be able to say that they had heard the orchestra under its famous conductor; (e) to learn something about music; (f) to really enjoy the music.

What gives people a love for good music? Do you consider inherited or consciously cultivated traits more common? Which do you consider most important?

Do you conceive of any means of evaluating a person's capacity to become a music lover? Do you know of any test for "music aptitude"? What do you believe would be the weaknesses of any such test? Could such a test be valid for non-performers?

CHAPTER 4

How We Like Music

ംട്ട്ട്ട്ട

APPRECIATION OF MUSIC

Strange as it may seem to a real music lover, there are people incapable of liking music; evidently Charles Lamb, the English essayist of the Romantic period, was one of these. You may remember his experiences as related in his *Essays of Elia* (1823-1833):

> It is hard to stand alone in an age like this (constituted to the quick and critical perception of all harmonious combinations, I verily believe, beyond all preceding ages, since Jubal stumbled upon the gamut), to remain, as it were, singly unimpressible to the magic influences of an art which is said to have such an especial stroke at soothing, elevating, and refining the passions. Yet, rather than break the candid current of my confessions, I must avow to you that I have received a great deal more pain than pleasure from this so cried-up faculty.
>
> I am constitutionally susceptible to noises. A carpenter's hammer, in a warm summer noon, will fret me into more than midsummer madness. But those unconnected, unset sounds are nothing to the measured malice of music. The ear is passive to those single strokes; willingly enduring stripes while it hath no task to con. To music it cannot be passive. It will strive—mine at least will—'spite of its inaptitude, to thread the maze; like an unskilled eye painfully poring upon hieroglyphics. I have sat through an Italian opera, till, for sheer pain, and inexplicable anguish, I have rushed into the noisiest places of the crowded streets, to solace myself with sounds which I was not obliged to follow, and get rid of the distracting torment of endless, fruitless, barren attention! I take refuge in the unpretending assemblance of honest common-life sounds; and the purgatory of the Enraged Musician becomes my paradise.
>
> I have sat at an oratorio (that profanation of the purposes of the

cheerful playhouse) watching the faces of the auditory in the pit (what a contrast to Hogarth's Laughing Audience!) immovable, or affecting some faint emotion, until (as some have said, that our occupations in the next world will be but a shadow of what delighted us in this) I have imagined myself in some cold Theatre in Hades where some of the *forms* of the earthly one should be kept up, with none of the *enjoyment*; or like that

> —Party in a parlor
> All silent, and all DAMNED.

Above all, those insufferable concertos, and pieces of music, as they are called, do plague and embitter my apprehension. Words are something; but to be exposed to an endless battery of mere sounds; to be long a-dying; to lie stretched upon a rack of roses; to keep up languor by unintermitted effort; to pile honey upon sugar, and sugar upon honey, to an interminable tedious sweetness; to fill up sound with feeling, and strain ideas to keep pace with it; to gaze on empty frames, and to be forced to make the pictures for yourself; to read a book, *all stops*, and be obliged to supply the verbal matter; to invent extempore tragedies to answer to the vague gestures of an inexplicable rambling mime—these are faint shadows of what I have undergone from a series of the ablest-executed pieces of this empty *instrumental music.*

Fortunately, there are few who have such intense feelings. Most of those who do not like music simply beg the question and protest: "It is all beyond me; music is too full of technicalities which I cannot understand. I know what I like, so why should I bother with trying to learn more about it?" A full response to music is the result of native capacity *plus* experience and training (which are so often wanting), and any device—for example, this book—which will increase our musical experience and train our musical reactions cannot but add to our enjoyment.

VARIOUS APPROACHES TO APPRECIATION

As Edwin Alden Jewell has said in an article on "Reaching the Man in the Street":

Art is beyond nobody who cares. Technicalities are but means employed by the artist in expressing what he has to say, and it is the expression that counts. Besides, once you have really *heard* what the artist has expressed, it is simple—and fascinating—to work back, step by step, through the technique. Thus may one share in the task of creation. And no one who has learned really to share in that can be thence-

forth indifferent. Learning to share and learning critically to dis-
criminate may well end in learning to love.[1]

Here is the crux of the whole matter. This is what is meant by
learning to "appreciate music." This expression has been criticized
for its ambiguity, since it can mean so many different things to so
many different people. But until a better one is invented, we must
continue to use it. *Appreciate* means, Webster says, "to set a just
value on; to esteem to the full worth of; to approve of; to be grateful
for; to be sensitive to the aesthetic values of." These are exactly the
meanings we give to this word in connection with music.

An appreciation of music covers a number of different factors
and can be gained in a number of different ways.

THE PERFORMANCE OF MUSIC

One of the commonest ways is through learning to *do* something
in music—to play an instrument or to sing. No one in his proper
senses would wish to deny the importance of the performing
amateur. Active participation in music gives a kind of interest that
can come in no other way; it fosters an admiration for and an understanding of the skill of a composer that can rarely be gained through
hearing alone. Amateur playing or singing is one of the most
pleasant and beneficial means of occupying leisure time, and it often
leads to a real knowledge and understanding of music. But there are
obvious dangers which have to be considered; anyone who has
observed at all carefully will have noticed that sometimes the process
of acquiring mental and physical dexterity and powers of co-ordination sufficient to perform music with any degree of facility weakens
the very thing that should above all else be developed—a love for
the music itself. What is more, the faculty of performing, once
acquired, often occupies the interest and attention of the player or
singer to the exclusion of attention to what he is playing or singing.
Too few singers, for instance, after they have spent years in acquiring a technic, know or care about the finest things in vocal literature
—the songs of Schubert, Franz, or Wolf. Too few pianists pay
much attention to the supreme things in piano literature unless they
happen to provide an abundant opportunity for exhibiting technical
prowess. There have been many movements for stimulating active

[1] *New York Times*, July 27, 1941.

participation in music in recent years—massed singing movements, choral and instrumental contests, and such—but the net result of all these activities, insofar as concrete gains in musical knowledge and consequent improvement in taste are concerned, are often dubious. A stimulation of activity does not always mean an attainment of worthwhile results; localities which have shown the greatest activity may exhibit the poorest taste in the music they have chosen to perform.

No, the ability to perform music does not provide an open sesame to an awareness of its beauty or an understanding of its message. If cultivated properly, performance is assuredly a stimulating and fructifying influence, but we must not confuse our issues here. The ability to perform music and a knowledge of and love for the best music are individual attainments, and the second is by no means always the consequent of the first.

Music's Rhythmic Appeal

The most natural approach to music is through its rhythmic appeal. As we will see later, rhythm is one of the most fundamental aspects of music. Even the unmusical person can usually feel the essential power of repeated rhythms—witness the present-day appeal of the drumbeats of the African savage or their more sophisticated modern counterparts, the rhythms of American jazz. It is obvious enough that the world-wide appeal of this type of music is due almost entirely to its strong rhythmic backgrounds. Learning to "hear with our feet" is easy, but we must realize that it is only one of a number of gateways through which we may enter into the beauties which music possesses.

Music as Sound

Another approach is through the development of the physical capacities by which we receive musical stimuli. Music is physically a matter of *sound*, and until we can learn to recognize its physical attributes clearly, we are certain to be more or less in the condition of the man who is blind and to whom any appreciation of painting is impossible. We have to learn to *listen*, in the literal sense: to hear accurately and acutely, to differentiate between the various pitch levels, to recognize various rhythmic patterns, melodic ideas, and so on. This is difficult and requires the greatest concentration on the part of the listener. It cannot be emphasized too strongly that it is *impossible to listen to music while doing something else.* With so much music available everywhere today, on records, radio, and television, it is almost inevitable that we hear rather than listen. Music is commonly used as a background for reading, study, and so on, without the hearer's awareness of it other than as an aural accompaniment of his personal activity. We must remember that it is necessary to concentrate on music itself in order to appreciate its particular qualities.

MUSICAL MEMORY

The listener should try to develop habits that will enable him to retain musical stimuli as meaningful musical ideas; once he has started to develop the powers of pitch discrimination, rhythmic recognition, and so forth, he must learn to relate them to the musical apparatus used by composers. He must be able to realize how creators of music combine various pitches into groups called chords and from these invoke the mysterious magic of harmony; how they weave complex musical fabrics out of a number of separate themes; how they relate various parts of their compositions to the whole. In short, the listener must learn to recognize the simple facts of musical construction—its grammar, structure, and form.

In doing this, his greatest help will come from the development of his musical memory. Music is unlike any other art in that it goes past us like a flash, and not every particular piece may be immediately available again. (Here, obviously, is the advantage of the phonograph.) One may stand before a piece of sculpture, the Parthenon, or a painting and take time to enjoy its details. But even if a piece of music is played over many times, one may not remember all its fine details; and from one hearing the less experienced listener, however eagerly he may desire to absorb it, may well come away baffled. Patience, time, and the cultivation of the memory—not only for tunes, but for what the composer does with them—for the structural logic of a musical work are needed. A symphonic movement may last a quarter of an hour or more; symphonies often last for fifty minutes, some of them even longer. It is obvious that only the impatient and thoughtless listener would expect to understand all such a work has to tell him even after two or three hearings. The best resource of all, undoubtedly, is the power to read the printed score, but we shall not presume that power to exist in our readers. We congratulate those who have cultivated or are cultivating this valuable exercise, and offer them every encouragement to persevere. The novice can soon make headway if he starts with simple scores. One of the best mottoes a group of musical amateurs could adopt would be: *Poco a poco*. If the music is worth our attention at all, it is worth being taken seriously, like any other study in which we seek to educate ourselves and by which we wish to make ourselves whole and balanced.

THE EMOTIONAL SIGNIFICANCE OF MUSIC

We must learn to recognize and apperceive the different emotional reactions engendered by music and to evaluate these in comparison with their other elements. This is a matter of nice discrimination and avoids the extremes of being completely absorbed and abjuring the emotional significance of music on the other. Music's effect on us is one of its important powers and should be neither overemphasized nor neglected.

THE COMPOSER'S EXPERIENCE

The listener should try to make the composer's experience his own, crystallizing it as definitely as possible so that he can seize it, reflect upon it, and even, perhaps, use it as the basis for an imaginative creativeness of his own. We have said that all art is communicative; we should prepare ourselves so that we stand ready on the receiving end, qualified to make part of our own experience whatever the music can give. The development of a certain ability to describe such experiences in words may help. When Charles O'Connell writes of Beethoven's *Fifth Symphony*, we know that he has made the music's experience his own.

> The bitterness and violence of this movement have no parallel in music. The sheer power that moves it, the utter logic and inevitableness and finality of this music almost remove it from the manipulations of the conductor; given instruments and knowing hands, it plays itself. Many a conductor has found that there is but one interpretation—Beethoven's—and *that* one speaks, rudely and clamorously and suffi-

ciently, for itself. This is an utterance of the supreme and ruthless ego, momentarily frustrated but unconquered, and it does not brook interference.[2]

EXTRA-MUSICAL MEANINGS

In music, sounds often have other-than-ordinary significance, and we should try to realize these special meanings—in other words, to learn to relate music to other experiences. This involves understanding such things as national idioms in music, certain qualities of musical atmosphere (the aesthetic tone or mood or harmony of effects in a work of art), and the like. When we argue whether Tchaikovsky's symphonies are or are not Russian in character, when we demonstrate, to our satisfaction at least, that Dvořák's *New World Symphony* has more of a Bohemian than American[3] flavor, or when we speak of Debussy's music as being impressionistic, we are relating music to experiences and ideas outside itself. As we progress we shall see how really important this single phase of musical understanding is.

MUSIC IN LIFE

Finally, we must relate music to other values of life. We should realize how it has developed historically, how it parallels other phases of man's development, what it stands for now, and what are its possibilities for the future. This historical aspect of music's development is a lengthy study in itself and involves much careful reading and patient listening, but it is absolutely necessary if we are to obtain anything like a proper perspective in listening. To know why and how Palestrina's *Missa Brevis* differs from Beethoven's *Missa Solemnis* is necessary to our appreciation of the qualities of these two different works. If we are to take any reasonable view of present-day developments in music, we must know how these have grown out of the past and how they point towards the future. Otherwise, we may become confused and lose our way altogether.

GOALS

These, then, should be our goals. The process of discovering

[2] Charles O'Connell, *Victor Book of the Symphony*. New York: Simon and Schuster, Inc., 1948.
[3] See Chapter 20.

music, we shall find, is nothing more or less than the process of becoming aware of the various aspects of music's rich and complex structure. The more we can make them a part of our intellectual and artistic experience, the deeper will be our understanding and the fuller our enjoyment of the music we hear.

Into all appreciation some degree of criticism must come. We shall not attempt to make this a specialty, but we should not forget that the real meaning of appreciation is to sum up, to strike a balance. There is a world of amusement, and much profit not yet gained, in the study of bad music, but, mercifully, we shall not pursue it—we are already overtaken by too much bad music every day. We suggest that stern criticism may well be left to mature with time and experience. As for "knowing what we like," we do our readers the courtesy of presuming that they are too wide-awake to mistake this for criticism. In the right man, it may be, but for Everyman it is usually no more a manifestation of artistic appreciation than is his preference for mustard over ketchup, or his dislike for olives or tomatoes.

It is a commonplace among music lovers that, in distinguishing among qualities—in even the mildest form of criticism—it is essential that we do not decry a work for failing to do what its composer did not set out to do. We do not blame the lightweight boxer for failing to stand up to the heavyweight champion or the butterfly for being apparently less industrious than the bee. Each works according to his nature. But an essential question must not be omitted here: Is what the composer is striving to do worth doing?

George Sampson, a discerning critic of literature, has a wise word on this: The good student is not to be taken in by novelties, or to be put off with accidentals. Confronted by the mass of Walt Whitman's work, with all its disconcerting irregularities and inequalities, he does not waste time by asking painfully and fruitlessly, Is this poetry? Is this prose? Is it both, or neither? He asks what is, after all, the real question for critics: Does this succeed artistically? In days when religion was decisively a part of life, there came suddenly to certain men rare moments when they felt strangely uplifted in spirit and moved beyond themselves. Such moments of ecstasy come also from the great creative arts of poetry and music. The moments that make you catch your breath, the moments in which you are carried beyond space and time, and feel as if the powers from afar had touched you with their wings—these supreme moments of beauty are, in plain terms, the moments of artistic success. To create such moments is the prerogative of the artist; to share them is a privilege of the humble receiver. Could we have a better ideal than that in our search for significance in the beauty of music?

LIST OF SUGGESTED MUSIC

The following are good examples of how the development of a musical memory will help you realize the real musical content of a piece.

Lohengrin, Prelude   WAGNER

Notice how this entire piece grows out of this single theme, heard high on the strings near the beginning and repeated at various descending and ascending pitch levels throughout the selection:

Make note also of the scale of dynamic changes from a very soft beginning to a big build up of the whole orchestra in the middle to a very quiet ending. The developments may be diagrammed in this way:

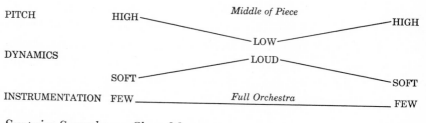

Surprise Symphony, Slow Movement   HAYDN

Here a musical idea is presented first in its simplest form and then differently, in a series of variations, without losing any of its own identity.

Theme:

In following the different presentations of this idea, we learn to listen with concentration to what is going on in the music; we learn to develop the power of musical memory as we constantly compare the new shapes of the theme with the old. The germs of the four variations are:

Eine kleine Nachtmusik (Serenade for Strings), K. 525   MOZART
Slow Movement—Rondo

This beautiful movement can be followed easily, if one keeps the
main theme in mind.

As the piece develops, other themes are interpolated:

but the first always returns in its original form and at its original
pitch level, as if to say, "Well, here I am again!" The scheme of the
rondo is A–B–A–C–A Coda. (The coda is simply a tail-piece or brief
closing section.)

Overture—The Year 1812   TCHAIKOVSKY

This has been called the world's noisiest overture. It was written
to celebrate a great event in Russian history—the repulsion of
Napoleon's armies. Try to work out its structural scheme. The
main themes are:

Symphony No. 5, in c minor, First Movement   BEETHOVEN

Reread O'Connell's paragraph on this (p. 29) and see how well his description fits the music. Again this movement is built up out of two contrasting themes, followed by a development section and then their restatement as at first. We shall have more to say about this particular "form" later.

TOPICS FOR DISCUSSION

Which of the various approaches to musical appreciation seems to you the most obvious for the average person who is entirely ignorant of music's scope? Which do you think the most important and influential?

Discuss the difference between literary and musical criticism. Which is more attractive? Why?

Why is vital, persuasive criticism of music difficult to produce? Can a very young critic be useful to his readers? Why?

What keeps many people from enjoying serious music? What do you think is the most direct remedy for any lack of appreciation of music?

What has brought about the enormous interest in jazz by even the most serious journalists? Is this beneficial or detrimental to the cause of serious music?

As an aid to remembering music heard, prepare a small card index or notebook and alphabetically record each composition you hear. A few comments on the characteristics of the music and composers may be added. Information about the composers may be found in a standard reference such as:

Percy Scholes, *The Oxford Companion to Music.*
The Everyman Dictionary of Music.
Pratt, *The New Encyclopedia of Music and Musicians.*
Thompson, *International Cyclopedia of Music and Musicians.*

CHAPTER 5

"Getting Behind" The Music

⋙ ⋘

ENJOYMENT, EMOTIONAL AND INTELLECTUAL

If one were rash enough to begin a catechetical inquiry into the subject of aesthetics, his first question might well be, "What is the chief end of art?", and the answer, "To be enjoyed—in the literal sense of the term, to give pleasure, to be delighted in." A painter plans his canvas or distributes the elements of his mural decoration to produce a design, appealing in its proportions, balance, rhythm, and use of color. The writer fashions his prose or poetry to give pleasure to the reader, either an intellectual satisfaction in the ideas conveyed or an aesthetic one through the beauty of their expression. Even the most practical of the fine arts, architecture, if it is true to its principles, must formulate its designs so that they are structurally proportioned, and thus pleasing to the eye as well as practical.

So it is with music; unless it gives the listener enjoyment it is of very little value to him. There are, of course, various ways of enjoying music, just as there are various ways of enjoying life. We may approach it through the senses, in the manner of those who seem to feel that sensual enjoyment is the great end of all existence. Music possesses tremendous powers of sensual appeal through its rhythms, its melodies, its charm of sound. Even the most unmusical person feels the essential appeal of the repeated rhythms in the nervous drumbeats of savages. We all react to the appeal of a sentimentally turned tune, to the trumpet's wild blare, or to the seductive strains of muted strings. On the other hand, we may enjoy our music primarily from the intellectual standpoint by understanding how it is constructed, how it develops logically through various stages to a final climax, how it succeeds in varying its constituent parts to provide variety and achieve unity. This sort of enjoyment is like that of the intellectual who derives his greatest pleasure in life through the processes of his mind, and who distrusts the pleasures of his senses.

Both these ways of enjoying music are legitimate and need to be cultivated. They are, however, only the means through which we come in the end to the fullest sort of enjoyment, that which comes through sharing the feelings which impelled the creation of the music in the first place. Our greatest art productions are obviously the result of their creator's overwhelming enjoyment of an idea, a formal design or color pattern, a state of mind or a feeling. Something which he cannot resist takes possession of the creator, and we feel that the music or the painting or the poem which he produces forms itself without conscious effort, that the creative artist is a mere instrument in the hands of some power outside of himself. Every great work of art has been born in such a glow of creative enthusiasm, whether the result was an immediate one, such as a Schubert song or a Mozart symphony, or whether the effort was spread over a long period of time, such as Brahms' *First Symphony* or Goethe's *Faust*. Centuries may have elapsed between the beginning and the finishing of a work of art, such as the medieval cathedrals. But the delight in each case is the same, a delight so keenly felt that the artist is driven to share it with posterity through the mysterious powers of creation. Through his abilities as a craftsman he has been able to communicate his delight to others, and the greatest joy that can come to us as listeners or beholders of his work is sharing this delight and experiencing a glow similar to his, even if, necessarily, a much feebler one. Aldous Huxley has reminded us that of all the arts, music is the one which has the least connection with what we call reality, and that, like mathematics, it is an almost unadulterated product of man's inner world. It is this inner world that will best understand it and derive the greatest pleasure from it. We should be able to experience such a sense of pleasure in hearing music that we go out from it with "joy in our hearts and like the poor cripple in the story, walking the streets like a god," as Edward Dickinson tells us in his fine book *The Spirit of Music*.[1]

Our study of the technic of musical construction, necessary as it is to the full comprehension of what we hear, must be used as a means to help this spiritual understanding. The full meaning of music and the pleasure to be derived from it are gained only when to analytic dissection of its structure we add the evaluation of it as an expression of human experience. To paraphrase William Blake, we must learn to hear *through* not *with* our ears. Lewis Mumford has observed that painting is an organization of human experience by image, as literature is by the word; and we may add, as music is by sound. And music, because of its essential characteristics, is able to communicate this experience even more significantly than do its sister arts.

ADVANTAGES TODAY

One of the peculiarities of music, which distinguishes it from the other fine arts, is the necessity for the interpolation of a third person, the interpreter, who establishes a link between the minds of the creator and the listener; in the other arts, a piece of literature, a painting, or a building itself establishes the link. It is perfectly possible, of course, to re-create music directly from the printed page, just as we would read a poem,[2] but this requires extraordinary powers of concentration as well as a tremendous technical facility. For most of us music must be re-created each time it is enjoyed, a fact that has given the re-creator a prestige somewhat out of proportion to his true significance in the scheme of musical things. It is obvious that the listener's impression of the music he hears depends on the re-creator's interpretation, and that a poor interpretation can change the whole complexion of the music and distort the composer's intentions. Thus a great deal of the effect which music has on the listener is due to interpretation.

Until the advent of the phonograph at the end of the nineteenth century, unless one were a Maecenas able to pay for a personal

[1] New York: Charles Scribner's Sons, 1925.

[2] Poems, although they can be comprehended more easily through silent reading than music, are nevertheless greatly improved through proper interpretation by a skilled reader.

musical establishment, the only means of apprehending music were attending an occasional concert or listening to one's own or a friend's efforts at reproduction. Now the phonograph and radio give us invaluable opportunities for repeated hearings of music whenever we desire them. In their present stage of development they are able to give us the greatest music of all ages, interpreted by the world's greatest artists with startling fidelity of reproduction. Thus, insofar as the listener is concerned, the performer in a personal sense is no longer the necessity he once was.

THE LISTENER'S PITFALLS

All of the foregoing are true enough, and we should be ready to take every advantage of the marvelous opportunities for studying music and increasing our appreciation of it which are offered to our generation. There are, however, obvious dangers to be avoided in the process. Even in music, an art which is above all things to be enjoyed, the full glories are revealed only to those who have shown some proof of their worthiness to comprehend. By this we mean a willingness to exert some active desire. The idea of mere hearing suggests a superficial and passive process, rather than the necessary personal effort in learning to hear what is in the music. The old idea of "appreciation" of an art was largely that of exposing oneself to it, of perhaps putting oneself in the same room with it, and then daring it to exert some influence upon him. In the great majority of cases, of course, nothing happened. Music, by its ability to dispense with the aids of reality and fact, especially tempts us to enjoy it in passive and sensual ways. As a writer in the London *Musical Times* says,

> We love to sit dozing in a symphony just as we sit dozing and bathing in the warmth of the sun. And when an art that is both too difficult (because of its spiritual qualities) and too easy is made suddenly accessible to everybody by the pressing of a switch, it is likely to lose at least as much as it gains. That is the danger of music today; there is so much of it and it is so promiscuous that it is being heard rather than listened to. And there are ninety passive listeners to ten live (participative) ones, because listening calls for knowledge as well as effort, and only ten (or even less) have been given the knowledge. Since taste is largely dependent upon knowledge, it follows that the ninety either prefer bad music, or don't know the difference between good and bad.

If you are inclined to doubt the truth of such a statement, consider the parallel case of literature. Never before have there been so many books published; they are spread far and wide by the activities of both author and publisher. And yet there is probably less reading today—that is, reading with real understanding—than in the times when books and magazines were less easily available.

The mere presence of such a mass of literature and music may act as a deterrent to putting forth personal effort in trying to understand them. Probably the very extent of the flood does some good, but the proportion of value, of virtue absorbed into the reader, is apparently small. Things these days seem to be turned on like a tap—reading, seeing, hearing—and the senses become completely dazed. In art appreciation, as in all phases of human activity, the truth holds that we get just as much out of our efforts as we put into them.

Another danger that we must guard against as we take advantage of mechanical devices in the reproduction of music is that such processes are liable to short-circuit our experiences. When we seem to be transported at once to where we desire to be, we may forget that we actually may not be there, that we can really get there only by the slower process of going around. Basil de Selincourt puts it well:

> While discussing mechanical musical devices we should note that the music they reproduce cannot be expected to sound in small rooms as it does in a concert hall. A listener who has received his musical experience only through the medium of even the best recordings is always surprised by a "live" concert. How different the music sounds; how much more vibrant and powerful is his experience!

There are a number of reasons for this: the acoustical qualities of the hall, the sense of direct communication established between the interpreters and the listeners, even the occasional mistake inevitable in all human endeavor. In making recordings the music is played through a number of times to erase all interpretative slips and mistakes, and then a composite recording of the best results is made. Usually there is no audience present to establish any sense of rapport with the players or singers, and the engineer can—and usually does —intervene to control all details of volume, timbre, and so on. Much of the reproduction's quality depends on the material used in making tapes or records. Finally, the nature and efficiency of the engineer's apparatus definitely determines the results obtained. If the recordings are broadcast, further possibilities of distortion are present. The cumulative hindrances to direct contact between composer and listener when sound is recorded and transmitted are the quality of its interpretation, the nature of its recording, the sensitivity of materials used, the fidelity of the reproducing machine, the type of broadcasting apparatus (again in the hands of engineers), the effectiveness of the receiving set, and the acoustics of the room in which the music is heard. No wonder some of the essential, original effectiveness is lost!

TYPES OF LISTENERS

Psychologists tell us that in general there are four different ways in which music affects listeners.

1. To many people music appeals largely as a sensory, emotional, or conative experience.[3] In such works as Tchaikovsky's *Symphony pathétique*, Beethoven's *Eroica* or *Ninth Symphony*, or Sibelius' *Second Symphony*, the listener may follow the different aspects of the composer's experience, may suffer and rejoice with him, may be moved perhaps to hope, perhaps to despair, at the same time that he is thrilled with the colorful sonorities and appealing charm of the melodies.

2. For others music arouses all sorts of associations, many of them having little or nothing to do with music itself. A certain phrase or rhythm may remind them of a day in the country or a trip to the mountains and awaken some very intimate, personal associations connected with such events. One thing leads to another, and often the listener reflectively connects these personal associations and experiences with universal moods and feelings, thus giving the music a larger, more human significance. This is as true of music like Beethoven's *Pastoral Symphony*, as it is of Copland's *El Salón México*.

3. There is also an objective method of enjoying music, by considering its value *per se*, without reference to anything else. Those

---

[3] The psychologists are careful to distinguish here: *conation* means the power or act of striving, with or without a conscious goal. *Joy* and *sorrow* are emotional states; *hope* and *despair* are conative attitudes.

who enjoy music in this fashion refrain from an individual response; to them, matters of form and technique are of paramount importance, and they criticize music largely, if not entirely, from this viewpoint. Good examples of compositions this type of listener especially enjoys are Bach's *Art of the Fugue* and his *Trio Sonatas* for the organ.

4. Perhaps the simplest response to music—in this case the listener does not "get behind the music" at all—is through personifying its character—that is, thinking of it in entirely personal terms, as morbid, joyful, light, heavy, and so forth. Very little discrimination is needed for this kind of listening and, of course, comparatively little satisfaction results.

One listener may, and often does, react in all these different ways according to his mood and to the type of music he is hearing. Generally speaking, however, listeners fall naturally into only one classification.

LIST OF SUGGESTED MUSIC

In order to ascertain the ways in which you listen to music, you might review some of the pieces already listed and add to them the following. Try to classify your reactions according to the categories of listeners.

Afternoon of a Faun (L'Après-midi d'un faune)   DEBUSSY

This is a fine illustration of the possibility of "getting behind" the music and sensing it as an experience in sound. Before listening to this, read Chapter 23.

Suite in b minor for Flute and Strings   J. S. BACH

Here is a delightful set of eighteenth-century dances in an exhilarating piece of music by one of the greatest composers.

TOPICS FOR DISCUSSION

Can too much talk about music harm a work of art or weaken appreciation of it?

Discuss the belief that "the great composers always held their art as an open one," without anything mysterious about it. Is the cult of the mysterious a modern development? How does painting fare in the present-day craze for publicity and stunting?

Obviously, it is possible for many of us to appreciate music we could never perform. Is it also true that a skilled performer may not understand fully the music he plays? How should a performer guard against this possibility?

Some people argue that technical knowledge may interfere with pure enjoyment of music. Need this be true? Do you think that it is often true? Compare music and sports in this respect.

Is it true in music that the "onlooker sees most of the game"?

Appreciate can mean to evaluate pro and con. Do you find present-day musical criticism weak in either type of evaluation? If you do, what do you think are the reasons for this defect?

To which of the listening types do you belong? Do you fit into more than one category? What were the influences which made you the type you are? Is it possible for a person to belong to different categories at different times?

CHAPTER 6

Instruments: The Means for Making Music

❧ ❦

BUILDING A BACKGROUND

An accurate taste in poetry, as in all the other arts, is a talent which can be acquired only by severe thought and a long continued intercourse with the best models of composition.

It is well to keep this idea of Wordsworth's in mind when we hear people question the sincerity of those who try to improve their taste and enrich their lives through a study such as the appreciation of music. We have already indicated that there are no short cuts to culture, and that the listener's concern from the very first should be with the acquisition of enough musical background to make his listening intelligent. (This does not imply the superficial sort of knowledge which is so often evidenced in the persons who *know* practically nothing about music, but who *talk* about it with an authority quite astonishing to the professional.) The aspiring listener should direct his musical education toward gathering all the information and meeting all the experiences necessary to make him a sensitive recipient of music. His first interest will naturally be in the instruments which produce this music, the means used by the composer to impress the sounds he conceives on the consciousness of the listener.

THE INTERACTION OF GROWTH: INSTRUMENTS AND EMOTION

Since music outgrew its early savage state, its development has been surprisingly conditioned by the instruments available for its production. Up to the beginning of the seventeenth century it was produced largely by the human voice; as soon as the possibilities of music made by instruments were thoroughly understood, the new art of instrumental music arose, and the most glorious period in the whole development began. The reasons for the choice of a particular instrument for the expression of the ideas of a composer have always been a source of interesting speculation for the musical amateur; in listening to good music we must realize that a great deal of its poignance and effect is due to the instrumentation chosen by the composer. (In this connection it is important to realize that the composer of serious music, in contradistinction to most of the writers of popular music, writes his own orchestration, which is never changed in interpretation.) It is difficult to imagine Beethoven choosing any instrument other than the orchestra for the *Fifth Symphony;* a string quartet would have been inadequate and the piano almost ridiculous. On the other hand, many of the best compositions of Haydn and Mozart belong to the string quartet and would lose their essence if transposed to any other instrument. We should remember that the symphony orchestra, although composed of a large group of individual instruments, is really an instrument itself, co-ordinated and played upon by the will of a conductor, and that a string trio or quartet—combinations of violin, viola, and violoncello, or two violins, viola and violoncello—are likewise instruments in an individual sense. A great deal of Schumann's and almost all of Chopin's music sprang directly from their love for and understanding of the piano. The majestic dignity and architectural splendor of Bach's organ works are due to his careful cultivation of the resources of that huge instrument and are unthinkable on any other, unless it be the modern orchestra. Furthermore, each age seems to have selected its own particular instrument, one which definitely expressed its own characteristics and which was developed for its needs. The lute suggests the romantic spirit of the sixteenth century; the organ, in spite of many modern improvements which have made it more easily playable, is a quiescent instrument today—its period of great glory extended from the late seventeenth century to the early eighteenth.

THE INFLUENCE OF POLITICS

The eighteenth century was the great period of the string quartet and other "chamber" (room) music. The nineteenth was the century of the piano—an age of individualism, of star performers demanding a solo instrument capable of complete, single mastery, and suitable for great displays of virtuosity. The choice of these instruments for the varying periods was no haphazard one; political changes and economic conditions had a great deal to do with it. The organ reached its dominance and achieved its importance during the seventeenth century because Germany at the time (immediately following the Thirty Years' War, 1618-1648) was a poverty-stricken country, unable to support the elaborate and costly court music to which France and Italy were accustomed, and looked to the stimulating influence of the strong Protestant Church to satisfy its love for music. Opera had its genesis (the first opera was written in 1600 for the celebration of the marriage of Henry IV and Marie de' Medici in Florence) and was developed during the following years largely through the demands of the luxurious European courts for amusement. The division of eighteenth-century Europe into various petty courts, each with its own prince and royal establishment, made possible the system in which chamber-music organizations flourished so widely. The democratic idea in government swept away the petty prince and, with him, the string quarter and chamber-music organizations maintained for his court concerts. The passing of nineteenth-century Romanticism with its great individualistic figures—Liszt and Chopin—sounded the death knell of the piano as the deified deliverer of self-conscious soul-strivings.

It is no accident that the great bulk of the music we have chosen for illustrating these chapters has been orchestral music; the symphony orchestra is the instrument of our time, and its music, although almost incredibly complex in many instances, is better understood and more easily appreciated today than music written for instruments of another period. Not so many years ago it was thought to be a mark of cultural distinction to be a regular attendant at symphonic concerts; now, rather unfortunately in some ways, orchestral enthusiasts are only too common. The orchestra, because of its size, its capacity for varying tone color and all shades of dynamics, appeals to all types of listeners, to the musically trained and to the musically untrained. As someone has well said, it is as modern as present-day industry—one big thing made up of many parts—and it suits our age as the simpler instruments suited handicraft times.

THE GROWTH OF THE ORCHESTRA

Most of us are not aware of how new an instrument the modern symphony orchestra is. We are so accustomed to the fine orchestras of today, with their almost unbelievable perfection of technic, that it seems as if they must have been in existence for many centuries. As a matter of fact, we have to wait until the Baroque period to find any real grouping of instruments which resembles the present-day orchestra. Giovanni Gabrieli in his *Sacrae symphoniae* (c. 1600) was the first composer to use a specific instrument for each part. Claudio Monteverdi's orchestra for his opera *Orfeo* (1607) was the first to treat instruments individually and for special expressive purposes. It may be of interest to note the composition of Monteverdi's orchestra: two harpsichords, two double bass viols, ten viols, three bass viols, one harp, two violins, two bass lutes, three portable organs, four trombones, two cornets, one small recorder, one high trumpet. Obviously, these were the instruments available to the composer at the time, and there was little consideration of balance or ensemble.

The first attempt at developing an orchestra in the present-day sense was made by a German prince, Karl Theodor (1743-1799), Elector of Pfalzbayern, whose court orchestra at Mannheim developed a beauty of tone, a unison, and a degree of dynamic shading entirely unknown before. In quality as well as in type of music played, this orchestra can be said to have been the first "symphony orchestra," according to modern terminology. Most historians consider this group of musicians the experimental laboratory from which our present ideas of symphonic music come.

From that time until the present the orchestra has developed consistently. Instruments have been added from time to time, and more and more complex music has been written for it, until we have the great colorful instrument we know today. The four divisions of the modern orchestra are: the strings, in which stretched strings are set into vibration by bows or plucking; the wood winds, in which vibrations are produced in a hollow tube, usually by reeds; the brass winds, in which the player's lips act as the vibrating medium; and the percussion—drums, cymbals, gongs, and so on—in which the vibrations are caused by striking. We may best remind ourselves of the qualities which these instruments give to the orchestra by dividing them into "families" or choirs. This is the distribution usual in the larger orchestra:

Strings, about 66:	18 first violins
	16 second violins
	12 violas
	10 violoncellos
	10 double basses
Wood winds, about 15:	3 flutes, 1 piccolo
	3 oboes, 1 English horn
	3 clarinets, 1 bass clarinet
	3 bassoons, 1 double bassoon
Brass, 11:	4 horns
	3 trumpets
	3 trombones
	1 tuba
Percussion, 5:	2 kettledrum players
	3 men for bass and side drum, glockenspiel, celesta, xylophone, triangle, cymbals, tambourine, and so on.

THE INSTRUMENTS

THE STRINGS

VIOLINS.   The violin is the smallest and highest pitched string instrument. Normally, it plays the top (soprano) or next to top part. Its smooth, singing tone is universally admired and is the standard for all other strings. Developed in Italy in the seventeenth century, the violin has a wide range, is capable of rapid passages and utmost precision, and can be made to sing lyrically or dramatically.

Illustration:

Scheherazade, Second Theme in First Section   RIMSKY-KORSAKOV

VIOLA.   The dark, somber tone of the viola is an excellent foil for the brilliant violin. It is about 26 inches long and, although it usually

Adrian Siegel

THE VIOLIN

Adrian Siegel

THE OBOE

Adrian Siegel

THE FRENCH HORN   THE ENGLISH HORN

Adrian Siegel

THE HARP   THE CONTRABASSOON

Adrian Siegel

THE TROMBONE THE DOUBLE BASS

Adrian Siegel

THE FLUTE THE TRUMPET

Adrian Siegel

THE VIOLA   THE CELLO

Adrian Siegel

THE TUBA   THE CLARINET

Adrian Siegel

THE PERCUSSION INSTRUMENTS

plays an inner part (alto or tenor), it can also be effective as a solo instrument.

Illustration: *Harold in Italy* (viola and orchestra)   BERLIOZ

CELLO.   The cello (a contraction of violoncello) is 45 inches long, and has a tone marked by a sonorous baritone resonance which can be made to sound both lyric and dramatic. It is one of the show instruments of the orchestra.

Illustration:
Schelomo, Rhapsody for Cello and Orchestra   BLOCH

DOUBLE BASS.   Largest of the strings, the double bass measures over six feet in length and has a range an octave below that of the cello. Awkward in solo passages, it is best suited to providing a solid foundation for the rest of the orchestra.

Illustration: *Symphony No. 5, in c minor,* Trio from Third
    Movement   BEETHOVEN
(Here the double bass is heard playing with the cellos.)

Wood Winds

The wind instruments, originally used for outdoor music and made of wood, are now used in concert orchestras and are often made of metal or plastic. They give color and flexibility to orchestral tone and are frequently used as solo instruments. In the wood-wind choir, the flute, oboe, and clarinet are sopranos; the English horn, the alto; the bassoons are tenors or baritones; and the double bassoon or bass clarinet are the deep bass.

FLUTE.   The player of the flute (and its smaller brother, the piccolo) produces the tone by directing his breath over the rim of a mouthpiece (*embouchure*) at the left end of the instrument. The flute, with a cool, clear, liquid tone in the upper register and a hollow one in the lower, has a range of three octaves. Though agile and brilliant, it is often swamped by the rest of the orchestra.

Illustration: *Suite in b minor for Flute and Strings*   BACH

PICCOLO.   The sharp, almost shrill tone of the piccolo is used to edge in melodies. Its high register gives the orchestra a brilliant glitter.

Illustration:
   The Nutcracker, "Chinese Dance"   TCHAIKOVSKY

In the double-reed wood winds, the tone is produced by two thin reeds, bound together, which are placed between the player's lips and set in motion by his breath.

OBOE. Although the least agile of the winds because of its double reed and the fact that it needs unusual breath and lip control, the oboe's penetrating and distinctive tone makes it one of the most useful solo instruments in the orchestra.

Illustration:
   Symphonie fantastique, Opening of Third Movement   BERLIOZ

ENGLISH HORN. Neither English nor a horn in shape, this instrument is an alto oboe with a pear-shaped bell. Its dark timbre makes it effective for solos, especially those suggesting melancholy moods.

Illustration: *Tristan und Isolde*, Solo, Third Act   WAGNER

BASSOON. The wide range (three and a half octaves) and characteristic timbres make this a most useful instrument. Its tone is rather thin at the top of its register, rich in the middle, and rough at the bottom.

Illustration: *The Sorcerer's Apprentice*   DUKAS

DOUBLE OR CONTRA BASSOON. Because of its sixteen-foot length this is the deepest voice of all the ordinary instruments. It adds depth and color to the whole ensemble.

Illustration: *The Sorcerer's Apprentice*   DUKAS

CLARINET. With the widest range of all the wind instruments (nearly four octaves) and a very distinctive variety of tone colors, the clarinet can play almost any kind of passage effectively. Its versatility makes it a favorite with composers of orchestral and chamber music. It uses a single reed.

Illustration:
   Symphony No. 3, in F Major, Second Movement   BRAHMS
   Quintet for Clarinet and Strings   BRAHMS

BASS CLARINET.   This sounds an octave below the regular B-flat clarinet and, in comparison, has a rather hollow sound.

Illustration: *Tristan und Isolde*, King Mark's Scene   WAGNER

Other clarinets, including a small E-flat, alto-, and contra-bass, are sometimes used for special effects. The saxophone, a hybrid, is not often used in regular orchestral scores; its family also includes instruments of all pitch ranges.

THE BRASS

In the brass instruments, the tone is actually produced by the vibration of the player's lips against the inner edge of the mouthpiece. With bulkier tones and smaller pitch ranges than the wood winds, the brass are used to give power as well as color to the whole. Mechanical improvements during the nineteenth century have made these instruments very agile and effective; their timbre is sometimes changed by inserting a mute or the player's hand into the bell.

TRUMPET.   The most brilliant of all the instruments, the trumpet is used in various pitches and usually as the soprano of the brasses. With its present system of valves controlling the length of the tube, it has wide range and flexibility. The older, "natural" trumpet, used in Baroque music, is very high in pitch.

Illustration: *Petrouchka*, Entrance of the Ballerina   STRAVINSKY

Brandenberg Concerto No. 2, Last Movement   BACH

FRENCH HORN.   The instrument is as expressive as the trumpet is brilliant. It has a wide range and a mellow, singing tone and is often used as a solo instrument.

Illustration: *Symphony No. 1, in c minor*, Last Movement   BRAHMS

TROMBONE.   Most often employed for broad and dignified effects, the trombone has a wide dynamic range, from softest *pianissimo* to powerful *fortissimo*. Devised in the fifteenth century, it is the oldest of the modern orchestral instruments.

Illustration: *Tannhäuser*, Overture   WAGNER

TUBA.   Its fat, ponderous tone makes this instrument ideally suited for use as the double bass of the brass. While the most frequently

used tuba is pitched in F, there are other sizes, some of them especially designed for use in Wagner's *Ring* music.

Illustration: *Also Sprach Zarathustra*   R. STRAUSS

Other brass instruments occasionally used include the cornet, a
standard instrument of brass or military bands which closely resembles the trumpet in tone; the alto horn or mellophone, which is
sometimes substituted for the French horn in amateur groups; and
the Sousaphone, a tuba developed for ease in carrying in marching
bands.

PERCUSSION

TYMPANI OR KETTLEDRUM.   The tone of these instruments is produced by striking the membrane-covered end of a drum with a soft
mallet. This results in a sharp thud with easily recognized pitch.
Both instruments have long been used by composers to punctuate
rhythmic effects. Before 1850 it was customary to use two kettledrums; since that time three, four, and even five have been employed
on occasion.[1]

Illustration:
   Symphony No. 9, in d minor, Second Movement   BEETHOVEN

XYLOPHONE.   The player strikes tuned wooden bars with a hard
mallet to produce the harsh, brittle tone of the xylophone.

Illustration: *Danse Macabre*   SAINT-SAËNS

MARIMBA.   A xylophone of Latin-American or African origin, the
marimba is used for exotic effects.

Illustration: *Latin American Symphonette*   GOULD

VIBRAPHONE.   This electrophonic instrument has resonators which
are kept vibrating by an electric current. It gives an oscillating tone.

Illustration: *Improvisation on Mallarmé, No. 2*   BOULEZ

GLOCKENSPIEL.   This set of tuned steel bars is played with hammers.

Illustration:
   The Pines of Rome, "The Pines of the Villa Borghese"   RESPIGHI

[1] In the "Tuba Mirum" of *Requiem*, Berlioz uses sixteen!

CHIMES.   The chimes, made of resonating metal tubes hung on a steel frame, give the effect of bells when struck with a hammer.

Illustration: *Symphonie fantastique*, Last Movement   BERLIOZ

TRIANGLE.   This metal rod bent into the shape of an equilateral triangle produces a clear, high, concentrated ping when struck.

Illustration:

Concerto No. 1 in E flat Major, Scherzo (piano)   LISZT

SNARE OR SIDE DRUMS.   These smallest of the orchestral drums are made by stretching pieces of wire or catgut across the head of the drum. They give a rattling sound when struck singly and an intense, military sound when rolled.

Illustration: *Ein Heldenleben*, Measures 45-75   R. STRAUSS

BASS DRUM.   The ponderous thud of this drum is used to accentuate rhythm and to produce noise effects.

Illustration:

The Pines of Rome, "The Pines of the Appian Way"   RESPIGHI

CYMBALS.   These metal plates, usually used in pairs, produce a dramatic sort of crash when struck. Occasionally, for special effects, they are struck with a stick.

Illustration: *Symphony No. 4*, Last Movement   TCHAIKOVSKY

   Afternoon of a Faun (small cymbals)   DEBUSSY

   There are other instruments of indefinite pitch used in the orchestra on occasion—for example, castanets, the tambourine, the gong, the wood-block, and the whip.

KEYBOARD INSTRUMENTS

   Unlike its eighteenth-century predecessor, the modern symphony orchestra does not regularly include a keyboard instrument. If one is used, it is usually a concerto instrument—that is, one used in solo against a background of the orchestra. The sound of these instruments is produced by keys which activate some tone-producing medium—string, wind, or (recently) electronic.

PIANO.   Taut wires struck by key-activated hammers produce the tone in this most commonly used keyboard instrument. Its ancestor, the harpsichord, had plucked strings and was commonly used in the orchestral groups of the Baroque period.

Illustration: *Concerto No. 2 in c minor* (piano)   RACHMANINOFF

        Brandenburg Concerto No. 5, in D Major   BACH

ORGAN.   The tone of this complex mechanism is produced by wind or in the latest design, by electronic mechanisms. It is not often used with the orchestra today except for grandiose or religious effects. In the Baroque period it was a constituent member of the orchestra.

Illustration: *Also Sprach Zarathustra*, Introduction   R. STRAUSS

        Concerti for Organ   HANDEL

CELESTA.   This little instrument, invented in the nineteenth cen-

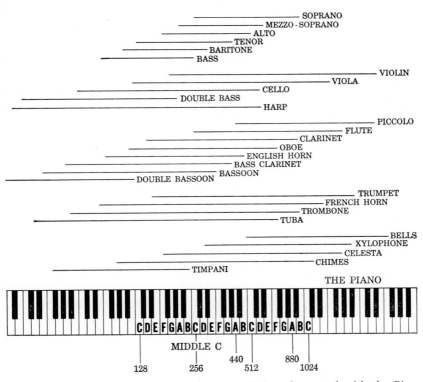

Ranges of Orchestral Instruments and Human Voices Compared with the Piano Keyboard

tury, produces a bright, tinkling sound by means of small hammers striking metal bars. It was introduced by Tchaikovsky in *The Nutcracker*.

Illustration: *Music for Strings, Percussion and Celesta*   BARTÓK

HARP.   Since its history goes back to the Sumerians and Babylonians, this stringed instrument is difficult to classify. It has been developed so that it can play in all keys and chromatically. A distinctive tone is given to glissandos and arpeggios.

Illustration: *Concerto in C for Flute and Harp, K.299*   MOZART

TOPICS FOR DISCUSSION

Do you know of any particular defects in or difficulties with the various instruments?

What are the obvious weaknesses in the function and tone of saxophones as they are used in jazz?

Which instruments of the modern orchestra appeal to you for their powers in solo work? On which instruments would you like to be a fine performer, if time and will allowed? Why?

Does any instrument of the normal orchestra *not* appeal to you? Is there any instrument which annoys you? Why?

CHAPTER 7

The Instruments and the Orchestra

❦

Recognizing the timbre of the different instruments, played singly or in combination, is one of the greatest pleasures to be had from listening. The most practical method of learning to do this is through first observing the qualities of the single instruments and then the various kinds of tonal ensemble—the sonorities of massed-string tone, the beauties of the wood-wind group, or the glories of the brass choir. We may do this by listening to recordings or by attending concerts, where we see as well as hear the locations of the various groups of players. Looking at any orchestra, we notice this seating plan, which is more or less standard for all American orchestras.

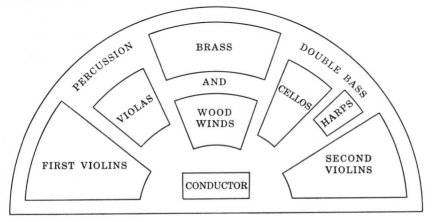

Recognition of the various orchestral timbres may be aided by a study of the many fine recordings now available. Take such a familiar composition as Wagner's *Tannhäuser Overture*, for example; before the music has run the course of fifty measures, the listener has obtained the essential color of the different orchestral choirs. In the first fifteen measures the wood winds are heard alone; (the French horn is often counted as a wood-wind instrument because of its peculiarly smooth tone); then for some twenty measures we have the wood winds blending with the strings; and finally we hear some of the brass choir sounding the melody of the Pilgrims. The beginning of the Waltz from *The Nutcracker* suite is also a good tonal illustration of the wood-wind ensemble. There is a flowing background here supplied by the harp, an instrument that belongs to none of the regular orchestral classifications but is used for occasional effects.

Another example is the beginning of the second movement of Brahms' *Third Symphony*. Certainly there are few better illustrations of the richness possible from the wood-wind ensemble; there is an occasional interpolation of one or two measures from the strings to set off the peculiar wood-wind timbre desired by the composer. In fact, this whole movement is played almost entirely by combining wood winds and strings; only occasionally a trombone enters to help sustain the whole and tie it together. This is music worthy of many hearings; in trying to realize just how the composer uses these two groups of orchestral instruments, the hearer will incidentally become familiar with some of the world's noblest music.

Another place for recognizing the contrasting colors of strings and wood winds is at the very beginning of Tchaikovsky's *Symphonie pathétique*. After a slow introductory melody on the bassoon, accompanied by low-toned strings, the whole string section suddenly bursts into animated action, followed immediately by the wood winds taking up the same phrase.

INSTRUMENTAL CHARACTERISTICS

The strings are the foundational group of the orchestra; they take up its main burden and are helped and relieved by the other choirs. Here, as we found to be true in the case of the wood winds, there is a diversity of duties. The violins are divided into two groups, firsts and seconds, and generally take the melody; the violas take an alto part, the cellos, a broad flowing tenor or baritone part, and the basses supply the foundation for the whole. Listen to the beginning measures of Beethoven's *First Symphony*: the strings have the main say, the violins on top sounding the melody. They are joined occasionally by the wood winds, but the chief color is that of the strings, forming a background for the characteristic qualities of the other groups. What a portentous beginning the deep-toned strings (cello and bass) give to Schubert's *Unfinished Symphony!* There is a lightening of the mood when the violas and the violins are added a few measures later, and the whole section forms a background for the melody sung by the blended oboe and clarinet. In all orchestral compositions the strings often are heard alone; sometimes the composer writes a whole composition for them, as Mozart did in his *Eine kleine Nachtmusik*, composed for a special occasion in Vienna. From the four movements of this serenade we can gain a good idea of the varied possibilities of the string choir, ranging from the introspective rendering of sentiment to a light fleet celerity of which no other instruments in the orchestra are capable.

The brass, with its impressive choir of trumpets and trombones, can on occasion "roll up the heavens like a scroll." Witness the opening measures of the last movement of Beethoven's *Fifth Symphony*, or the introduction to the last movement of Brahms' *First Symphony* (measures 30-60), where the effect of the whole is determined by the golden weight of this important family of instruments. But this brass group can also speak eloquently with a still, small voice; what more suitable opening can be imagined than the beginning measures of Weber's *Oberon* Overture, with its faint "horns of elfland, softly blowing"? Wagner uses the brass choir for tremendous, resounding effects, as well as for delicate, imaginative ones. The Funeral March from *Götterdämmerung*, for instance, gains its almost overpowering poignancy through the inexorable way in which Wagner uses the brass here—four horns, three trumpets, a bass trumpet, four trombones, a tenor tuba, two bass tubas, and a contrabass tuba. The effect of all these sounding together is unforgettable, cataclysmic, a fit prelude to the destruction of the gods. On the other hand, the composer's delicate use of the horns at the beginning of the second act of *Tristan und Isolde* gives exactly the proper mood for the moonlit scene that follows in the lovers' garden.

A fact the orchestral listener is likely to forget is that, because of difficulties inherent in their construction and mechanism, wind instruments (both brass and wood-wind) have to be kept in tune with one another and with the rest of the orchestra by "main force." Every note on all the wind instruments used in the orchestra must be tempered by the breath and lips of the player if it is to sound in tune with the rest of the ensemble.[1] And this is true today, even after considerable improvements which the makers (particularly the Belgian C. J. and A. J. Sax and the German Theobald Boehm) have made in the methods used in constructing instruments. No wonder that Bach, Haydn, and Mozart used the oboes, bassoons, flutes, trumpets, and horns of their day so sparingly, and that it was not until Beethoven's scores that the clarinet became a regularly functioning member of the symphony orchestra. The problems—adjustment of valve lengths, proper breath and lip pressure, the correction of deflection from pitch due to temperature changes—connected with the playing of wind instruments are so complicated that they have never been completely solved. The mechanical imperfections of these instruments are still so great as to make necessary a great deal of lip and breath control on the part of the player. This makes these sections the most temperamental departments of the orchestra; even in the best of ensembles out-of-tune playing by these instruments is sometimes noticeable.

The percussion family is probably the oldest of all the orchestral divisions. Most of its members contribute to the rhythmic, coloristic, or dynamic qualities of the ensemble rather than to its harmonic or melodic enrichment.

SPECIFIC ILLUSTRATIONS

Every opportunity to observe these and similar tonal groupings should be taken. Only in this way can the listener learn to understand the parts played by the orchestral voices in various combina-

[1] The slide trombone, however, because of the infinite number of positions possible with the slide, can be played in perfect tune, without tempering by lip and breath, with any instrument or combination of instruments.

tions. Benjamin Britten has given us what has been well called a "painlessly educative" method of doing this in his piece *The Young Person's Guide to the Orchestra*.[2] This music introduces the listener first to the sounds of the various choirs, and then to the different instruments one at a time. Britten uses a theme from music written for a play by an earlier English composer (Purcell's rondeau from *Abdelazer*), and lets us hear it first played by the whole orchestra.

Then he repeats it played by the various choirs in turn: first the wood winds, then the brass, followed by the strings, and finally, very cleverly, by the percussive instruments. At the end, just to remind us, he gives it to us again by the whole orchestra.

There follows a series of variants of the tune, thirteen in all, each emphasizing one instrument. Here is the scheme:

Variation 1. For the highest of the wood-wind group, the clear, sweet flute and its rather shrill brother, the piccolo, have a background of first and second violins.

Variation 2. This slow variation on the plaintive oboe (which, as the music shows us, can be forceful) has an accompaniment of strings playing an unmistakable rhythm.

Variation 3. Two clarinets, beautifully smooth and mellow, are heard over an accompaniment of strings and (of all things) a tuba!

Variation 4. Here the tune is given to two deep-voiced bassoons, again with a very distinctive string accompaniment.

Variation 5. First and second violins soar above a polonaise rhythm on the brass.

Variation 6. The violas are heard next against short, repeated chords in the wood winds and brasses.

Variation 7. Warm, rich, smooth cello tones are heard with clarinet and viola accompaniment.

[2] Excerpts reprinted by permission. Copyright 1947 by Hawkes & Son (London) Ltd.

Variation 8. The score here calls the double basses the "grandfathers of the string family with heavy, grumbling voices." They are played against a wood-wind background.

Variation 9. The harp, with its range of six octaves and a fifth, shows what it can do; it is heard above a soft string *tremolo*.

Variation 10. The four horns, rich and full, are played in harmony.

Variation 11. Two trumpets, with a military-like section, are accentuated by a strong drumbeat.

Variation 12. This displays the heavy, brassy voice of the trombone and the still heavier tones of the tuba.

Variation 13. Parts are included for the most familiar percussion instruments: tympani or kettledrums; bass drum; cymbals; tambourine; triangle; the side drum; Chinese block; xylophone; castanets; gong; whip.

Having taken the orchestra apart, Britten proceeds to put it together again in a fugue, adding instrument after instrument in the same order as before, starting with the piccolo. At the very end comes the original theme thundered out on the brass, with the rest of the orchestra whirling madly about it—a most exciting and original finish to the whole piece.

Another good practice piece for the same purpose is Ravel's famous, though overplayed, *Bolero*. Written as a sort of stunt, this number employs a two-part Spanish dance tune as a theme, repeating it over and over again throughout the course of the piece; the only change, except at the very end, is in orchestration. Here is the plan of the various solo instruments as they bring out this rhythmic tune:

(a) refers to the first part of the tune (b) to the second.

1. (a) Flute
2. (a) Clarinet
3. (b) Bassoon
4. (b) E-flat Clarinet
5. (a) Oboe d'amour (an obsolete type of oboe, tuned a little lower than the usual one used in the orchestra. Not in general use since Bach's day).
6. (a) Flute and Trumpet
7. (b) Tenor Saxophone
8. (b) Soprano Saxophone
9. (a) Horn, Celesta, Piccolos
10. (a) Oboes, English Horn, Clarinet
11. (b) Trombone

12. (b) Same as 10 plus Flutes and Piccolo
13. (a) Same plus First Violins
14. (a) Same plus Second Violins
15. (b) Same minus Clarinets and plus Trumpet
16. (b) Same plus Clarinets, Soprano Sax, Violas
17. (a) Wood Winds, Saxes, Trumpets, High Trumpet, First Violins
18. (b) Incomplete, modulating into a great loud explosion, with Trombone

THE SCORE AND SCORE READING

One of the many mysteries of musical composition is the composer's ability not only to create his themes, compose their harmonies, and decorate them with counterpoint and other technical features, but also to hear them in their most effective instrumentation and incorporate them, by means of symbolic signs on a sheet of paper, in a score. The actual writing down of all the parts involved in a musical work is called its *scoring*, or *orchestration*.

The usual practice in scoring is to consolidate the various horizontal lines containing the individual parts on a large, ruled sheet of paper. The score is arranged from the topmost piccolo part to the lowest string bass, and is placed so that the complete metrical units of the music (the *measures*) are directly underneath each other. The names of all the separate instruments are placed at the left of the lines: the wood winds at the top, the brass next, the percussion third, and finally the strings. Thus the score reader or conductor has in front of him what might be called an aural picture showing exactly what the composer expects to be going on in all the instruments at any one particular instant.

It must always be remembered that the process of orchestration—the treatment of the structure, compass, and timbre of the different instruments and their effective combination in a balanced whole—is an essential part of the composer's original concept. He writes down what he wants each instrument to play, with proper directions for dynamics and shadings, and it is intended that these be followed exactly by the players under the guidance of the conductor.

The ability to read a complexly organized score is acquired only through a great deal of study and practice—as is the capacity to hear mentally what the composer has written physically. Such a specialized skill is absolutely necessary for the conductor, and it helps the amateur who possesses sufficient technical background and natural musicality to grasp the innermost significance of the music. The average listener, however, is neither able to hear what he sees before him in an orchestral score nor to see what he is hearing in the performance; and it will be better for him to concentrate on one-line scores such as we have provided for Beethoven's *Fifth Symphony.* (See pages 397-416.) By connecting the musical sound with the notation and observing the instrumentation as given, the listener's enjoyment and understanding will be increased through a general realization of how the composer wrote and orchestrated the music.

WHAT THE CONDUCTOR DOES

We may well ask, what is the actual relationship between the full score (and the instruments that play it) and the conductor who directs its production. Before any piece can be played, even in rehearsal, the conductor must master the score completely, determining how he wants it to sound in every detail. His functions are keeping the group together, securing unanimity of execution through the signals he gives in beating time, indicating cues and so on. He is also responsible for obtaining the effects intended by the composer and marked in the score—interpreting the music, as we say. It is hardly necessary to add that this interpretation is a tremendously important factor in the impressions received by the listener—so important that very often the interpreter gets more credit for the effects produced than does the composer. Music is a unique art in that, as we have said, a third person must be interpolated between the composer and the listener for the latter to receive the impressions desired by the former. This has made possible the present-day overemphasis on the conductor as a musical influence, especially since most hearers of orchestral music do not know what the real functions of the conductor are. Some listeners seem to think that through some occult means, while the performance is in progress, the conductor is moved by brilliant inspiration which he transmits to his men as they are playing. And the showman-like gyrations of many of our conductors don't help disillusion the public!

EUGENE ORMANDY
Conducting the Philadelphia Orchestra.

Adrian Siegel

A good conductor studies his score carefully, decides just what effects are to be desired in various places, the proportions and balance of tonal effects desired, and the shaping of the various musical phrases. In long and very often laborious rehearsals, he impresses these ideas on his men so that they know exactly how they are expected to play each phrase, how their parts are to balance the others, and so forth. Henderson tells us that he once asked Arthur Nikisch, one of the world's great conductors, if he was accustomed to making changes in the reading of an orchestral work during the course of its performance. Nikisch replied that if he realized that the music was going rather heavily, he might increase the pace, but otherwise he made no attempt to change details or general outlines. At the concert performance the conductor can work his men into a frenzy of inspired playing, but to do this he has to build on the solid foundation of careful rehearsals. Today's magnificent orchestral performances are the result of constant and painstaking rehearsals and are in strong contrast to the conditions at the time when Beethoven conducted the first performance of his *Fifth Symphony* in

Vienna, which was then (1808) the musical capital of the world. Not one full rehearsal for the program had been held; Beethoven had to stop the orchestra in the middle of a passage when a player lost his cue. The response of the few people in the unheated hall, Beethoven tells us, was anything but enthusiastic because of the wretched performance his music received.

LIST OF SUGGESTED MUSIC

In learning to listen to the various instruments of the orchestra, we all will have our favorites, and the recognition of their voices will add the refinement of personal pleasure to orchestral experience. Perhaps we are enamored of the horn; if so, the theme for four horns from Weber's *Oberon* Overture will work particular magic. A sensitive critic called this instrument the romantic poet of the tonal world and said that, like Blake's evening star, it can "bid the wind sleep on the lake and wash the dusk with silver." The voice of the cello, eloquent amorist and imposing rhapsodist of the orchestra, is like that of a friend bringing comfort in trouble in the passage at the beginning of the second movement of Beethoven's *Fifth Symphony*. Yet the same instrument, if not treated with respect and given music suited to its inherent capabilities, can sound like a Hebrew prophet doing handsprings, as someone has put it. The crystal clearness of the clarinet melody in the *Oberon* Overture, the pastoral sweetness of the oboe and the flute in the third section of Liszt's *Les Préludes*, the nostalgic longing of the English-horn melody in the second movement of the César Franck *Symphony*, and its prophetic sadness in the shepherd's tune at the beginning of the third act of *Tristan und Isolde*, are all highlights of unforgettable beauty. The violin is a universal favorite, for it can "dance and mock and flirt like Columbine, as well as sigh and glow like Juliet"; it is an instrument equally capable of light-hearted gaiety, empty-headed brilliance, or soulful discourse on things of mighty import. It can be the means of suggesting playful badinage, as in the first measures of the last movement of Beethoven's *First Symphony*, or of conveying such grave commitments as are entrusted to it by Brahms in the second movement of his *First Symphony*.

Tannhäuser Overture   WAGNER

Götterdämmerung, Funeral March WAGNER

Tristan und Isolde, Prelude to Act II WAGNER

Tristan und Isolde, Shepherd's Tune, beginning Act III WAGNER

The Nutcracker, Waltz TCHAIKOVSKY

Symphony No. 6 (Pathétique), First Movement TCHAIKOVSKY

Symphony No. 1, in c minor, Second Movement BRAHMS

Symphony No. 3, in F Major, Second Movement BRAHMS

Symphony No. 1, in C Major, First and Last
Movements BEETHOVEN

Symphony No. 5, in c minor, Second Movement BEETHOVEN

Symphony in b minor (Unfinished), First Movement SCHUBERT

Eine kleine Nachtmusik, K.525 MOZART

Oberon Overture WEBER

Les Préludes, Pastoral section LISZT

The Young Person's Guide to the Orchestra BRITTEN

Bolero RAVEL

INSTRUMENTS OF THE ORCHESTRA

Examples have been compiled by various recording companies, demonstrating the characteristics of the principal instruments that comprise the modern symphony orchestra.

TOPICS FOR DISCUSSION

Someone has claimed that almost all instruments are defective, even the violin. Discuss this general charge.

One able musician has suggested that saxophones may take the place of clarinets in the symphony orchestra. Would this be an advantage?

What factors must we remember when considering even the best phonograph records as representative of the effects produced by the orchestra?

Discuss the instrumentation used by the following composers:

Stravinsky, Richard Strauss, Wagner, Berlioz, Beethoven, Haydn, Bach, Monteverdi.

Discuss the differences which most readily strike a listener when he hears the instrumentation of Richard Strauss after that of Haydn, or Wagner after Bach.

What are the most distinctive features of the orchestrations of Berlioz, Richard Strauss, and Stravinsky?

What is your opinion as to the degree of perfection of reproduction achieved by phonograph records? How highly do you esteem stereophonic recording? Do you prefer monaural or stereophonic apparatus? Why?

CHAPTER 8

The Composer's Materials

❧❦

THE RAW MATERIALS OF MUSIC

All the arts make use of materials of one sort or another, materials which the artist selects, organizes, and interprets for his particular purpose. The heaven-soaring ideals of the medieval architect were carried out through the organization of such simple materials as wood and stone, shaped into forms relating mass to mass through the genius of the builders. Our masterpieces of literature are formed from words used in ordinary speech, shaped through the power of poet or novelist. The raw materials of sculpture consist of certain three-dimensional blocks of various materials—stone, wood, clay, and so on—capable of assuming, under the skilled hand of the artist, the shapes he desires. The world's greatest paintings, insofar as their materials are concerned, are simply colored pigments applied to canvas, wood, or plaster.

But there is something beyond these purely physical substances that we must consider when we think of materials with which artists work, something all the more important because it cannot be seen, something on which the real quality of any work of art depends. For example, we cannot truthfully say that the materials of architecture are merely the wood and stone, the bricks or concrete that have gone into the building we know. Beyond these and the physical laws which enable man to use them as he wishes are all those necessities and inducements that have led him to plan and erect buildings—such necessities as those of providing shelter from the elements, or

73

depositories for his goods, or temples for the worship and glorification of his gods. Without these spiritual and social necessities the art of architecture as we know it could never have come into being.

Similarly, we realize that what we call literature would never have been created if man had not been impelled to use words in a manner that far transcends their ordinary purpose of communicating simple ideas. We can say that the desire of man to acquaint his fellows with his reactions to the world about him or his reflections on his own inner and personal experiences constitute as important a "material" of literature as the significance and symbolism of the words he uses.

So it is with music. The physicists tell us that the raw material of music is auditory sound[1] having variations of pitch, intensity, timbre, and duration. And to a certain extent they are right. These musical materials can be studied as laboratory apparatus—that is, the structure of sound can be analyzed and stated in scientific and mathematical formulas. It is important that the listener, if he aspires to anything like a real understanding of music, be familiar with them in a general way. But he must always remember that in themselves these physical materials do not necessarily constitute music. There are certain spiritual concepts and ideas without which music is merely an interesting physical phenomenon, a dead series of tonal relationships and mathematical ratios with no power to stir the imagination or move the hearts of men. It is necessary that we consider both these aspects of music's materials; let us take the physical first.

THE PHYSICAL CHARACTERISTICS OF TONE

The physical material of which music is composed is sound[2]—tones, vocables, and noises—with an occasional use of silence, what the musicians speak of as a "rest." For systematic purposes, and in order to account fully for certain of their characteristics, the physicists are careful to describe these variations of auditory sound—pitch, intensity, timbre, and duration—as being both physical

---

[1] They mean sound that is produced by some sort of vibrating medium, transferred through alternate compressions and rarefactions of the atmosphere, and registered in the auditory centers of the brain through the human ear mechanism.

[2] As one writer puts it, "Sound is the auditory experience, the stimulus for which is the vibratory motions of some elastic body." Schoen, *The Psychology of Music*. New York: Ronald Press Co., 1940.

phenomena (pulsations in the ear) and psychological effects (sensations) perceived by the listener. This careful reasoning need not concern us too much as practical musicians, since we naturally assume that the one implies and causes the other.

Long and detailed experimentation has shown that the vibratory motion producing the sound has four important characteristics:

1. *Frequency*: a certain number of vibrations per second. The term *cycle* is used to designate one of these complete vibrations.

2. *Amplitude*: a certain extent or range.

3. *Form*: the series of pulsations which transmits sound through the air. It is called a "train" of sound waves and consists of longitudinal vibrations of the air molecules. The physicists have devised machines which graphically represent these linear motions of the sound waves, and these graphs show that the vibratory motion has definite form that is sometimes simple and sometimes complex.

4. *Duration*: the time a vibratory motion lasts.

The sound waves produced by any single tone possesses all four of these characteristics; and since any two waves may differ in one or more of them, we can see how complex is even a single tone on any one of the musical instruments.

Each of these physical properties has a certain psychological effect on us, and it is these concepts with which we as listeners are concerned. What we have come to know as the *pitch* of a tone depends largely on the frequency of the sound wave it generates. The quality of a tone that we recognize as *volume* depends on its amplitude; *timbre* or *tone quality* depends on the form or overtone structure of the sound wave; and the existence of a tone in time, its persistence as an auditory experience, depends on the objective fact of *duration*.[3]

A change in any of the physical characteristics of a tone thus produces a reciprocal change in what we hear; this is simply another way of saying that the experience of listening to music is an exceedingly complex one, made up of a number of experiences that unite to form a single impression.

[3] Also, to a much less degree, on other physical characteristics. Certain changes in the form of a sound wave produce definite changes in pitch; the intensity of a tone likewise affects its pitch to some extent. Experiments have shown that the loudness of a tone depends on the frequency and form of its sound wave.

These properties of tone are not merely of theoretical interest: they underlie the most fundamental concepts of music. As we shall see, the scales which are at the base of our present-day musical structures are simply expressions of certain intrinsic arrangements of pitch relationships. The dynamic quality in music, on which so much of its beauty depends, is a matter of degrees of loudness and softness. The specific tone qualities of the various instruments, qualities that color and condition all the music we hear, are a matter of overtone arrangement. And rhythm, that life force of music, depends to a great extent on the relationships of tonal durations. All these factors are basic to musical organization of even the simplest form.

PITCH

By pitch we mean the relative highness or lowness of a tone, though strictly speaking, the terms are incorrect, since there are no such spatial relationships in music.[4] What we call high and low pitches are in reality differences in frequency of vibrations, but for practical reasons these attributes of space are applied to music, the art which exists only in time. About 550 B.C. the Greek philosopher Pythagoras showed that the pitch of any tone depends on the number of vibrations per unit of time set up by the vibrating body. Every body capable of being set in vibration—be it string, reed, elastic membrane, or air column—has its own frequency of vibration (number of vibrations per second), depending on the materials of which it is made, its size, its density, its degree of tension, and its shape. Experiments have shown that the human ear at its best is capable of hearing anything from deep bass rumbles of about sixteen cycles per second to high treble overtones of about eighteen to twenty thousand cycles per second. The frequency range of the fundamental tones on the piano keyboard is shown below for comparison. The compass of ordinary spoken language is quite limited and is pitched to the natural placement of the different speaking voices.

[4] Technically, tone is sound that is produced by regular vibrations and having fixed pitch; it is thus distinguished from "noise," which is produced by vibrations that are scattered and irregular.

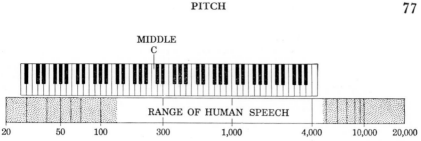

MIDDLE
C

RANGE OF HUMAN SPEECH

20   50   100   300   1,000   4,000   10,000   20,000

Man has come nearer agreement on the matter of pitch than he has in most other fields of endeavor; most countries using the European system of music have finally agreed on a uniform standard of pitch for their music-producing instruments. According to this standard, A when sounded in a temperature of 68° F. has 440 cycles of vibration per second. This has not always been agreed upon; a standard reference book on the subject, Helmholtz's *Sensations of Tone*, gives a seventeen-page compilation of the listing of pitches throughout Europe and the United States from 1360 to 1880; during that time the range of A was from 373.3 to 567 cycles—an enormous difference.

Several factors have operated to resolve such wide differences. The human voice, by holding pitch to the usual ranges of the respective voices—soprano, alto, tenor, and bass—has had a great influence. In 1711, an English musician, John Stone, invented the tuning fork, with a pitch of 419.9 cycles per second for A; this gave a dependable and easily determinable source of pitch. Thus while there was a difference ranging from about 415 to 428 cycles for A during the two centuries which we call the Classical Age, when many of the foundations of music were laid by the great masters, there was some sort of mean-pitch agreement at a level considerably below that today. (This might well be taken into consideration and the pitch changed accordingly in present-day interpretations of the music of the period.)

During the nineteenth century the standards of pitch rose steadily because of efforts of the makers and players of wind instruments to secure a more brilliant tone; this naturally handicapped singers who had to produce their music at a pitch considerably above that for which it was originally composed. In 1859, a French commission fixed the normal pitch of middle A as 435 vibrations per second at a temperature of 59° F., or 68° F. (the latter is considered to be the

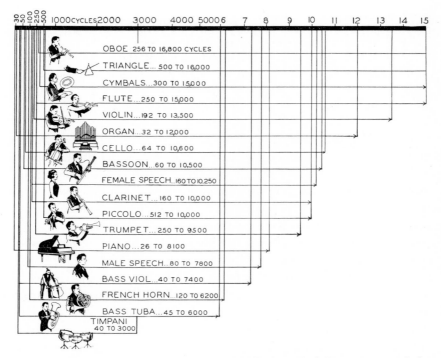

The Complete Frequency Range of the Principal Musical Instruments and the Human Voice. (Includes fundamentals and overtones.)

temperature of the average concert hall). This was established as "international pitch" at Vienna in 1889, and later an absolute frequency of 440, independent of temperature, was adopted as standard throughout the world.

The important thing for the listener, however, is what happens when an instrumentalist or a singer uses a scale from any tone such as A, going up a tone at a time. As the pitches become higher and higher, their wave lengths become shorter and shorter, and the number of waves which reach his ear per second becomes greater and greater. Finally, he will recognize a tone which bears a strong resemblance to the original tone from which the player started; this relative of the first tone, the physicist will show him, has a wave length exactly half that of the original and a frequency exactly twice that of starting note. This second tone we call the "octave" of the first. To make this more concrete: if the length of the sound wave set up by an oboe sounding A is 31.02 inches, measured from the crest of one wave to that of the next, the wave length of A above will measure exactly 15.51 inches; if the frequency of vibration of the first is 440 cycles per second, that of the second will be 880.

The relationship between a tone and its octave, discovered by Pythagoras, is one of the most important phenomena in all music. There would be absolute chaos in a world in which so many vibrations are capable of being recognized by the ear, were it not for this happy relationship of the octave. The fact that doubling or halving the number of vibrations set up by any tone produces another tone, so like the first that we can immediately recognize it as its twin brother, reduces the vast range of sound waves at our disposal (from about 16 to 18,000, remember) to a workable unit that is repeated over and over again at various pitch levels. The eighty-eight different tones represented on the modern piano keyboard give vibrations from $27\frac{1}{2}$ to 4186, covering only part of the range of audibility; thus they are conveniently divided into a seven-octave system, with a few notes left over. One can readily realize this by playing through this entire piano range, taking note of the number of times the same tone is repeated in octave relationships. How much more difficult the recognition of pitch relationships would be if there were no such interrelationships and we had to relate each tone directly to all the others.

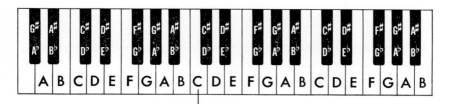

MIDDLE C

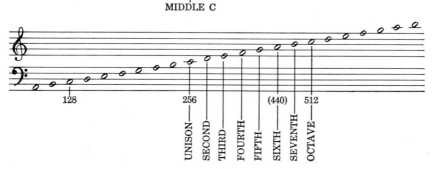

Notation of Pitch in Three Octaves of the Piano Keyboard.

It is possible, even within the octave, to obtain an indeterminate number of pitch variations. If musicians had not agreed on the necessity of using only a certain few of these pitches for their musical systems, there would be much confusion. The number and character of these within-the-octave pitch relationships have varied in different parts of the world and at different times in history. From these pitches we have formed certain basic tonal relationships called *scales* (see page 102), for which we use two names:

(a) Absolute, based on the number of vibrations per second—A, B, C, D, E, F, G.

(b) Relative, based on the relationships of one tone to another, such as octave, second, third, fourth, fifth, sixth, seventh. (These terms refer to the interval or ratio of vibration-frequencies between the tones.)

These relationships, common to all Western music, may be expressed in mathematical-physical ratios. The most commonly used intervals—that is, pitch-distance between tones— are:

Octave, for example, from c to c^1	2:1
Fifth, for example, from c to g	3:2
Fourth, for example, from c to f	4:3
Third (major), for example from c to e	5:4
Third (minor), for example, from c to e flat	6:5
Sixth (major), for example, from c to a	5:3
Second, for example, from c to d	9:8
Seventh (major), for example, from c to b	15:8

Our present-day usage employs twelve pitches within each octave —count them on your piano keyboard—and makes them all equal in size. This practical system arranges these pitches (called semitones) so that they have the same value in all keys. Although it puts all the intervals slightly out of tune according to the actual mathematical ratios, the system is a necessity for modern keyboard music because of its use of modulation—the practice of shifting from one key to another.

In a theoretically perfect system of arranging these intervals within the octave so that they correspond exactly to the mathematical series of proportional ratios, it would be possible to use only one such scale in a piece of music, since modulation from it into another similar scale would be almost impossible. To avoid this difficulty, an acoustical compromise called *Equal Temperament* was adopted during the eighteenth century. In this, all the intervals except the octave are only approximately in tune but the discrepancy is hardly noticeable and the compromise satisfies three incompatible requirements: true intonation, complete freedom of modulation, and convenience for use on keyed instruments.

VOLUME

As the arc of the swing of a vibrating body increases (that is, the extent to which it moves away from its normal state of rest), the energy of a tone increases, and it becomes louder. If we pluck a violin string or strike a piano string lightly, a certain number (say, 256) of slight vibrations per second will be set in motion; if we strike harder, the same number of vibrations per second will result, but their amplitude will be wider, and thus the tone will be louder.

The relationship between physical cause and psychological effect here is a peculiar one; it has been shown by experiment that the sensation of loudness does not vary directly as the intensity of the vibrations but as the logarithm of the intensity. For example, if we increase the intensity of a sound from ten to a hundred times, the resulting loudness is increased only from one to two times.[5] In non-mathematical terms, doubling the intensity of a sound does not double its loudness. The practical results of this experiment are important: two flutes playing together are not twice as loud as one flute; ten pianos are not ten times as loud as one. It has been estimated that twenty players must be added to an eighty-piece orchestra to produce an appreciable difference in loudness.

These facts suggest the reason why comparatively few degrees of dynamic intensity are needed by musicians: it has been argued that seven different degrees of dynamic intensity are all that are necessary to cover the extremes of *fortissimo* and *pianissimo* used by a pianist in interpreting ordinary music for his instrument.[6] Other theorists would insist that there are more; but in any event, compare this with the eighty-eight different degrees of pitch relationships that are at the disposal of the pianist.

[5] The logarithm of 10 to the base 10 is 1, and that of 100 is 2.
[6] Guy Montrose in *The Journal of Applied Psychology*, April, 1928.

TIMBRE

The scientist can take us into his laboratory and show us that the characteristic quality of a tone, or its *timbre*, is determined by vibrations. By means of a specially constructed instrument called a *phondeik*, invented by Professor Dayton C. Miller of the Case School of Applied Science, he can produce graphs which trace the distinctive patterns of various kinds of tone. For example, a tuning fork, which produces almost pure tones, forms this sort of graph:

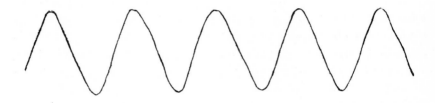

Most elastic bodies (which includes all musical instruments) produce, on the other hand, complex sound waves resulting in graphs like these:

Phonodeik Graph of Violin Tone.

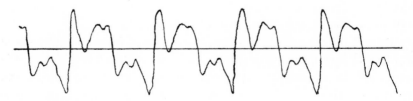

Phonodeik Graph of Clarinet Tone.

Properly interpreted, this means that a body which produces this sort of wave vibrates not only as a whole, but also in parts or segments, and that it therefore produces not only a fundamental tone but also a number of supplementary or "partial" tones. The vibration of the body as a whole is the strongest and loudest of the compound tones we hear when a note is produced; this is what we call its *fundamental*. When we speak of the pitch of a tone we refer to the number of vibrations of this fundamental. The tones produced by the fractional vibrations of the body are called *overtones* or *harmonics*. These stand in simple ratio to the vibration of the whole (producing the fundamental)—namely, 1 : 2 : 3 : 4 : 5 : 6, and so on—and vary in intensity and number according to the composition of the vibrating body, the manner in which it is sounded, and so forth. It is the number and relative intensities of the overtones which determine the quality of any musical tone. When we hear a tone such as is produced by a piano or an orchestral instrument, we may think that we are hearing only one tone—the fundamental; in reality, we also hear many other tones of lower intensity. It is the presence or absence of these in combination with the fundamental which determines the *timbre* of the instrument.

Taking any note, G, for example, as the fundamental produced by a vibrating string or an open-air column, we find that the overtones produced in conjunction with it would be, according to the most commonly accepted theory, as follows:[7]

The pure qualities of the upper tones of the flute are caused by the fact that practically no overtones are heard except the second (that is, the octave above the fundamental); the characteristic quality of the tone of the clarinet is due to the presence of the odd-numbered harmonics—the third, fifth, seventh, and so forth. We find that the orchestral horn gives out a strong fundamental tone with more than twenty overtones. Since the first investigations of Helmholtz (1821-1894) into these physical bases of tone quality, a great deal of research has been done, and we now know that there are other factors which help determine timbre. In the main, however, his theories are still considered correct.

[7] The overtones present in any tone depend partly on the instrument producing the tone and partly on the manner in which the tone is produced.

DURATION

The duration of a musical tone is obviously the time which elapses between the beginning and the end of vibrations. It has been estimated that the shortest possible period that can give rise to any consciousness of existence is about 1/20 of a second. Periods of silence are indicated by symbols that have a time relationship to notes. We say, for example, that the duration of a whole note or rest is twice that of a half note, and four times that of a quarter note. The symbols used in modern notation to indicate the relative values of duration are:

	WHOLE	HALF	QUARTER	EIGHTH	SIX-TEENTH	THIRTY-SECOND	SIXTY-FOURTH
NOTES	𝅝	𝅗𝅥	𝅘𝅥	𝅘𝅥𝅮 or	𝅘𝅥𝅯 or	𝅘𝅥𝅰 or	𝅘𝅥𝅱 or
RESTS	𝄻	𝄼	𝄽	𝄾	𝄿	𝅀	𝅁

Successive notes are connected by the tie to sound as one tone.

WRITTEN	SOUND	WRITTEN	SOUND
𝅗𝅥‿𝅗𝅥	𝅝	𝅘𝅥‿𝅘𝅥	𝅗𝅥

A dot increases by half the duration of the preceding note or rest.

$$\text{𝅗𝅥.} = \text{𝅗𝅥‿𝅘𝅥} \qquad \text{𝅘𝅥.} = \text{𝅘𝅥‿𝅘𝅥𝅮}$$

In practical use, the sense of duration also includes tempo—the rate of speed at which a piece of music moves. This may be indicated either by an Italian term, such as *adagio, andante,* or *presto,* affixed to the music or by a definite reference to the metronome, an instrument devised for marking exact speeds.

The system of *notation* which has been developed in Western music during the centuries is really a system of written signs which indicates the prescribed pitches and duration values of the tones to the interpreter of the music. The pitch is graphically represented by the vertical pattern of the note-signs on a horizontal indicator (called the staff or stave) consisting of five parallel lines, each of which signifies a certain pitch. The pitch of the various lines and the spaces between them is determined by a *clef* sign, placed at the left-hand edge of each staff, denoting high (treble, 𝄞), medium (the C clef, which can be placed on several different lines, 𝄡), and low (bass, 𝄢) pitches, thus:

Duration is indicated by the character of the notehead used (whether open or closed), and that of the stem (see above).

This common alphabet came into use in European music around 1600, and every listener who wishes to come into close contact with music should at least learn to read it. It is no more difficult to learn than the multiplication table and opens, like the learning of the alphabet, the gateway to an entirely new and wonderful world.

THE SPIRITUAL FACTOR IN MUSIC

It was Beethoven who defined music as the "link which connects the spiritual with the sensuous life"; what he meant was that in addition to its existence as sound, music is a means of communication by which something of the processes of a man's inner life is revealed to his fellow men. The composer expresses, not what lies outside him, but what goes on inside him. Through the external physical means which we have just outlined, he communicates his inner feelings and spiritual concepts in such a way that they can be perceived through the senses of those who listen. As someone has said, "The musical composition which a composer makes is the expression in musical tones of his inner life."

On the afternoon of the day before this was written, the authors had an experience which should furnish sufficient proof, if such be needed, of the validity of the statements just made. In a large metropolitan concert hall an audience that taxed the capacity of the auditorium had gathered to hear one of the world's great orchestras interpret the music of one of the greatest composers. As the program progressed, it was evident that the audience came more and more under the spell of the music. Forgotten were the immediate sur-roundings, the discomfort of the crowded hall, the technical perfection of the playing, even the sympathetic interpretation of the orchestra. Here was a great man speaking simply, from the depths of his spirit, with a direct vigor and forcefulness of utterance that could not be denied, of things that matter today just as they mattered when they were first put on paper and as they always will throughout the history of the human race. There was a great deal more to this music than "auditory sound organized with variations of pitch, timbre, intensity, and duration." Something was being communicated from composer to listener so forcefully, so directly that, to quote a poetic observer of the occasion, when the finale of the last symphony came and the "portals of the skies swung asunder and the great chant of victory and defiance was heard," the audience crashed into applause and wild cheers.

That is what we mean when we say that there are spiritual as well as physical materials to be reckoned with in music. This audience listening to the Boston Symphony Orchestra playing Sibelius' music would never have received the impressions it did had it not been for the physical means used to convey the ideas of the composer—the superb timbre of orchestral tone, the carefully adjusted matters of pitch relationship, the intensity of tone, the correct relations of tempo, and so on. Had there been nothing else, however, the music would have been but sounding brass and tinkling cymbal; what made it memorable was the fact that the conductor and the orchestra were able to convey, through physical means, what the composer had put into the music—the full expression of his inner life. To paraphrase St. Paul: Music is an art not only of the letter, but also of the spirit; and he said, "The letter killeth, but the spirit giveth life."

LIST OF SUGGESTED MUSIC

A number of records illustrate the technical points made in this chapter. Among the most valuable are:

The Chromatic Scale	COOK
Frequency and Intermodulation	COOK
Sounds of Frequency	FOLK
Theory and Practice of Just Intonation	MUSURGIA

TOPICS FOR DISCUSSION

What effect do you think modern interest in the physical characteristic of tone may have in the development of music as an art? Give illustrations of present-day instruments illustrating this interest.

Discuss Beethoven's idea that music connects the spiritual with the sensuous life. Which of these elements do you think is the stronger in the average life? Can you define any means by which music acts as a link?

Discuss St. Paul's dictum about the letter and the spirit in the light of your own experience of musical interpretation by others.

CHAPTER 9

How Materials Are Made into Music

❦

As we listen to a piece of music, there are certain factors which organize the raw materials of physical sound in ways that heighten our understanding and increase our enjoyment. Although we may not realize it, our interest in a composition depends on one or more, perhaps all, of these factors; we may not be conscious of a single one of them, but it is their combined effect that makes music capable of being apprehended. Therefore, one of the first needs in learning to listen to music is to train our ears to recognize the fundamental factors by which its raw materials are organized: *rhythm, melody,* and *harmony*. These might well be called the elements of the language of music, and a complete understanding of them demands much study and belongs to the higher intricacies of the art. But even if the music lover is enabled only to hear how their use helps shape the composition to which he is listening, his appreciation will be tremendously advanced. These factors are present in all music, and the importance of great masterworks results partly from the significant ways in which a composer employs them.

RHYTHM

Rhythm is the most easily perceived of these fundamental factors. There is good reason for this, for rhythm is one of the most funda-

88

mental elements in nature. A famous musician is quoted as saying that "in the beginning there was rhythm," and if we stop to consider the universe in general we will see that this is true in other things besides music. Our life is being sustained constantly by the rhythmic beating of our heart, the beats occurring in pairs, one accented and the other unaccented. Our breathing is rhythmical, the inhalations corresponding to unaccented beats, the exhalations to accented. Our walking and running are rhythmical, as is, indeed, the natural pace of all animals. The larger operations of nature occur in rhythmical sequence—the succession of the seasons, the movements of the stars and planets, the flow of the tides, the beating of the waves on the shore, and so on.

Thus an art is merely conforming to a universal truth in insisting that the elements of which it is composed be arranged in some sort of harmonious correlation. The rhythmic schemes of the space arts —architecture, sculpture, and painting—are rather easily discernible to the eye, just as those of the time arts—music and literature— are to the ear. Every work of art worthy of the name is arranged according to some pattern of weak and strong units that gives it interest and makes it intelligible to the mind of the beholder or listener. The façade of a building, the arrangement of details in a painting, the distribution of the elements of a piece of sculpture give grace and serve to stimulate the interest; they are among the most important means which serve to make the art work intelligible to the beholder. In music and poetry there is need for even more careful organization of rhythmic elements if we are to have a sense of order and balance. We do not have to listen to a piece of poetry or music long before we realize that its constant flow is marked by a succession of beats or pulses, arranged into definite groups by means of heavier stress coming every so often. For instance, in the nursery rhyme that begins:

> Bobby Shafto's gone to sea
> Silver buckles on his knee

there are four periods of stress or accent in each line. In the first line they fall at the first syllable of "Bobby" and of "Shafto," and on "gone" and "sea." This point of stress we call an accented (strong) beat, as opposed to the others, which are unaccented (weak). We

can diagram the above lines thus, letting ↓ represent a **strong beat**,
and ◡ a **weak beat**:

$$↓ ◡ ↓ ◡ ↓ ◡ ↓ (◡)$$
$$↓ ◡ ↓ ◡ ↓ ◡ ↓ (◡)$$

The following tune has exactly the same general rhythmic
scheme, which we may call duple, since the meter consists of two
beats or pulses, a heavy and a light, with the first in each group
accented:

On the other hand, these lines will be found to have quite a
different scheme:

> Spotted and veinèd with various hues
> Through the clear realms of azure drift

$$↓ ◡ ◡ ↓ ◡ ◡ ↓ ◡ ◡ ↓ (◡ ◡)$$

and a tune like this famous one represents the same pattern:

This is what we call triple meter, consisting of three beats or
pulses, with the first in each group accented.

It will be found that most of the more complicated regular
rhythmic schemes may be resolved into these two elemental ones,
duple and triple. For example, in this line

> Sandy cat by the Farmer's chair

$$↓ ◡ ↓ ◡̆ ↓ ◡ ↓ (◡)$$

the heavy accent really comes on the first beat of each group of
four, with something of a secondary accent halfway between.
Obviously this is an elaboration of duple rhythm. In music we have
this well illustrated by a tune such as the old round:

The following scheme is clearly a modified triple meter, with the main accent coming on the first beat of each group of six and a secondary accent midway between:

Often I think of the beautiful town

↓◡◡ ↓   ◡ ◡ ↓◡◡ ↓ (◡◡)

The old French folk tune illustrates this well:

The fundamental time units which occur in music are called *measures;* they are assumed, in ordinary music, to be of equal length and to be made up of a certain number of beats, organized and bound together by the principal accent with which they begin. Thus, in duple time we speak of two beats in a measure; in triple, of three; in quadruple, of four. The vertical lines which are placed on the music score to designate its division are called *bars* or *bar lines,* while the divisions themselves bear the name *measure.* When writing or printing music, the general rhythmic scheme is indicated at the very beginning by means of a fraction placed before the first note; the numerator indicates the number of beats that there are to be in each measure, and the denominator, the kind of note which represents each beat. Thus, 2/4 has two quarter beats to a measure; 4/4, four quarter beats to a measure; 6/8, six eighth beats to a measure; 9/8, nine eighth beats to a measure, and so on.

Music's Meter

This aspect of music's rhythmic structure may be called its *meter*[1] (or measure), since it is concerned with its division into units called *measures,* each of which consists of a certain number of beats or pulses. The principal meters used in present-day music are:

2/4 meter: two beats to a measure, each a quarter note

♩ ♩ | ♩ ♩ |

---

[1] This is often erroneously spoken of as *time;* the latter is not a musical term at all, but refers to "that which elapses while music is being played."

2/2 meter: two beats to a measure, each a half note

$$\text{𝅗𝅥 \quad 𝅗𝅥 \quad | \quad 𝅗𝅥 \quad 𝅗𝅥 \quad |}$$

4/4 meter: four beats to a measure, each a quarter note, the accent coming on the first and third beats, with the third-beat accent slightly weaker than the first

$$\text{♩ ♩ ♩ ♩ | ♩ ♩ ♩ ♩ |}$$

3/4 meter: three beats to a measure, each a quarter note

$$\text{♩ ♩ ♩ | ♩ ♩ ♩ |}$$

3/2 meter: three beats to a measure, each a half note

$$\text{𝅗𝅥 𝅗𝅥 𝅗𝅥 | 𝅗𝅥 𝅗𝅥 𝅗𝅥 |}$$

3/8 meter: three beats to a measure, each an eighth note

$$\text{♪ ♪ ♪ | ♪ ♪ ♪ |}$$

6/8 meter: six beats to a measure, each an eighth note, the accent coming on the first and fourth beats, the fourth being slightly less accented than the first

$$\text{♫♪ ♫♪ | ♫♪ ♫♪ |}$$

9/8 meter: nine beats to a measure, each an eighth note, dividing itself into three groups of three eighth notes each

$$\text{♫♪ ♫♪ ♫♪ | ♫♪ ♫♪ ♫♪ |}$$

12/8 meter: twelve beats to a measure, each an eighth note, dividing itself into four groups of three eighth notes each

$$\text{♫♪ ♫♪ ♫♪ ♫♪ | ♫♪ ♫♪ ♫♪ ♫♪ |}$$

It is possible, of course, to have 2, 3, or 4 beats in a measure with *any* length of note as the unit; this note length may be simple (divided into halves) or compound (divided into thirds). The 6/8, 9/8, and 12/8 meters are illustrations of this—multiples of simple meters with 2, 3, and 4 units in measures that have internal divisions of thirds.

Regular patterns of meter, when used with invariable regularity, lay the music open to the charge of being monotonous, and so composers use various means for avoiding this overdose of regularly recurring down beats. One of the most popular of these is syncopation—the shifting of an accent in a measure so that it does not come where we expect it naturally. For example, instead of having the accents in a measure occur according to the usual scheme,

↓ ᴜ ↓ ᴜ │↓ ᴜ↓ ᴜ│, we may have ᴜ↓ ᴜ↓ │ ᴜ ↓ ᴜ ↓ │ ; or instead of
1 2 3 4 1 2 3 4   1 2 3 4   1 2 3 4

↓ ᴜ ᴜ │↓ ᴜ ᴜ │ we often have ᴜ ↓ ᴜ │ ᴜ ↓ ᴜ │, or even
1 2 3   1 2 3   1 2 3   1 2 3

ᴜ ᴜ↓ │ ᴜ ᴜ ↓ │.
1 2 3   1 2 3

This device seems either to dull our rhythmic sense by confusing us as to where the strong pulse actually should come (and thus to give a certain flagging or rhythmically dulled character to what we hear), or, by strongly stimulating our curiosity as to where the beat will fall, to heighten the effect and make the music more interesting. (Watch the feet of those listening to popular music, which contains so many interesting syncopated effects.) In passing it should be noted that, despite the belief that it is peculiar to contemporary popular music, syncopation has been in wide use since the time of the Renaissance. For a good illustration listen to the first movement of Beethoven's *Eroica Symphony*, beginning with measure 250.

Some composers, especially the more modern, avoid monotony by inserting a measure or two of different metrical pattern into the regular flow of pulsation—for instance, a three-beat pattern into music that is regularly in two-beat measure. Tchaikovsky does this most effectively in the principal tune in his *Andante cantabile* from the *String Quartet*, Op. 11. (See page 245.) Composers from Debussy on have not hesitated to mix the metrical pattern of their measures more or less indiscriminately; in Debussy's *Afternoon of a Faun* the meter fluctuates between 9/8, 6/8, 12/8, 3/4, and 4/4, and in Stravinsky's *Sacre du printemps* one page may contain as many as four metric patterns.

A new rhythm is sometimes superimposed on the regular one, a device often used by Brahms, in this fashion: │ 1 2 3 │ 1 2 3 │ .
                                                          1 2 1 2

Sometimes in these superimposed rhythms the first beats of the succeeding measures do not coincide; then we have an even more striking polyrhythmic effect, thus: $\left|\frac{1 \quad 2 \quad 3 \quad 1 \quad 2 \quad 3}{1 \quad 2 \mid 1 \quad 2 \mid 1 \quad 2}\right|$.

In good jazz music, over a fundamental, unchanging bass rhythm, the composer places freer rhythms which often seem to play havoc with the underlying pulse of the piece. Again this is nothing new, for the same device was used, and very cleverly, too, by the scores of madrigal composers who flourished all over Europe before the time of Shakespeare; some of these madrigals contain most ingenious conflicts of meter between their various parts.

PRACTICE IN METER

The metrical pattern of a piece of music is comparatively easy to recognize, since this sort of rhythmic pulse is largely physical and our response to it is almost a reflex action. Everyone can be taught to "keep time" to a metrical beat, even if some of the other fundamentals of music persist in escaping him. Here are some suggested examples for practice in determining the difference between duple, triple, quadruple, and sextuple meters. Hum or whistle the tunes, tapping out the heavy beats with a pencil or your foot.

"Old Black Joe"
"America" (God Save the King)
"Humoresque"
"Long, Long Ago"
"Abide with Me"
"Onward, Christian Soldiers"
Sur le pont d'Avignon (On the Bridge at Avignon)
"The Last Rose of Summer"
"Annie Laurie"
O Tannenbaum (Maryland, My Maryland)
Ach! du lieber Augustin
Minuet in G by Paderewski

OTHER ASPECTS OF RHYTHM

It should not take much listening practice to make one realize that there are rhythmic schemes in music other than purely metrical ones. In other words, the recurrence of some readily recognized metrical pattern is not the only way by which the features of a musical conception may be organized to "produce a harmonious whole through the correlation and interdependence of its parts."

(See the definition of *rhythm* accompanying the picture on this page.) There is, for example, the rhythm of note duration which music imposes on the underlying metrical scheme of a composition. We do not necessarily have a note for each beat of the meter; some notes are held for one or two beats, while often a beat is divided among several notes.[2]

South Door of Twelfth-Century Kilpeck Church in Herefordshire, England.

Rhythm is a characteristic common to all the fine arts. It may be defined as the regular recurrence of like features in an artistic composition, producing a harmonious whole through the correlation and interdependence of parts.

In the familiar tune "Old Folks at Home," we can easily establish the underlying metrical pattern as being 4/4; but if we tap this out rhythmically while singing the melody, we will find that the note values of the melody are in the following proportions:

[2] Silence, regarded as the mere absence of sound, is an important factor in music; its length of duration is indicated by rests, which, as we have shown, have values that correspond to the length of the notes.

The nature of these note values contributes another rhythmic scheme to the whole effect which we gain from listening to music and has a great deal to do with the impressions we receive.

There are other rhythmical designs in music, many of them intricate and difficult to hear, for they are made up of melodic and chordal features; these we may leave to the carefully trained expert to recognize and enjoy. The idea that several kinds of rhythmic schemes exist side by side in an art work may be difficult for the listener to grasp at first; but if we compare music with literature, which also have various types of rhythmic organization, the realization may be made easier.

Reciting Housman's lines from "A Shropshire Lad," stressing the regular beats of the metrical scheme, we get the following:

With rue my heart is laden

For golden friends I had,

For many a rose-lipt maiden

And many a light-foot lad.

Notice (1) that there is a certain rhythm in the line lengths—lines 1 and 3 have four metrical units in them, but lines 2 and 4 only three; (2) that in order to get the real sense of this verse we must continue without pause (we must "phrase," as the technical term has it) from line 1 into line 2 and from line 3 into line 4. Full comprehension of these lovely lines comes only when we combine, as we read them, all the rhythmic elements they possess.[3]

---

[3] In order to avoid confusion we should apply the term *rhythm* in general to the organizational schemes by which the various features of a piece of music or poetry are formed into an integral whole—the organization of tones of differing lengths, the subtleties of placing measure against measure, phrase against phrase, sentence against sentence. Meter should be used to describe that type of rhythm which is measured by dividing the flow of music or poetry into units made up of definite arrangements of pulses or beats.

So, too, with music; it is made up of many subtle interactions of the various rhythmic elements. This is easy enough to prove; listen to these examples of duple meter, all of them chosen from Beethoven's scores. Notice how all the elements which make up the rhythmic impression are responsible for the total effect you receive from the music.

(1) *Symphony No. 3, in E-flat Major (Eroica)*, Second Movement (at the beginning). Here the slow tempo (pace of the music) and the way the notes are grouped in the measure give a solemn, heavy, funeral-march effect.

(2) *Symphony No. 7, in A Major*, Second Movement. Here a quicker tempo and a broad arrangement of the notes give an effect that is not so overpowering and oppressive.

(3) *Symphony No. 5, in c minor*, Fourth Movement. The dignified tempo and the exultant melody combine to give a joyous, buoyant effect.

It is the same with ¾ measure:

(1) "Tales from the Vienna Woods" by Johann Strauss or any other good waltz, such as Tchaikovsky's from *The Nutcracker* suite. The lively tempo and the enticing melodic patterns make us want to dance.

(2) *Largo* by Handel. Here the slow tempo and the dignified arrangement of the notes give a sort of religious effect. If you look at the melody carefully, you will find that only two measures of those which contain more than one sound have the rhythmic pattern. This theme *grows*. In the hands of an ordinary patterner, measures 5-8 would probably have reproduced the lengths of measures 1-4, but Handel was after real rhythm, and so he subtly varied his theme. This subtlety is an essential part of musical form.

LIST OF SUGGESTED MUSIC

If further time allows, you may be interested in determining the metrical schemes of such examples as these:

Tannhäuser, March	WAGNER
Mazurka in c sharp minor, Op. 63, No. 3 (piano)	CHOPIN
Polonaise in A Major, Op. 40, No. 1 (piano)	CHOPIN
Symphony in g minor, Minuet, K.183	MOZART
Bolero	RAVEL
Pavane pour une infante défunte (Pavan for a Dead Princess)	RAVEL
Tango in a minor	ALBÉNIZ

Enough suggestions have been given here to enable the hearer to realize how some recognition of the rhythmic structure of a piece of music will help his enjoyment. The important thing to remember is that in learning to listen, not everything can be grasped at once; a general conception of the rhythmic flow is all that is necessary for the amateur.

TOPICS FOR DISCUSSION

Devise your own definition of rhythm. Is an all-inclusive definition practicable?

"Cross-rhythm" always pleases musicians; Brahms was fond of using it. Compare the manner in which Brahms used it with Beethoven's use.

"Rhythm music" as used in popular music has little or no meaning for the serious musicians, who take for granted that rhythm is vital. They complain that popular, ephemeral music is rhythmically weak. What is the meaning of this criticism? Is the accusation true? What is rhythmic weakness?

Discuss the far greater possibilities for elaboration of rhythmic complexity in music as compared to lesser possibilities in poetry.

How does Stravinsky's *Le sacre du printemps* bring its rhythmic complexity to a climax? Is the result clarifying or confusing?

CHAPTER 10

How Materials Are Made into Music (continued)

ॐ ॐ

MELODY

If, as we have said, "in the beginning of music there was rhythm," the element of melody could not have been far behind; it is impossible to discuss one of these primary factors of present-day music without considering the other. *Melody*, defined as a *successive sounding of tones related to each other in such a way as to make musical sense and coherent expression*, has an emotional significance in music, just as rhythm has a physical significance. Neither can be thought of as separate, independent entities, except in the most primitive music (such as the exciting examples brought to us from Africa by the recording companies). Whenever we think of rhythm we think also of the shadow of the melody associated with it. You can easily prove this for your own satisfaction: try to think of the rhythm of even such a simple piece as "Old Folks at Home" or "Tales from the Vienna Woods," and you will find yourself humming the melody in order to do so. These two elements might be called the Siamese twins of music.

All compositions are made up of some sort of melodic and rhythmic patterns, repeated and varied in different ways throughout the course of the music. And so if we are to gain an adequate knowledge of the music we hear, it will be necessary for us to train ears and minds so that we become conscious of these musical *themes*

99

and remember them. Such simple tunes as we have mentioned above are recognizable to us readily enough because we have heard them from our earliest days. But what about those others with which we are not familiar—those hundreds of themes or motives, sometimes only a few notes in length, sometimes several measures long, which occur in the compositions that are unknown to us—how are we to learn and remember these?

MEMORY HINTS

Here are some hints for assisting your memory.

(1) Notice the peculiarities of the melodic flow—whether, for instance, it is limited, as is the case of this theme from the slow movement of Beethoven's *Seventh Symphony* (the interest here is almost entirely rhythmic):

Or whether it skips about more or less adroitly, as in these two examples from the first movement of Mozart's *G Minor Symphony*:

(2) See whether the quality of the melody is essentially vocal or instrumental—whether it was meant to be sung or played.

Such a theme as this, from Beethoven's *Ninth Symphony*, first movement, is obviously instrumental in style. Its wide range and great leaps make it almost impossible to sing:

The following theme, from Verdi's *Rigoletto*, was, on the other hand, meant for singing:

La don-na è mo - bi - le Qual più ma al ven - to

Mu - ta d'ac - cen - to E - di pen - sie - ro

Such themes as that from Handel's opera *Xerxes*, quoted on page 97, from Schubert's *Unfinished Symphony*, first movement (page 107), or Dvořák's *New World Symphony*, second movement (page 108) are suitable for either singing or playing. They are naturals in this respect, a fact which accounts for their unusual popularity.

(3) Observe the characteristic rhythmic patterns of the themes.

The theme from Beethoven's *Seventh Symphony*, quoted on page 100, has a rather monotonous rhythm—probably Beethoven intended this to emphasize its quality. On the other hand, notice the rhythmic vitality of this melody from Mozart's *G Minor Symphony*:

The slow movement of Beethoven's *Fifth Symphony* is one of the most carefully organized melodies in all music, so far as its rhythmic patterns are concerned. Even a first hearing will tell you that Beethoven begins with a complicated "dotted" rhythm and then follows with a broad, simple one.

(4) Finally, listen carefully to the characteristic tone quality of the instrument or instruments producing the melody. Try to memorize themes *in their instrumental timbres;* an oboe theme, for example, stays in the memory longer if we can remember it as being played on the oboe and not just a succession of notes.

We have already discussed *timbre* at some length; here we simply remind the listener that the ability to distinguish "tone color" (this phrase is used because no better is available) or quality of the various instruments and voices singly and in combination is one of the most obvious pleasures to be derived from listening.

Scales

To further aid your memory, take notice of the *scale* or *scales* used by the composer in forming his melody. As suggested by the meaning of the Italian *scala* (a staircase), *a scale may be said to be the pattern according to which the octave is divided into a specific succession of tonal steps.* There can be a wide diversity of scale patterns; a famous theoretician has said that it is possible to construct a hundred scales within the tonal space of an octave. Fortunately for the listener, only a few of these are in practical use, evolved by grouping together certain formulas common to melodies through the ages; but it is important for everyone who listens to music to know something about these scales, for on their structure depend the character, expressive quality, and style of the melodies and harmonies he hears. The notes of most familiar melodies are arranged not only in relationship with each other in the scale but also in relationship to a pitch, which we feel to be foundational, upon which the scale is based. The relationship with this central pitch, the *tonic*, is called *tonality;* the way the notes of the melody are arranged within this tonality gives the melody its particular, individual character.

In our Western music system the smallest interval used in scales is the half tone or semi-tone—the tonal distance between B and C, or E and F on the piano, for example. Twice this tonal distance we call a whole tone—the intervals between C and D, or F and G are good examples. Most present-day scales consist of these intervals arranged in varying combinations, starting from the different notes as tonics. The much-used major scale consists of this series, making up the octave: tone, tone, half tone, tone, tone, tone, half tone. If we go to the piano and, starting from C as tonic, use this formula, we will hear what we call the major scale of C.

Major Scale

whole whole half whole whole whole half
tone tone tone tone tone tone tone

Starting from any other note as tonic the same sequence will give the major scales of D, E, F, G, and so on. It will be found necessary to use the black keys occasionally, in order to keep the proper sequence of tones and half tones. Much of the music we know well is written in one of these major tonalities; the use of this pattern gives a bright, rather full and cheerful character to the music, as is evident in this major tune, already quoted, from the second movement of Haydn's *Surprise Symphony*:

Now listen to the brooding opening melody of Tchaikovsky's *Symphonie pathétique*, first heard low in the wood winds—dark in color and somber and melancholy in character.

Minor Scale

Here, obviously, the composer used a scale based on a different arrangement of steps and half-steps. This scale is called a minor scale. There are different kinds of minor scales in which, while the interval between the second and third steps remains consistently a half-step, that between the fifth and sixth steps and between the seventh and eighth steps may be either a half or a whole step. (See Glossary: Minor.) Minor scales have by no means been confined to somber, melancholy melodies such as the Tchaikovsky passage—note the first theme of the first movement of the Mendelssohn *Violin Concerto*.

The major and minor scales determined much of the dance and song type music of the seventeenth, eighteenth, and nineteenth centuries. Later, wide use was made of the *chromatic* (highly colored) scale, which is comprised, in succession, of all the twelve available semi-tones into which the octave is divided.

Chromatic Scale

This gives the music a peculiarly agitated, gliding, questioning, sensuous character, well-suited to the Romantic period. A good example is found in Rimsky-Korsakov's *Sadko*:

The *pentatonic* scale, with its familiar gaps and jumps, makes use of only five tones (instead of seven) in the octave. There are many patterns of this, the easiest to find on the keyboard being that of the five black keys, starting from the lowest of the three-group. This gives F sharp, G sharp, A sharp, C sharp, D sharp (F sharp). If we transfer this pattern to the white keys, starting on C, we have:

Pentatonic Scale

This scale seems to satisfy the needs of simple as well as sophisticated peoples; it is known to all music systems, both Eastern and Western, and is responsible for much of the charm and exotic character which we associate with the music of distant lands. Chinese, Indonese, Javanese, Scottish, Russian melodies all use it. Here are two simple examples:

From the oriental music which he heard, Debussy devised a six-tone scale comprising six whole tones in the octave thus:

Whole-tone Scale

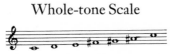

This scale, which has a peculiarly exotic character, gives a certain color to many things of Debussy. For example, this from his First Book of *Préludes*[1] for the piano:

This is a good place to note the occasional scales, other than those already mentioned, to be found in contemporary music. If we listen to Vaughn Williams' popular *Fantasia on a Theme by Tallis*, we are immediately aware of a somewhat different, detached, and archaic flavor. It is due to the composer's use of modality, that is, harmonic and melodic formations based on the church modes, in distinction to those based on the major and minor scales. Modes were used primarily for ecclesiastical music (the Gregorian Chant used in the Catholic Church today is almost all "modal") and therefore were also naturally employed in secular music. Their distinguishing feature, to be clearly heard in this rousing "chanty" tune, "The High Barbary," is the use of a whole tone between the seventh scale step and the tonic:

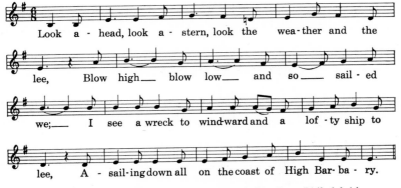

Look a - head, look a - stern, look the wea-ther and the lee, Blow high___ blow low___ and so___ sail - ed we;___ I see a wreck to wind-ward and a lof - ty ship to lee, A - sail-ing down all on the coast of High Bar- ba - ry.

[1] Excerpt reprinted by permission of Elkan-Vogel Co., Inc., Philadelphia.

A special kind of scale making use of "tone-rows" was evolved by Arnold Schönberg about 1921 to give an effect of "atonality," music without any sense of tonality such as is produced by the major and minor scale systems. These rows are arbitrary arrangements of the twelve notes of the chromatic scale in a particular order, different for each composition. Schönberg used this row as the basis of the last of his *Five Piano Pieces*, Op. 23:

Some modern European music, as well as Indian and other Eastern music, makes use of scales that are composed of intervals called microtones, smaller than the semitone. These, of course, require special instruments or systems of tuning, and a different kind of notation.

If a melody stays mainly in the chromatic scale, we call it a *chromatic* melody; if it does not stray often from its major and minor outlines, we speak of it as being *diatonic*. If it sticks to one of the modes, we call it *modal*. There is as much difference between music that is based largely on chromatic melodies and that which is diatonic in character as there is between major and minor melodies. Chromatic tunes are bland and lush; in comparison, diatonic melodies are severe and plain. Compare, for example, Rimsky-Korsakov's well-known "Song of India" with the melody quoted on page 103 from Haydn's *Surprise Symphony*, and you will quickly hear this difference. Or notice the difference in effect (carefully calculated by the composer) between such diatonic themes of Wagner's as that of "The Sword" from *The Ring of the Nibelung*

and his famous chromatic theme from *Tristan und Isolde*, portraying with relentless intensity the burning anguish and longing of the two famous lovers:

This last is one of the most famous themes in all music, and no better or more appealing example of how melodies are wrought into larger wholes could be found. It gives us a definite illustration of the fact that one of the best means for getting an "ear-hold" on music is through learning to recognize good melodies, and listening to hear how the composer weaves his musical fabric out of them. This little germ theme is at the basis of nearly all the Prelude to Wagner's opera *Tristan und Isolde.*

PRACTICE IN MELODY

Here are some fine melodies on which to practice. Get them firmly fixed in your mind, and then notice how they are used by the composer to build up a larger organized piece. You will realize the necessity of holding fast to melodic units when listening to music.

Although consisting of but two notes repeated at different pitch levels, this motive can easily be remembered because of its strong rhythmic pattern:

It is the first theme (or melody) of the opening movement of Beethoven's *Fifth Symphony* and, as used here, is in minor mode. It is followed shortly by this beautiful longer melody in the major, the second theme:

Listen to the whole movement and you will hear how it is built up largely of manipulations of such germ themes.

A still longer melody, but one easily remembered, nevertheless, is a theme from the first movement of Schubert's *Unfinished Symphony,* which is in the minor. Notice that the third and fourth measures are exactly the same as the first two measures:

The next theme of the same movement is one of the best-known melodies:

Listen to the movement as a whole, and you will hear these two tunes used constantly throughout.

This is a fine example of a lively minor melody taken from Dvořák's *New World Symphony*.

Notice how the composer follows the first four measures with an answering four measure theme; then repeats the first in a higher register, followed by the answering theme in the major. Thus small themes are extended and expanded. More about this later!

HARMONY

Since it is common practice to use the word *harmony* to mean a pleasing concord or a musical consonance, it is necessary, at the beginning of our discussion of this most sophisticated element of music, to say that the musician defines harmony as the *simultaneous sounding of tones* as opposed to their successive sounding in melody. Both melody and harmony use the same materials: melody gives contour and color to the structure; harmony provides it with body and substance. A good example of this is to be found in the first four measures of the melody just quoted from Dvořák. They are made up of only three notes which, when sounded together as a *chord*, provide a harmonic support to the same notes spread out successively as a melody in a lively rhythmic pattern.

Although we must here treat these factors individually, melody, harmony, and rhythm are interdependent in actual practice. The detailed consideration of harmony is hardly a matter for the amateur listener, although he can readily realize that most of the music he hears is dependent on harmony for its effect. Harmonic support is given to melody through forming and connecting simultaneously sounding clusters of tone. The science of harmony consists of the study of the ways in which these chords are built and related to one another.

There are different ways of putting these tone clusters together; the most common is by building a three tone chord (triad) above a fundamental pitch, called the root. Since a great deal of music employs four part harmony (one for each of what would correspond to soprano, alto, tenor and bass voices), one member of the chord is usually sounded in two voices.

The simplest triads are made up of *consonant* intervals which suggest a static feeling of repose. This is, of course, a matter of training and experience, musicians' ears reacting in different ways at different periods in musical history. Traditionally, these intervals are the ones classed as consonant:

Consonant Intervals above C

All others, such as seconds, sevenths, diminished fifths, are dissonant and give a sense of stress or tension.

Dissonant Intervals above C

When triads are extended by adding dissonant intervals, particularly those which lie a seventh or more above the root, we call the resulting chords *dissonant*. The degree of dissonance is determined by the number of dissonant intervals they contain. Here is a very mild one:

There are other ways of producing dissonant chords.

1. Chords are sometimes erected using intervals other than the third; for example, in quartal harmony they are based on fourths:

2. When arbitrary scales such as the tone-rows are used, the chords are constructed from the notes of those scales:

Chords based on a Schönberg Tone-row

3. Two or more triads are sounded together to produce a poly-chord:

4. Tone clusters or complex sonorities are achieved by notes sounded without consideration of anything but sonority; they occur in contemporary piano music, where the player is instructed to depress a group of notes with his fist, elbow, or forearm.

It is the constant flux between consonance and dissonance, the constant production and resolution of dissonance, that adds a great deal of interest to the music we hear. As the course of music has changed during the centuries, composers have turned more and more to dissonant harmony. The works of composers of as late a period as the eighteenth century consist largely of consonant harmonies, with dissonances used from time to time to heighten interest and provide tension. This process is almost exactly reversed by the composers of the twentieth century, many of whom use dissonances entirely.

If you listen to the overture to Wagner's *Tannhäuser*, you will quickly realize that the effect of the opening strains is due as much to the chords that Wagner uses as to the suitable rhythm and impressive melody. When the change of mood comes in the middle of the overture, you will notice that the type of harmony changes as well. Much of the broad effect that we receive from Handel's *Largo* is due to the fine, straightforward, majestic chords employed.

A review of the excerpts already quoted as illustrations of melodies and rhythms will show how much the chords employed in each example contribute to our interest in the music. Perhaps the most striking example of this is the Schubert melody, quoted on page 107. Hearing it alone gives us a great deal of pleasure, but when we put chords beneath it, it seems almost like another thing in the fullness of its beauty.

In general, when the chords used in a composition conform to the major or the minor scale, we say that the piece is "in the major" or "in the minor." When the chords used are built out of the tones of the chromatic scale, the harmonization is said to be *chromatic;* or if the notes used keep in the diatonic scale, we speak of the chords as being *diatonic*. In the *Tannhäuser* overture the opening measures are in diatonic harmony; the middle section is decidedly chromatic in its harmonization.

TONALITY

Even the briefest consideration of music from the viewpoint of its harmonic context must include a mention of *tonality*, one of the most subtle and yet powerful assets of the art. Practically all the music we hear (except that of some contemporary composers) is in one "key" or another. By this we mean that the notes which comprise our tonal system are grouped in specific sets of relationships to a tone which serves them as a sort of axis, a tone from which the movement within each of these sets of relationships (called *Keys*) starts and to which it returns as a final resting place. This tone, as we have seen, is the tonic. Since any one of the twelve tones within the octave can serve as a tonic, the composer has at his disposal twelve different tonal planes in which to write his music. Suppose he chooses one—the key of C, for example—he may decide to write music composed of melodies and chords that use the major scale which begins on that tonic, as Beethoven did in his *First Sym-*

phony, or he may write music using the minor scale starting on that tonic, as Beethoven did in his *Fifth Symphony*.[2]

And so with all the other tones within the octave—C sharp, D, D sharp, and the rest; each can serve as a tonic for either a major or a minor scale. Since each of these scales has its own set of tonal relationships and its own groups of chords, composers have twenty-four tonal levels on which to erect their music, twenty-four keys, twelve major and twelve minor. When we speak of the tonality or the key of a piece, then, we describe (1) its specific tonal level, that is, the tonic around which its tonal structure is centered; and (2) the set of tonal relationships (the scale or the mode) which generally prevails. The title of Bach's *Suite No. 1 in C Major* means simply that its prevailing tonality centers around C as a tonic and that the scales, chords, melodies, and so on which go to make up its fabric are in the major mode. His second suite, on the other hand, centers about B as a tonic (its pitch level is thus half a tone lower than that of the first suite), and it is written in the minor mode. When Bach wrote the two great collections of clavier music which comprise his *Well-Tempered Clavier*, he deliberately used each of the twelve major and twelve minor keys as tonics for the pieces, thus making a total of twenty-four in each collection.

This may seem intricate enough to the amateur listener, but it is not all that he should learn about the subject of tonality. Pieces have tonality not only as wholes but also in parts; in other words, a composer does not keep to the same tonality (or, putting it into other words, does not keep to the same key) throughout the course of a piece. He purposely uses changes of key (called *modulations*) to hold and increase the interest as the music progresses; a simple song usually contains several changes, and a great work, such as a Beethoven or a Brahms symphony, contains scores of them. The constant shifting of tonal levels, now lower, now higher, revives our interest as we listen to a long work, much as a hiker's progress up and down a mountain affects his appreciation of the view that greets his eye as he walks. In each case the general impression received is not altered, but the continual change of points of view gives renewed interest and freshened enthusiasm.

[2] In the case of large works, such as symphonies, sonatas, and quartets, the tonality is determined by the prevailing key of the first movement—thus we have Beethoven's symphonies in C Major and c minor, in E-flat Major, in B-flat Major, and so on.

On the part of the composer, these modulations must be skillfully and effectively wrought; any violent or awkward change from one key to another may destroy rather than create interest. It is a tribute to the technical skill of the great composers that most of us, in listening to their music, are quite unaware that such changes arc taking place until they are pointed out to us. We have been affected by them unconsciously; they have increased our enjoyment of the music and heightened our imaginative realization of its content; and yet they have been so unobtrusively accomplished that we probably never knew that they existed. Any attempt which the listener may make to realize the manner in which a composer takes him on these tonal adventures cannot but increase his enjoyment of the music he hears. It may be difficult to follow all the devious paths and windings, but that is hardly necessary. Just to realize what is happening adds zest to listening.

TOPICS FOR DISCUSSION

Make your own definition of melody and compare it with other definitions. If there are differences in definition, how do you account for them?

How did the Romantic conceptions of melody originate? Do you consider them final?

Can there be any clear or generally accepted definition of melody in the most extreme modern music? How do you think the composers of this music might define melody? Would they be likely to admit that the present-day concept is not acceptable to older musicians?

Do you think that the days of melody are over? Do you expect a return to the older style? What has taken its place, if melody is "out"?

Review the major stages in the development of the idea of harmony.

When two melodic lines were sung together in medieval times, did they make *intentional* harmony? If not, why were they used?

What are some of the values of the ability to follow changes of tonality in music? Name any specific instances of changing tonality which give you special pleasure.

CHAPTER 11

How The Composer Works

ೆ§ ೯ಎ

Everyone who has come under the spell of a great picture, a powerful novel, or a moving piece of music has wondered what it was that impelled the painter or the writer or the composer to create. What is there about an artist that makes him so different from his fellow men that he can paint as El Greco did, write as Milton did, or compose as Bach did? Granting that such creative artists are endowed by nature with certain abilities which, when trained, enable them to excel their fellows, does this fact in any real way explain the qualities of El Greco's *The Penitent St. Peter*, or Milton's *Paradise Lost*, or Bach's *B Minor Mass*? What constrained the artist to bring such things into being; how was he able to give his work the meaning it has for us; what were the processes of his creation? These are the questions the amateur is likely to ask as he becomes more and more familiar with art.

THE CREATOR, A UNIQUE FIGURE

Such questions are not easy to answer. The first thing we must realize, in trying to arrive at some explanation of how a creative artist "out of nothing brings a world into being," is that such an individual is far apart from those about him. He is no ordinary man interested in the world merely as it appears to his senses; rather is he one who searches for significance in the scheme of life. He gathers the subject matter for his painting, his writing, or his music partly from his own experience as a sensitive member of human society,

Courtesy, The Fine Arts Society of San Diego

EL GRECO: THE PENITENT ST. PETER

The penitence of the Apostle who denied his Lord was a favorite subject of this great painter. This picture shows St. Peter awakening from a dream of despair. Hope for his forgiveness fills him with ecstasy, and reaches him in the form of spiritual light, even after he had denied his Master.

partly through his sympathetic observation of the actions and reactions of such a society. His greatest endowment—aside from technical aptitude—is his ability to extend and develop his own experiences, which necessarily are limited and fragmentary. Such a power in itself gives the creator an insight into human experience far superior to any participation he may have at first hand. It explains El Greco's ability to project so vividly St. Peter's suppliant hope of forgiveness, or Beethoven's powerful concept of man the hero, bestriding the narrow world like a colossus.

Most of us are too closely concerned with life and its difficulties and joys to see things in perspective; we lack imagination to link what we experience today with what we have experienced in the past or what will follow after. Such specialists as the scientist and the historian are too far removed from realities to sense, or even comprehend, the quality and purport of life. The artist is the only one who seems able to see life steadily and as a whole, who is able to look at is as a "human being and yet not merely as a single individual, with passionate intensity, yet with dispassionate lucidity." That is what we mean when we say that men such as El Greco and Beethoven were inspired when they painted or composed; there is something in their best work—something put there by their very attributes as artists—that far transcends technical achievements or artistic proficiencies. It is this that distinguishes them from their less fortunate fellows.

Most professional artists would probably deny that they have any such spiritual basis for creation. A contemporary American musician has said that, to a composer, composing is like fulfilling any other natural function such as eating or sleeping; he composes because he feels that he was born for the job—because he can't help it.[1] Of course, he adds, after the thing is done, everyone, especially the composer, hopes that it will turn out to have been "inspired."

This is true enough, so far as generalities go, as everyone who has had any experience with creative workers must acknowledge. As a rule, artists do not sit around waiting for the divine afflatus; they turn to their creative tasks, whatever they may be, day after day, simply doing the best job they can. The difference between the great and the minor artist is that the great artist, once the creative process is started, is likely to produce something of real significance to the world because of his greater sympathy with its experiences and his keener imaginative ability to extend and develop these sympathies—in a word, because of his ability to "apprehend the man in men." Insofar as the actual physical processes of

[1] Aaron Copland, *What to Listen for in Music*. New York: McGraw-Hill Book Co., 1957.

creation are concerned, the great men do not differ from those who produce merely competent work.

VARIOUS COMPOSER TYPES

We have to face the fact, at the beginning, that there can be no such being as a typical composer and no such thing as a "regular" method of composing. There have been some composers—only a few—who have written music as if they were possessed of some Apollonic daemon. Music simply welled out their consciousness as water from spring; their greatest difficulty seems to have been finding time enough to put it on paper. For them there were few problems of choice or arrangement of materials; whole works seem to have been spontaneously created in their minds with little or no conscious effort. We have evidence of such prolific spontaneity in two of the greatest composers, Mozart and Schubert, who must always remain the outstanding examples of the inspired composer writing music because nothing else in life seemed important or necessary.

Then there are those who have labored carefully and long over their works, starting with a few germinal ideas and painstakingly weaving them into an imposing and closely designed musical fabric. Beethoven may be cited as the characteristic example of this type, and most of the outstanding men since his time—such composers as Brahms, Wagner, Strauss—have followed him in this respect. The record shows that Beethoven was busy with his *C Minor Symphony* for over five years, and that it took Brahms over twenty-five years to write his great symphony in the same key.[2]

Some composers have given very little thought to any sort of constructive process; they simply took traditional patterns which had become well established by the time they arrived on the musical scene and used them to suit their own purposes. The composers of the Renaissance—such men as Byrd, Di Lasso, and Palestrina—used only the patterns and formal molds of their time: the motet, the Mass and the madrigal. Neither did Bach, when he started on the tremendous project of writing the forty-eight preludes and fugues

2 An early draft of Brahms' *C Minor Symphony* dates from 1850; the work was finished in 1876.

THE WAY FROM THE INAUGURATION OF THE PAINTER TO THE IMAGE

These sketches are excellent examples of the manner in which Michelangelo evolved the various sections of his great mural painting on the ceiling of the Sistine Chapel in Rome. Compare these sketches for the figure of the Libyan Sybil with the finished painting. Then contrast this method of painting with that of Winslow Homer, the American artist, who, in painting his water color of a West Indian scene, obviously did so without any hesitation, putting his idea on paper as quickly as possible.

THE LIBYAN SYBIL

Courtesy, Metropolitan Museum of Art

WINSLOW HOMER: "TORNADO"

in his *Well Tempered Clavier*, or the *Brandenburg Concertos*, depart from the accepted models of his time.

There have been pioneering spirits however who, dissatisfied with the musical styles in which they had been reared, revolted—often at the expense of the quality of their music. In different centuries, Monteverdi, Berlioz, Debussy, and Schönberg are examples of composers who sought, through experimenting with new resources, to develop a different, nonconformist type of writing. Naturally their methods of working would differ greatly from those of the traditionalists.

First, the Idea

There are certain practices common to all composers; the first of these is getting started. How is the creative process actually begun? A famous old recipe for rabbit pie, written in days when meat was not so plentiful, starts with the admonition: first, you must catch your rabbit. Similar advice must be followed by every composer who would set about concocting tonal delicacies. All com-

positions, whether short or long, whether traditional or experimental, start with a music idea.[3] Perhaps the idea first occurs to the
composer as a melody that he can hum to himself, as a rhythmic
pattern, or merely as a suggestion for an accompaniment. Whatever
it is, or however it may come, this theme (the name we give to such
a musical idea) is the real *germ* from which the composer later
fashions his whole piece. It is, as Copland rightly says, a "gift from
Heaven which comes almost like automatic writing"—the composer
has no control over it except to write it down as quickly and as
accurately as he can, adding it to his collection of similar items.

Obviously, an important part of the composer's creation of such
a musical theme is his evaluation of it in what might be called its
emotional and musical terms. He is aware of its emotional value
instinctively, realizing whether or not it provides the starting point
for, or helps to develop, the type of human expression with which
he is concerned at the moment. He examines it as music, noting its
outline, its possibility for later "development," and perhaps alters
it here and there so that it may better fulfill his musical requirements. It may be that he is quite unconscious of the process, but the
composer, once his thematic material has been revealed to him, immediately sets out to determine its nature and then sees what can
be done with it.

A theme may carry some emotional suggestion which the composer feels called on to develop; it may well be the other way about,
that some sort of emotional background is realized first, and that
out of it comes the musical idea; or it may be that the whole creative process takes place on a largely formal plane, the composer
thinking of his music as music, without paying much attention to
its expressive values. There are examples of all three of these different processes of composing. The sketches left by Beethoven may
be interpreted to show that many of his themes came to him in
purely musical form, and that such expressive ideas as those dealing
with the "awful powers of Fate and ending with a triumph song
of the human will" were evolved afterwards, during his long struggle with his material. We know, on the other hand, that, in such
works as Richard Strauss' *Don Juan* and *Don Quixote*, the whole

---

[3] Sometimes these ideas come to the composer in the most incongruous circumstances. It was the Austrian composer Bruckner who, pointing out the theme of a
movement in one of his symphonies, is said to have remarked that it had come to
him on a picnic, just as he was unwrapping the sandwiches.

of the extramusical program was achieved first, and that out of it came the musical material. It is difficult to believe that Bach had anything other than the formal manipulation of his material in mind when he composed some of his great works.

It is impossible to know whether the composer chooses the medium he will employ—whether he will write a string quartet, a symphony, an opera, or a piano sonata—before or after the time he catches his musical rabbit—that is, conceives his thematic material. Here again we have conflicting evidence. Instead of pondering whether his theme belongs in a symphony or in a string quartet, many a composer has evolved his themes directly for some work he had in mind. No medium other than the opera could ever have been intended for the delineative themes that Wagner created; he evolved them for particular dramatic purposes. Schubert's lyric melodies, in whatever the medium used, always sound as if they had been conceived as songs. On the other hand, we have Brahms hesitating whether to use the thematic materials which finally went into his first piano concerto in a sonata for two pianos, a symphony, or a concerto. Some of the most effective thematic material in Bach's great choral work, the *B Minor Mass*, had been used in earlier works, sometimes in a quite different medium.[4] His contemporary, Handel, did not hesitate to lift themes from his own works and sometimes from those of another composer whenever they seemed to fill some particular need.

Generally speaking, however, the composer has little trouble satisfying himself as to either the inherent value or the essential quality of the ideas he has conceived. Once he has decided what he is going to write, his immediate problem is what to do with his thematic material, for, significant and suggestive as it may seem, it is far from being a piece of music. How is he going to spin it into a composition that will last anywhere from several minutes (in the case of a song) to an hour (in the case of a symphony) or to several hours (in the case of an opera)?

PRINCIPLES OF DESIGN

In following the conventional means of writing music the composer instinctively uses certain principles of design which are the

---

[4] The theme of the *Osanna*, for instance, was originally used in a composition written as a welcome song to Bach's monarch, the King of Saxony.

THE RUINED PARTHENON

foundation of all good art. If we examine any outstanding work of art—a finely designed building, a beautifully executed painting, a good piece of sculpture, a poem or a drama—we shall find certain general principles of design that control the use of its structural elements. The creator may have followed these principles consciously or intuitively; the one thing for us to realize is that he did follow them. The most important of these principles are

1. *Repetition*, usually according to some rhythmic scheme
2. The dominance of some particular feature of design and the subordination of others, so as to secure *Unity in Variety*
3. *Balance* or *Symmetry*, by means of which the various elements are held together and yet synthesized and organized into a harmonious whole

No definite rule or formula can be given for the use of these, or any other, artistic principles, but there exists within us a certain innate sense for good design, which, if we cultivate it, will grow into a power of discrimination of which we can be strongly conscious. We all react, for example, to these structural principles as they have been exemplified in the Parthenon; we instinctively know that this must have been a *good* building. Even today, some twenty-four hundred years after it was built, this magnificent structure still holds our attention and arouses our enthusiasm.

Notice the rhythm of the repeated vertical columns; the builders definitely established this sense of verticality as the dominant feature of their building. See how carefully they used it in contrast to the horizontal lines above and below the repeated upright columns. The manner in which the various structural details are balanced and symmetrized, each having its part in the harmony of the whole, shows how keenly sensitive to beauty the Greeks were, and how highly developed were their tastes.

REPETITION

The composer, if he wishes to create a musical work of lasting value, pays careful attention to the same schemes of design. The principle of repetition is essential to any real intelligibility in music; such a transient art must have certain features that can be grasped easily and recognized pleasurably by the listeners. If you are inclined to doubt this, listen to some well-known and easily followed melody such as Foster's "Old Folks at Home," and see how its phrases are repeated, contrasted, and combined to make up its structure.

First 4 measures: phrase.   First 8 measures: period.   All 16 measures: double period.

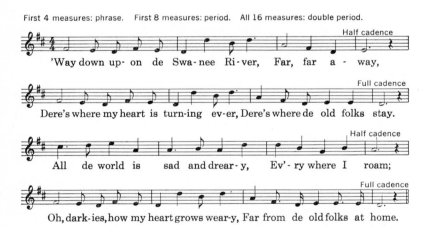

By *phrase* in music we mean certain melodic sections which come to a natural pause at their end through a sort of musical punctuation called a *cadence;* phrases are discernible by such exterior means as the number of measures they contain between cadences. If the cadence suggests a permanent conclusion, it is a full cadence; if only a temporary cessation of flow, it is a half-cadence. Two phrases may be said to constitute a period, and two periods, usually sixteen measures in length, a double-period.

This procedure is one of the simplest and commonest forms of musical repetition, but there are many kinds of structural devices which are not confined to simple and popular music. Composers of all sorts and in all periods have woven their musical fabric out of a repetition, expansion, and diversification of some melodic or rhythmic pattern, and the more we learn to follow them, the better is our enjoyment of music. Instead of repeating a theme exactly, for example, a composer may imitate it in another part, as Bach does here in the *Fugue in c minor:*

He may play it against itself, at a later time, in the form of a canon. For example, Franck uses this device in the fourth movement of the *Sonata in A Major for Violin and Piano:*

A composer may "vary" a theme as Mozart does in *Batti, batti,* from *Don Giovanni:*

(*b* is a variation of melody *a*)

He may change the rhythmic pattern of a theme by lengthening the duration of each note (augmentation) or shortening it (diminution). Bach employs this device in *The Art of the Fugue,* opening theme:

Theme

Theme in augmentation

Theme in diminution

The character of the music may be changed by turning it upside down (inversion).

Theme in inversion

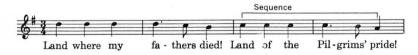

The theme may be repeated at various pitch levels in sequence, as in "America":

Land where my   fa - thers died! Land of the   Pil-grims' pride!

(The opening melody of Tchaikovsky's *Symphonie pathétique* is another example of this device. See page 103.)

While keeping its characteristic features, a theme can be transformed by the composer into a quite different type, thereby glorifying it, so to speak, as Liszt does here in *Les Préludes:*

Theme
Transformation

Finally, using all these and any other mechanism which his power of invention suggests, the composer may develop a theme—a process difficult to describe in words, although it can be recognized readily enough when heard. Listen to the middle section (that immediately following the double bar) of the first movement from Beethoven's *Fifth Symphony,* and you will find that the composer views his original theme in a number of different aspects and puts it through a number of metamorphoses. Development is a logical and almost inevitable process which, when well used, adds greatly to our listening enjoyment.

There are a number of different ways the composer may obtain balance and symmetry of design in his music. In fact, the musical *forms*—such as the fugue, the sonata form, the theme and variations—about which we will have much to say later, are simply convenient and well-tried devices for achieving this end. They have changed through the centuries and are still in process of evolution; they have been variously used by different composers, but they all help solve the same problem: attaining good balance and effective symmetry.

All these devices must be used by the composer so as to secure an intelligent and pleasurable whole. The skill of the composer appears in this welding together of disparate elements according to the structural principles of good design. He does not necessarily follow any rules, but he must so order his music that the listener can find his way around in it, can realize at any given moment what is going on. The piece, no matter how long it may be, should proceed logically from its beginning to its end; there should be a sense of relation of parts that leaves no room for confusion in the hearer's mind; and the music should be so cunningly put together that it shows none of the seams by which it is joined, to use Tchaikovsky's picturesque phrase. Above all else there must be, in Mahler's words, "abundance and continuous *flow*," if the music is to be any good. This all sounds easy enough in the telling; as a matter of fact, it is a tremendously difficult achievement, and to a large degree the real quality and staying powers of a composition depend on it.

TOPICS FOR DISCUSSION

Discuss how the composer's environment influences his music. For example, consider Beethoven's *Pastoral* Symphony, Schubert's songs, or Chopin's piano music.

Tabulate the elements of unity and variety in any simple compositions you may like.

Variety-in-unity is sovereign in composition. Compare this idea in music and architecture, or in painting and sculpture. Similarly, compare development in a symphonic movement with development in a play or novel.

A novelist is often asked, "How do you start a book? Do you begin with the plot, the setting, or the characters?" The same questions might be asked of the composer of music. How are these processes paralleled in music?

CHAPTER 12

Our Way of Approach

❦❧

ART AND LANGUAGE

A poetic critic, Romain Rolland, has said that music can be all things to all men: tonal architecture in certain centuries and among certain peoples; design, line, and plastic beauty to such nations as have cultivated a sense of form—to painters and sculptors like the Italians; an intimate poetry, a lyric efflux, a philosophical meditation to a poetic and philosophical nation such as the Germans; an *art de coeur*, gallant and graceful to Francis I or Charles IX; a weapon of faith and combat to reformers such as Martin Luther; a matter of princely pride and royal pomp to kings such as Louis XIV; an art of the salon during the eighteenth century; a lyric expression of tremendous personalities during the nineteenth. It is obviously not only an art but a language, capable of expressing widely divergent ideas and conceptions, including some of those generally regarded as belonging to the spheres of the other arts.

MUSIC'S WORLD OF THE SPIRIT

A moment's reflection, however, will show us that music has its own distinct province and that while it perhaps can go as far as embodying moral ideas, it expresses some things much better than others. Its great strength lies in depicting emotions rather than thoughts, in realizing intangible moods rather than concrete forms, in depicting ideality rather than reality, and, most of all, in appealing to the spirit rather than to the senses.

We readily follow a great man like Beethoven when his music stirs our emotions as it does in the *Fifth Symphony;* but we are not so sure of him, or of ourselves, even when he places mottoes like *tantôt libre, tantôt recherche, or muss es sein?—es muss sein* at the beginning of certain movements in his last quartets, as if he would convey some metaphysical concept in his music. We quickly respond to the melancholy brooding of Tchaikovsky in his *Symphonie pathétique,* or to the alluring Eastern colors of Rimsky-Korsakov's *Scheherazade,* or to the healthy vigor of Brahms' *First Symphony;* it is more difficult for us to realize the comparatively simple structural design of these compositions, and thus to appreciate their architectural proportions.

In these materialistic days there are many listeners who may find it easier to appreciate Honegger's realistic description of mechanical power in his *Pacific 231* than Schubert's romantic search for a spiritual home in *The Wanderer.* Wagner in his great series of operas, *The Ring of the Nibelung,* and Debussy in his tone poem *Afternoon of a Faun* appeal mightily to our spirits, but it would be difficult for some of us to get much "sense" from these works.

Furthermore, the fact that music, as distinct from its associated arts, is largely independent of exterior associations constitutes one of its chief glories, or its most confusing difficulties, according to our point of view. The static arts are easier of comprehension. No matter how imaginative the treatment, in order to convey his meaning the painter, architect, or sculptor commonly uses means that are closely associated with the consciously experienced world. Even literature, which comes closest to music as a means of emotional and imaginative suggestiveness, must use a medium closely associated with everyday life language.

Everyone knows the story of Turner, the English artist, and the woman who told him she had never seen such sunsets as he painted. "No, but don't you wish you could?" was certainly the right answer to such a comment. Music does not even need to try to explain the lack of such relationships. Although it works with two familiar yet intangible factors, rhythm and sound, it uses them for the most part in ways entirely different from those in which they occur in nature. Their combination in music affects our senses in ways different from those of the other arts, ways which we hardly understand and which have no counterparts in our other emotional experiences. They make of music a peculiarly dynamic art; instead of allowing it to be examined at any length, they cause it to rush precipitately at us, sometimes with the passionate eloquence of a great orator, sometimes with almost intangible persuasiveness. In any case, it is gone almost before we are conscious of its having existed, and must be re-created before we can again be aware of its qualities.

PROGRAM MUSIC

Various types of music differ in their extra-musical associations. All of us can remember music which definitely imitates sounds such as bird-calls, storms, and so on, and many an older musician has in his listening career suffered under the "storms" of the sensational organ player's making. Such definite imitations of nature are not necessarily the resort of cheap musicians only; no less a composer than Beethoven makes use of these very devices. In his *Pastoral Symphony* we find the mood of the music heightened by a musical suggestion of a peaceful brook rippling over the stones, the calls of various birds, the growling of the thunderstorm. We all know that certain sounds suggest certain states of mind to us; in fact, these sounds may induce these states of mind. The hunt is suggested, for example, by the sound of the horn as it is heard at the beginning of the second act of Wagner's *Tristan und Isolde*. In the last section of Liszt's rather oversensational *Les Préludes*, the blare of brass, delivered in all the enthusiasm of this composer's style, excites us to martial ardor. The plaintive longing of the English horn, wonderfully expressed in the shepherd's tune at the beginning of the last act of *Tristan und Isolde*, awakens our consciousness to an answering mood of brooding melancholy. In the "Roaring Twenties" Arthur Honegger made a tremendous sensation with his orchestral description in *Pacific 231* of the "visual and physical enjoyment" (his own words) produced by a powerful steam locomotive at top speed. Full of never-ceasing dissonance and cacophony, until its very conservative cadence brings the engine to a full stop, this is a most effective essay in descriptive mechanism.

And so a composer, using these means and coupling them with the various devices of composition, may easily give music an extraneous implication, may make it set forth a sequence of pictures, tell a story, or what you will. This kind of music, having connection with something outside itself, we know as *program music*.

Here again we must consider the composer working within the natural limitations of his material, for program music does require an intellectual approach. Since tone, the natural sensuous element of music, does have duration in time, it would seem aesthetically justifiable to relate, by means of a "program," what is happening at any particular moment in the music to what has already happened and to what is going to happen. Provided—and this is the crux of the whole matter—the composer conveys the objective quality demanded by the program of the music itself. In other words, in works inspired by a literary association, if the music as music (and not because of its intellectual program) communicates to us a conception of inherent beauty and organic unity, our enjoyment of it cannot be questioned even on the strictest aesthetic grounds. Beethoven's *Eroica Symphony*, written in memory of a great man, is an outstanding musical triumph because the music is essentially heroic in itself. Strauss' *Till Eulenspiegel* and *Don Juan*, Wagner's "Siegfried's Funeral March" or "Isolde's Love Death," all frankly programmatic to the utmost degree, can nevertheless be ranked as among our greatest masterpieces. In all of them one can sense the spirit of their program *in the music itself;* an intellectual reading is not needed to give them meaning.

In order to clarify the issue, it may be well to define here precisely what is usually meant by "program music." Ever since the time of Berlioz and Liszt, the beginning of the nineteenth century, the term has been applied to instrumental music that not only is intended to express ideas outside the realm of the art but also is conditioned and shaped by extra-musical ideas rather than by primary considerations of proportion and form. Although it covers a wide range of styles and schools, from Berlioz to Richard Strauss, the term is never applied to *opera* or *song*, forms which associate music directly with words.

ABSOLUTE MUSIC

In direct contrast to program music is the pure or absolute type of music, based on definite laws of structure and development rather than an appeal through associations with literary or illustrative ideas. In this music the ideas must be good, the proportions well-balanced, the harmonies clear. Nevertheless, it is difficult to draw a line between these types and say that on one side is program music, on the other absolute. A Bach fugue (the organ *Fugue in G Minor* is a good example), in which the structure of the music is a matter of paramount importance as the whole thing grows to tremendous climax under the structural genius of its composer; or a Haydn quartet (the one in F major, Op. 3, No. 5, for instance), with its detached, impersonal attitude to everything except the weaving together of tonal patterns—these are as near to absolute music as we can get. The materials in these compositions are arranged in certain sequences, and their significance is one of aesthetic beauty rather than of emotional content. But music which seems to have been written with the idea of pure tonal concepts may contain dramatic and impressionistic material, and vice versa, so that definite boundaries are not easy to establish.

The subject of program versus absolute music has given rise to many vigorous debates. One of the best discussions of it will be found in Ernest Newman's *Musical Studies*. We need not attempt to summarize further the arguments here; the topic makes an excellent one for debate among music lovers. It will suffice to suggest that since program music has always existed (there are naïve examples in the earliest art music), it evidently springs from a deep natural desire to relate music to life. Obviously, such music is likely to appeal in its own terms. If one is really musical he works through the more simple forms of program music pretty quickly, but only a sadly pedantic person would refuse to open his heart to *Till Eulenspiegel* because of cast-iron convictions about the inferiority of program to absolute music! We must consider all music on its merits. A good program should not allow poor music to scrape through; on the other hand, we must not expect a program piece either to declare its program without the use of words or to be as impressive without its program as with it. In the best program music, the composition so richly interprets or suggests the verbal ideas that the two are inseparable. An example of this is Vincent d'Indy's *Istar;* the music suggests by its structure the story of a goddess, who, to free her lover, must pass through seven doors at each of which a demon robs her of adornment.

It is well to remember that the novelty of an exciting program may attract for a while, but that then the music may become stale with familiarity. Hence we should give program pieces a good many hearings before deciding whether they wear as well as nonprogram favorites.

In listening to program music we have a double task because we have to take in the program plus the music; we must decide all along how the music carries out the literary idea. There must be *form* in both, and the comparison of the two provides an enjoyable task.

WE TAKE THE ROMANTIC ROAD

We have now arrived at a point from which it is possible to see the best approach to the difficult problem of learning how to listen. It lies naturally through that music which recognizably maintains a connection with things outside itself, things which can be definitely recognized and easily understood. Most of the works known and loved by the intelligent amateur in music belong in this category. This is a realm of beauty and interest,

> a land bounded on one side by the austere peaks of the classics and on the other by the broad plains of conscientious mediocrity. It is an irresistably lovely tract, its valleys and mountains perpetually varied by the wandering clouds of romanticism, its streams darkened by winds blowing from the other world of mysticism; a land where sensuous beauty, the immediate delight of the ear, is of primary importance and logic a reluctant necessity (Hubbard Hutchinson in *The New York Times*).

Using this kind of music first of all to establish a delight in listening and then, as a means for acquiring familiarity with the problems of technical structure, details of melody, harmony, rhythm, orchestration, and so on, the would-be listener can soon enter into the more abstract difficulties as well as the greater beauties of absolute music. Using his days in the delectable land of romantic beauty as a preparation, he should gird his loins and quicken his spirit for the journey to the rarer heights and wider visions of the "austere peaks of the classics."

Throughout his whole journey the musical wayfarer must keep in mind his ultimate goal—the acquisition of the ability to listen to music in its own terms, without the outside props that have helped him get started. He can do full justice to its glories only by giving it a fair opportunity to work in its own particular field. It is in its very being-itself-ness that music becomes most difficult—when it is most necessary to understand it (that is, when it is "purest"), it is most difficult to grasp. This applies, of course, to the more complex works. At the same time, we must point out that there is ample music that is only slightly complex and yet is as absolute as can be. The complexity of the music is a real necessity, not a feature put in by the composer "to make it more difficult," like a mis-lead in a crossword puzzle. A student starting to learn to listen to a piece of complex absolute music is apt to think that the composer has intentionally made it as difficult as possible, whereas all good composers strive to make their utterances as clear as they can, consistent with the magnitude of the ideas they are expressing. Complexity in music is more obvious than in the other arts, and more difficult to grasp, because of music's fleeting character and its appeal to the least trained of our senses.

But we have already warned the student that he has not set forth on an easy journey, even though it is a very delightful one, and that too rapid progress cannot be expected at first. Once his attitude towards the art is an active rather than a passive one, the listener can gradually learn to get from the music the sense that the composer would convey. By developing an ability to remember musical phrases and patterns, by trying to train his powers of discrimination and by keeping an open mind and a sympathetic attitude towards all kinds of music, he will greatly forward his progress. By confining the music he hears to that which, because of its content, can justify its existence as a means of "enriching and sanctifying life," he will educate himself in the real sense of the term. In a valuable essay on *Music and the Cultivated Man*, Gilman quotes William Orton's definition of education as an initiation of the mind to ever new and finer types of experiences. Music will give us these new and finer types of experience if we learn to choose it carefully and to listen to it properly.

LIST OF SUGGESTED MUSIC

Symphony No. 6 (Pathétique)   TCHAIKOVSKY
The last movement especially should be heard because it is illustrative of "melancholy brooding."

Scheherazade   RIMSKY-KORSAKOV
The third movement has "alluring Eastern colors."

Symphony No. 1, in c minor   BRAHMS
The last movement is full of "healthy vigor."

Der Wanderer (The Wanderer)   SCHUBERT
The following translation of the German will help you follow the varied beauties of this mastersong:

Ich komme vom Gebirge her,	From mountain summits I come,
Es dampft das Thal, es braust das Meer.	Through foggy vales and ocean's foam.
Ich wandle still, bin wenig froh,	I wander on, am full of care,
Und immer fragt der Seufzer wo, immer wo?	And always ask in sorrow, Where, where, where?
Die Sonne dünkt mich hier so kalt,	The sun seems here so wan and cold,
Die Blüthe welk, das Leben alt,	The flowers are dead, and life is old,
Und was sie reden, leerer Schall.	And what they tell me, empty sound.
Ich bin ein Fremdling überall.	I am a stranger everywhere.
Wo bist du, wo bist du, mein geliebtes Land,	Where art thou, my beloved land?
Gesucht, geahnt, und nie gekannt!	I've sought, I've dreamed, yet never known.
Das Land, das Land so hoffnungsgrün,	That land where all my hopes are new,
Das Land wo meine Rosen blühn,	That land where all my roses bloom,
Wo meine Freunde wandelnd gehn,	Where live the friends I dearly prize,
Wo meine Todten auferstehn,	Where all my dead will one day rise,
Das Land, das meine Sprache spricht,	The land that knows the tongue I speak,

O Land, wo bis du?	O land, where art thou?
Ich wandle still, bin wenig froh,	I wander on, am full of care,
Und immer fragt der Seufzer wo,	And always ask in sorrow, Where,
* immer wo?*	where, where?
Im Geisterhauch tönts mir zuruck:	In spirit tones there comes reply:
"Dort, wo du nicht bist, dort ist	"There, where thou art not, there
* das Glück."*	joy is found."

TOPICS FOR DISCUSSION

Discuss Charles Morgan's dictum that "Art is news of reality not to be expressed in other terms."

Most beginners in appreciation enjoy program music more than absolute music. Why do you think this is so?

Discuss the permanent value of any such piece (assuming it to be well composed) as Arthur Honegger's composition about a railway engine, *Pacific 231*.

Paul Bourget gave this recipe for artistic creation: "*Sois belle, et tais-toi*" ("Be beautiful, and let it go at that"). Is this a valid argument for the study of music? Why or why not?

Some people speak of "purely musical emotion" as distinct from other human emotion aroused by the arts or experience. Do you think there are emotions peculiar to music, or do you think the emotions which arise from music are already familiar to us?

We have spoken of the high service of music in enriching and sanctifying life. What other services do you prize in music?

CHAPTER 13

Till Eulenspiegel's Merry Pranks

ಆ§ ೬ઐ

A GAY BEGINNING FOR OUR JOURNEY

Our musical journey may well begin with one of the most significant pieces of program music ever written, *Till Eulenspiegel's Merry Pranks*, by Richard Strauss. On hearing this, even for the first time, we can hardly fail to be impressed with its greatness. It is very evident that the orchestra is telling us a story in which something is happening every minute. What is perhaps not so immediately evident is that the composer's ability in construction is on a par with his imaginative facility. Here is music inspired by the liveliest of imaginations and created by the most consummate skill imaginable.

Strauss, who wrote this music in 1895, tells us that his original intention was to let the music speak for itself, giving the hearer the title and letting him guess the details and enjoy the music for its own sake. This was said with tongue in cheek, for no one knew better than Strauss that if the hearers are to share a composer's enjoyment in the treatment of a programmatic subject, it is necessary that they know something of the story unfolding in his mind as he writes the music. So he later gave us his program.

"Till Owlglass," to use an English translation of the fanciful name, is not very well known in this country, but in Germany

RICHARD STRAUSS IN
1895

every schoolboy can relate the adventures of this medieval hero. A fifteenth-century book tells of his journeys through life and of how he managed to live by his wits. He is supposed to have lived in Brunswick and died in 1350 at Mölln, near Lübeck in the north of Germany. During the Middle Ages he came to be recognized as a personification of the triumph of nimble wit over bourgeois dullness. An amusing rogue as amoral as Punch, jack-of-all-trades, a universal swindler, yet he was able to ingratiate himself with everybody by his hail-fellow-well-met gusto. Something of a poet with a streak of childish heedlessness, ramshackle, a danger to the community, yet he had a likable turn to his folly. (Likable, perhaps, mostly in retrospect; not so much when his insolent pranks drove nearly frantic the honest dullards on whom he delighted to exercise his wits.) "When he was grabbed by the collar and hauled along to the gallows, he went as a matter of course, without knowing why. He took life after the manner of a poet, just as he took the goods of others" (Eugene Bacha).

AN IDEAL PROGRAM

What a program for a creative musician of Strauss' imaginative power and technical resource! In working it out, the composer makes his music not only an apotheosis of this medieval character, but a running commentary on life in general and on the individual who dares to stand out against generally accepted opinions. Coming as he did after Liszt and Wagner, Strauss was able to develop the foundations laid by these giants. Possessed of a most unusual talent in writing for the orchestra, he was able to make this huge instrument obedient to every dictate of his thought. Even a casual hearing of this music will prove that its pictures are very clearly drawn, the instruments saying exactly what the composer wants them to say. There is a strong sense of folk-feeling pervading this work; in the first bars we hear two themes which seem to suggest to us that "once upon a time there lived a wag named Till Eulenspiegel." Strauss carries these themes throughout his whole work, weaving them in the most manifold guises, moods, and situations, right up to the catastrophe where Till, after he has been condemned to death, is strung up to the gibbet. We can learn a great deal as we enjoy this vivid, vigorous score. Observe how the composer builds his music out of the manipulations of the two main themes, and follow in as much detail as possible the various phases in the process.[1]

[1] By way of practical suggestion: There is much to be said in favor of the listener following this and other music which will be suggested later in this book with the printed score before him, even though he may not be able to read musical notation and can only follow the general trend of the composer's thought. Picking a detailed structure apart is as good a way to discern how it is put together as can be found; the more technical knowledge the observer acquires, the better his appreciation. The logical build-up and "feel" of the music can better be obtained in this way than any other. If the hearer can only find the places in the score where the principal themes occur, he will gradually learn to read the printed page more

The two themes are strikingly characteristic; they are both heard at the very beginning of the composition. The first four notes from the orchestra (measures 1-2) vividly suggest the rogue-hero, the quirk of the notes describing him as exactly as music can describe anybody or anything. Almost immediately after the first little theme, we hear a rising, quickly repeated, humorous theme played on the horns (5-12). The ability to recognize such tone color in the orchestra will give added pleasure to our listening! *Keep these two Till themes in mind*, for out of them is fashioned the fabric of the whole piece.

TILL IN THE MARKET PLACE

As the music gets under way, notice how the second theme (the rising, repeated horn theme) gradually becomes more lively (25-35); it is taken up by the various instruments in turn and finally proclaimed in a *fortissimo* passage by the whole orchestra (35-40). "The milieu is thus given by which we are enabled to recognize the pranks and droll tricks which the crafty schemer is about to bring before our ears." (This and following quotations are from the analysis of the score made by Klatte and approved by the composer.) A clearly marked drop of an octave (44) suggests that the rogue is really off on his adventures. Till is suddenly before us; the clarinets sound his theme, and there follow a few sharp chords for the wind instruments (49-50). It is not difficult to recognize

the outlines of the story which Strauss tells us were in his mind: Till, his clothes tattered and torn, puts on his best manners, slyly

---

eloquently. To help him in this process, figures referring to the numbers of the measures in which the feature under discussion occurs are inserted in the text in this and following chapters. The piano scores of most of the works discussed in this book are readily available, and they are best for the amateur reader, for they are condensed versions of what the whole orchestra is doing. Later on, he may learn to use the orchestral score, in which all the parts for the various instruments are laid out before him. Reference is not usually made to the different recordings which are available, but no music is used for illustration which is not easily available in one or more recordings, and which is not likely to remain permanently in the lists.

passes through the gate of a city and enters the market place. It is market day; the women sit at their stalls and prattle. Hop! Eulenspiegel springs on his horse, gives a smack of the whip, and races into the midst of the crowd. Clink, clash, clatter! A confused sound of broken pots and pans, and the market women are put to flight. In haste the rascal rides away, an incident which is suggested by the trombones in a loud phrase, and secures a safe retreat.

The jogging market tune (51-54) heard in this incident is obviously a variant of the second theme, using many of its very notes. As Strauss works this scene up to a climax, notice how he plays with the first theme, making it serve in different ways, breaking it up into little two-note groups (110-120), and expanding it to fit the situation exactly (135-150).

TILL THE PRIEST

The first prank is followed immediately by a second. A straightforward tune, strongly resembling a German folk tune, is suddenly heard in the midst of the whirling music (179-182):

Thus the scene changes for us. Till is disguised as a priest, dripping with unction and morals, Strauss tells us. Note the sudden interpolation of the quirky Till theme on the clarinet (191) in the midst of the bourgeois folk tune; it is as if the preacher's mask has slipped and suddenly Till's mocking, grinning face is revealed beneath. He begins to get qualms at having mocked religion and fears for the success of his scheme. A veiled proclamation of the horn theme suggests that perhaps he does not feel any too comfortable in his borrowed glory. He makes up his mind—away with all scruples, he is himself again.

TILL IN LOVE

A sort of shuddering phrase for a solo violin (207) marks the beginning of a new adventure, and the music which immediately

"THE PROFESSORS," COSTUME SKETCH FOR THE BALLET
Till Eulenspiegel

In 1916 Diaghilev commissioned a ballet, using the Strauss music. The American scene designer Robert Edmond Jones made the settings and designed the costumes. The choreography was by Nijinsky.

follows shows its character. The principal theme is brought forward in lively time, but subtly metamorphosed and chivalrously colored (209):

There is no doubt about it, Till is in love. "He has become a Don Juan and one pretty girl has made quite an impression." Hear how now, glowing with zest, the violins, clarinets, and flutes sing! (229) But all this ardor is in vain; Till's advances are received with derision, and he goes away in a rage, swearing vengeance on all mankind. A tremendously loud passage on the brass (267) developed from the first short theme, with a change of rhythm, and repeated several times, leaves us in little doubt about this.

TILL AND THE PHILISTINES

After a short pause another adventure begins, the violoncellos announce, with a peculiar hopping insistence (293), the arrival of

some strange personages, who are honest, worthy doctors and professors. In an instant Till's anger is forgotten in his joy at opportunity for making fun of these solemn, old, self-important dry-as-
dusts. The second theme suits itself to the rhythm (303-305), as if
to suggest how easily Till falls in with the ways of living and thinking of his new companions. He begins to propound a few amazing
theses to them. This is apparent from the way fragments of the
theme come from various parts of the orchestra. There follows a
rhythmic phrase (344) representing the dull stodginess of the Philis-
tines and the rapid quirks of the Till motive. It is as if Till were pro-
pounding one amazing idea after another so quickly that he leaves
his hearers open-mouthed in astonishment. He works himself up
into a perfect frenzy of excitement, but after he has had his joke, he
loses interest in the whole thing and leaves the professors and doctors behind in amazed stupefaction.

TO BE OR NOT TO BE HIMSELF

Now comes material more suited to the real domain of music than
these pictorial elements with which we have been concerned up to
now. A happy *gassenhauer* (a street song) is heard (375), its short
staccato phrases emphasizing Till's essential naïveté:

Then follows a sort of psychological struggle in the hero's mind
between the various elements in his character. The different themes
are taken up and bandied about in various rhythms, as if Till sometimes thinks he ought to reform his ways and settle down, but
decides against it. The arch villain "gets the upper hand and the
merry jester, the born liar goes wherever he can succeed with a
hoax. His insolence knows no bounds; the Till themes fairly dance
in unholy glee (555). Finally the street tune is heard again, sung by
the whole orchestra as if in jubilation at the hero's final determination to be himself again."

TILL'S SAD END

Suddenly comes the denouement. "The drum rolls a hollow roll (575); the jailer drags the rascally prisoner into the court room." This is one of Strauss' happiest characterizations, this Court of Justice theme—heavy, pedantic, threatening chords on the woods winds and lower strings (577-580). The impudent Till theme (582) replies brazenly to these somber thunderings of the court; it sounds as if the prisoner were thumbing his nose at the solemn-faced jury. Finally he realizes that the jig is up and his pranks are over. Fear seizes him as he is marched to the gallows. There he swings as the trap is sprung; this rather gruesome incident is marked by a peculiar drop in the pitch of the orchestra. A last, piteous struggle, suggested principally by the clarinet and the flute (615), and his soul takes flight. The mortal Till is no more.

After a sad *pizzicato* passage for the strings (625), the composer adds a delightful epilogue, a sort of improvisation on the opening measures. It is as if he says, "Till thus becomes a legendary character; after all, there was a lovable side to his ramshackleness, and the people will always tell tales about him, 'Once upon a time,' etc." But in all the retrospective affection with which Strauss clothes Till, he does not let us forget that he was a devil and an immoral rogue. To this appraisal of his character the final measures, sounded by the full orchestra, testify most eloquently.

FEELING BEFORE ANALYSIS

No matter whether he can read the score or not, the listener should always keep clearly before him the necessity of cultivating an eloquence of heart if he is to come to a real understanding of this magnificent music. He must realize the necessity of getting back of the music, of sensing its spiritual communication, of letting himself be "reminded by the instruments," as Walt Whitman put it. This does not mean that he should give himself over merely to the summoning of vague, shifting, sentimental images when he listens to the music. This sort of thing is ridiculed by the purists in art, and with good reason. But the more one hears, sees, and reads, the more one must be convinced of the necessary and salutary relationship between art and life. All art must spring from nature; art for art's sake is nonexistent, nor can it be produced. If art is to maintain itself and assure its own existence, some kind of moral and spiritual stimulus must be given. It is the sharpening of his faculties of apperception, so that he can realize this relationship, that is necessary for the listener as he hears this music. He must learn to respond to the emotion in such music as this, to feel its beauty, before he attempts to explain it. He should sense its connection with life in general, its "ulterior and philosophic meaning"; in this particular case he must realize, as we have said, that this music is jubilantly conscious of that which "soars high above and beyond prison bars or scaffolds, or even the excellent rulings of worthy people." Then he can proceed to analysis and appraisement, a mental process which will no longer hinder his progress by assuming undue importance; rather will it increase his enjoyment by rendering his possession of the music more sure. This process of developing from a purely sensual and subjective state of hearing into a more objective and analytical type of listening is a glorious experience.

Till Eulenspiegel should awaken within us a new understanding of life and the universe; in realizing the humor as well as the tenderness, the eloquence as well as the joy of life that is in this music, in signalizing its triumph of the spirit over material obstacles, we open our hearts to new powers of feeling and understanding. And, having cultivated such power of understanding, we can learn to appreciate the effective arrangement of idea and event within this music, its masterful descriptive ability, and its outstanding scheme of construction. Only then can we say that we have really made it our own.

ADDITIONAL EXAMPLES OF PROGRAM MUSIC

The Sorcerer's Apprentice   DUKAS

This is a humorous translation into music of a ballad by Goethe. Based on a theme popular since the time of the Romans, it is the story of a magician's lazy apprentice who, while his master is away, uses the incantations he has learned to bring brooms and buckets to life and make them work for him. The magic spell is suggested by a muttering theme:

Strings muted

answered happily by the response of the broom:

Wood winds   Brass

These are the two main themes out of which the work evolves. After the apprentice utters the incantation, we hear:

The music works up steadily. The various themes are tossed about more and more feverishly to suggest that things are gradually getting out of control, and that the apprentice has forgotten the spell which will make them stop. Frightened, he chops the broom in two but the halves begin sweeping and the activity mounts to a new climax. The master, announced by brass blasts, returns suddenly and puts things right, and the apprentice assumes his proper place. Radiantly orchestrated and highly imaginative, this has long been a very popular program piece.

Danse macabre[2]   SAINT-SAËNS

Written in 1874, this symphonic poem is a description of verses by a contemporary French poet. Considered the utmost in "intense and coarse realism" in its day, it sounds rather tame and antiquated today. The brilliant orchestration and vivid descriptive writing, however, make it good listening practice.

Death (playing a violin) summons the skeletons from the graveyards to midnight revels. After tuning his fiddle, he calls up the specters as midnight strikes and gives them two contrasting tunes to dance to:

Violin Flute

[2] Excerpts reprinted by permission of Durand et Cie, Paris, France; Copyright owners: Elkan-Vogel Co., Inc., Philadelphia.

These are presented in numerous variants; for example the xylophone is used to depict the creaking bones of the skeletons. A derisive version of the *Dies Irae*, a medieval plainsong melody associated with the Judgment Day, is heard:

The whole thing builds to a tremendous climax. When the cock crows at dawn, the spirits speed back to the shades, and the piece ends suddenly with two plucked chords on the strings.

TOPICS FOR DISCUSSION

What else has Strauss done in the field of program music? Do these works equal *Till* in vividness, truth, and the balancing of description and imagination?

Do any of the episodes in any of these pieces seem to you less completely successful than others? If so, which, and why?

Why is *Till* so widely esteemed as a perfect work of art? What elements in its form, story, and musical treatment seem to you to entitle it to so high a place?

Why is *Till* obviously a better work of art than *Danse macabre*?

CHAPTER 14

Romanticism: LISZT'S
LES PRÉLUDES

❧ ❧

A NEW SPIRIT DEVELOPS IN MUSIC

Having enjoyed a piece of program music such as *Till Eulenspiegel,* in which the composer carefully elaborates a detailed program, the listener may well turn to music which extends into a wider imaginative realm and does not of necessity follow an exterior programistic outline. Liszt's *Les Préludes* will do well for an example, although it can hardly be ranked with the Strauss work as a musical masterpiece. Play through a good interpretation of this music of Liszt's. You will find it introspective and contemplative as well as external and pictorial; the composer is dealing with emotional states as well as with events—more so, in fact. In this sense this music belongs to the real realm of art, since it presents us with images rather than ideas, and these images produce in us definite states of feeling. It was written at a time when men were not ashamed to feel deeply and express themselves luxuriantly. Full of color, possessing dramatic force, with melodies of frank and robust sentiment, *Les Préludes* is characteristic of the Romantic Movement which gave it birth, and in which its composer played so prominent a role.

Every significant work of art is, of course, an unconscious picture of its contemporary world. In this case it was a world which revolted against the more formal, aristocratic elements of the seventeenth and early eighteenth centuries and which, in direct contrast to that period, emphasized the development of personal freedom and aggressive individualism. Shaped through aspirations developed from the experience of the new political ideals, it was a world which insisted on more freedom for the individual, whether he was the bourgeois member of the new industrial society or an artist striving to defy what he felt to be the stultifying conventions of the day. The intellectuals and artists of this period came to look on the world not so much from the point of view of how it had been affected by the past, but rather in the light of how the world would affect the life of the individual. "I am different from all men I have seen; if I am not better, at least I am different," boasted Rousseau, one of the leaders of the Romantic Movement and its first great spokesman.

It was the self-conscious attempt to give expression to those qualities which determine the personality that typified the artist of this era; intensity of feeling and picturesqueness of effect were what he strove for above all else. The absorbing interest in the perfection of technique, a hallmark of the art of the old regime and a manifestation of the elevation of the business of living to the stature of a fine art, was subordinated by the Romanticist to the emotional and subjective expression of self. This does not necessarily mean that the artists of this period (roughly from the end of the eighteenth to the middle of the nineteenth centuries) were not interested in technique, or that they lacked skill in craftsmanship. Goethe, Schiller, Beethoven and Wagner in Germany; Stendhal, Berlioz, and Delacroix in France; and Wordsworth, Byron, Coleridge and Shelley in England—to name only a few of the greatest Romantic artists—are enough to refute such an idea. But, these artists were so preoccupied with self, so immersed in the social patterns of their age, that they plunged into a passionate, surging conflict with life and came out of the struggle with a strong sense of dissatisfaction with their existence and an overwhelming desire to escape from it.

To escape reality, the Romantic artist voyaged in his imagination to distant lands glimpsed through "magic casements opening on the foam of perilous seas." By looking back to the remote past or ahead to the distant future, he was able to release spiritual forces which had been pent up for centuries, and in so doing produced some of the greatest art ever created. A quotation from Shelley's *Ode to the West Wind* is an example:

> *If I were a dead leaf thou mightest bear;*
> *If I were a swift cloud to fly with thee;*
> *A wave to pant beneath thy power, and share*
> *The impulse of thy strength, only less free*
> *Than thou, O uncontrollable! If even*
> *I were as in my boyhood, and could be*
> *The comrade of thy wanderings over heaven,*
> *As then, when to outstrip thy skiey speed*
> *Scarce seemed a vision; I would ne'er have striven*
> *As thus with thee in prayer in my sore need.*
> *O! lift me as a wave, a leaf, a cloud!*
> *I fall upon the thorns of life! I bleed!*
> *A heavy weight of hours has chained and bowed*
> *One too like thee—tameless, and swift, and proud.*

It is all here: the apotheosis of self, the pessimism, the sense of passionate struggle, the poignant dissatisfaction with life, the nostalgic longing for the past, the struggle against destiny and the final resignation. We could well choose a motto for Romantic art from the above lines: "I fall upon the thorns of life! I bleed!" It is this exaggeration, this insistence on the picturesque and extravagant, that has brought the whole Romantic Movement into disrepute in more recent years; our present-day attitude of realism rather mercilessly exposes these very evident weaknesses.

Because of its very nature, music became the most significant of all the arts during the Romantic period. It has been estimated that at least 75 per cent of the music we hear today was either inspired by or came under the influence of Romanticism. Before that time the basis of music's life was a sort of disciplined intellectualism, the beauty largely of an abstract, classical type. The emphasis was on form, a carefully maintained balance between manner and matter that subordinated (though by no means rejected) personal feeling. The two great writers of eighteenth-century music, Haydn and Mozart, while they showed some romantic tendencies in their later works, wrote largely in the classical style. With Beethoven came a change. He marks the transition to Romanticism; after him came the deluge. Schubert, Schumann, Liszt, Chopin, Berlioz, Wagner, Brahms, Bruckner, Mahler, Sibelius, Strauss, even such men of the

EUGÈNE DELACROIX: LIBERTY LEADING THE PEOPLE

Here the spirit of Romantic revolt is portrayed in a setting dramatizing the French uprising of 1830 which deposed the Bourbon king. Note the bold, personalized treatment characteristic of Romanticism.

late nineteenth century as Delius and Schönberg (in his earlier works)—all were possessed of the Romantic spirit. They spoke with vigorous power on trenchant themes and did not hesitate to use whatever means they felt necessary to achieve their effects. (Symphonic resources increased tremendously during this period.) They revelled in colorful sonorities; their dynamic ranges were much wider and the intensity of their climaxes more powerful than those of the classical composers. Their formal structures were not always as clearly defined as those of their predecessors, but they increased the range of their expression to include program music as a means of conveying sensuous and passionate ideas. Their music makes frequent use of dissonances and modulates freely and often. In a word, their qualities were destined to make Music a more human goddess, and one more immediately appealing.

Certainly there were shades and degrees of intensity in Romantic expression; not all composers of the era used the style or expressed the ecstasy of Wagner. The quiet heart-searching of Schubert, the resigned nobility and autumnal glow of Brahms, the warm, personal brilliance of Richard Strauss are as characteristically Romantic as the continuous surge and overpowering sweep of Wagner. There were definite courses into which the mighty flood waters were finally channelled: *Realism*, a kind of artistic temper concerned with drawing art as close as possible to life; *Nationalism*, the desire of the artists to express something of the spirit of their people in what they created; and *Impressionism*, an indirect communication of emotion is made by creating intangible and atmospheric moods. But all these styles of expression, while possessing qualities of their own, are in essence only variations of the Romantic temper.

ROMANTIC DRAMA IN SONG

A good idea of the stimulation given the early artists of the time by the spirit of Romanticism may be gained from observing their treatment of such a subject as the Erlking. Legend has always been a fruitful source of artistic inspiration, and the Romantics found it especially congenial. One of the most famous treatments given a legendary subject is the ballad which Goethe (1749-1832) made out of the German folk-specter which was supposed to inhabit the dark forests and lure people, especially children, to their destruction.

This poem so impressed the eighteen-year-old Schubert that he made out of it one of his and the world's greatest songs. His wonderfully imaginative setting depicts in turn the wild ride through the night of the father with his sick child in his arms, suggested by the pounding rhythm of the accompaniment throughout the whole song; the voices of the *dramatis personae* of the poem describing the scene, each with his own characteristic tone: the terror-stricken boy, the beguiling Erlking, the reassuring father, and the dramatic poet; and the final heartbreaking climax as the father, exhausted and trembling, reaches home only to find that the child in his arms is dead.

One of Schubert's closest friends and confidants in his life as a young musician in Vienna was the painter Moritz von Schwind; he

MORITZ VON SCHWIND: THE ERLKING

too was struck by the dramatic possibilities of this story and made a Romantic painting out of it. If we compare the three versions— poem, song, and painting—we get an excellent suggestion of what is meant by the Romantic spirit in art.

Der Erlkönig (The Erlking)
Words by JOHANN WOLFGANG VON GOETHE (1749-1832)
Music by FRANZ SCHUBERT (1797-1828)

Wer reitet so spät durch Nacht und Wind? Es ist der Vater mit seinem Kind; Er hat den Knaben wohl in dem Arm, Er fasst ihn sicher, er hält ihn warm.
"Mein Sohn, was birgst du so bang dein Gesicht?"
"Siehst, Vater, du den Erlkönig nicht? Den Erlenkönig mit Kron' und Schweif?"
"Mein Sohn, es ist ein Nebelstreif."

Who rides so late through the stormy night? A father holding his child tightly to keep him warm.

Father: Son, what frightens you so?
Son: Father, can't you see the Erlking with his robe and crown?

Father: Son, what you see is only a streak of mist.

"Du liebes Kind, komm', geh' mit mir! Gar schöne Spiele spiel' ich mit dir; Manch' bunte Blumen sind an dem Strand, Meine Mutter hat manch' gülden Gewand."

"Mein Vater, mein Vater, und hörest du nicht, Was Erlenkönig mir leise verspricht?"

"Sei ruhig, bleibe ruhig, mein Kind; In dürren Blättern säuselt der Wind."

"Willst feiner Knabe, du mit mir gehn? Meine Töchter sollen dich warten schön; Meine Töchter führen den nächtlichen Reihn, Und wiegen und tanzen und singen dich ein."

"Mein Vater, mein Vater, und siehst du nicht dort Erlkönigs Töchter am düstern Ort?"

"Mein Sohn, mein Sohn, ich seh' es genau; Es scheinen die alten Weiden so grau."

"Ich liebe dich, mich reizt deine schöne Gestalt; Und bist du nicht willig, so brauch' ich Gewalt."

"Mein Vater, mein Vater, jetzt fasst er mich an! Erlkönig hat mir ein Leids getan!"

Dem Vater grauset's, er reitet geschwind, Er hält in den Armen das ächzende Kind,

Erreicht den Hof mit Müh' und Not; In seinen Armen das Kind war tot.

The Erlking: Dear boy, won't you come with me? Such merry games I'll play with you; gay flowers are blooming in the meadow, and my mother has golden raiment for you!

Boy: Father, oh father, can't you hear what the Erlking is whis-\pering to me?

Father: Be quiet, my boy, it's only the wind in the trees.

The Erlking: Won't you come with me, my fine boy? My daughters will wait on you, and play with you, dance with you, and sing to you!

Boy: Father, oh father, can't you see the Erlking's daughters in that dark place?

Father: My boy, there's nothing there but the old grey willows.

The Erlking: I love you, I must have you, and if you're not willing, I will carry you away by force!

Boy: Father, oh father, he is touching me now! The Erlking has hurt me!

The father shudders, he rides like the wind, holding the pale sobbing child in his arms.

He reaches home, full of fear and horror; in his arms the child lay dead.

Les Préludes—TYPICAL ROMANTIC ART

Another outstanding example of Romanticism in music is Liszt's tone poem *Les Préludes;* it suggests both the strength and the weakness of this type of art. Its very program is somewhat extravagant; it melodies are overluxuriant and nostalgic to a generation so thoroughly removed from the vapors of Romanticism as to incline to the other extreme, demanding art without expression. But Liszt was no precious *poseur;* he knew how to make his music telling, and he had a thorough command of the technic of musical construction. He may have been exotic and picturesque, but he was never disorderly or flabby. We may well examine this tone poem, not so much as an example of great music as of consistent, well-ordered construction in the Romantic vein. A realization of its fervor and exuberances should not deter us from gaining a helpful insight into the processes of its musical composition.

Liszt chose a quotation from Lamartine as his program:

> Is our life anything but a series of Preludes to that unknown song of which death sounds the first and solemn note? Love is the glowing dawn of all existence, but in whose destiny are not the first delights of happiness interrupted by some storm whose blast dissipates its fine illusions? And where is the cruelly wounded soul, which on issuing from one of these tempests, does not endeavor to find solace in the calm serenity of country life? Nevertheless man can hardly give himself up for long to the simple beneficence which he at first finds in nature, and he hastens to the dangerous post wherever war calls him to its ranks, in order to recover at last in the combat full consciousness and entire possession of his energy.

This obvious program gives us life viewed first from the aspect of Love, its greatest fulfillment; second, as a struggle for an Ideal, and the inevitable disillusionment that follows; third, as an opportunity for regaining spiritual equilibrium in the solitude of Nature; and finally, as a glorious re-entry into Conflict. Liszt wrote his tone poem in a single continuous movement, but divided it into four contrasting sections which conform to the four varying moods of the program and correspond to the four separate movements of a symphony. Most of the work is evolved from a three-note germinal theme (which seems to have been popular with many other composers) first heard in the third measure of the introduction (to mark its identification, we have indicated it in the excerpts):

The music which follows is obviously developed from this idea and is self-propellant, moving towards the definite goal of the first main love theme. Before this is reached, the germinal theme is sounded *ff* in the trombones, cellos and basses:

Then comes the first main theme, broadly sung by the strings:

As if to make sure we will not forget it, the composer repeats it almost immediately, this time with brass. The second love theme follows shortly, a quiet but intense tune intoned softly by divided French horns and violas and then repeated on the wood winds:

This too is evolved from the germinal theme. There is no doubt that Liszt—*l'homme d'amour*, as Pourtalès called him—is here discoursing at length on a subject dear to his heart.

The cellos and clarinets unite to give us the first inklings of the storm which occupies the second section of the musical form. A series of chromatic rumblings, again based upon the three-note theme, presages the storm:

When the storm finally arrives, the keen listener will note that the material from which these passages is built is another, intensified, version of the three-note theme. This all moves to a climax in which the second main theme is brilliantly used (161). Unfortunately, this Lisztian storm is more objective than subjective; we are reminded of the rushing roar and muttering outbursts of a storm in nature rather than of the tempestuous, spiritual struggle suggested by the program. Nor does it help the general effect that these chord progressions, used nearly a century ago by Liszt, have come into the current repertory of the movie-mongers; today the whole episode has a melodramatic, cheapened aspect undreamed of when it was written.

The next section (201-344) contains some of the most colorful music in the whole tone poem. Corresponding to the lyrical slow movement of a symphony, it is introduced by a languorous, pastoral oboe theme followed by a lively main theme for the clarinet:

Here is really

> Beauty clear and fair
> Where the air
> Rather like a perfume swells

In this section Liszt sings his charming *bergerette* with great skill and colors his themes with unfailing good taste.

Once again the mood changes, and we hear the two themes (346 and 370) in a quick martial rhythm, delivered with so much pompous grandeur as to make them sound like different tunes from those heard in the first episode.

All is bustle and stir; the struggle and glory are, however, again purely objective. It is in the pomp and circumstance of war that Liszt's hero recovers his individuality and regains possession of his energy. A vigorous coda (405 to end), already mentioned as suggestive of the introductory measures, brings the work to a close; in it notice how the reference to the thematic material with which the piece began rounds out the whole and gives the effect of unity.

FRANZ LISZT

This portrait of the young composer has a romantic quality about it in its powerful, aggressive confidence and self-assurance.

A DOUBLE PERSONALITY

Liszt once jokingly referred to himself as a musician-philosopher, born on Parnassus, coming from the Land of Doubt, and journeying towards the Land of Truth—a description more accurate than his sometimes rather tawdry music would lead us to believe. Ernest Newman in one of his articles in the London *Sunday Times* wonders

> how there came to be so much originality, so much distinction, so much downright commonness in Liszt. Somewhere or other in the course of even his best and most sincere thinking the old *cabotin* will rise up in him again and he becomes, once more, the flashy, flowery, too-effusive Liszt of the Paris salon. Here in *Les Preludes,* for instance, we can see, again and again, the self-conscious and self-approving air with which, in the days of his handsome and seductive youth, he was wont to throw back his mane, put his whole romantic soul into his fingers and his eyes, and slay a gushing countess with a glance.

ADDITIONAL EXAMPLES OF ROMANTICISM IN MUSIC

The Moldau (Vltava)   SMETANA

Smetana, the Czech composer (1824-1884) who was the most notable nationalistic musician of that country before Dvořák, told in his score how in the deep Bohemian forest two streams rise, one warm and swift, the other cold and quiet. Rushing down from the rocks, they unite and flow happily in the rays of the morning sun.

In time, the swift brook becomes a river, the Vltava or Moldau, which, hurrying through Bohemia's valleys, grows into a mighty stream:

It flows through dark, mighty forests, where the huntsman's horn is heard:

It streams through rich pastures in the plains and hears the songs of peasants at a village wedding:

By moonlight the water nymphs play in its waters:

Upon its bosom are mirrored the towers of castles that in past days resounded with the clash of arms and great deeds of warriors:

In the gorge of St. John, rocks seek to oppose it, but it bursts through in foaming torrents:

Then, broadening out into full majesty, it sweeps nobly on past Prague

greeted by the ancient fortress of Vysehrad:

Finally, in all its power and splendor, it is lost to the poet's vision.

The Fountains of Rome   RESPIGHI

Though Italy, unlike some of the Middle European nations, new and old, has not developed a strongly self-conscious school of composition based on folk music, those of its writers who have turned to orchestral rather than to operatic expression have upheld the country's reputation for brilliant, colorful, dynamic depiction. Among them one of the most notable is Ottorino Respighi (1879-1936). Though he wrote for the theater, much of his best-known work is in the form of tone poems, a series of which is devoted to the glories of Rome. Typical of a certain pictorial luxuriousness which may well be compared with Liszt's is his *Fountains of Rome*. There may be some correspondence between this type of program music, with its flowery, literal, prose style (as distinguished from Liszt's poetical searchings) and some aspects of modern life and thought.

In his clever depictions, which date from 1916, the composer (in his own words) "endeavored to give effect to the sentiment and vision suggested by four of Rome's fountains, contemplated at the hour at which their character is most in harmony with the surrounding landscape, and in which their beauty appears most impressive to the observer."

1. The Fountain at Valle Giulia at Dawn. "A pastoral landscape. Droves of cattle pass and disappear in the mists of a Roman dawn." Muted violins suggest the fountain, wood winds the pastoral scene.

2. The Fountain of the Tritons, in the Morning. "A sudden loud and insistent blast of horns . . . is like a joyous call, summoning troops of Tritons and Naiads, who . . . pursue each other and mingle in the dance between the jets of water."

3. The Fountain of Trevi, at Noon. "A solemn theme from the wood and brass assumes a triumphal character. Trumpets peal across the radiant surface of the water. Neptune's chariot passes, drawn by sea-horses and followed Sirens and Tritons. The procession vanishes. . . ." The magnificence of the fountain, with its waterfall, its statues of Neptune, and those illustrating the legend of the discovery of the Virgin's Spring, gives the composer fine scope for elaborate, gorgeous writing.

4. The Fountain of the Villa Medici, at Dusk. "A sad theme rises above a subdued warbling. The air is full of tolling bells and birds twittering; then all dies peacefully in the silence of the night." The music suggests the chaste dignity of the fountain in its oak-guarded seclusion—a scene meet for half-sweet, half-melancholy meditations as the day is dying.

Carnival of the Animals   SAINT-SAËNS

A bulwark of conservatism and a believer in the value of absolute music, Saint-Saëns (who died in 1921 at the age of 86) did not allow this "grand zoological fantasy" to be published or performed during his lifetime. One hearing will show why; it is a most unconventional piece (it was originally written as a sort of musical joke), and its realism has become famous. In the sketches the composer not only reproduces the sounds made by the various animals but also delights in satirizing the music of his own day. The orchestration includes a two-piano part and a well-known solo for cello. The sections are labeled

Introduction and Royal March of the Lion
Hens and Cocks
Wild Asses

Tortoises (The composer here mocks an Offenbach cancan by playing it very slowly.)

The Elephant (The tune to which the elephant lumbers is Berlioz' *Waltz of the Sylphs!*)

Kangaroos

Aquarium

Personages with Long Ears

Cuckoo in the Woods

Birds

Pianists (Concert players, with their phenomenal runs and crashing chords, are here put in their place.)

The Swan (This is the most famous of all sketches, and includes the famous cello solo, "The Swan.")

Fossils (Saint-Saëns does not hesitate to ridicule himself, for he includes a theme here from his *Danse macabre.*)

A brilliant Finale, in which all the animals are passed in review.

The whole thing is not much more than a well-done pre-Disney "Silly Symphony," but it is clever and witty music and has found a place on concert programs.

TOPICS FOR DISCUSSION

Liszt's romanticism now seems overdone to many people; some have even called it "hysterical." In its day, it was revered. Can you account for the considerable change in outlook toward Romanticism in the past century?

Do you think a revival of Romanticism is possible? Would it be desirable? Could it have value to offset the present-day scorn for sentiment in music?

Which of the composers since Liszt seem to hold the balance in this matter of Romanticism?

Apart from his romanticism, what are Liszt's artistic weaknesses and contributions, technically and otherwise? Can you ascribe to his nature, upbringing, or environment definite influences in Liszt's art?

Compare *Les Préludes* with *Till*. Which do you think is the finer work of art? Why? Which would attract the unskilled layman more easily?

Can you hear in Liszt's tone poem elements which he persistently uses in other works? Are these, in your opinion, the strong or weak elements in his work?

CHAPTER 15

The Question of Form

ళ§ ৡల

Form in art means exactly what it means in life in general—the successful co-ordination of elements to produce the most effective results possible. When we speak of the form of an athlete, we refer to the intangible something that enables him to bring all his powers into proper relationship to attain the greatest possible effectiveness. Form in art means the organizing process—in plain terms, the plan —by which all the fundamental elements of that art are arranged to make the maximum impression on the consciousness of him who perceives. A piece of music, for example, may have good melody, with well-arranged rhythmic patterns, and may be well harmonized, with effective combinations of timbre; but unless it has, in addition, a good plan of organization by which its materials are significantly ordered, it fails of full effect. This ability to organize his materials effectively is the most intellectual part of a composer's equipment; it may be acquired to a certain degree, but it must be present if a man is to write good music. The greatest composers have been those who have had consummate skill in creating great ideas and an organizing ability to present them well.

We have already suggested the need for design and form in all art; that need is even more necessary in the immaterial and transient art of music than in the material arts of painting, sculpture, and architecture. A composer must know how to present his ideas so that they arrest our attention and hold it. The various elements that make up his whole composition must be contrasted in a way that will give effective balance, without being so diffuse as to make them difficult to remember. A composer must have some design or formal scheme in his mind when he writes or his music will be simply a hodgepodge of ideas, unintelligible to other minds.

TEXTURE IN MUSIC

One of the chief elements of formal structure in music is what may be called its texture, the characteristic quality resulting from the composer's integration and blending of its various parts. In general, the texture of music may be said to be of three different kinds: *monophonic*, *homophonic*, and *polyphonic*. Derivatively, the first two of these words mean the same thing: sounding alike, of the same pitch; technically, they have two quite different meanings. The third word means, literally, "many-voiced" and in general is used synonymously with *contrapuntal*.

Monophonic Music

Monophonic Music is the simplest we know—a one-voiced, unaccompanied line such as is found in Chinese, ancient Greek, or Hindu music, or, in our Western system, in the Gregorian chant of the early Church.

Homophonic Music

Homophonic texture in music can easily be recognized in such selections as Handel's *Ombra mai fu* (Largo) from *Xerxes*, the second movement of Dvořák's *Symphony No. 5*, and in fact, in most of the music written from the end of the sixteenth century to the present day. Its distinguishing characteristic is that it consists of a principal melodic line supported by a *chordal* accompaniment, the sort of thing we discussed in our earlier remarks about harmony.

Symphony No. 5, in E Minor
Second Movement

Dvořák

The accompaniment may consist of simple successions of block chords, as above, or the chords may be broken up, their tones sounded not simultaneously but one after another, in some sort of *arpeggio* formation:

POLYPHONIC (CONTRAPUNTAL) MUSIC

There is a third kind of texture, one that is much more difficult to recognize and hear than the two we have just described. Since it is not used in music making today as much as it was in earlier times, our ears have to become accustomed to its peculiar characteristics. This kind of music texture was employed by composers before the general ideals of the homophonic style were adopted around the beginning of the seventeenth century. We call it *polyphonic* or *contrapuntal*, because it is made up of a number of separate and independent melodic strands, each with its own rhythmic values, which, taken together, form harmonies. This is the way all part music before 1600, and a considerable amount of it for some time afterwards, was written. It is necessary to learn to listen to this type of music in a different way from that which is used for the works of later composers. In polyphonic music we should try to hear separately the various strands sung and played by the different parts instead of being content to hear the customary main melody, supported by chords in vertical fashion. Here is a fine excerpt from a sixteenth century composer:

Grátia vobis.

HOMOPHONIC AND POLYPHONIC MUSIC

A piece of music does not necessarily keep strictly to any one of these textures. Generally speaking, the earlier it comes in the line of historical development, the greater the probability that it will be written with only one kind of texture. We have said that the earliest European music we know consists of a single unaccompanied melodic line, and that up to the beginning of the seventeenth century music was almost entirely polyphonic. After that there was a graceful blending of the homophonic and the polyphonic manners of writing until the nineteenth century, when composers began to emphasize the basic homophonic style. Of late, because of a neo-classic reaction against the romantic excesses of the nineteenth century, there has been a revival of interest in counterpoint (a term synonymous with polyphony).

A good example of distinction between homophonic and polyphonic styles is in the chorus "Glory to God" from Handel's *Messiah*. This is written at first in harmonic blocks and then, at the words "good will towards men," it is changed to polyphony. This is easy both to hear with the ear and to see with the eye, in the score. Another outstanding example of the practical use of these various textural styles is the slow movement of Beethoven's *Seventh Symphony*. The earlier part is almost entirely homophonic—all chords, with hardly a suggestion of melody. The middle part is partly contrapuntal, partly homophonic, because of a new, fully expressed melody woven against the chordal background. Later on there are several short, purely contrapuntal sections where the violins weave a distinctive counterpoint against the melody heard in the opening measures. This distinction between polyphonic and homophonic styles is a vital one, and it is necessary to understand it thoroughly if we are to realize the fundamental qualities of music written in different historical periods.

FORM IN PROGRAM MUSIC

Another element of formal structure in music is its consecutiveness—the way its various parts follow each other so as to attract and hold the hearer's interest. The composers of the program music we have just studied were not greatly concerned with the problem of "making their music last." They simply took a suitable story or philosophical concept and, using a few themes as generative material, let the music they wrote follow the necessities of the program. We can be sure, however, that when Liszt and Strauss chose programs, they kept a weather eye out for genetic possibilities; they made sure that the program itself was constructed so that the arrangement of contrast, balance, and unity made an arresting start and led through a number of consecutive episodes to a convincing finish. Hence the music with which they clothed their programs possesses the quality of good formal design. (Review briefly the programs of *Till Eulenspiegel* and *Les Préludes*, and see how true this is.)

These compositions are called *symphonic* (or *tone*) *poems*, a term invented by Liszt, who wrote thirteen works of this kind. The listener should be able to realize that their formal structural plan follows the program, without having any set outline. A work of this kind having several movements, such as Rimsky-Korsakov's *Scheherazade* suite (to be studied soon), is called a *symphonic suite*. There is usually little thematic development in these works; its place is taken by alterations and paraphrases of the themes to fit the program.

FORM IN ABSOLUTE MUSIC

An even greater concern with the principles of good construction is necessary in writing absolute music, for in it there is nothing in the way of an underlying poetic program to carry us along. The best way to sense this is to listen carefully to a well-constructed piece of absolute music where the formal patterns are comparatively easy to follow—again the first movement of Beethoven's *Fifth Symphony* is an ideal example. On hearing music such as this, even for the first time, you will observe that there are several well-defined themes, such as were found in the program pieces, that occur and recur frequently. In absolute music these themes are presented in a logically and carefully ordered manner so that they may be readily grasped; they have, of course, no connection with any story. It is not difficult to see, then, that some understanding of this controlled imaginative thinking, as form has been defined, is necessary if we are to increase our enjoyment of music through comprehending it.

Photograph by Muller

CAPITAL FROM THE CHURCH OF ST. MICHEL-DE-CUXA,
ROUSSILLON, FRANCE

*Showing a twelfth-century sculptor's understanding of form. Abstracting the
shapes of well-known animals and birds, this unknown artist made them into a
beautifully shaped capital, or head of a pillar designed to support an archway.
Here, indeed, "all the fundamental elements are arranged so as to secure the maximum impression upon the consciousness of him who perceives" and incidentally
to make a most functional architectural design.*

Before we try to explain the rather intricate details of musical
design, it will be well to clear up one prevalent misunderstanding as
to the general nature of form. In discussing the problems of the composer we have said that he has at his disposal a number of structural
plans or molds, evolved by his predecessors through the centuries,
which aid in the coherent organization of his material. We are apt
to think that a composer chooses one of these formal molds which
seems best suited to his purpose and then designs the substance of his

music to fit its requirements. It is customary to suggest in this respect that in art there are *form* and *substance*—the vessel and what the vessel contains. This is not true; an examination of any great masterpiece of music, painting, or architecture will show that it seldom fits neatly into a prearranged scheme of formal design such as is laid down by textbooks. In art, form and substance are one, inseparable, born together in the mind of the creator and growing together as do the veins and arteries, and the blood they contain, in our bodies. Rightly considered, any study of the formal element in music or in any other art is made in order better to understand the living thing, a process similar to that undertaken by the medical student in order that he may better understand the living organisms with which he must deal. We must realize that a composer can work within a formal mold and yet be independent of it. Almost every great symphony written is a good example of this; while keeping to the general formal outlines laid down by his predecessors, Beethoven did not hesitate to depart from them whenever he felt that such a procedure would make his music more effective. It may truly be said that the "form of any genuine piece of art is unique."

It would seem foolish for any composer to discard completely the well-tried and proved formulas that had been developed through the combined effort of generations preceding him. These predetermined formulas are in the back of his mind as he writes, acting as guides and incentives. But it would be even more foolish for him to attempt anything in the way of absolute fidelity to such formulas; this could only result in what the Germans realistically call *Kapellmeistermusik* —music that is correctly written but that possesses no spark of life. The character of the composer's thought and the exigencies that develop as he proceeds in his work make it necessary that he use any formal scheme he may choose only as a prop, discarding it whenever it does not seem to suit his particular and personal need. In this sense we can see that each masterpiece makes its own rules.

All this does not mean, however, that the listener cannot profit greatly from an understanding of these design patterns that have been used by the composers. There are a number of ways in which we may classify these forms to better realize their full significance. Below are listed the three main types of musical form and the categories within each form:

Vocal Forms

IN SECULAR MUSIC:
1. The song
2. The opera
3. The madrigal
4. The cantata

IN SACRED MUSIC:
1. The chant
2. The song
3. The hymn (chorale)
4. The motet (anthem)
5. The mass (communion service)
6. The oratorio (Passion; cantata)

Forms That Are Both Vocal and Instrumental

1. *Contrapuntal Forms* based on a *cantus firmus* (literally "fixed song")
2. *The Fugue*

Instrumental Forms

SECTIONAL FORMS (Forms in relation to separate, short divisions of a work)
1. Unitary form (One-part form)
2. Variation form
3. Rondo form
4. Binary form (Two-part form)
5. Ternary form (Three-part form)
    (a) in songs
    (b) in short instrumental pieces—the minuet, scherzo, and so on
    (c) in small piano pieces—nocturne, waltz, impromptu, and so forth
    (d) in slow movements of sonatas and symphonies
    (e) in first movements of sonatas and symphonies (sonata form)
6. Free forms: overture, fantasia, prelude

Conjoint Forms (Form in relation to the piece as a whole.)

1. The march
2. The waltz
3. Small instrumental pieces (nocturne, étude, and so on)
4. The suite
5. The sonata family
    (a) the sonata
    (b) the symphony
    (c) the concerto
    (d) chamber music; trio, quartet, quintet, and so forth
6. The symphonic poem (program-music form)

VOCAL FORMS

It is difficult for most listeners to realize that vocal music reached a height of perfection long before instrumental music, for our attention is largely centered on the latter type. Naturally, form in vocal music follows the words; the composer of vocal music takes a series of words—a poem, a liturgical text, or a dramatic libretto— and sets them to music. The result depends so largely on the character of the text that the first requisite in following the vocal forms is a complete understanding of the words used. We come here upon a difficult and vexatious problem, one that is of great importance for the English-speaking listener who would familiarize himself with vocal music: the outstanding examples of the various types of vocal form—song, oratorio, opera, mass—have foreign texts. Fashion and usage have decreed that nations such as the United States and England, where the people generally have little experience with any language other than their own, must listen to their songs, operas, and oratorios in Italian, German, French and Latin. (In recent years the use of English, especially in opera, has greatly increased.) It is because of this language problem that opera in English-speaking countries has been slow in developing, whereas in European countries like Italy and Germany it has become a part of everyday experience.

SECULAR MUSIC

Literally, a *song* is any musical composition for the voice; every individual, whether or not he is really musical, has experienced the satisfaction of expressing his feelings through song; it is man's most immediate and intimate musical manifestation. As a form of musical expression, the song is of indefinite antiquity. The earliest recorded examples in Western Europe date from the tenth century, but long before music was performed by professional composers or musicians, songs and dances flourished among the people as a natural, spontaneous expression of their common ideas and feelings. From this beginning there developed a tremendous collection of songs which are the equivalent of the stories, myths, and sagas of literary history. Both of these forms of expression are, in essence, the natural products of the national groups from which they sprang.

Folk songs are generally of unknown authorship and have been handed down by word of mouth. Folk songs which have been preserved in printed texts and have an original author—for example, those bearing the name of Stephen Foster—are called *composed folk songs*, in contradistinction to the traditional folk songs.

The so-called *art song*, on the other hand, is one which has been put together by a composer who, in writing a musical setting for voice with piano accompaniment, fuses song, poetry, and instrumental music into a whole. This union has produced the distinctive form usually known as the *Lied* (literally, song), so called because Germany has produced more and better works of this kind than any other nation.

An *opera* is a dramatic work in which the whole or the greater part of the text is sung with instrumental accompaniment. Originating in Italy at the beginning of the seventeenth century, opera has largely maintained the traditions established at that time and in that country, although it has become the most international of all vocal forms.

The principal distinctions to be made here are those between the semi-spoken portions, called recitatives, which are more closely related in pitch and rhythm to dramatic speech than to song, and the song-like *arias*, symmetrical pieces of vocal music designed to exploit and display the capabilities of the singing-actors performing the opera.

A *madrigal* is a secular piece for several voices, with or without instrumental accompaniment (usually without). Written in a woven polyphonic style (see p. 165) in which one part or voice largely imitates another, it was extremely stylish during the sixteenth and seventeenth century, when various courts delighted in its sophisticated word painting and symbolism.

A *cantata* is, literally, a piece which is sung, as opposed to a sonata, which is played. In practical use, however, the name *cantata* is applied to an extended piece of music (secular or sacred) for one or more voices consisting of a number of movements such as arias, recitatives, duets and choruses based on a continuous text. The secular cantata first appeared in Italy where it took various forms and styles; later it developed in France and especially in Germany, where it was widely adapted for religious purposes.

SACRED MUSIC

There are a number of forms of religious vocal music. The simplest and earliest is the chant, a general term for monophonic, unaccompanied liturgical music in free rhythm. In particular, it refers to the unaccompanied vocal music used in the services of the Christian Church. Most common is the *Gregorian Chant* or so-called plainsong of the Catholic Church, although the liturgical melodies of other rites, such as the Ambrosian, Byzantine, Greek Orthodox, and Anglican, are usually referred to as chants.

The distinction between *sacred* and *secular* songs is largely one of style, determined by the difference in the words used as text. The tradition of a sacred solo song accompanied by an instrumental ensemble (or organ) derives from English usage of the late sixteenth century.

A *hymn* is a stanzaic religious song composed in a style that is effective for mass singing. Hymns have been used by all civilizations and have become an integral part of the Christian liturgy. The type introduced by Luther into the Protestant Church at the time of the Reformation—the *chorale*—is without the unfortunate sentimentality found in so many English hymns and constitutes one of music's greatest treasures, especially as elaborated and harmonized by J. S. Bach.

A *motet* may be defined as the sacred counterpart of the madrigal; a sacred song for a number of voices, it has no fixed place in the liturgy of the Church. Its English counterpart is the *anthem*.

The *Mass*, speaking musically, is the setting given to those fixed portions of the Eucharistic rite of the Roman and Greek churches which are appointed to be sung by the choir. Some of the world's finest music has gone into these settings, most of them unheard today because of their specific ritualistic character. Beginning with those unknown composers who wrote Gregorian chant settings of the Mass in the early centuries of the Church's existence, almost every composer up through the seventeenth century gave attention to this form. Even such outstanding men as Bach and Beethoven wrote Masses, compositions which, considered as music, rank high among the works of these composers, although they are not suitable for liturgical use. The *Requiem Mass* is a special type sung for the repose of the souls of the dead. The *Communion Service* consists of the translated parts of the Catholic Mass that have been retained in the ritual of the Anglican churches.

An *oratorio* may be described as a sort of non-acting version of opera with a dramatic text or libretto (which may be sacred or secular), recitatives, arias, and choruses with orchestral accompaniment, but without stage action, scenery, or costumes. The *Passion* is a special form of oratorio developed in the German Lutheran Church; the text, drawn from the gospel narratives, is descriptive of the sufferings of Christ between the night of the Last Supper and his death. The religious *cantata* is a small-dimensioned oratorio for solo voice (or voices) and the usual performing apparatus—solos, chorus, and orchestra. J. S. Bach wrote almost three hundred of this type of composition for use in the churches where he directed the music.

Irwin Edman wrote some verses for the *New Yorker* magazine which he called "Varieties of Musical Experience"; these contain such good, humorous descriptions of some of the most used forms that we are quoting them in this and following chapters.[1] Of the cantata he says:

> *No person's more persona grata*
> *Than he who's penned a sound cantata;*
> *Would there were lots of him! But ach,*
> *There are few, and none like Bach!*

FORMS WHICH ARE BOTH VOCAL AND INSTRUMENTAL

It does not take a great deal of musical experience to realize that most of the forms employed by composers through the ages have been either vocal or instrumental. A few forms, however, were developed at the time when vocal music was gradually being supplanted by instrumental. Early instrumental music was merely the playing on instruments of that which had been written originally for voices; through trial-and-error experimentation, there gradually developed a style that was characteristically suited to instruments.

CANTUS FIRMUS

An examination of these overlapping forms will show that they are all *contrapuntal* in character. In writing for voices, composers naturally chose the polyphonic style because of its intricate weaving of parts. When the instrumentalists began to develop an independent

[1] Quoted by permission.

style which would realize the possibilities of their instruments, they started with some of these vocal contrapuntal forms; thus, certain forms were used both vocally and instrumentally. Based on some clearly defined theme which could easily be recognized and followed throughout the course of the music, they consisted of ingenious contrapuntal manipulations of a fundamental generative idea called the *cantus firmus*. Composers of the great polyphonic period (the fifteenth, sixteenth, and seventeenth centuries) did not consider themselves as much inventors as builders; sometimes they did not even use their own themes for the foundations of the imposing tonal structures they reared. Many of the countless Masses and other church compositions written during this time were based on themes taken from Gregorian chants or from the works of other composers —or, strange as it may seem to us today, on the often incongruous tune of a popular song of the day. Later, in the Lutheran church, the same practice was followed, except that the *cantus firmus* was usually a chorale tune well-known to the congregation for which the music was written. Many of Bach's church cantatas contain elaborate contrapuntal numbers for voices and orchestra constructed entirely on a chorale *cantus firmus*. Bach and his predecessors and followers also wrote a large number of *chorale preludes*, service pieces for the organ with a chorale as *cantus firmus*. These little works, many of them programmatic in character, since they often depict some idea suggested by the words of the hymn, show Bach's genius at its zenith.

The Fugue

One of the most popular of these overlapping vocal-instrumental styles, the fugue, may be said to have been the outstanding form for both vocal and instrumental music during the seventeenth century. Technically, the fugue consists of an elaborate polyphonic texture —it can hardly be called a set *form*—evolved during the fifteenth and sixteenth centuries from the simple principle of imitative writing.

Everyone knows the *round*—or *canon*, as it is more formally called—a sequential presentation of one musical phrase by various voices. This simple idea underlies the construction of the fugue, but in this elaborated presentation, each of the two, three, or four voices in which the fugue may be written has equal participation in the general effect. Just how this is done may be seen by analyzing a typical Bach fugue and comparing it with the simple canon or round which was its structural ancestor. In a three-part round, the melody as given by one voice is usually imitated tone by tone by each of the other voices:

Sometimes one of the voices, in order to keep the melody within singing range, has the tune transposed into another key:

This idea was in time developed so that by bringing in the theme (the *subject*, we call it in the fugue) in different keys, built up into a unified whole by the use of episodes, a work could be produced which was compact and meaty, one which could keep the listener keenly interested in its fashioning, and—if the composer was a man of strong feeling, as was Bach—by no means devoid of emotion.

The subject is generally short and always characteristic, easily remembered because it is to be followed in various appearances, wholly or in part, throughout the fugue. The answer is the name given to the same theme's second appearance, this time in a dominant key and in another part or "voice." This answer is accompanied by the counter-subject. If there are only two parts performing in the fugue, we get just the subject followed by the answer with its accompanying counter-subject. If there are three parts (as in the example below), one has the subject, the second the answer (the same tune, remember) and the third the subject again. If four, the fourth has the answer again—in the dominant key, like the former answer. A short diagram of a typical fugue from Bach's great collection called *The Well-Tempered Clavier* (known for short as *The Forty-eight*, because that is the total of its preludes and fugues— forty-eight of each) will show the general scheme:

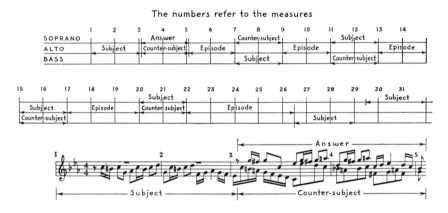

It may be said that this simple setting forth of the one main theme with an accompaniment makes the first section of the fugue. In the second (which follows without a break) things begin to happen to both subject and its accompaniment tune. The composer begins to build with subject entries and episodes as materials. Since these are of the same fabric, there is high unity in the fugue, and the composer's skill must provide variety and cumulative interest. As long as everything he does contributes to the fashioning of the unified piece, he can do anything he wishes—even introduce fresh ideas, although this is not very common. If you examine *The Forty-Eight*, you will find an amazing diversity of methods, although the amount of *material* used in any one fugue is very small. There are far more ways of treating the subject and counter-subject than one might at first imagine. They may come in longer or shorter notes than at first—augmentation or diminution. They may be upside down, tail foremost, or in any other guise. A good part of the intellectual pleasure in listening to the fugue comes from observing how the parts are blended and woven together for the common good.

A device for tautening the excitement is *stretto*—letting the theme answer itself in a shorter time sequence than it did at first. This device may be used several times in a fugue, and if it is, the time interval is almost always shorter at each appearance in order to build up the excitement. The closest stretto generally comes just when we are entering the home stretch—the third section of the fugue. Here, after the adventures of the middle section, the subject generally enters, like a giant refreshed, in the original key. Thereafter to the end of the fugue the "coda spirit" prevails, and we receive the definite impression that our flight is about to be ended.

> *In fugues the listener rejoices*
> *To follow keenly several voices*
> *And at the close greet with a shout*
> *The way they neatly all work out.*

It might be thought that such a complex musical pattern, more or less strict in its fashioning, variable only through the amount of musical invention the composer puts into it, would be stiff and academic. But Bach was able to make this complicated process yield some of his most imaginative and surprisingly beautiful music. It has appeared, usually written in a rather free style, only occasionally since his time.

LIST OF SUGGESTED MUSIC

FOLK SONGS

"I Wonder as I Wander"
"Wayfaring Stranger"
These are American mountaineer ballads which can be traced to English, Scottish and Welsh sources. They are sung in traditional manner by such folk singers as John Niles and Burl Ives.

ART SONGS

Der Erlkönig (The Erlking)   SCHUBERT

Der Wanderer   SCHUBERT

OTHER FORMS

ARIA: *Cielo e mar!* from *La Gioconda*   PONCHIELLI

MADRIGAL: "Sweet Honey-Sucking Bees"   WILBYE

HYMN: "Onward, Christian Soldiers"   SULLIVAN

CHORALE: *Ein' feste Burg*   LUTHER

MOTET: *O Bone Jesu*   PALESTRINA

ANTHEM: "The Bell Anthem"   PURCELL

MASS: *Assumpta est Maria*   PALESTRINA

ORATORIO: *Messiah*   HANDEL
            St. Matthew Passion   BACH

CANTATA: (Sacred) *Christ lag in Todesbanden*   BACH
         (Secular) *Nell' dolce dell' oblio*   HANDEL

MONOPHONIC MUSIC: Any part of the Gregorian setting to the Mass
            Lux et origo

HOMOPHONIC MUSIC: *Ombra mai fu* from *Xerxes*   HANDEL

POLYPHONIC MUSIC: Any part of the setting of the
            Missa Papae Marcelli   PALESTRINA

MIXED STYLES: (both homophonic and polyphonic)
            Symphony No. 7, in A Major,
            Second Movement   BEETHOVEN

FUGUE: *Fugue in g minor* (*Little*)   BACH

INSTRUMENTAL TREATMENT OF A CANTUS FIRMUS

Chorale Prelude: *Das alte Jahr vergangen ist*   BACH

Chorale Prelude: *Liebster Jesu*   BACH

TOPICS FOR DISCUSSION

Many laymen find polyphony dull because they are unfamiliar with it. What examples would you choose to convince them that it is not?

Discuss the ways in which early musical forms were suited to the powers and limitations of early instruments.

It has been said that the development of instruments and that of forms in composition have always reacted with each other. Can you name instances?

Some say that the old forms such as the symphony are outworn and will not be used in the future. What is your opinion: can the symphonic form be rejuvenated, or are fine symphonies still being written?

Can you separate form and substance or shape and meaning in any work of art? Discuss.

Discuss the vitality of key in form by analyzing the key moves in a number of simple pieces. Note how they give pleasure, and try to explain how this is done.

Do you see any way in which the fugue might extend its boundaries and still remain a free (and yet not indefinite) style?

CHAPTER 16

Instrumental Forms

⊸§ ¿⊱

When we listen to music that has no association with words, it is often difficult to recognize the various units which go to make up its formal architecture, for we do not have the structural outline of the poetry to help us. Just as in this book words have been put together to form phrases, phrases joined into sentences, sentences grouped to make paragraphs, paragraphs molded into chapters, and chapters combined to form the whole work, composers deal with structural units in building their music. The smallest unit is a little melodic or rhythmic group, sometimes containing only a few notes, such as the famous so-called Fate *motive* in the first movement of Beethoven's *Fifth Symphony*. These motives are usually combined into larger units, forming a more complete melody of several measures, called a *theme*. These themes can be extended and enlarged with congruous material into *sections*. And sections can be gathered together to form what is called a *movement*, the very meaning of which suggests that it is a structural division of an even more extended composition such as a *symphony*.

A description such as this cannot be exact, and you will find in reading about musical form that there is by no means any uniform agreement about these terms. In studying form as a help in listening, we should be content with finding generalities and approximations, and "look for exactness only so far as the nature of the subject permits," to borrow an Aristotelian phrase. General methods of procedure can be deduced from observing individual works of art, but no genuine art work can be formulated according to exact prescription. If it were, it would certainly cease to be art. Although there are general formal principles that underlie the construction of all instrumental music, each composition, large or small, elaborate or simple, must in reality make its own rules.

UNITARY FORM

The easiest musical forms for listeners to recognize are those which are put together sectionally, each section being made up of material that hangs together naturally.

SINGLE DIVISION FORM

The simplest of these sectional forms is that which consists of a single division—a short composition that was conceived all of a piece, without break from beginning to end. This form is not very usual and when employed is limited to small pieces in which there is no need for contrast. The first prelude in Bach's *Well-Tempered Clavier* and Chopin's *Prelude Number One* in his Opus 28 can be cited as effective examples.

VARIATION FORM

It would be perfectly possible to make an extended piece of music from an indefinite repetition of one of these single-division forms, but the result would hardly be interesting. Basically, as the early composers of instrumental music quickly found out, one of two things can be done to a tune to stretch it into an extended composition: repeat it or vary it. And since literal repetition is dull, they soon found how to repeat it with diversity. Edman puts it neatly:

> *It's fun to watch while a musician*
> *Dotes on a theme by repetition.*
> *There is no other art I know of*
> *Where anyone can make a go of*
> *Saying once, then ten times more,*
> *The same thing one has said before.*

So we find the *theme* and *variations* (which may be represented to the literal-minded by the formula: $A—A^1—A^2—A^3$, and so forth) used by many examples of the earliest instrumental composers. Some of the first examples of this form are not very exciting to modern ears; such things as Byrd's "The Bells" and Morley's

"Goe from My Window" are variations done according to formula, and they tend to become tiresome. The seventeenth-century and eighteenth-century *air with doubles* (so-called because each successive variation was written with faster notes), although not profound, contains some interesting technical devices. The most famous example of this type of variation is the one called "The Harmonious Blacksmith," from Handel's *Suite in E Major*. Other early variation forms were two varieties of the *basso ostinato* (literally, obstinate bass, since a short phrase is repeated over and over in the bass), the *chaconne* and the *passacaglia*, forms which consist of a series of variations built around the reiteration of a melody or a set of chords. All these were widely used by the "pre-classic" composers; Frescobaldi and Purcell wrote some of the best we know.

With the advent of the classic composers, Haydn, Mozart, and Beethoven, the theme and variations became a more interesting form. The theme was usually straightforward, and the variations followed it closely in melodic outline, dimensions, and structural relationships. Haydn's well-known set in the second movement of his *Surprise Symphony*, the first movement of Mozart's *A Major Piano Sonata*, the slow movement of Beethoven's *Kreutzer Sonata*, Op. 47 should be listened to carefully as excellent examples. Even the nineteenth-century composers found this form exceedingly useful although they did not follow it closely; their compositions might better be called "meditations" or "divagations" than "variations." Schumann's *Études Symphoniques*, Brahms' *Variations on a Theme* [formerly believed to be] *by Haydn*, César Franck's *Symphonic Variations*, and above all others, Elgar's *Enigma Variations* are works of considerable length and great interest. Such modern writers as Stravinsky (in his *Octet for Wind Instruments*), Roy Harris (in a string quartet), and Hindemith (in his *Schwanendreher*) have used this oldest of all instrumental forms for shaping their musical thoughts.

RONDO FORM

The *rondo* form is another way of organizing an extended piece out of a single-sectioned form. Here we have a scheme in which a section is literally repeated a number of times, with extraneous material in well-varied keys (which play a considerable part in the interest of the work) inserted between each repetition: A—B—A—C—A—D, and so on. There are different kinds of rondos, but they are all symmetrical in construction; they probably derived from the literary *rondel*, invented in the fourteenth century and used largely by medieval French poets. There was a certain rhyme scheme in its fourteen lines, as shown in this nineteenth-century example by Dobson:

A   Love comes back to his vacant dwelling
     The old, old Love that we knew of yore!
     We see him stand by the open door,
B   With his great eyes sad, and his bosom swelling
     He makes as though in our arms repelling
     He fain would lie as he lay before:

A   Love comes back to his vacant dwelling
     The old, old Love that we knew of yore!
     Ah, who shall keep us from over-spelling
     That sweet, forgotten, forbidden Love?
C   E'en as we doubt, in our hearts once more,
     With a rush of tears to our eyelids welling
     Love comes back to his vacant dwelling
A   The old, old Love that we knew of yore!

    This exact structural scheme was used by Bach in the Rondeau of his *Suite in B minor for Flute and Strings:*

Rondeau (ABACA)
Allegro

Unfortunately, the relationship of the details of the rondo when applied to larger forms may be difficult to determine, because the A section (called the *refrain*) and the contrasting sections (called *episodes*) are often sub-divided into schemes that are complex and confusing. (The most common of these, the *sonata-rondo*, is discussed later.) In general, it can be said that the principle of the rondo is much clearer than its application, and that the only sure principle to follow in listening is to recognize the more or less regular return of the refrain in whole or in part.

BINARY FORM

A sectional form that has been widely employed, especially by composers of an earlier time, is the *binary* or *two-part* form (represented symbolically by the formula A—B), consisting of two consecutive divisions.[1] Sometimes the second is entirely different from the first; sometimes it is simply a new aspect or rearrangement of it. The A section usually ends in the key of the dominant; B leads back to the tonic. The tune "America" is an illustration of simple binary form; the musical phrases to which the first three lines of the text are sung comprise the first section:

My coun-try, 'tis of thee, Sweet land of li - ber-ty, Of thee I sing

Those set to the last four lines make up the second division:

Land where my fath - ers died; Land of the pil-grim's pride,

From ev' - ry moun-tain-side Let free - dom ring!

[1] Either or both of these divisions may be repeated, but it is customary in analyzing forms not to take these literal repetitions into account.

The binary form was extremely popular in the seventeenth and eighteenth centuries and was often used by such composers as François Couperin and Domenico Scarlatti in the pieces they wrote for the harpsichord. Listen to some of Couperin's fancifully titled clavecin pieces or to one of Scarlatti's brilliant sonatas, and you will have heard this form in its best estate. Bach's *Suite in b minor for Flute and Strings* has a fine example of this form:

Sarabande: Binary form.
[Andante]

TERNARY FORM

Still another easily recognized scheme is the *three-part* or *ternary* form (A—B—A), perhaps the most universally used of all. Listen to the French folk song *Sur le pont d'Avignon*.

The two sections marked A are exactly alike except at the end; the second has a more final air about it than the first. This is likewise true of the German folk tune *Ach, du lieber Augustin:*

But if you follow these tunes through, you will find that their composers were not satisfied with just this simple repetition of ideas. In the French song, a new contrasting idea is inserted, consisting of two short phrases, the second an exact duplicate of the first and after this the first section, A, returns again:

So with the German song:

This gives us a basic picture of the pattern which is used continuously throughout music, in all kinds of simple and complex ways:

1. The statement of an idea or a section
2. The placing in contrast of a new idea or section
3. The restatement of the first idea to give unity and finality

We find examples of this form in music of many styles and periods:

SONGS

It has been employed by the composers of many simple songs. Hum or whistle through the following tunes, and you will find that they are all built according to this three-part form:

"Ye Banks and Braes," Scots folk tune
"The Flight of the Earls," Irish folk tune
"All Through the Night," Welsh folk tune
"Drink to Me Only With Thine Eyes," English folk tune
"Turkey in the Straw," American folk tune
"O Tannenbaum," German folk tune
"Humoresque," Dvořák

MINUET AND SCHERZO

These were used by composers of the classic period for certain of their short instrumental pieces, particularly the minuet. Of all the dances developed during the course of European history, this seems to have had the greatest effect on music. Starting as a French peasant dance, the minuet was developed by the aristocratic court circles and then taken over by the writers of instrumental music. Almost from its earliest existence it has been written in ternary form—a first stanza, followed by a second, and then the first again. In Bach's time the two contrasting sections of a minuet were thought of as separate pieces and so labeled: Minuets I and II. These were played successively, after which Minuet I was repeated (again see the Bach *Suite in b minor for Flute and Strings*). To provide a better contrast, the second minuet was written for three instruments or in three-part harmony, and so came to be known as the *trio*. This name stuck, even after the reasons for it had been lost. So the plan came to be

1. Minuet
2. Another minuet called a *trio*
3. The original minuet repeated intact

When Beethoven supplanted the minuet by the *scherzo* in his piano and orchestral pieces, he kept the same general form and merely changed its mood and speed. Some of his most characteristic contributions to symphonic literature took the form of *scherzo* and *trio*—for example, the third movement of the *Eroica* and the *Seventh Symphony*. Many composers since his time have followed his example in using the *scherzo* in their symphonies.

Small Piano Pieces

The three-part form, with slight adaptations, was used for many of the small pieces popular with the nineteenth-century piano composers: the nocturne, the waltz, the prelude, the impromptu and so on. It makes an ideal form for this purpose, for in a limited scope it offers plenty of opportunity for ingenious architecture and strong emotional contrasts. Here are characteristic examples from Chopin:

Nocturne in F Major, Op. 15, No. 1
A beautiful slow melody (marked *adagio cantabile*) is the feature of the opening section (1-24); the middle section (25-48) is marked by a fiery series of broken chords and brilliant runs for the left hand; and then the quiet, peaceful melody returns in its original mood.
Nocturne in F Sharp Major, Op. 15, No. 2
Here again the A section (1-24) is marked by one of those slow,

rather melancholy melodies that Chopin knew so well how to write. The middle section (25-48) has in contrast a series of interlocking chords supporting a melody that moves twice as fast as the original. Then the first section is again heard almost exactly as before.

Prelude in D Flat Major, Op. 28, No. 15

Here the contrasting section (28-75) is carried over logically from the first (1-27) by a clever device: the almost maddening repetition of a note that has been very prominent in the melody and harmony of the first section. Upon its return, A is somewhat shortened.

Étude in F Major, Op. 10, No. 8

The different sections are now always clearly defined. Here the middle section (41-60) is marked out, not by the introduction of new material, but by the reshaping of the ideas of the first part. A (1-40) is distinguished by a running figure in quick time in which the accent is heavily marked out at the beginning of every second measure. In B we seem to sink to a new tone level, and the rhythmic pattern is obscured by the bright chromatic harmonies, making a blaze of color which quickly subsides when A (61-86) is reintroduced. There is a distinct coda (87), a prolongation of the section, due to the natural tendency of an artist to end whatever he attempts in as impressive and complete a way as possible.

Slow Movements of Sonatas and Symphonies

An extended ternary form is sometimes used for the slow movements of sonatas and symphonies; when this is the case, the result is simply a lengthened song form such as that employed by the unknown composers of *Sur le pont d'Avignon* and *Ach! du lieber Augustin*. Grieg used this extended three-part song form most effectively in the second movement of his *Sonata in c minor* for violin and piano, Op. 45. In this, the first division of 44 measures is played by the piano alone and then repeated by the piano and the violin together; the B section offers new material in decided contrast to the A; then A returns, this time with the violin part an octave higher than before.[2]

[2] Wagner, the great opera composer, had a peculiar name for this form: he called it a *bogen* and used it frequently during the course of the musical development of his great works. He also frequently used a slightly different three-part form consisting of two identical or similar parts (each of which he called a *stollen*), completed by a third part, known as the *abgesang*—A-A-B instead of A-B-A. This unit Wagner called a *bar*, taking the name from the old nomenclature of the medieval guild of the Mastersingers. Indeed, his whole opera *Die Meistersinger* is filled with *bars*, varying in length from phrases a few measures in length to others occupying many pages of score. Notable among these is the music which fills the Prize Song section in the last act of which accompanies Walther's *Am stillen Herd* in the first act.

SONATA FORM

The most complex and at the same time most widely used of the tripartite forms is the *sonata form*, generally used in the first movements of sonatas, symphonies, and quartets. Musical nomenclature is here sadly at fault because it gives plenty of opportunity for confusion in the use of this term: we use it when we speak of the form of the sonata as an entire work, consisting of three or four movements; we use it also when referring specifically to the structural plan which is generally used in the first (and sometimes in the last) of these movements.

The listener must keep the distinction clearly in mind between (1) a type of composition—the sonata as a whole—and (2) a movement form—*sonata form*, sometimes termed *first-movement form* or *sonata-allegro form*. This form was first developed by the generation of composers following Sebastian Bach, especially by one of his sons, Carl Philipp Emanuel, and his contemporaries. It reached full maturity at the hands of still another generation centering around Haydn and Mozart; from their time on it became the usual form for the first, quick movement of sonatas, symphonies, quartets, and other instrumental music. Followed in general by Beethoven, it was sometimes sorely strained by his innovations, and later on, as Romanticism developed, it became somewhat modified by such composers as Schumann and Liszt. It can be said to be one of the soundest structural schemes used by composers, satisfying the needs of men as widely different as Haydn, Beethoven, and Brahms. Some of the greatest music has been composed in this form, and it has proved to be a stimulant for important composers to do their best work.

The cardinal principle of this sonata form is that of the manipulation of two main thematic groups of contrasting character, the one vigorous (masculine, it is sometimes designated), the other (feminine) gentler and more lyrical. These groups are usually, but not very accurately, described by the term *first theme* or *subject* and *second theme* or *subject*. The first group centers about the home or tonic key, the other about a contrasting, related key—almost always the dominant in a major-key movement, and the relative major in a minor-key movement. Each of these thematic groups has room for connecting and subsidiary themes.

The general scheme of procedure in the sonata form is as follows: There is a first thematic group in the tonic, followed by a transitional or bridge passage to another key, when a second or subsidiary group which comes to an end in a definite final manner appears. This part thus far is what is called the *Exposition* or *Statement* of the theme and is often repeated, especially in classic symphonies and sonatas. A section called the *Workingout* or *Development* follows; the previous materials are shown in new ways and there are some new groupings of parts of the themes with a number of changes of key; and sometimes, new material is introduced. Eventually this leads back skillfully (if the composer knows his business) to the tonic key and the *Recapitulation*. This section restates the Exposition but this time puts it all in one key. The Development and the Recapitulation often are followed by a *Coda* which brings the whole movement to a fitting conclusion.

The basic construction of the *sonata-allegro* form may be diagrammed in this fashion:

AN INTRODUCTION (Not an essential part of the scheme, and not found in many instances after Haydn)

A: THE STATEMENT OF THE THEMES (Exposition)

Tonic key (1) First theme group connected by means of a bridge passage to

Dominant key (*Relative major, if first theme is in minor*) (2) Second theme (or group of themes), complementary in character, sometimes (as in developed Beethoven style) closely connected with a

(3) Closing passage. This may consist of a new theme (which would then be called the third theme) or of a modification of the other themes. This part brings the whole section to a definite close.

B: THE DEVELOPMENT OF THE THEMES

Many keys Here the composer re-creates his themes in new ways, often pulling them apart and re-combining them in new patterns, letting his skill and imagination deal with them in various ways. This section is marked by many changes of key, thus providing constant new interest.

A: THE RESTATEMENT OF THE THEMES (Recapitulation)

Tonic key   (1) Restated as before, and connected with
                   (2) Restated, and in turn often connected with
                   (3) Restated, after which the movement is brought
                       to a close.
The coda, or post-oration, often follows, thus providing a final climax.

This, it must always be remembered, is a simplified, skeletonized plan of sonata form; many deviations from it are possible and have been made by various composers. Actual listening practice will show that the sonata form is not so simple as the above outline might lead us to believe.[3] For instance, what we have called the first and second *themes* are often not so much clear-cut themes as a series of compacted fragments of themes. The important thing to realize is that the section which we have labeled "The Statement of the Themes" contains one group of themes which are similar in character, in juxtaposition with another group of themes which are similar in character; the strong contrast between these two groups provides dramatic interest and the material for this section of the movement. The first group is usually powerful, aggressive and vital, and stands in strong key contrast to the second group which is exactly opposite in mood—relaxed, lyric. The last theme or themes may be of almost any nature, so long as the material is sufficiently conclusive to indicate the end of this whole "statement" section and suggest that the "development" is about to begin. We may note that this A or exposition section is sometimes repeated (as was the custom in earlier times), or the interpreter may go on directly to the development. The bridge passages may be short or long, but they should always be consistent, really leading out of one set of thematic ideas into another. The tendency with some composers has been to use rather meaningless musical figuration in such passages—what Wagner (in speaking of Haydn's symphonies) rather pointedly described as the "clatter of the dishes between the courses at a royal feast." Most of Beethoven's bridge passages are striking examples of what can be accomplished.

The great second or B section of the sonata form, instead of con-

[3] No better example of this form can be found than the first movement of Beethoven's *Fifth Symphony*. Here everything is as clear and forthright as it possibly can be. See Chapter 32.

sisting of new material such as we found to be the case in the other tripartite forms, features the development of materials already presented. This feature of evolving new musical substance from old ones challenges the skill of every composer because it requires not only technical resources but outstanding imagination. All sorts of expedients are available; fragments of the themes with which the listener has become familiar are tossed about, pulled apart, recombined in different ways, put into new key relationships. Sometimes all the themes are treated, sometimes only one or, more usually, two. There are no fixed rules or set patterns other than that the section usually opens with at least a suggestion of the first theme to orient the listener, and, after modulating through a varied series of keys, finally arrives at the end back in the original key level of the first theme to be ready to start the recapitulation. Almost anything may happen in between; even new themes are sometimes introduced. In the hands of a skilled composer such as Beethoven, whose architectural sense was matched by his imagination, the development section can be the source of the greatest possible pleasure and excitement for the listener.

The restatement or recapitulation follows the development section without pause; in the classic sonata form it is almost exactly like the statement, except that all the themes are now in the same key to give a sense of unified finality. The bridge passages have to be altered somewhat, since it is no longer necessary to lead from one key level to another, and the tendency of modern composers has been to shorten this section. Even those who do so, however, take care that the recapitulation ends with a definite culminative impact, sometimes in the shape of a forceful coda, sometimes without it. Beethoven, especially, wrote mighty codas, containing sometimes almost a new development. A well-constructed first movement should leave us with a satisfied sense of arrival home after a series of colorful and exciting adventures.

Composers, ever seeking freer forms, devised the so-called *sonata-rondo*, a combination which is much more fluid than the rather square, older, simple rondo type since it contains elements of both sonata and rondo forms. The usual plan for this sonata-rondo is as follows: A—B—A—C (a third section in place of the development) —A—B—A. It was this type of rondo (with slight variants) which was often used by Mozart and Beethoven. Examples may be found in the latter's piano *Sonata in B flat*, Op. 22, the piano *Rondo in G*, Op. 51, No. 2, and the piano and violin *Sonata*, Op. 12, No. 2.

FREE FORMS

Strictly speaking, there is no such thing as "free" form. No matter how free a piece of music is, it must always have form; that is, it must have some basic structural plan if it is to make any sense for the listener. There are certain kinds of musical writing, however, which do not fall naturally into the basic formal types. These, for lack of a better term, we call *free forms*.

OVERTURE

One of the most important of these is the *overture*, literally "an opening piece." In essence it is closely connected with the theater: it may be the opening selection before a play, provided to heighten emotional mood; more likely, it is the introduction to an opera with themes taken from the score. Sometimes it merely sets the mood—suggests whether the work to follow is a light comedy (*vide* Mozart's inimitable overture to *The Marriage of Figaro*, which is in modified first-movement form, without development)[4] or a deep tragedy (such as the music provided by Wagner for playing before his *Tristan und Isolde*). It may foreshadow the events to come, as in the overtures which Beethoven wrote for his one opera, *Fidelio*,[5] (thereby, as someone has sagely remarked, making the opera itself unnecessary). Composers have also applied this term to independent concert pieces composed in the style of an operatic overture, as Brahms did in his "Academic Festival" and "Tragic" overtures.

Originally, overtures were written without any great concern for form; they just "grew." In the seventeenth century they crystallized into two general types, the Italian and the French overtures; both were in more than one movement. The Italian type (popularized by A. Scarlatti, 1659-1725), was composed of

---

[4] Mention should be made here (this is as good a place as any to introduce such an irregularity) of this sort of first movement that has no real inner structure, the sort of thing that is used in many *sonatinas* (sonatas of less serious, or less developed, character) and opera overtures. Other examples may be found in Mozart's *Piano Sonata* in F (K.280) and Schubert's *Rosamunde Overture*.

[5] The composer made four attempts at writing an overture for this work.

> A quick movement
> A slower movement
> A quick movement

The French overture (most effectively used by the composer Lully, 1632-1687), on the other hand had

> A slow movement (played twice)
> A quick movement
> A slow movement, usually part of the first, sometimes
> a new, slow dance form

These types, especially the latter, were in use for a long time (the overture to Handel's *Messiah* is a good example), but were gradually pushed aside by the development of the sonata form, which became the accepted type of overture form during the nineteenth century. Later composers freed themselves again from formal considerations in writing overtures, as, for example, Wagner did in the overtures to his operas *Lohengrin* and *Parsifal*.

As a matter of fact, Wagner called the overtures we have just mentioned "preludes"—the word in this sense meaning the same thing—an introductory piece played before an opera. The term is also applied to small, independent orchestral or piano pieces and to introductory pieces played before a fugue; in both these cases the free form of the prelude is a distinguishing feature.[6] A *chorale-prelude*, based upon the tune of a chorale, is a contrapuntal composition popular in eighteenth-century organ music. Usually transcribed for orchestra, *preludes* are often found on modern concert programs.

FANTASIA

A *fantasia* may be defined as a composition in which the formal demands are subordinated to those of imagination or perhaps pure willfulness; one dictionary definition goes so far as to say that a composer uses the term *fantasia* when no other name occurs to him. There is always a suggestion of the imagination in this term. Rousseau, in the great dictionary of music he published in the eighteenth century, defines *fantasia* as "a piece of instrumental music that one performs as one composes it" and adds that a *fantaisie* can "never be written, because as soon as it is written or repeated it

[6] Some *preludes*, as we have seen, are in strict three-part form.

ceases to be a *fantaisie* and becomes an ordinary piece." This is not strictly true because Beethoven, Chopin, Brahms, all left us fantasias, some of them quite informal in character, others rather strict as to form. As always, Edman is to the point here:

> *Yes, the sonata form is neat,*
> *But on occasion it is sweet*
> *To wander freely here and yon*
> *As melodies meander on.*

> *For this fantasias are the stuff;*
> *They wander artlessly enough,*
> *Relaxed and tender, casual, human,*
> *Most notably when they're by Schumann.*

Classic examples of the fantasia are two which Bach wrote as introductory movements to organ fugues, one in G minor, the other in C minor. (The complete titles are *Fantasia and Fugue in g minor; Fantasia and Fugue in c minor.*) Mozart wrote three fine piano fantasias, two in C minor (K.396 and 475), and one in D minor (K.397); the first of these is strangely prophetic of Beethoven's style. Vaughan Williams' *Fantasia on a Theme by Tallis*, written in 1910, is one of the most popular modern examples of this form. The term fantasia has had rather too many meanings, good and bad, over a long period of years; in its tawdry sense, this form can descend to a very low level, as, for example, when the name is applied to strings of tunes from an opera or a musical comedy, hashed together and served in unappetizing fashion.

THE VALUE OF RECOGNIZING FORM

By this time the musical neophyte is probably thoroughly confused in his attempt to grasp the underlying principles of so many different kinds of form. He is, in fact, probably tempted to turn his back on the whole matter and ask, "After all, what is the use? Can I honestly expect to enjoy music any more by trying to follow these architectural plans and understand all these technical terms, many of them so confused and inexact in meaning?"

The only answer we can give is that even a slight acquaintance with the way in which music is put together will help to remove this sense of bewilderment and futility from which so many suffer when listening to great music. In its place there will come—gradually, to be sure, but none the less surely—the pleasure of observing a composer's designs and of realizing how they are (or are not) being fulfilled. This sense of the design and plan of the music becomes an almost intuitive part of the listener's equipment and, when added to the sensuous pleasure he gets from what he hears, helps his experience and cultivates his taste. Form is by no manner of means all there is to music; but the more one understands it, the surer he is of his musical judgment.

LIST OF SUGGESTED MUSIC
UNITARY FORM

Prelude in C Major	BACH
Suite No. 5, in E Major (harpsichord)	HANDEL
The Bells	BYRD
Surprise Symphony, Second Movement	HAYDN
Kreutzer Sonata, Op. 47, Second Movement	BEETHOVEN
Variations on a Theme by Haydn	BRAHMS
Symphonic Variations	FRANCK
Enigma Variations	ELGAR
Octet for Wind Instruments	STRAVINSKY
Der Schwanendreher	HINDEMITH
Chaconne: Violin Partita, No. 2	BACH
Piano Concerto in d minor, Last Movement	MOZART

BINARY FORM

Twelve Ländler, Op. 171	SCHUBERT
Waltzes, Op. 39	BRAHMS
Sonata in D Major	D. SCARLATTI
Suite in b minor for Flute and Strings	BACH

TERNARY FORM

Humoresque	DVOŘÁK
Nocturnes Nos. 1 and 2, Op. 15	CHOPIN

Prelude in D Flat Major, Op. 28, No. 15	CHOPIN
Sonata in c minor, Op. 45, Second Movement	GRIEG
From *Suite in b minor for Flute and Strings*	BACH
Symphony in g minor, Third Movement	MOZART
Symphony No. 7, Third Movement	BEETHOVEN
Symphony No. 4, Third Movement	TCHAIKOVSKY
Symphony No. 5, First Movement	BEETHOVEN
Rondo in G Major, Op. 51	BEETHOVEN
Sonata in B Flat, Op. 22, Last Movement	BEETHOVEN

FREE FORMS

The Marriage of Figaro Overture	MOZART
Fidelio Overture	BEETHOVEN
Academic Festival Overture	BRAHMS
Semiramide Overture	ROSSINI
Tristan und Isolde Prelude	WAGNER
Symphony No. 3	HARRIS

FANTASIAS

Fantasia in g minor (organ)	BACH
Fantasia in c minor, K.396 (piano)	MOZART
Fantasia on a Theme by Tallis	VAUGHAN WILLIAMS

CHAPTER 17

Instrumental Forms (continued)

⋘§§⋙

CONJOINT FORMS

Having obtained an idea of the sectional forms used by the composers through the centuries, the listener now should investigate some of the larger aspects of form—how it shapes the composition of a piece as a whole. A great deal of the instrumental music one hears consists of compositions of extended length—sometimes lasting well over an hour—that are made up of a number of separate elements, or "movements," as the musician calls them. When these are grouped together under a single title, they may be given one of several names, depending on the general character of the composition and the instrument for which the music was written.

THE MARCH AND THE WALTZ

Among the simplest of these conjoint forms is the *march*, a piece of strongly rhythmical music designed or fitted to accompany marching and used from early times to "enliven the spirits and minimize fatigue." As used today, it consists of a sort of rondo with a strongly melodic principal section that comes round again and again, separated by intervening tunes, which are sometimes called, with as little reason as in the minuet, *trios*.

Another simple conjoint form is the *waltz*, which, while designed for dancing, is often played in concerts. It consists of a string of seven or eight different short waltz themes, the whole being prefaced with a suitable *introduction* and often followed by a *coda* recapitulating some of the tunes used in the body of the work. (See Johann Strauss' *Wiener Blut* and *Geschichten aus dem Wiener Wald*, two of the finest waltzes ever written.)

THE SUITE

Still another of these simple conjoint forms is the *suite;* the literal meaning of this word gives us its musical definition: *a series or group of things belonging together and forming a unit.* Just as we have suites or rooms or of furniture, so in music we have suites of compositions, each complete in itself. These separate units may be written in any form—binary, ternary, rondo, theme with variations, sonata—that the composer may choose, and can be played and enjoyed as entities, without relationship to any other music. The composer, however, intends that they be played in sequence, and they give their full effect only when so programmed.

In the early days of instrumental music, suites were invariably comprised of dance tunes all in the same key. The convention was that there be four of these tunes—the allemande, the courante, the saraband, and the gigue. Between these, the composer was at liberty to insert as many other types of dances as suited his fancy— gavottes, minuets, polonaises, rigadoons, bourées, and so on. Usually a prelude or an overture was added, and the whole work was arranged to secure the maximum contrast in tempo and style. The form was thus actually quite free. It may best be studied in the suites of Purcell, Bach, Handel, and Corelli. Other names were often given to the suite by some older composers: *serenade, partita, divertimento,* and *cassation.* All these have the same general structure and were written for a wide variety of instruments, singly and in combination.

Today suites are, of course, often written on the same free lines as in the eighteenth century, although the classic dance forms are no longer used. Sometimes composers try to evoke the spirit of former times, as in Ravel's lovely suite, *Le Tombeau de Couperin;* sometimes they simply string together materials from theatrical or ballet music, as Grieg did in his much-played *Peer Gynt* suites or Tchaikovsky in his *Nutcracker* suite; sometimes they merely try to provide a series of entertaining and contrasting movements, as in Dohnanyi's *Suite for Orchestra,* Op. 19.

THE SONATA FAMILY

A whole group of compositions, including some of the greatest things ever written, may be classified under one generic category. These works are of an extended type and consist of a number of separate divisions or movements (usually four, quite frequently three), each of which, while maintaining its identity, is an inherent part of the whole. These compositions have been given different names, according to the use for which they were designed:

Sonata (literally, a composition that is sounded or played, in contra-distinction to one that is sung) is a work of this type written for one or two instruments.

Symphony is a sonata for orchestra.

Concerto is a sonata for solo instrument (or instruments) with orchestra.

Trios, quartets, quintets, sextets are sonatas for three, four, five or six instruments.

Here again, although there are no fixed rules, tradition has dictated that each movement of these works be written according to a different form. The usual procedure has been as follows:

The *First Movement* (of a vigorous, quick, *allegro* character) is written in sonata form (perhaps better designated here as sonata-allegro or first movement form). It introduces the general mood and character of the entire work, and its themes are *sometimes* used in other movements. Its outstanding characteristic is good architectonic structure and effective thematic manipulation.

The *Second Movement* (usually *andante* or *adagio*) is, in contrast, slower and more lyric in character. It may be in sonata form, a theme with variations, or in ternary (song) form. In accordance with its general character, its themes are melodic and personal in character; the whole section stresses emotional rather than structural content.

The *Third Movement* is strongly rhythmic and provides relaxation. Vigorous and lively, in reality it is a dance movement, almost always in triple meter. With Haydn and Mozart it took the form of a minuet and trio; Beethoven substituted a scherzo, in which the tempo of the minuet was speeded up and the general mood of the movement lightened. Later composers in general followed Beethoven's example.

The *Fourth Movement* is again rapid and complex, something like the first but with more of an air of finality. It is usually in rondo or sonata form, although a theme with variations is sometimes used. The great objective is to provide a final sense of climax to the work as a whole. *Sometimes,* it contains references to other movements.

What a common-sense procedure this is! The first movement is designed to arrest our attention; the second to set us dreaming, or at least contemplating; the third gives us a chance to relax; and the fourth puts us in a cheerful or exalted frame of mind. All composers, from Haydn to Shostakovich, have realized the effectiveness of this traditional scheme and have followed it more or less closely—to date it has been impossible to think up a better one. The greatest composers have excelled in maintaining the essential character of each of these movements while weaving them into a congruous and climactic whole. They have been, as Lawrence Abbott has said, master architects and dramatists in the opening movement; imaginative poets and tender lyricists in the second; rhythmic dance musicians in the third (with plenty of boisterous rhythms up their sleeve); and eloquent prophets and effective spellbinders in the fourth. Study such works as Beethoven's *Fifth Symphony* or Brahms' *Second Symphony*, and you will hear how effectively the plan has been used by the great men.

There are some changes from this general procedure that certain composers have made familiar. The order of the second and third movements is sometimes reversed, the scherzo coming second and the slow movement third (as in Beethoven's *Ninth Symphony*). There is often, especially in sonatas, only one middle movement; usually it is the scherzo that is omitted, or the slow movement and the scherzo may be telescoped into one.

It should not be thought that, because their general formal patterns are the same, there is no difference in the style of these extended compositions. The very meaning of the word *symphony* (sounding together) suggests the seriousness of purpose and high ideals associated with this form of writing. Generally speaking, although there are varying qualities of mood and purpose in the symphonies of the different periods, this form represents the best in musical thought throughout the years.

In a *quartet*, more attention is paid, naturally, to perfection of part-writing and delicacies of rhythm and nuance; it is meant for the delectation of a few listeners rather than of the many. Throughout the quartet (and its closely allied forms the trio and the quintet) there must be a constant interchange of ideas among the various instruments; if one is exalted too greatly at the expense of the others, the essential quality of the work is sure to be lost.

In the *concerto*[1] the listener must realize that there are two masterful forces in action throughout, the solo instrument or instruments and the full orchestra. Care must be taken by the composer that he does not slight one or the other, and that there are plenty of opportunities for drama in the interaction of the dominant powers. Since the same opportunities for dramatic contrast exist between the two themes of the concerto, this form may be said to be a sort of heightened or intensified symphony with two important kinds of dramatic interactions being developed. So too, in a sonata for violin and piano the two instruments are on an equal footing and are supposed to share the honors evenly. The best way to familiarize oneself with the characteristics of these compositions is to listen to a number of representative examples of each and compare them.

To complete the record, we add here Professor Edman's verses on the *tone poem*, the form which program music takes, as we have already shown in an earlier chapter:

THE TONE POEM

This is the music that demands
Always a program in your hands,
So that on hearing Section VIII
You know if it is Love or Fate
You're hearing, and if Section VII
Speaks of the sea, or war, or Heaven.
The program helps you to enthuse
With learned—and surprising—clues:
The muted trumpets, these are death;
The treble flutes, Spring's earliest breath!
I am among the louts, I fear,
Who do their listening by ear,
And, leaving program notes unread,
Don't care much what the music's said.
Don't care much what the music's said.

LIST OF SUGGESTED MUSIC

MARCH

Semper Fidelis; The Stars and Stripes Forever;

The Washington Post; El Capitán   SOUSA

[1] We refer here to the three- or four-movement concerto; *concerti grossi*, an earlier type, are really suites for solo instruments and orchestra.

WALTZ

Wiener Blut   J. STRAUSS

Tales from the Vienna Woods   J. STRAUSS

Be sure to obtain authentic Viennese interpretations of these, not modern, streamline versions; there is all the difference in the world.

SUITE

(Early)

Suite No. 1 in G Major   PURCELL

Sonata for Flute and Strings   A. SCARLATTI

Suite for Strings   CORELLI

(Later)

Holberg Suite, Op. 40   GRIEG

Le Tombeau de Couperin   RAVEL

Suite, in f sharp minor, Op. 19   DOHNÁNYI

Caucasian Sketches, Op. 10   IPPOLITOV-IVANOV

The first three of these attempt to catch the spirit of the old suites but employ more modern idioms; the last is a descriptive program suite.

Peer Gynt, Suite No. 1   GRIEG

L'Arlésienne, Suite No. 1   BIZET

The Nutcracker   TCHAIKOVSKY

Daphnis and Chloe, Suite No. 2   RAVEL

Pulcinella Suite   STRAVINSKY

Lieutenant Kije Suite   PROKOFIEV

Incredible Flutist   PISTON

These are all based on concert treatment of theater music.

SONATA

Sonata for Piano No. 8, in c minor, Op. 13
   (*Pathétique*)   BEETHOVEN

Sonata No. 9, in A Major (Kreutzer)
   (violin and piano)   BEETHOVEN

Trio

Trio, B flat Major (piano and strings)	SCHUBERT
Trio, E flat Major (French horn, violin and piano)	SCHUBERT

Quartet

Quartet No. 1 in F Major, Op. 18, No. 1	BEETHOVEN
Quartet No. 1 in g minor, Op. 25 (piano)	BRAHMS

Quintet

Quintet in A Major (Trout), (piano)	SCHUBERT

Sextet

Sextet in B flat Major, Op. 18 (strings)	BRAHMS

Septet

Septet in E flat Major (for strings and winds), Op. 20	BEETHOVEN

Octet

Octet in F Major (for strings and winds), Op. 166	SCHUBERT

Symphony

Symphony No. 5, in c minor	BEETHOVEN

Concerto

Concerto No. 20, in d minor, K.466 (piano)	MOZART
Concerto No. 4, in G Major (piano)	BEETHOVEN
Concerto in D Major for Violin and Orchestra, Op. 35	TCHAIKOVSKY

TOPICS FOR FURTHER DISCUSSION

Have any composers been equally successful in writing both symphonic poems and symphonies?

Do you think that ability in writing one of these forms tends to cramp it in another?

Do you know of any symphonies that have more than four movements? If so, where are the extra movements added?

Compare the symphonic poem with the symphony in freedom of form. What might be a drawback of the symphony in the hands of the less skillful composer?

Compare the two forms again for suggestive power. Are the advantages of the symphonic poem all to the good?

Can you define the essential differences between a titled symphony and a symphonic-poem?

Some people are annoyed by cadenzas in concertos. How can these be artistically disadvantageous? What is your own feeling about cadenzas?

If you can, hear some of the late Beethoven works in the variation form (for example, Op. 109 and the string quartets, Op. 127 and 131) and consider whither Beethoven's variations were tending, and what spiritual qualities they seem to express.

Define the basic differences between simple binary and ternary forms.

Why do you think that variations are not cultivated by today's composers? Do you like the idea of choral variations (which are also infrequently used today)?

Compare some sets of variations by Mozart or Haydn with some by Brahms, Elgar, or Franck. What are the broad differences between usages of the two periods?

Compare typical overtures of romantic operas with the Gilbert and Sullivan type.

State the advantages of the sonata-rondo form over the simple rondo.

Can you name instances of sonata-rondo form where the sonata predominates, and vice versa?

CHAPTER 18

Russian Nationalism

❦

THE FORCES IN NATIONALISM

As we have seen, Romanticism meant a revolt against the accepted traditions of the past, an intensification of the qualities that determine the characteristics of the individual, and a revolution that changed the intellect of Europe from a monarchical to a popular state. Among the Romantic artist's greatest sources of material in his struggle against heritage and convention were the half-forgotten folk tales and colorful legends of the various countries. The search for these really represented a movement towards national freedom, a movement greatly aided by the series of European wars stirred up by Napoleonic ambitions. The nineteenth-century wars aroused feelings of national consciousness and hopes of revolt in all the countries, hopes and feelings which were, after all, but magnifications of the times, developed into an artistic chauvinism from the effects of which we still suffer today.

Thus in the latter part of the nineteenth century we find the peoples of the different countries turning their attention more and more inward, striving in every possible way, practical as well as spiritual, to advance their national ideals and cultivate their national resources. It was natural for the artists of each country to fall in with such a movement, and so we find them struggling to free themselves from the bondage of the foreigner, using every means they could devise to stimulate their own national expression. The unique environment of each land, its physical and climatic conditions, its historical vicissitudes, its future possibilities—all were excellent grist for the nationalistic mill.

Insofar as the production of music was concerned, Italy, France, and Germany had made the major contributions up to the beginning of the nineteenth century. In 1843 Robert Schumann, an outstanding musical *litterateur* as well as composer, realizing that the nations bordering on Germany were desirous of freeing themselves from the influences of German composers, had perspicacity enough to advise the musicians in these countries to develop the qualities found in their own native music. Composers in countries such as Spain and England, which formerly had been very prolific musically, turned their attention to the development of their native resources in the hope of attracting more attention. Thus a new and important phase of Romanticism developed, a phase that we call Nationalism, the manifestation of a people's characteristics through their art.

The great ideal of this new development in music and art was to present to Europe in general the national characteristics—the melodies, rhythms, and so on—that were part and parcel of the individual life and living of each country. This had a sensational effect: "exoticism," the admiration for everything introduced from a foreign country, became the fashion. This tendency was especially obvious in the literature and music of Russia, a country which had been so completely isolated from the rest of Europe that it had never been affected by the Reformation, the Renaissance, or the French Revolution; a country which, on the other hand, because of its long Asiatic land frontier and its close contacts with the Turks, Persians and Chinese, had strongly been influenced by Oriental ideals. No wonder that the strange and unfamiliar rhythms, the unusual and different harmonies of this non-European music had such an effect upon European listeners. The lethargy of generations is to be heard in its strains, and its spell transports us as a magic carpet to lands that are far beyond our ken just as the intense introspection, the penetrating portrayals of strange life, and the skillfully drawn character sketches in the novels and plays of such Russian nationalists as Dostoevski (1821-1881), Tolstoi (1828-1910), and Chekhov (1860-1904) seem somehow to let us escape from the commonplaces of our lives.

Also appealing was the less spectacular nationalism of Bohemia, a country (now known as Czechoslovakia) which in the middle of the nineteenth century was struggling to throw off the oppressive power of a neighboring state. The triumph of such men as Smetana and Dvořák was achieved not only because of the innate vigor, charm, and color of their music, but also because they represented a conscious struggle on the part of a suppressed people to assert national ideals. During the Renaissance, Spain and England had been among the most brilliant musical nations of Europe, but for one reason or another their creative musical power declined during the centuries that followed. It was not until the nationalistic strivings of the nineteenth century that creations of world significance again were manifest in these countries: Albéniz and Granados in Spain and Vaughan Williams and his successors in England.

THE REVELATION OF RUSSIA

The effects of musical nationalism may best be observed in the Russians among whom it worked most strongly. The sources of Russian music are obvious: an irregularly rhythmed, deeply melancholy folk music, suggestive of the limitless plains, the great rivers, and the impenetrable forests of this vast land; and a religious vocal music, based on the Byzantine chant, related to pre-Christian, Asiatic melodies, and developed in opposition to European ideals. Until the time of Peter the Great, eighteenth-century Czar, the church represented the chief cultural force in Russia and regulated every national development; popular amusements, including singing and dancing, were frowned upon. Since then, music, like all the other arts, has been subjected to political orientations.

At first this orientation was strongly toward European influences; Italian and French painters, architects, and musicians were the favorites. Every attempt to foster national music, contemptuously referred to as "coachmen's music," was strongly discouraged. It was not until Glinka (1804-1857), a friend of the first great nationalistic author, Pushkin, animated by a desire to "write something Russian, comprehensible to every Russian," composed his opera *A Life for the Tsar* in 1836 that the Russian musical awakening came.

Following in Glinka's footsteps and emulating his desires there arose a group of composers called at first derisively the *Kutchka* (a little heap—handful), usually translated in French and English as The Five: Balakirev, Cui, Borodin, Rimsky-Korsakov, and Moussorgsky. None of this gifted group had originally intended to become a musician; the training of all of them, with the exception of Rimsky-Korsakov, and Moussorgsky, was somewhat desultory and sketchy. But under the leadership of Balakirev they became united by a strong patriotic wish to create a real Russian art; and the geniuses among them succeeded in doing so: Moussorgsky, one of the most wayward but interesting personalities in musical history, in his opera *Boris Godunov*, his program cycle *Pictures at an Exhibition*, and his wonderful songs; Rimsky-Korsakov in his symphonic suite *Scheherazade*, in which all the fairy tales from *The Arabian Nights* seem somehow to come to life.

SCHEHERAZADE

Having studied in particular a piece of program music built on specific themes, with each new twist of the story closely detailed by their development (*Till Eulenspiegel's Merry Pranks*) and one whose themes are more generally related to changes of mood and feeling than to specific events (*Les Préludes*), we now choose for study a third program piece of even more generalized character, one in which the composer selected his themes to stimulate the listener's imagination rather than to delineate specific program events or ideas—Rimsky-Korsakov's symphonic suite *Scheherazade*. This kaleidoscopic fairy tale is based on random items from that greatest of all folk-tale collections, *The Arabian Nights' Entertainments*. A strong Russian sense of color and rich interpretative fantasy give this composition its nationalistic flavor.

Rimsky-Korsakov has given us this preface to his music, all the program that we really need:

> The Sultan Schahriar, convinced of the faithlessness of women, had sworn to put to death each of his wives after the wedding night. But the Sultana Scheherazade saved her life by diverting him with stories which she told him during a thousand and one nights. The Sultan, conquered by his curiosity, put off from day to day the execution of his wife, and at last renounced his bloody vow. Many wonders were narrated to Schahriar by the Sultana Scheherazade; for her stories the Sultana borrowed the verses of poets and the words of folk songs and fitted together tales and adventures.

The composer's additional information, given to the public at the time this music was first performed, is helpful. He suggested the following titles for the four movements of his suite:

I. The Sea and Sinbad's Ship
II. The Story of the Kalendar Prince
III. The Young Princess
IV. Festival at Bagdad—The Ship goes to pieces on a Rock surmounted by the bronze figure of a Warrior—Conclusion

There is no logical sequence to such a program. Rather, we have a series of incidents which stimulated the composer's imagination as he planned the various musical sections of his work. There is no difficulty in following the poetic suggestiveness of his music, however; its direct appeal and beautiful orchestral speech assure its immediate popularity everywhere. It will be of interest for us to examine this music in detail so that we may observe the manner in which a composer weaves his fabric out of simple materials.

Rimsky-Korsakov uses several principal themes in his composition, but they are not, as we found them in the Liszt or the Strauss tone poems, directly linked with the fixed poetic ideas of the program. Here they are "purely musical material, themes for musical development," to use the composer's own words, and we find that sometimes the same theme is used to suggest quite different incidents in the program.

First of all there are two themes:

These occur throughout the whole suite, providing a sort of unifying thread to connect the different sections: (1) a harsh, threatening phrase (I, 1-4), heard at the very beginning—Rimsky-Korsakov tells us that it is meant to suggest the stern Sultan, always ready to listen to the fair Scheherazade's stories, but just as ready to cut off her head should she fail to interest him; (2) the theme of the Sultana herself (I, 14-17), graceful, lithe, given to the violin with accompanying chords on the harp. The two are repeated again and again in the course of the music, as if to keep us properly oriented. Then there are other motives which thread through the various sections, alternating and twining each with the other, appearing in different contexts and different moods.

In the first section, after the introduction of the Sultan and the Scheherazade themes, we hear an undulating arpeggio figure (I, 18-23), suggestive of the roll of the sea:

Listen to what the composer does with it after first bringing it to our attention: first heard low in the orchestra, it mounts steadily, growing more and more intense, to a loud climax; after this quite another development of it is heard, with a different instrumentation. The climax this time leads to a new (I, 70-75) series of detached chords on the wood-wind instruments, using this theme:

Then follow fragments of the sea theme, to which is later added the violin figure of the Sultana motive (I, 94). Finally the Sultan motive comes thundering in the bass (I, 110). A vigorous development follows; the different themes are tossed about in various parts of the orchestra, they are heard in varying keys and in different orchestral combinations, sometimes loud, sometimes very soft. The whole section gives a fine idea of the manner in which a skilled composer can treat germane material. This corresponds in manner of treatment, of course, to the development section of the sonata form. Listen to this part several times, trying to fix in your mind the intricate weavings and manipulations of the melodies, and you will have ideal practice in listening. Naturally, as we learn more of these methods of how music is put together, our admiration of the composer's craftsmanship will add another element to our capacity for enjoyment.

The second movement, after a brief reminder that the Sultana is still busy at her life-preserving task (II, 1-4), launches into a story told by a wandering Oriental beggar. The bassoon takes the center of the orchestral stage and sings us a theme (II, 5-25) suggestive of the burlesque, sometimes of an almost pathetic mock heroism:

The oboe takes up this theme (II, 26), followed by the violins (II, 48), and then the brass and wood winds (II, 71); the pace quickens and there are furtive suggestions of the Sultan and Sultana themes. Suddenly a brilliant fanfare of the brass (II, 105) announces a new twist to the story; Rimsky-Korsakov has wisely left us in the dark as to what particular incidents figure in it. The trombones give us a new theme of brilliant character (II, 108), and it is answered as if in echo by muted trumpets:

A lively development follows, interrupted by two graceful, arabesque-like reminiscences of the Sultana theme, the first of them given to the clarinets (II, 161) and the second (II, 421) to the bassoon. The section between is given over to a rapidly moving development of the brilliant trombone theme heard shortly before. Fragments of these various tunes follow thick and fast, and the whole section ends with a solemn pronouncement of the Sultan theme.

The third movement is a romantic love idyl. Like all ardent lovers, the Prince speaks first; his theme is a light folk-like passage for the strings (III, 1-8):

There is a rushing, oriental-like passage for the clarinet (III, 21), and then the Prince theme is repeated, with an oboe added to the strings in a lower, darker register of the orchestra (III, 25). When the rushing theme comes again, it is given to the flutes (III, 46). These two themes are now alternated, one answering the other until, with a sudden change in color, the Princess is heard, her theme given to the clarinet with an accompaniment of snare drum, tambourine, and triangle (III, 70-78):

The two principal themes are as much alike as lovers' themes should be; their distinguishing characteristics are their rhythms. They are now heard intermingled in lovers' discourse, only to be suddenly interrupted (III, 142) by the Sultana theme, as if to remind us that, after all, this idyllic story is a product of the Sultana's lively imagination.

The motives of the Sultan (IV, 1-4) and the Sultana (IV, 8-9) are heard at the beginning of the last movement. Then we are suddenly in the midst of a colorful festival at Bagdad in the days of the mighty Caliph, when the city was at the height of its gorgeous splendor (IV, 30 ff.):

The metropolis of a huge empire, Bagdad was a city of pleasure, the Paris of the ninth century, and Rimsky-Korsakov gives us a colorful picture of its busy streets. A riot of milling crowds, shrill Oriental instruments—the music is ablaze with the color and radiance of Asiatic cities. Suddenly, as in a sort of unbelievable dream, we are no longer on the hot Bagdad streets, but aboard Sinbad's ship, headed for the fateful rock on which it is doomed to crash (IV, 595). The undulating sea theme and the giant Sultan theme have joined forces, and we get a vivid picture of the menacing storm, the winds whistling through chromatic passages for clarinet and flute (IV, 605-610 and 615). The waves seem to have risen with increasing force, and the vivid description of the incident as given by Henley is recalled to our minds:

> *Tearing their beards*
> *The sailors wept and prayed; but the grave ship,*
> *Deep laden with spiceries and pearls, went mad,*
> *Wrenched the long tiller out of the steerman's hand,*
> *And, turning broadside on,*
> *As the most iron would, was haled and sucked*
> *Nearer and nearer yet:*
> *And, all awash, with horrible lurching leaps*
> *Rushed at that Portent, casting a shadow now*
> *That swallowed sea and sky; and then,*
> *Anchors and nails and bolts*
> *Flew screaming out of her . . . and she lay*
> *A broken bundle of firewood, strown piecemeal*
> *About the waters.*

The whistle of the wind in the storm, the shattering of the ship, the following peaceful calm, all are clearly delineated in Rimsky-Korsakov's music. And then in the silence, Scheherazade's "appeasing fiddle" is once more heard as she comes to the end of her tale.

And the Sultan of the Indies could not but admire the prodigious and inexhaustible memory of the Sultaness, his wife, who had entertained him for a thousand and one nights with such a variety of interesting stories.

His temper was softened and his prejudices removed. He was not only convinced of the merit and great wisdom of the Sultaness Scheherazade, but he remembered with what courage she had suffered to be his wife, without fearing the death to which she had exposed herself, and which so many Sultanesses had suffered within her knowledge.

These considerations, and the many other good qualities he knew her to possess, induced him at last to forgive her. And so they lived in all pleasure and solace of life and its delights, till there took them the Destroyer of delights and the Severer of societies, the Desolator of dwelling places and the Garnerer of graveyards, and they were translated to the ruth of the Almighty Allah.

TOPICS FOR DISCUSSION

What elements have made *Scheherazade* one of the most popular Russian nationalistic pieces?

Why is Rimsky-Korsakov often spoken of as a "non-professional" musician, although he wrote one of the great classic works on orchestration? In addition to *Scheherazade*, what were the important contributions which Rimsky-Korsakov made to Russian nationalism?

How does Russian nationalism in music spring from other nationalistic impulses? How much of it springs from the history of conflict in the country?

How much of the Russian character in music is influenced by the climate and remoteness of the country?

Why were Russian composers so fond of making music about legends, fairy tales, and national history?

What do you find most attractive about the Russian musical pioneers? Does anything in their writings seem tiresome?

On which of the other European composers can you see the influence of Russian works? Was this influence healthy?

Why is Tchaikovsky a perennial favorite with the average music-lover?

CHAPTER 19

Wagner as a Nationalist

_◆§ §◆_

A MASTERPIECE OF FORM AND FEELING

We have noted that the _Scheherazade_ suite is a fine example of the type of program music in which the composer is more interested in developing his musical structure than in carefully following the details of an elaborate program. We are now to consider a piece of program music which concerns itself entirely with musical development. We know that it is program music and that it concerns a personal episode of tremendous import to the two personages involved because Wagner has told us this. But we do not know anything more about its "story," and so we are left free to study its musical evolution without much concern about extra-musical associations. Those who are familiar with the great operas of Wagner— music dramas such as _Die Walküre, Siegfried, Götterdämmerung_ —will perhaps be surprised to see the _Siegfried Idyll_ cited as an example of German nationalistic music. Most of Wagner's works, though derived from Germanic sources, have transcended the narrow borders of nationalism because of their tremendous scope and the universality of their appeal. Wagner based the stories of his operas on material gathered from the great medieval poems which were the heritage of the Scandinavian and the Germanic peoples. His treatment was such, however, that these operas appeal not alone to the German, or to other nations because of their peculiarly Teutonic qualities. They belong rather to the whole human race; the music of these works is understood as well in New York and London as it is in Munich or Berlin; their emotions are those of humanity in general, glorified and epitomized. Men of all kinds know this music to be of themselves, and warm to it because they can sense in it their own personal characteristics.

The little instrumental piece we are about to study, the *Siegfried Idyll*, is full of a quiet German beauty quite outside the general run of Wagner's other works. Built on themes associated with the greatest of the German folk heroes, it suggests to us the cool depths of the dense, dragon-haunted forests. Overflowing with the happiness of domestic felicity, it celebrates the family ideals of the typical German bourgeois. The intensity of feeling, the acute sensitiveness, the fundamental reflective character of this nation is felt throughout this piece. If we stop to inquire into the history of its writing, we shall find the reason for its unique position among Wagner's works.

SOME WAGNER HISTORY

Wagner's career, overwhelmingly successful as it seems to us today, was an intermittent series of struggles, disappointments, and triumphs. His works were written during a long period of strife, sometimes with little hope that they would ever be performed. Their tremendous scope, their unusual technical requirements, the difference of their constructive principles from those to which the public was accustomed, did not make for immediate popularity with a people steeped in the traditions of the Italian opera. Nor did Wagner's personal idiosyncrasies help in establishing his work in public favor. Possessing luxurious habits and expensive personal tastes, he constantly involved himself in financial difficulties; of choleric, irascible temperament, he needlessly made many public and private enemies, and resentment against him rose on various occasions to such a pitch that it was necessary for him to leave his native land. His personal affairs, even when viewed from the vantage point of distant years, seem inexplicably confused. For years he lived a troubled existence with his first wife, Minna, whom he married in 1836, and who died in 1866. Coming under the spell of one woman after another, he lived with Cosima von Bülow, wife of one of his most ardent disciples and eloquent interpreters, in a villa just outside Lucerne, Switzerland, during the years 1866-1870. At the end of this period, Cosima obtained a divorce, and Wagner was able to establish her as his wife in the eyes of the law; they were married on August 25, 1870. His happiness at this time knew no bounds. He had finished five of his great works, *Tristan und Isolde, Die Meistersinger von Nürnberg, Das Rheingold, Die Walküre,* and *Siegfried,* works which he knew would go down to posterity even though he could not secure production of them immediately in the German theaters. No one knew better than Wagner himself that it was the loyalty, devotion, and sympathetic understanding of the amazing Cosima that enabled him to go ahead with the enormous tasks and face the terrific difficulties of his later years.

A CHRISTMAS BIRTHDAY GIFT

The birth of his son Siegfried in 1869 was a significant event for Wagner. (It is rather remarkable that both Cosima and Siegfried died within a year of each other, the one in 1929, the other in 1930, after devoting their lives to carrying on the traditions of the theater established by Wagner at Bayreuth.) Richard resolved to write a piece of music in commemoration of the birth of his son and as a graceful tribute to his wife. He prefaced it with verses which gave his reasons for writing this music:

> *Thine was the loving, sacrificing thought*
> *That gave a habitation to my art,*
> *And through all the conflicts that I fought*
> *Gave refuge that was constant and apart.*
> *As we dreamed, our Teuton heroes came to us*
> *Out of country's past reviewed in mind and heart,*
> *Till in my life there rang in glad acclaim:*
> *"We have a son—and Siegfried is his name."*
> *This music now gives thanks for him and thee—*
> *What greater prize could Love have hoped or had,*
> *Within our souls what joy could greater be*
> *Than now is voiced within this music glad?*
> *For I within this offering hold united*
> *Thou and Siegfried—wife and lad.*
> *In all its harmonies stand revealed*
> *Our own sweet thoughts, till now concealed.*

Could any music have a more general, and yet a more personal program? No wonder Wagner was able to write a composition

RICHARD AND COSIMA
WAGNER

which is a wondrous outburst of joy at the termination of his bitter struggles and full of tender thankfulness for the haven of Cosima's love and understanding. Taking from his just-finished opera, *Siegfried*, themes which suggest the love of the hero of that work for Brünnhilde, Wagner produced a musical work of unusual beauty and quiet loveliness. That he was writing program music is certain; we have it on the evidence of the music itself, as well as the testimony of Glasenapp, one of the composer's "official" biographers. We know nothing of the details of the program which stimulated Wagner's imagination (a fact which one critic thinks may be the reason several transitions in the music seem rather abrupt), nor do we need to know. Wagner's imagination caught fire at the idea of picturing his great love for his wife and newborn son, and there "was no staying it until the fire had burned itself out."

The *Idyll* was composed during the autumn of 1870, in preparation for Christmas Day, which happened to be Cosima's birthday. Local musicians from Lucerne were gathered together for the first performance. The score called for a small orchestra: two first violins, two seconds, two violas, one cello, one double bass, one flute, one oboe, two clarinets, one bassoon, two horns, and one trumpet (played by Hans Richter, who was later to become the outstanding Wagner interpreter of Germany). This small band was secretly rehearsed, and early on Christmas morning its members came to the Wagner villa, set up their music desks on its broad stairs, and after quietly tuning their instruments in the kitchen, took their places. Wagner, standing at the top of the stairs, conducted. Below him were the violins, violas, wood winds, horns, and at the bottom, out of his sight, the cello and bass. Everything went well, and Cosima tells us in her diary that the performance was a complete success. She was awakened by the music; at first she thought herself dreaming, but, as consciousness gradually returned, she realized the graceful tribute that was being paid her. When the music died away, Richard came to her room, and offered her the score of the symphonic poem. "I was in tears," she writes, "but so was all the rest of the household."

PECULIARITIES OF STRUCTURE

It will not take a great deal of listening to realize that the methods of construction in this piece are different from the others we have heard so far. Wagner's unending melody, the peculiar method by which he built his musical structures—repetition and elaborations of the same themes—gives a cohesion and homogeneity found in few other music works. Once started, it seems as if this music must run on to an inexorable conclusion. By means of themes that are in themselves marvels of beauty and suggestiveness, Wagner weaves a seamless web of music, always suited to the constantly changing worlds of his dreams. But though there is repetition, there is no monotony, for the composer is constantly giving us the same material in new guises. By shifting the harmonies that accompany his themes, by changing the keys, by alternating the rhythmic design, or by combining a theme with others so that they form a complex whole, the composer achieves a marvelous variety and yet a complete unity.

One of the great joys of listening to this music is being able to recognize not only the themes as they are used but also the manner in which each is treated and woven into the fabric of the enormous tapestries. Those who are at all familiar with the opera *Siegfried*

will recognize most of the themes in the *Idyll*; but, as that great
Wagnerite Ernest Newman has shown, some of them were originally
conceived for a string quartet that Wagner meant to write for
Cosima, and were later transferred to the opera. Newman thinks
that "much of the substance of the quartet has been taken over
bodily into the *Idyll*"; this makes it a striking example of the composer's power of symphonic structure—a type of writing which,
had he lived longer, it seems reasonable to suppose that he would
have developed.

The opening of the *Idyll* is a fine little study in free counterpoint,
just the thing for anyone to ponder who doubts the value of studying this important element in composition. Notice what Wagner
makes of the theme

first heard in completeness in measures 29 and 30, how he repeats
it and what he develops out of it. Shortly after, we hear the slumber
motive (37), and then the cradle song (91) (the only theme that is
not the composer's own):

At first it is sung by the oboe and then quickly joined with the
theme heard at the beginning. These original themes are joined later
(148 ff.) by new motives which we find in the closing scene of
Siegfried (259 ff.).

From internal evidence Newman believes that the theme of measure 148 was also originally part of the never-completed quartet and
adapted, rather awkwardly, to the opera. But the 259 theme "was
certainly written first for the opera." As you listen, notice how
Wagner manipulates these various motives; they are the roots from
which the music beautifully grows. Near the end we hear added the
"slumber motive" of Brünnhilde (287), given to the oboe, followed
by the call of Siegfried's forest bird (303 ff.). Through all the music

the love themes form a dominating influence, weaving, in their
varied forms, a background for the whole piece.

After you have heard the different sections several times and have
a knowledge of the music's imaginative and constructive background, forget this side of it entirely and put yourself into the mood
for Christmas morning, 1870. Hear the whole thing again, thinking
of the intimate, affectionate meaning the music would have for
Cosima—music not intended for publication but as a private gift in
celebration of the baby's birth. You will then appreciate to the full
the clarity and eloquence of the music, from the pastoral-like beginning to the sighs of peace at the end. The *Siegfried Idyll*, one of the
world's masterpieces of loveliness, is the sort of music to which we
can surrender ourselves unhesitatingly, confident that it will never
disappoint.

SCENES FROM OPERAS

This little masterpiece of Wagner's happens not to be in the main
stream of his life's work, which, as we have intimated, was the splendid flood of a new style of opera which he called "music drama."
(The specific nature and style of these Wagnerian operas are discussed in the supplementary chapter on opera.) It remains necessary
to remind the reader who has just enjoyed the *Siegfried Idyll* that
its small orchestra and intimate manner are not characteristic of the
Wagnerian music dramas, although its method of weaving its musical fabric is similar.

We will cite a few examples from the mature works of this great

Romantic to show how he achieved his effects. Like all other composers who grew and developed throughout their careers, Wagner did not achieve his full effects in his earlier operas (up through *Lohengrin*). The works beginning with the Ring cycle (including its four operas), *Tristan und Isolde, Die Meistersinger,* and *Parsifal* are all built upon the principle of "leading themes" or *leitmotives,* and these closely wrought works may truly be said to represent Wagner at his best (again see the opera chapter for details).

PRELUDE TO *Tristan und Isolde*
FINALE (*Liebestod*: LOVE DEATH) FROM *Tristan und Isolde*

Since these portions of the greatest of all love dramas, its opening and its close, are often played together in the concert hall as one piece, they may well be briefly described together here. The tragedy of Tristan's passion for the Princess Isolde, whom he escorts over the sea to be another man's bride, has been called one long love duet. Its theme, epitomized in the *Prelude,* as Wagner stated it, is the unappeasable longing for love and death.

The prelude is woven from several of the chief themes; first there is the one given out by the cellos, which, although it seems to sound like one theme, is in reality two, the one melting into the other:

Another impassioned theme, given to the oboe, is that of the "Love Glance," heard in the opera itself when a potion makes the two aware of their love:

It should be interpolated here that careful annotators have given names to all these themes, relating them to the ideas, actions, persons, or things in the opera with which they are associated. It is perfectly possible, however, to enjoy Wagner's music without having any but a general idea of what these themes represent.

The "Deliverance by Death" theme is the climactic point of the Prelude; after it, the music droops in weariness.

The concert performance usually joins this without interruption to the *Liebestod*, Isolde's farewell to the dead Tristan at the end of the opera. It is poignant with memories of their duet in the second act and ends with the motive of "Desire":

"FOREST MURMURS" FROM *Siegfried*
SIEGFRIED'S JOURNEY TO THE RHINE AND IMMOLATION SCENE FROM
Götterdämmerung

Siegfried is the third, and *Götterdämmerung* (Dusk of the Gods) is the final of the series of four operas called *The Nibelungen Ring*, which Wagner built out of old Scandinavian and Teutonic legends. These great *Gesammtkunstwerke*, as they came to be known, are an attempt to combine the various arts into one unified whole. They center around the story of the magic ring made out of gold, stolen from the depths of the Rhine, and the curse it brought upon all who owned it. The first opera in the series (which Wagner originally intended to be given on four successive days), *Rheingold*, tells the story of the theft of the gold, the making of the ring by Alberich, chief of the Nibelungen dwarfs, and its theft by two of the gods, upon whom the curse immediately begins its work. *Die Walküre* (The Valkyries), the second in the cycle, traces the ancestry of Siegfried, the hero of the whole saga, and tells the story of his parents, Siegmund and Sieglinde, the children of Wotan. In *Siegfried*, the hero, after slaying the dragon Fafner, guardian of the hoard of gold which includes the ring, secures this magic circlet and goes forth to conquer the world through love. In "Forest Murmurs," Siegfried rests in the woods just before his encounter with Fafner, musing on the fact that he does not know who his parents were and his hope of somewhere finding a mate. As background to these emotions, Wagner sketched in a lovely woodland scene: the rustle of the leaves in the tree overhead, the song of a bird, the murmur of a stream. The whole thing is as naturalistic a description in sound as music is able to give. At the end of this opera Siegfried, in true fairy-tale fashion, finds his princess, Brünnhilde, rescues her, and makes her his bride.

In the final Ring drama, Siegfried's last adventures and his death are depicted. In the first selection from *Götterdämmerung* chosen here, Siegfried starts forth at daybreak seeking further adventure, leaving the magic ring with his bride. We hear his horn call as he leaves Brünnhilde and journeys down to the Rhine. The bold, striding, pealing theme which follows, "Love's Resolution," suggests his hopes as he goes forth into the world. A rolling theme represents the mighty Rhine; we hear the song of the maidens who dwell in its depths and who once guarded the gold from which was forged the ring, source of so much woe. The ring theme, and others reminding us of earlier parts of the story, are introduced; there is, at the end of this orchestral interlude, a hint of the tragedy to come.

Through a magic potion given him by his enemies, Siegfried forgets Brünnhilde, who denounces him and enters into schemes of revenge. The great hero is killed at a hunting feast; his body is brought to the banks of the Rhine and placed upon a mighty funeral pyre. As the flames mount heavenwards, Brünnhilde, before sacrificing herself and her beloved steed in them, delivers an impassioned sacrificial ode (the *Immolation*) telling the whole, long story of her love for the dead hero. This is a magnificent example of Wagner's use of the solo voice in these later operas, not in the Italianate manner of the aria but as a sort of *recitative* without measured melody, which reinforces the dramatic communication given by the orchestra. We must always remember that it is the orchestra in these mature Wagner works which is the real medium for the conveyance of the dramatic ideas. In reality, here it tells us the story of Siegfried's long career, bringing in, one after another, the *leitmotives* representing the various events associated with him, weaving them all into a gorgeous, glowing musical fabric without any seams at all. Many of the references in the text are obscure to those who have not followed the whole development of the Ring story; but no better method of understanding Wagner's characteristic style of combining voice and orchestra, using the *leitmotive* as the basis of construction, can be found than through this thrilling *Immolation*.

TOPICS FOR DISCUSSION

Why does Wagner's music seem less appealing today than at the turn of the century?

Indicate why Wagner was one of the greatest of musical revolutionaries.

What are the possibilities of adapting such modern means of mass communication as television and the cinema to Wagner's ideals of opera?

Why has Wagner always been one of the most controversial figures in musical history?

CHAPTER 20

The New World Symphony

A SYMPHONIC NATIONALIST

Composers who have been interested in the various nationalistic movements have turned naturally to the writing of program music as the style best fitted to the fulfillment of their ideas. So, to a small extent, did Anton Dvořák, the Bohemian nationalist; but most of his compositions, although they are full of the color, rhythm, and melody of the Czech folk music, are cast in forms used by the composers of the earlier Classical school. He started his career in the traditions of the German Romantic school of Beethoven and Schubert, and although this greatly influenced his choice of forms, the first years of his artistic development coincided with a determined effort on the part of a group of older Czech composers to develop a school of nationalistic writing. The young Dvořák found this idea congenial, and from 1874 he threw himself body and soul into the new movement, filling his music with the spirit of his country.

Like Schubert, Dvořák was a man who lived only in the world of music. This gives spontaneity and freshness to everything he wrote and makes it very easy to enjoy. His genius was most at home in melodies and rhythms that have a folk flavor, and he was able to weave these into a fabric of real musical worth through his mastery of the older forms. In other words, he was at his best when writing absolute music, unhindered by programs of any sort. He had a flair for striking and effective instrumentation, and his best music proceeded from his ability to use resources in the most natural manner possible.

THE FIFTH SYMPHONY

Without doubt his greatest work is his last symphony, the one in E minor generally called the *New World Symphony*.[1] It was written during the composer's short stay in New York as the head of the National Conservatory of Music (1892-1894) and was undertaken in an attempt to show American composers what might be done in the way of writing music in the larger forms, using folk-style themes as material. There has been a great deal of discussion as to whether Dvořák employed in this work melodies suggestive of the American Indians and Negroes. It is known that one of his talented pupils, the Negro singer and composer Henry T. Burleigh, introduced Dvořák to the beauties of the Negro spirituals, and it seems probable that the second theme of the first movement may have been suggested in this way. But, according to Dvořák's friend, Josef Kovarik, who made the first copy of the score of this famous symphony, every note and theme are Dvořák's, and no one else's. All of the themes seem curiously like others Dvořák wrote before going to America; and, in any case, in Dvořák's hands they lose any peculiarly New World characteristics they may have possessed.

[1] Excerpts from *New World Symphony* are reprinted by permission of Associated Music Publishers, Inc., New York.

The First Movement

The first movement of *From the New World* is as strict in form as if it had been penned by some classical writer—Haydn or, perhaps, Mozart. The sonata form can be seen here as a logical, clear-cut, and very effective means for the expression of a composer's ideas and the ordering of his musical materials. Only after a rather long introduction, which contains several foreshadowings of the main theme, does Dvořák plunge into its leaping rhythms. We hear on the horns:

There are a number of interesting things to observe about this theme: (1) it is written in the pentatonic scale, which uses only the first, second, third, fifth, and sixth tones of our usual scale; (2) it employs the folk-song "snap," a short, snappy note placed before a long one (see the second measure of this theme); (3) there are two distinct parts to the tune, the up-and-down arpeggio given to the horns and the answering part given to the wood winds (much use is made of both these parts in the building up of the movement).

The connecting passages linking the main themes of this work are obviously suggestive of the lilt and quality of folk music. The ingratiating second theme, with its cellos thrumming a bag-pipe-like bass, sounds as if it had been taken directly from Czech folk music:

Yet, it has the personal color and characteristic features (for example, the lowered seventh step which is a peculiarity of the Negro folk songs known to the composer) that are Dvořák's signature and belong to no one else.

The third theme, when it finally arrives, sounds somewhat like the famous spiritual "Swing Low, Sweet Chariot":

Like most of Dvořák's themes, it is short and very individual, making it easy to remember and its development easy to follow.

There are just short of a hundred measures in the development section; the first and third themes are used, but the second gets only a look-in in the rhythmic pattern, now and then. It may be felt that we get rather a lot of the opening measures of the first theme—that aspiring arpeggio—and that the devices are somewhat overworked. Dvořák is not afraid to drive home a rhythmic pattern by repetition —a touch, perhaps, of the peasant mind. (Compare it with the sometimes almost maddening repetition of Russian composers.) Color interests this writer more than discourse; on the whole, the development does not lead us far down the garden, and we spend most of our time admiring the flowers.

In the restatement section, Dvořák wisely makes less use of the first theme than he did in the statement. This is what we want, for although we have enjoyed its company, we have had enough of it for this time. The second theme comes back in regular order but in a different key, which adds interest to our listening, even though we may not realize the reason for it. The third theme is, of course, again stated, and shortly after there begins a fine coda, based largely on the first theme.

THE SECOND MOVEMENT

The second movement is one of the most famous in all symphonic literature; its principal theme is known to everyone in some arrangement or other. There have been many suggestions as to its inspiration: one writer thinks that this haunting song of the English horn could have been a Negro spiritual, for it is in that vein and has a typical melancholy and pathos; another says that everybody knows it took shape "after Dvořák had been thinking of the story of Hiawatha's betrothal to Minnehaha." Dvořák's sons are authority for the statement that this tune was suggestive of their father's homesickness for his native land, a homesickness expressed while he was in the midst of a strange and unappealing environment. This explanation seems as good as any that might be offered, if we must have reasons for the writing of beautiful music. It is not difficult to feel the nostalgia and longing that pervade this music, and for this reason it will always appeal. The movement is of particular interest to us, however, because it is a beautiful example of the form which has so often been employed by composers for the second movements of their symphonies—what has come to be known as "song form."

An expressive movement such as this does not need very detailed analysis; if we listen carefully to it as a whole, we notice that it divides into three sections, and that the first section is repeated once the second has been finished. There is a short, sustained, chorale-like introduction, and then we hear the well-known tune, given to the English horn, which distinguishes the first section:

The middle section is marked by a quicker tempo and has a beautiful wood-wind and string scoring, with a plucked bass a great deal of the time:

Then, after a curious and unexpected interpolation with a light-hearted, open-air flavor, the first and third themes from the first movement are heard. After this the slow, expressive *largo* tune enters again, this time with some effective hesitations which have the effect of making us wish that it would continue just a little longer. The section closes with the same beautiful chords heard at the beginning. The scoring throughout is a triumph of aptness, and the formal design is handled with masterly skill.

THE THIRD MOVEMENT, A TYPICAL SCHERZO

It is hardly necessary to remark that the various movements of a symphony are purposely varied to provide new interest and hold the attention of the listener from beginning to end. After a vigorous opening movement, the second (almost always called the *slow* movement), comes as a refreshing contrast. It is in the second movement that the composer usually displays his emotional powers; lyric in character (hence the name *song form*), the slow movement has a depth of feeling from which we in turn need relief. Thus the third movement is always brisk, more or less cheerful, and decidedly rhythmic. We have seen that the older writers (Haydn and Mozart) employed a classic dance—the minuet—as a pattern for their third movements; and that Beethoven introduced a freer feeling and a livelier pace in his third movements and called them *scherzos*— literally "jests." Most symphony writers since his time, following his example, have used this form for their third movements. Dvořák is no exception; his scherzo here is a humorous, lively movement, again in three large sections with the same general idea predominant —restatement after contrast. Each of the sections has two main themes, and close listening will show that the formal scheme is this:

A: First part, principally employing theme 1:

Second part, principally employing theme 2:

First part again.

B: First part, principally employing theme 3:

Second part, principally employing theme 4:

First part again.

All of part B is then repeated.

A: An almost literal repetition of the whole first section, followed by a coda made up largely of the first theme from the first movement.

The middle, or contrasting, section (B) of the scherzo (as well as of the minuet) is called the *trio* because in the early days it was written in three parts. The different sections in this Dvořák scherzo are easily recognized but, as if to ensure recognition of these divisions, at the end of A, just before we hear B, the composer introduces an interpolation from the first movement's first theme.

THE LAST MOVEMENT

The final movement of a symphony is very often again in sonata form, although other types of construction are sometimes used— the rondo, or the variation form, for example. In the *New World Symphony* we have a fairly strict use of the sonata form, with constant interpolations of themes from earlier movements; the composer seems to want us to renew our acquaintance with these older friends as the work comes to an end.

The listener may have noted that many of the themes used in this work have been in the minor key, but by the way he has used them, Dvořák has demonstrated very clearly that the minor need not necessarily express a sad or doleful sentiment. The first theme of the last movement, again in minor, shows that peculiar thrusting, nervous energy and directness characteristic of this composer.

There are two parts, and the second, almost jiglike in character, gives us a hint of the rhythm which is strongly felt throughout the movement. The second theme is played by a clarinet over a delicate string tremolo:

Then follows a third theme (this is the end of it):

(The last measure plainly says "Three Blind Mice"; just what the connection is, no one knows—perhaps just a bit of Dvořákian foolery.) In the development section not only are the two main themes of this movement treated, but some from the other three are also heard. The restatement follows, and the final coda brings other suggestion of earlier themes.

Perhaps the middle movements stand on their own feet best; the *largo* is unequaled in its quiet beauty. Although the ideas throughout the whole work are not broadly or philosophically worked out (as we find them in the Beethoven and Brahms symphonies) and the tune material is brief, there are ingratiating features in this symphony, and we cannot imagine that it will ever pass from the concert repertoire. No more engaging introduction to the literature of the symphony can be found.

ADDITIONAL EXAMPLES OF DVOŘÁK'S MUSIC

In addition to Dvořák's fine string quartet, discussed in a later chapter, listen to his sixteen *Slavonic Dances* in order to get a complete picture of the musical soul of the Czechs, a soul sorely tried during many oppressive years of the country's long history. Colorful and rhythmic, alternatingly gay and sad, these short works are a monument to what the Czechs can produce. They are especially stirring if heard in the recording by the Czech Philharmonic Orchestra.

TOPICS FOR DISCUSSION

Why is Dvořák so popular a composer? Can you name one or two of the weaknesses in his music? Why is it that these rarely bother anyone?

Estimate the influence of America on Dvořák's works and words after his stay in the United States. Consider this influence on the music written after his departure and on American music of today. Can you trace definite elements in American composers today which are the results of Dvořák's work?

What is your opinion of the composer's idea that American composers should build a native music on Negro music? Would the music of the Indian have been a good influence?

CHAPTER 21

Chamber Music, "The Music of Friends"

❧ ❦

CHAMBER MUSIC IN THE HISTORICAL SENSE

One of the most pleasurable and satisfying forms of music which European civilization has produced, chamber music, has often been referred to as "the music of friends"—that is, music produced for a small group of real music lovers, whether in the princely courts of England, Spain, or Italy during the Renaissance, the great houses of the eighteenth-century gentry, or the informal chamber-music parties of present-day amateurs. In 1622, when all instrumental music was what we today call chamber music, Henry Peacham wrote in his *The Compleat Gentleman*, "There is no one Science in the world that so affecteth the free and generous spirit with a more delightful and inoffensive recreation."

Yet this "friendly" music is not very well known today, even by rather accomplished listeners, and certainly is not understood by the general public. Witness such slips as those that have appeared in reviews in small-town newspapers when reference was made to "chamber of commerce music"; or the regret expressed by a backwoods critic that a certain piece of Beethoven's written for a string quartet—the most common of all chamber-music organizations— had not been "played by a larger band." The expression *chamber music* (literally "room music") originally signified the kind of music

238

A TYPICAL EIGHTEENTH-CENTURY COURT ORCHESTRA

The Hofkapelle of Herzog Friedrichs des Frommen, Ludwigslust, painted by Georg David Matthieu.

that was written to be played in the salon of a prince, as distinguished from that written for performance in church or theater.

Up to the time of the Renaissance the growth of music had taken place almost entirely under the protecting care of the Church; from 1600 on, it developed largely under the patronage of princes and royalty. The earlier church music was vocal, with little attention to any instrumental accompaniment. In the seventeenth century, as instrumental music came more and more into vogue, each prince gathered around him his own musical establishment for the pleasure and edification of his court as well as for the increasing of its reputation for brilliance and splendor. Just as in more recent years the great manufacturing barons often placed an organ (the more expensive, the better) in their show houses, so in the late seventeenth and eighteenth centuries most of the European princes and princelings had chamber-music groups for the delectation of their guests.

Some of these musical establishments were of considerable size and importance; a typical and probably average one, with the exception of its leader, was that of Prince Leopold of Anhalt-Cöthen, which Johann Sebastian Bach directed from 1717 to 1723. This organization comprised some eighteen players: violinists, violists, cellists, a bassist, an oboist, a flutist, bassoonists, trumpeters, an organist, a drummer, and a copyist to prepare the music. The prince played the clavier himself, and Bach wrote much music for the various combinations possible within this group of players. This, chamber music in the real sense of the term, was played in the great room of the castle on certain days each week after dinner, for invited guests and some of the prince's subjects who were known to be lovers of music. Frederick the Great, master of the art of music as well as of war, head of the more elaborate Prussian court at Potsdam, had his own chamber-music organization, with which he played the flute in the music room of his palace every evening he was in residence.

IN THE MODERN SENSE

The modern meaning of the term has changed somewhat; princes no longer have a monopoly on music of this sort. It is now played almost entirely at public concerts, but its range is still limited to music suitable for rooms of moderate size, and *it is usually played by not more than one instrument to a part.* Modern chamber music may be said to date from the middle of the eighteenth century, when composers began to write for various instrumental combinations without including the clavier to hold the music together, as had been common practice. Even though we know little of this earlier type of chamber music in which the harpsichord or the clavichord (called the *continuo*) played an important role, we do know that its quantity was enormous. In fact, much more of this earlier kind of chamber music was written than has been produced since Haydn (1732-1809) laid the foundations for our modern style.

Not content with having a miscellaneous grouping of varied instruments held together by a harpsichord, Haydn selected the string quartet as the norm and worked out for it certain principles which have since proved their validity for all other chamber-music organizations. First of all, he developed a form, using in general the same scheme he had worked out for the symphony: four movements, each of them contrasting in mood and structure. He felt that the instruments in a small combination must be of equivalent musical capacity and on equal tonal terms. It would be useless to match a slow-speaking, relatively awkward instrument with others more agile and facile—a double bass with a violin, for instance—or it would be poor taste to introduce into a group any instrument, such as the trumpet, that would shatter the tonal ensemble. Furthermore, and this was of great importance for future developments, the individual parts were written for each player, and every note written for the various instruments was intended to be heard as written. There was to be no filling-in by an instrument such as the piano, which was liable to smear the general effect while binding it together. In the style of chamber music initiated by Haydn there is no opportunity for filling-in or thickening-up, as is so often the case with orchestral writing. This is one great reason why it is difficult to write good chamber music, and why this music is not the easiest to understand or, perhaps, to enjoy.

The society of the eighteenth century was comprised of only two classes: the privileged, governing class and the servile, governed class. This conception, whatever we may think of it politically or socially, had great value for the development of art, for it gave it an intelligent support that otherwise would have been lacking. This assorting of society gave way under the personal aspirations of the nineteenth century, when it was discovered that every man has a soul and a mind of his own, a right to freedom from oppression, and that there is a moral law directly opposed to the law of force. These new ideals led to the tremendous expressions that Beethoven gave us through the medium of the string quartet, expressions which no composer of his time, and very few since, have been able to equal. Beethoven regarded the string quartet as the purest of all musical forms and resisted those who appealed to him to write more oratorios and operas; instead, he applied himself with enthusiasm to this most difficult form of pure music.

Other composers have carried on the traditions of chamber music started by Haydn. Schubert wrote some of his finest things as chamber-music works. Schumann, pianist and poet, also wrote chamber music, with somewhat indifferent success in spite of the real power of his thought. Johannes Brahms was one of the great composers who seemed to find this kind of music especially congenial; he wrote twenty-four important works in this form, nearly all of them very fine. There is everywhere in his chamber music a noble elevation of ideals, a virile strength, and a depth of feeling that make it one of the glories of German art. Other writers of chamber-music works deserving mention, even in such a cursory survey of the field, are César Franck, Dvořák, Debussy, Ravel, and Schönberg (who carried his radical tendencies into this classic field).

What is it that makes chamber music particularly appealing to some musicians who have had a great deal of practice in listening and equally baffling to others who have not versed themselves in the niceties of listening? There is no doubt that chamber music has gained a supreme place in the affections of many music lovers, nor that the average listener is left cold by the lack of dramatic appeal in this music and is puzzled by its intricacies.

Sir Henry Hadow, a writer well known for his musicianship as well as for his understanding of the average listener's position, has this to say:

> Among all forms of composition, chamber music is that which to my taste is the most complete and satisfying. Its transparent texture makes it easy to hear and understand; one is never distracted or bewildered by overcharged sound or overemphasized emotion. And this very transparence renders it necessary that the composer's drawing should be perfect and his design sure. With a very wide range of emotion, it is vowed, in the first instance, to the sense of pure beauty—to beauty of melody, of harmonization, of structure, in which every point tells and every phrase is significant. Heine speaks of Goethe's prose as a pellucid ocean through which one can see his golden thoughts: that simile seems to me wholly suitable to the great classics of chamber-music composition.[1]

TYPES OF CHAMBER MUSIC

Before we take up the study of some representative pieces of chamber music it will be well for us to acquaint ourselves with the general characteristics of this kind of writing. In passing, a word about the development of the stringed family of instruments will be helpful. The medieval "fiddles," variants of the bowed-string principle, all led to the viols, which, from the fifteenth century until

[1] Reprinted, by permission of Oxford University Press, from Cobbett's *Cyclopedic Survey of Chamber Music*. Oxford: 1930.

the coming into power of the new violin tribe in the middle six-teenth, first held mastery, then contested it with the violins, and finally went under, as far as popular use was concerned. We can occasionally hear the old viols at their best in the hands of such players as the Dolmetsch family or the *Société des instruments anciens*. In Tudor and Stuart times viol-playing was popularly cul-tivated as part of the education of every gentleman. The violin family came from Cremona just at the right time. Amati, Stradi-varius, Gasparo da Salo produced instruments of incomparable beauty, and for three hundred years the design of these instruments has remained virtually unchanged.

The most usual chamber-music combinations in use at the present time are the trio, the quartet, and the quintet. Some of the world's greatest music has been written for these combinations. German musicians seem to consider that it takes at least three instruments to constitute a chamber-music group, but general consensus admits the duet to this classification. The usual duo combinations are those of violin and piano or cello and piano, but many duets have been written for the piano and some wind instrument, such as the horn or clarinet. Trios for piano, violin, and cello contain some of our loveliest chamber music, probably because this combination offers a fullness of tone that is unusual. (Haydn, Mozart, Beethoven, Schubert, and Brahms all wrote such trios.) There are string trios for violin, viola, and cello (a difficult combination), for piano, violin, and horn, and for piano, clarinet, and cello. (Both the latter combinations were tried by Brahms with great success.)

In the string quartet for two violins, viola, and cello we have the purest and highest form of chamber music, perhaps of all music. There is another type of quartet for piano and strings (violin, viola, and cello), but this combination does not rank with the pure string quartet for beauty of tone, since the use of the piano necessarily confines the other players to its tempered intonation. String quintets differ very little from quartets; the extra instrument is either another viola (Mozart has given us the outstanding work for this com-bination) or a cello. Both Mozart and Brahms wrote quintets com-bining the clarinet with the string quartet, and there are popular piano quintets, notably those of Schubert (the *Forellen* quintet) and Schumann. Composers have attempted to write for groups of five wind instruments, such as flute, oboe, clarinet, horn, and bassoon. Brahms has given us two great string sextets for two violins, two violas, and two cellos.

There are many different combinations for other instruments, most of them grouping the strings with one or more wind instruments, such as Schönberg's beautiful sextet *Verklärte Nacht* and his *Pierrot lunaire* (for piano, flute [piccolo], clarinet, violin, cello, and voice). Stravinsky's *Octet for Wind Instruments* indicates the trend of modern ideas toward new chamber-music combinations.

In hearing such a group play, the amateur is almost always disappointed; his natural mistake is in confusing volume with quality of tone. He is disappointed, perhaps, at hearing only three or four instruments instead of a hundred, as in one of the great orchestral works. He misses the overpowering magnitude and splendid weight of the orchestral mass; there is no flashing contrast of colors, no surge of composite tone, no tremendous contrast in dynamics. The very picture before his eyes is disappointing; instead of a large group of instrumentalists, each of them blending his personality and activity with a hundred others under the kindling fire and burning enthusiasm of the conductor, he sees only three, four, or five players huddled in the middle of the stage, each of them engaged in reading his own music without the magnetic stimulus of a visible leader. Everything seems cool, calculated, cerebral.

Let him listen for other things—the clear sonority of the various instruments as they blend together or answer one another in dialogue or repartee; the strength of the whole, due to the equal importance of each part; the weighty matters upon which the instruments discourse—all these are worth his careful attention. We do not have to disparage the greatness of the orchestral masterpieces to realize that chamber music is like Abbé Dimnet's description of sculpture: the art of the noble or heroically minded, the passion of the severely artistic. Despite the fact that the greatest success, and rightly so, perhaps, has always gone to the writers of orchestral music, chamber music will always afford a lasting and inexhaustible delight because of its clean sparingness, its lack of anything which approaches sentimentality, its disregard for virtuosity except as a means toward a perfect expression of great thought.

SOME EXAMPLES OF STRING-QUARTET STYLE

What is the best means for securing an introduction to this *sanctum sanctorum* of music? Opinions differ, but it seems natural that it should be through the medium of the most popular of all chamber-music groups, the string quartet: two violins, viola, and cello. Perhaps the most popular single movement in string-quartet literature is the *Andante cantabile* (literally, "leisurely singing") from Tchaikovsky's *Quartet*, Op. 11. This slow movement is full of a tender wistfulness enhanced by muted strings. The main theme is taken bodily from an old Russian folk song; it has a peculiar alternation of measures and a most appealing melody.

The second section, largely built over a repeated *pizzicato* figure in the cello, equals the first in beauty while providing a fine contrast. Then the first section returns; the whole movement is a good example of the three-part song form, similar in structure to the *Largo* of the *New World Symphony*.

We have already remarked Haydn's importance in the development of the modern quartet style. One of his best-known quartets is the so-called *Emperor Quartet*, which in its slow movement makes use of the Austrian National Hymn, a tune Haydn had written for the emperor's birthday celebration of 1797 and afterwards presented to the whole nation. This movement takes the form of theme with variations, a form that has always been popular with composers as a means for displaying skill and technic. We first hear the theme complete; some will recognize it as a tune to which a familiar hymn is sung:

After this we have a set of four variants followed by a short coda. In the first variation the second violin carries the tune while the first weaves a *staccato* embroidery above it; the other instruments are silent. In the second variation the cello has the melody while the second violin plays a counter-melody, and the first violin and viola supply an appropriate background. The viola takes the tune in the third variation, and there is some beautiful weaving of accompanimental threads by the other instruments. Notice the peculiar, veiled character of the viola here. In the last variation the melody is restored to its usual position on top and is sung by the first violin while the other instruments supply a rich background. The coda is short and quiet.

LIST OF SUGGESTED MUSIC

Trio in B flat Major (Archduke), Op. 97,
   Slow Movement   BEETHOVEN
   Many devotees of chamber music feel that this heroically conceived work for violin, piano, and cello is the ideal stepping stone for introducing initiates to the style. Belonging to Beethoven's most mature period, there is something about this music that seems to fuse its interpreters into one performing instrument, no matter how independent they may feel as virtuoso players. Two magnificent recordings of the whole trio have been made in which that rare achievement may be observed: "a virtuoso chamber-music performance in which the whole is equal to the sum of its parts." This work should be heard by everyone who has any doubt about the possibility of enjoying chamber music.

Octet in E flat Major, Op. 20, *Scherzo*   MENDELSSOHN
   Written when the composer was only sixteen years old, this deft, finely finished work is conceded to be the best writing ever done for eight strings. Light, staccato, and pianissimo throughout, it is said to have been inspired by a reading of the portion of Goethe's *Faust* which describes the Walpurgis Night revels of the witches and ghosts on the Brocken in the Harz Mountains, Germany. Later on, Mendelssohn orchestrated this *Scherzo* for a concert given in London, and orchestras throughout the world have been playing it ever since. To see the difference between orchestral style and chamber-music style, listen to a first-class recording of the original and con-

trast it with the revised form having wind and brass parts added to the strings.

TOPICS FOR DISCUSSION

Discuss the benefits and disadvantages of the old system of princely patronage of composers. By what could we best replace it today?

A newcomer to chamber music at first disliked the tone of the string quartet because it did not seem quite "in tune." Can you suggest the reason for his discomfort?

Can you compare the qualities of the numerous fine chamber-music organizations of today? What are your preferences among them? Explain your choices.

How did the fact that his princely master played a certain instrument influence Haydn's scoring?

Do you think it essential that a composer of string-quartet music play a string instrument? Do you know of any works written by non-playing composers?

CHAPTER 22

A Romantic Quartet and a Classic One

✥❦✥

DVOŘÁK'S *AMERICAN QUARTET*

No better introduction to the beauties of quartet style can be found than Dvořák's *Quartet in F Major*, Op. 96,[1] written just after the *New World Symphony* while he was a resident of the United States in 1893. Both these works, and his *Quintet in E flat*, Op. 97, are alike in color and style and in their attempt to use the flavor of local folk tunes. Hence they have become known as his "American" works, though they contain much that is innately Czech in flavor.

Dvořák came to teach in the United States during the seasons of 1892-3 and 1893-4; he settled down in New York, curious, excited, and yet perturbed by the swirling American life he found about him. He soon began sketches for the *New World Symphony* and, when it came time to finish the work and write out the score, he sought a quiet place where he could feel at home among his own people and still be under the influence of the atmosphere of the New World. His friend and mentor, Josef Kovarik, a young Czech who had been born in the Bohemian-settlement village of Spillville, Iowa, and had gone to Prague for training in music, recommended

---

[1] Excerpts from *Quartet in F* are reprinted by permission of Associated Music Publishers, Inc., New York.

Collection of The Metropolitan Museum of Art; Courtesy of the Downtown Gallery

JACK LEVINE: STRING QUARTET

this little town. Dvořák and Kovarik went there for the summer of 1893; the famous composer made himself completely at home, played the organ for the early morning Mass in the village church, talked to the farmers about their crops, and composed furiously. When the *New World Symphony* was finished and the score written out, Dvořák turned his attention to a quartet. Writing it quickly he played each movement over as soon as it was finished, with the help of three members of the Kovarik family; Dvořák himself played the first violin part. Thus this lovely "American quartet" came into being.

Although it follows in general the forms used by the classical writers of quartets, this work of Dvořák's can hardly be said to be typical. Its first movement has two main themes, both strongly rhythmic in a purely Czech manner and quite contrasting in key and color:

There is little development of these themes according to the manner of the usual first-movement (sonata) form; they are heard, together with subordinate themes, flashing in and out of the constantly weaving fabric and reappear at the end of the movement.

Three-part song form is an ideal mold for the *Lento* movement, just as it had been for the famous *Largo* of the *New World Symphony*. It is music suggestive of the deep woods (whether they are Bohemian or American makes little difference) and the melancholy songs of an oppressed race, perhaps the Czechs themselves or the American Indians, whose native music interested Dvořák so much. The main theme around which the first part of the movement revolves is

The middle section grows out of a nostalgic theme:

A beautiful coda for the cello brings to an end one of the most deeply expressive movements in all chamber music.

The third movement has the rather unusual form of variations on a very lively theme; the variations are mostly rhythmic, with some unusual twists of harmonic color so characteristic of this composer.

In the finale Dvořák comes as near to being natively American as he ever could; this gay sort of rondo has a main theme that somewhat resembles a "break-down."

But always in the background we see the smiling face of the Czech visitor, suggested by a subsidiary theme such as this, used later in the movement:

In the midst of this barn-dance jollity, there suddenly is heard a chorale-like section, as though the composer were improvising on the village organ at Spillville:

Then the dance is resumed, and the whole work concludes vigorously and happily.

HAYDN'S *QUARTET IN F MAJOR*, OP. 3, NO. 5

A good contrast to the Romanticism of Dvořák's work is the classical short *Quartet* of Haydn in F Major, Op. 3, No. 5. As far as we can determine, Haydn wrote eighty-three quartets, ranging in style from the rather tentative groping of his earlier experiments to the magnificent maturity of his later quartets. In them all there appears his peculiar genial quality, using the word in its English sense—warm and friendly—as well as in its Latin suggestiveness of the quality of genius. This Op. 3, No. 5 is typical, for certainly no more genial music has ever been written. The work is very short as quartets go, but its few pages contain some great beauties.

The first movement is characteristic of Haydn's gusto and verve; it is in sonata form with easily distinguishable themes: the first in measures 1 to 8, and the second in measures 41 to 45. The little development section of fifty measures contains a miniature "imbroglio," produced from a subsidiary figure in the bridge material connecting the two themes; yet it sounds perfectly logical and leads beautifully back to the recapitulation.

The second movement, one of the most famous in quartet literature, is called a serenade; it consists of two large sections, each of them repeated, with the melody given to the muted first violin and with the other instruments forming a *pizzicato* background. When played well it is a particularly lovely movement, inconceivable except in terms of the string quartet. The minuet and trio run true to form, with some interesting variants of the regularity of the usual minuet rhythm. The last movement, marked *scherzando*, is surely as rapidly running a sonata form as was ever written; the themes (three) are appropriately brief and snappy, and the whole thing is over almost before we know it. This is a perfect little example of Haydn's sympathetic treatment of the quartet style.

LIST OF SUGGESTED MUSIC

Quartet in D Major ("The Lark"), Op. 64, No. 5   HAYDN

Quartet in B flat Major ("The Sunrise"), Op. 76, No. 4   HAYDN

No other form of music has been better served by the long-playing record than the string quartet. The sustained and closely linked moods of this kind of composition should not be broken, as was inevitable in the older form of recording. Like many of his other quartets, these two works of Haydn have been given nicknames not only suggestive of the composer's intimate style but also descriptive of some feature of the individual work. The lark is suggested by the birdlike main theme of the first movement of Op. 64, No. 5. The sun rises on a lovely countryside in the B-flat-Major work and later sets with peaceful quietude in its slow movement. Both these quartets have been wonderfully served by the engineers; no better value in records can be found than the recordings of these quartets played by the Budapest String Quartet, which seems to have a special feeling for the music of this composer.

TOPICS FOR DISCUSSION

What is your personal opinion of chamber music? Do you think it will change as you hear more and more of this music?

Discuss the use of chamber music forms in modern jazz.

CHAPTER 23

Impressionism: Debussy Its Chief Exponent in Music

❦

The impressionist movement in art came into being during the latter years of the nineteenth century as a protest against the exuberance and excesses of the Romantics. Claude Debussy (1862-1918) was its chief exponent in music and his masterpiece, *L'Après-midi d'un faune (Afternoon of a Faun)*, one of its greatest productions. This work, although not strictly delineative in the manner of Strauss, employs definite themes suggestive of various episodes, quite in the manner of the Strauss tone poems. Instead of giving himself over to the direct evocation of emotional states in the manner of Liszt and the other Romantic composers, Debussy conveys his expression through suggestion. His music studiously avoids the dramatic and narrative aspects of his predecessors, just as they had avoided the formal and conventional aspect of the music of their eighteenth-century predecessors. While demonstrably an offshoot of Romanticism, *L'Après-midi d'un faune* represents a strong revolt against the overpowering and almost annihilating influences which the giants of the Romantic period bequeathed to their successors. We have already suggested that Romanticism was one of the most stimulating and virile influences ever to affect music and have said that its ideals shaped the output of one great composer after another: Weber, Schubert, Schumann, Liszt, and, finally, Wagner.

CLAUDE DEBUSSY

After the middle of the century the cry became "After Wagner, what?" And, as it so often has done in critical periods, history provided an ideal answer in the person of Debussy. The peculiar characteristics of his music which give it wings to send it soaring up to heights to which it could not possibly have risen otherwise were the results of an unusually effective blending of racial and environmental influences. Nature provided Debussy with an inquiring mind, a sensitive musical ear, and an unbounded imagination, and in so doing formed him as the ideal leader of a new musical movement. His music, with its aristocratic bearing, its shunning of commonplace exuberances, its essential restraint, its logic and balance, manifests typical Gallic qualities. And circumstances provided the ideal environment for the rapid development of Debussy's style.

SYMBOLISM—A PARALLEL MOVEMENT IN LITERATURE

Early in his creative life Debussy found himself in the midst of movements in the other arts, especially in literature and painting, which exerted a strong influence on the development of his music. It would hardly be too much to say that, just as the German poets of the beginning of the century precipitated Romanticism in music, so the French poets and painters of the last of the century left the very definite impress of their ideals and methods on the music of the next period. A group of poets—"symbolists" they called themselves —headed by Verlaine and Mallarmé, combined in a fight against what they considered to be the abuses of Romanticism to be found in such writers as Hugo and Lamartine. Delicate, tenuous poetry that stimulated the imagination, much of it frankly sensuous and voluptuous, expressed through extremely graceful means, was the aim of these new writers. Words were more than words—they became symbols suggesting rather than merely expressing; they were meant to evoke, by their sounds, certain subconscious sensations and ideas. The actual thought contained in a passage was less important than what one was led to read between the lines. Mallarmé said of these aims: "To name an object is to sacrifice three fourths of that enjoyment which comes from the pleasure of guessing bit by bit. To suggest, that is our dream." He and his followers, Rimbaud, Maeterlinck, Swinburne, and Yeats, wrote verse that is subtly sensuous in sound and suggestive in meaning.

A translation of one of Verlaine's short poems, "Serenade," will give some idea of the spirit that lay behind the whole movement:

> *The shepherd's star burns dim,*
> *Sinks in the night,*
> *The pilot fumbles for his light.*
> *Now is the time for him,*
> *Dark skies above,*
> *Whose hand seeks out for love.*
> *Sir Atys tunes his strings,*
> *His eyes to Chloris speak*
> *Of favors he would seek*
> *While the sad moon is up, and streams*
> *Down on the boat which glides and gleams*
> *Upon a sea of dreams.*
> —F. E. in the London Saturday Review[1]

A FAUN INSPIRES THREE ARTS

There is no better example of the poetry written by the symbolists than the famous "Eclogue" of Mallarmé (1842-1898), which

[1] By permission of the London Saturday Review.

inspired Debussy to write the music we are about to consider. Mallarmé's poem is said to have been inspired, in turn, by a little picture of the eighteenth-century artist Boucher, now in the National Gallery, London. This shows in a highly realistic way the leering face of a satyr who is pursuing two girls along the reedy bank of a river. (The distinction between mythological fauns and satyrs is not very clear; both terms are used to describe beings with tails, horns, goat's legs and feet, and furry, pointed ears, thus possessing both animal and human characteristics.) After he had seen it, Mallarmé was moved to write some of the most impressionistically vague and obscure evocations of emotion ever conceived, all the more beautiful because of their vagueness and obscurity.

> *Ces nymphes, je les veux perpétuer,*
>   *Si clair,*
> *Leur incarnat léger, qu'il voltige dans l'air*
> *Assoupi de sommeils touffus.*

> (I would immortalize these nymphs,
> So bright their sunlit coloring, so airy light,
> It floats like drowsy down.)

The poem was published in 1876; it is best known to American readers through the prose version made by Edmund Gosse, English poet and essayist, who has paraphrased this "miracle of unintelligibility" as well as anyone could. Even Gosse said that bit by bit, phrase by phrase, he did not understand the original; nevertheless, it gave him great pleasure and he was able to obtain from it "as solid an influence as Mallarmé desired to produce."

A faun, a simple, sensuous, passionate being, wakens in the forest at daybreak and tries to recall his experience of the previous afternoon. Was he the fortunate recipient of an actual visit from nymphs, white and golden goddesses, divinely tender and indulgent? Or is the memory he seems to retain nothing but the shadows of a vision, no more substantial than the arid rain of notes from his own flute? He cannot tell. Yet surely there was, surely there is, an animal whiteness among the brown reeds of the lake that shines out yonder? Were they, are they, swans? No. But naiads plunging? Perhaps. Vaguer and vaguer grows the impression of this delicious experience. He would resign his woodland godship to retain it. A garden of lilies, golden-headed, white-stalked, behind a trellis of red roses? Ah, the effort is too great for his poor brain. Perhaps if he selects one lily from the garth of lilies, one benign and beneficent yielder of her cup to thirsty lips, the memory, the ever-receding memory, may be forced back. So when he has glutted upon a bunch of grapes he is wont to toss the empty skins into the air and blow them out in a visionary greediness. But no, the delicious hour grows vaguer; experience or dreams he will never know which it was. The sun is warm, the grasses yielding; and he curls himself up again, after worshiping the efficacious star of wine, that he may pursue the dubious ecstasy into the more hopeful boscages of sleep.

IMPRESSIONISM IN PAINTING

For suggestions as to technical means for his musical expression, Debussy turned to another contemporary revolt against the traditional "high art" of the middle of the century, hedged about as it was with strict rules and limiting tradition. In reality, impressionism in painting was a new way of seeing the world, just as symbolism was another way of feeling and musical impressionism a new way of hearing. It was developed by a group of young and enthusiastic painters who (around 1869) revolted against the studio-produced art of the masters, as well as against the dynamic influence of the romantic-realist Courbet.

Although he was never a full-fledged impressionist, Édouard Manet (1832-1883) may be regarded as the precursor of the movement in his attempts to show that color and light alone have the power to provide form and composition in a picture. The real leader and the greatest figure in impressionistic painting was Claude Monet (1840-1926) who, in conjunction with his friends Renoir, Sisley, and Pissarro, developed its theories and invented its technical methods. Working entirely in the open air, largely at the Normandy beaches and the little bathing places and open-air restaurants along the Seine, these artists were intrigued by the vibrations of light set up by such fleeting images as the ripples seen in flowing water, the broken gleams of sunlight that played on its surface, the furtive movement of sails across the sea, the warm sun bathing the everyday objects of open-air life, or the cool, wind-ruffled leafage of the trees. They observed that these images changed constantly according to the varieties of light during different times of the day and conditions of the atmosphere; their great desire was to catch at all costs the *impression* of these fleeting, "colored moments."

IMPRESSIONISM AT ITS BEST: WESTMINSTER BY MONET

The peculiar quality of London's "faintly misted light" fascinated the impressionists and, together with their discovery of the English painter Turner's style, strongly influenced their work.

They tried to analyze these vibrations of light and air and to break them up into their constituent parts, calling in new scientific theories to back up their visual observation. In order to get these sensations onto their canvases, they based their idea of divided tones and color splotches on intuitive discoveries inaugurated by Delacroix some time before. These they juxtaposed in such a manner that they became mixed in the eye of the beholder, giving him a sense of light and air and color never before experienced in painting. The great discovery of the Impressionists was thus not only a new concept of space and time, but also a new rendering of light and movement. They avoided the usual subjects common to painting up to that time—literary ideas, classic subjects— as well as the traditional conventions of proportion and balance and form. They tried to make, by their attempts to reproduce the quality of light on various objects, a kind of "painted music." We do not get any idea of ordered structure or calculated design from these paintings—design such as we find in the Italian paintings of the Renaissance, for instance—but we do receive an impression of the scene at the moment the artist looked at it, vibrating with an effect of living light and air.

IMPRESSIONISM IN MUSIC

Debussy felt that this painted music could be of great service in helping him formulate new methods of expression in his own art. As a boy he had had dreams of becoming a painter, and as a mature musician in Paris he had come into direct and fruitful contact with the symbolist poets and impressionistic painters; thus he was particularly qualified to adapt some of their theories to his composing. In general it may be said that Debussy's ideal was to let music convey emotion without using a definite melodic or formal structure, as the impressionistic painters tried to convey their sensations through the eye without using conventional lines, patterns and form. Just as these painters were concerned with the constituent parts of light and were able to duplicate these on their canvases, Debussy turned his attention to the elements which make up chords. Using plenty of dissonances and paying little attention to the grammatical relationship of one chord to another, he placed these in combinations different from those that had been customary. Because of his unusually sensitive ear, he could single out the overtones that make up the timbre of the fundamental notes we hear, mixing and blending these to produce entirely new effects, much as the painters mixed their colors on the canvas. In this way he arrived at the new effects which, with other devices he used—the whole-tone scale (see Chapter 10), extreme fluidity of rhythm, and indefiniteness of melody—give his music its marked individuality. Thus Impressionism in music, especially in orchestral and piano music, developed as a style lacking the strict formal organizations of the symphony, sonata, and the like and intended to invoke a mood in the listener and convey associations outside the purely auditory meaning of the music. In both content and form, it paralleled the Impressionism of the painters.

L'APRÈS-MIDI D'UN FAUNE

Debussy's effects may be heard at their best in his masterpiece, *L'Après-midi d'un faune*,[2] written in the years 1892-1894, when his genius was in full flower. There is little that will trouble us in understanding and liking this wonderful tone poem today, although for many years after its first performance it was considered extremely daring music. This is program painting that conveys the emotional suggestions of a landscape rather than attempting to re-create it in musical terms. Prunières' phrase is a happy one: this is music which in order to be sensuous, poetic, and supremely effective is developed, not according to fixed formulas but simply and logically in accordance with the poetry it seeks to express. It is a synthesis by which one is transported to another world, one which can hardly be reached through either the art of poetry or music alone. Olin Downes speaks of his vivid remembrance of first hearing this music, the indescribable beauty and elusiveness of its instrumentation and the impossibility of recalling, at first, a single note. Probably everyone has a similar experience the first time he hears the piece. With the very first summons of the magic-flute passage at its beginning, Debussy's score takes us completely out of the mundane back to the sunlit slopes of Greece; this is music unlike any other in the world—pagan, full of the spirit of an ancient beauty. A dreaming faun, a child of nature in the shape of man with the horns and feet of a beast, lies slumbering in the noontime heat. The "arid" flute announces the principal theme (1-4):

Full of a desire in which there is a strange tenderness and melancholy (the "memory of the dream in the flute," as Debussy expressed it), oboes, clarinets, and French horns respond, and their chords, flooded with limpid harp tones, sustain the mood and heighten the impression of the opening measures. The rhythm fluctuates between 9/8, 6/8, 12/8, 3/4, and 4/4. The call becomes louder and more urgent, but dies away to let the flute again sing its song. A clarinet solo begins a new section (32), with a theme very much like the first in content, accompanied by fragmentary bits from the harp. Then we hear the oboe with a new theme (37), again strangely like the first in outline:

A lively dialogue follows (44); the music is marked *toujours en animant*, leading directly to a third theme on the wood winds: flute, oboe, English horn, clarinets (55)—a theme which could be said to suggest desire satisfied.

Then the principal climax of the whole is gradually built up, and the first theme returns, more languorous than ever (79); it is flutteringly repeated by the oboe and answered by the lightest chords imaginable from the whole orchestra. New chords are heard, as harp glissandi suggest the fleetness of the passing vision (86). At last a solo cello joins itself with the flute (100), and then an unforgettable passage for muted horns and strings brings the whole work to a conclusion in which the music seems simply to vanish. It hardly seems possible that there are only a hundred and ten measures in this score; never has such economy of means produced such wealth of beauty. Every measure is telling, nothing is wasted; the whole stands as fitting monument to a composer who was master of a style almost too fragile and delicate for survival in this practical world.

DEBUSSY'S *NOCTURNES*

Aside from *L'Après-midi d'un faune* and his great opera, *Pelléas et Mélisande*, Debussy's best-known work is a set of three orchestral nocturnes: *Nuages*, *Fêtes*, and *Sirènes*. These, on first hearing, may seem to lack the unity and coherence which is so striking a feature of the Faun; we hear melodies unlike any with which we are familiar, and the various sections of these nocturnes seem unrelated, the instrumental combinations without apparent reason. Yet if we consider these pieces as impressionistic suggestions with a sense of beauty that is only half uttered, as musical excursions into the realms of the imagination, their difficulties will quickly disappear. Of the three, the second is best known, perhaps because it is the most tangible. It is astonishingly vigorous for Debussy, for most of his music is so indefinite and intangible that it lacks force and power. Nevertheless, the pageants which the composer unfolds for us here are visionary ones; they are the imaginative and yet frightfully real spectacles such as are revealed only to the mind of the mystic. These are visions like Francis Thompson's *Hound of Heaven* or those of which William Blake spoke: "Is it not reasonable to suppose that we can create by the working of the mind forms stronger, clearer, and more moving than anything produced by nature? If not, what is the imagination for, and what in heaven's name is the use of art?"

In notes which he supplied for the first performance of these nocturnes in Paris in 1900, Debussy said that the title is "to be understood in a wider sense than that usually given it and should be regarded as conveying a decorative meaning." In *Nuages* he had in mind "the unchanging aspect of the sky, with the slow, melancholy passage of clouds dissolving in a gray vagueness tinged with white." How marvelously the music brings the sensations of this skyscape to our minds! *Fêtes* is meant to evoke the "restless, rhythmic dancing of the atmosphere, with bursts of brusque light." There is also the episode of a procession—a dazzling and wholly idealistic vision—passing through and blended with the festival. But always the background of the festival remains: "luminous dust participating in the rhythm of the universe." There is little use trying to explain this music—it belongs to the experience with which we are all familiar, experiences that border on the unconscious, hardly definite enough to be recognizable, yet strangely bewildering in their insistent appeal. The third nocturne, *Sirènes* (Sirens), is not often played because it requires a chorus of women's voices in addition to the orchestra. It has been the source of the mysteriously hummed backgrounds of many a moving picture; but it is wonderful music in its own right and should always be included with the other two when the set is played.

THE LATER YEARS

Later on, Debussy's music became somewhat more tangible and realistic: *La Mer* is a powerful evocation of the spirit of the sea in a big-scale, symphonic manner, full of the drama and color and mystery of its subject and showing how well the impressionistic style can fit large canvases. *Ibéria*, the middle work of his orchestral triptych called *Images*, is a dazzling summation of the spirit of Spain. Although Debussy did not know this country first hand, his imagination was so vivid and his art so subtle that we get from the three parts of this orchestral picture, "In the Streets and Byways," "The Fragrance of the Night," and "The Morning of the Festival Day," a vivid picture of the many aspects of this fascinating country, which seemed to be of special interest to the impressionists—its fragrant old gardens, the intoxicating spell of its nights, its riots of color, its animated rhythms, and its gorgeous national festivals.

Because the piano is an instrument peculiarly adapted to the manner of the impressionists, Debussy devoted a great deal of time and attention to the development of a characteristic piano style. He developed sonorities and effects quite at variance with the accepted traditions of the instrument up to that time, and many feel that the short program pieces he wrote for this instrument represent Impressionism and Debussy and the piano at their very best.

It is sad that in Debussy's later years his composing, which up to that time had seemed so fresh and spontaneous, degenerated into mannerisms and formalistic copying of earlier styles. Domestic troubles, sickness, and, above all else, World War I influenced his life and his creative powers. During the last six years of his life he produced in obvious haste, realizing that his days were numbered; none of these compositions compare with those written in the great days of his power. At his best, he was one of the great masters of his art, enveloping his music in a mysterious haze that is full of luminous color. He viewed the world largely from the viewpoint of the mystic, with little desire to mingle in it. There is also a peculiar sadness, a brooding for things that might have been, in much of his work. Certainly all its seeming mistiness and haziness is attained by means of a technical structure that is taut and clear, a structure that would seem to assure this music of immortality. How this was attained was a secret that perished with Debussy, for none of his followers was able to equal this phantasmal, chimerical, marvelously constructed music. Perhaps it is just as well; otherwise, as someone has wisely said, we might all become lotus-eaters!

CHARACTERISTIC WORKS OF DEBUSSY
(*not including the piano pieces*)

Printemps (Spring), 1886
An interesting example of the beginnings of the composer's personal style, this is the first work for orchestra which he permitted to be published. Written when he was still a student in Rome, it contains a not-too-well-digested mixture of romantic style and impressionistic technic.

Prélude à l'après-midi d'un faune, 1892-4
Why Prelude? Debussy expected to follow this with other evocations based on Mallarmé's poem: *Interlude* and *Paraphrase* were never written.

String Quartet in g minor, 1893
This has been called "the most distinguished piece of chamber-music writing in the French repertoire." Only faintly tinged with impressionism.

Pelléas et Mélisande, 1902
Fortunately for opera lovers, this masterpiece has been well recorded in full. One of the greatest of all operas.

La Mer, 1904
The titles of these three symphonic sketches are explicit enough:
1. *De l'aube à midi sur la mer* (From Dawn until Noon on the Ocean)
2. *Jeux de vagues* (Sport of the Waves)
3. *Dialogue du vent et de la mer* (Dialogue of the Wind and the Sea).

But otherwise there is not a programmatic idea in the whole work, even though a contemporary critic wisecracked that he liked particularly in the first movement the part at a quarter past eleven. A magnificent calling-up of sensations and images.

Images pour orchestre (Images), 1906-12
1. *Gigues*
2. *Ibéria*
(a) *Par les rues et par les chemins* (In the Streets and Byways)
(b) *Les parfums de la nuit* (The Fragrance of the Night)
(c) *Le matin d'un jour de fête* (The Morning of the Festival Day)
3. *Rondes de printemps* (Spring Roundelays)

TOPICS FOR DISCUSSION

Discuss the close interrelation between nineteenth-century French art forms—music, poetry, painting, sculpture.

Try to define the subtle elements in *L'Après-midi d'un faune* by which Debussy sought to arouse emotions similar to those engendered by Mallarmé's poem. Can you compare his methods here with those of his other works, for example, *La Mer*?

How far can Debussy convey his impressionism in a string quartet which is not based on a particular poem or program?

Discuss the differences between Debussy and Liszt.

CHAPTER 24

Impressionism (continued)

≈§ß≈

PIANO STYLES OF DEBUSSY AND RAVEL

A good connecting link between Debussy and his greatest contemporary (although not a real disciple), Maurice Ravel (1875-1937), is the music they both wrote for the piano. Most of the nineteenth-century piano composers—Beethoven, Schumann, Liszt, and even Chopin (although he did make some wider experiments)—wrote music that, lying largely under the fingers, came to be thought of as indigenous to the instrument. This conventional style of writing consisted largely of scale and arpeggioed passages alternating with sustained melodies and chords; it came off well, made a brave show, and thus was widely popular. Debussy and Ravel, both of them pianists of considerable ability, became impatient with this orthodox kind of writing and substituted ideas of their own: new and largely dissonant chords, with little attention to their "grammatical" progression; unusual melodies and accompaniments containing plenty of "alien" notes; the blending together of unusual and unexpected tonal and rhythmical combinations; and (like their contemporaries in painting) constant insistence on color as an important constituent in expression.

Such color effects could easily be obtained on the piano through the proper use of the damper pedal, and they came to be considered a hallmark of impressionistic pianism. New technical resources on the part of the player had to be developed in order to make these effective, and consequently we have had such impressionistic specialists as Walter Gieseking—strange to say, a German.

DEBUSSY

The development of Debussy's piano style can be easily traced, beginning with the rather romantically conventional *Arabesque* and the lovely *Suite bergamasque* (containing the popular *Clair de lune*), both of them quite in the salon style of the popular French composer Massenet, with but a touch of the genius that was to develop later. In 1902 he wrote a suite *Pour le piano*, which gave more of a hint of this genius, although there was nothing particularly startling except the *Sarabande*, with its archaic flavor, obtained through the use of an old dance rhythm combined with seventh and ninth chordal dissonances. Not until 1903 did Debussy, in the words of one critic, catch up with himself, insofar as piano music was concerned. By this time, we must remember, he had written *L'Après-midi*, *Pelléas et Mélisande*, the *Nocturnes*, and was busy with *La Mer*. In that year he published *Estampes*, consisting of three numbers: *Pagodes* (Pagodas), built on a five-toned Oriental scale and wonderfully atmospheric; *Soirée dans Granade*, in which Debussy, in his attempts to capture Spanish color, comes close to imitating an early Ravel *Habanera*, later incorporated into that composer's *Rapsodie espagnole;* and *Jardins sous la pluie* (Gardens in the Rain), with its shimmering aqueous effects that were certainly adapted, to say the least, from Ravel's *Jeux d'eau*, which had been performed two years before. *Estampes* is real Debussy, the creation of a temperament of a Chopin subjected to impressionistic influences; as someone has well said, Chopin makes poetry with the piano, Debussy paints with it.

Many of the twenty-four *Préludes* (1910-1913) are hardly more than miniatures, although the two books in these collections contain some matter of considerable importance. *La cathédrale engloutie* (The Submerged Cathedral) is based on an old Breton legend of a city submerged beneath the waves, with the myriad sounds of its daily life coming up from the bottom of the sea; bells toll, and the sound of a Gregorian Chant is heard. To obtain an idea of the difference between an essential piano style and an orchestral one, compare the orchestral arrangement which has been made of this piece with the original version. Such a comparison will by no means be all in favor of the orchestral version!

Another pertinent comparison is that between Debussy's idea of *Ondine* (*Préludes*, Book II, No. 8) and Ravel's program piece of the same name in his *Gaspard de la nuit*. *Ondine* is a version of the water sprite legend; in Debussy's piece she is graceful, sensuous, imaginative; in Ravel's hard, glittering, and detached. The difference is characteristic.

RAVEL

Ravel, born thirteen years after Debussy, was as essentially French as his predecessor (who delighted to sign himself Claude Debussy, *Musicien français*). Ravel made use of many of the same devices of impressionism in his writing, but his music has sharper outlines and more developed contrasts. In some ways it is easier to grasp, for he paid considerable attention to formal outlines, often using the conventional forms which classic composers had employed in their works. He had little of the Debussian sense of the mystery of life; rather, was he a detached, cool-headed, keen-witted observer, enjoying life sensuously in much the same way as did the Impressionistic painters. One feels that his aestheticism was very similar to that of Cézanne, who said that he wished to make of Impressionism an art that was "solid and durable." Certainly Ravel's best-known orchestral works are solid and durable in a sense that Debussy's are not.

Ravel's piano piece *Jeux d'eau* (The Fountain) has been mentioned; it is a lovely piece of program music with a program taken from a quotation descriptive of a fountain set in the midst of an old formal French garden, its figure of an ancient god happily spouting jets of water high into the air, where they are dissipated into soft rainbow clouds of vapor. Ravel has written music that carries out this poetic idea magically and yet carefully follows a set, formal scheme—the sonata form, if we dare to analyze it! The whole piece is largely an exploitation of one chord, the chord of the "ninth," as theorists call it. This chord may be found at the piano by starting with C and then playing in conjunction E, G, B flat, and D; out of it the composer weaves the loveliest of liquid sounds and color combinations. This is a dazzling little work, and it needs consummate technic on the part of the player who attempts it.

Pavane pour une infante défunte (Pavan for a Dead Princess) is another example of the combining of classic form and modern expression; one of Ravel's earliest popular works, it is an elaboration of a stately Spanish dance form current in the sixteenth and seventeenth centuries. Here again is a solidity of structure that readily allows us to understand the rather novel musical speech of the composer. The speech may be new and curiously original, but the language is the same as served the greatest of the old masters. Ravel makes use of the rondo form here, the leading theme returning time after time, like a sort of refrain.

Those who would familiarize themselves with this composer's stylistic development will find it clearly documented in his works, beginning with the *Rapsodie espagnole* (1908). This, a four-sectioned piece of program music, shows the Spanish influence which pervades so much of Ravel's writing, an influence natural enough, since he was born in the Basque country whose inhabitants show both Spanish and French characteristics. This mysterious, rapturous music is perhaps the best atmospheric musical picture we have of that strange land.

RAVEL'S ORCHESTRAL MASTERY

Daphnis and Chloe is the title of an ancient Greek pastoral poem, the story of two lovers, children of a goatherd and a shepherd. A more modern version written in the sixteenth century has been the inspiration for a number of works, among them the ballet for which the Russian producer Diaghilev in 1912 commissioned Ravel to write the music. This ballet was not a success, although the music shows its composer at his very best. He salvaged some of the music and made it over into two orchestral suites which, especially the second, contain a great deal of atmospheric and colorful music. The three sections of the *Second Daphnis and Chloe Suite* are: (1) *Lever du jour,* surely the most colorful sunrise ever suggested by music; in its suggestive rather than depictive powers, it can well be compared to Richard Strauss' stupendous beginning of *Also sprach Zarathustra;* (2) *Pantomime,* a necessary lessening of the tension before (3) *Danse générale,* a magnificently rhythmed, almost frenzied display of impressionistic technic. All three sections show Ravel's absolute mastery of his orchestra, an essentially aristocratic way of scoring, detached and cool, yet with the full exploitation of the possibilities of each instrument; the score glows with color and pulses with varied rhythms. In nothing else that he did was Ravel so human and warmly appealing.

La Valse, written in 1920, shortly after World War I, shows the natural disillusionment of the postwar period but is vivid with tonal hues and orchestral color. An inescapable feeling of bitterness and cynicism in its scraps of Viennese waltz tunes shining through an impressionistic mist makes a striking comment on the spirit of futility and nihilism that follows great wars. The *Bolero* is largely a mechanical, crescendo repetition of a rather obvious Spanish-like tune. Written in one key throughout, the instrumentation piles up in intensity and explodes, with a sudden change of key, at the very end. It was composed on the particular order of a rather eccentric dancer featured in Paris in the 1920's; and because of its strong rhythmic appeal, it has become popular—another example of a composer's being best known by one of his weakest works.

A SYMPHONY IN THREE SPANISH GARDENS

Manuel de Falla's music is a happy combination of Impressionism and Nationalism. Making use of many of the technical devices of Debussy and his followers, this composer infused a peculiarly Spanish idiom into all his work. To most of us the very name Spain spells romance—the land of the fabulous adventures of Don Juan; the magic stage on which Don Quixote and his faithful Sancho played out their immortal drama; the trysting place of the gypsies of Borrow's fascinating travel tales; the home of Carmen and her castanetted rhythms, of the multicolored, cruel bullfight, of proud arrogance and fiery love. Spain arouses in our minds memories of soft music sounding through warm nights, visions of the Alhambra outlined against the radiant Andalusian sky, reminiscences of a glory that is past forever. It is this sort of thing that we listen for in Spanish music—and with good reason. One of the most important factors which influence the popular conception of a nation's characteristics is the music it has produced. Naturally, the connection between the songs (together with the verses to which they are set) and the thoughts and feelings of those who sing them is very close. It was a wise rather than boastful historian who said: "Tell me what sort of songs a nation has produced, and I can tell you what sort of nation it will become." The music Spain has given the world is full of a soft, undulating, poetic suggestiveness quite in line with the popular conception of the country as a land of romance. This is meant in no derogatory sense; despite the fact that she has produced no great international figures in music, Spain is a musical country. Her genius has been for glorified dance forms, descriptive music, and charming, graceful, sentimental songs. It is in her sense of rhythm that she stands supreme, and much of the attractiveness and appeal of Spanish music arises from this.

Luckily for us, the popular music of Spain has not been ruined by academic influence, but has been preserved almost intact and unharmed. Before any movement for the cultivation of the music of the Classic composers of other countries could gain much headway among the Spanish, they had become aware of their own genius, and educated composers made no attempts to write after the manner of Bach and Beethoven. The music of the best modern Spaniards, men like Falla and Albéniz, although showing unmistakable influences of their neighbors the French, is peculiarly indigenous to Spain. The three numbers in Falla's suite *Nights in the Gardens of Spain* seem like a re-creation of the popular soul of the composer's native land. Although based on rhythms, scraps of melody, and cadences peculiar to the folk songs of Andalusia (the southernmost part of modern Spain), this music never copies these songs exactly. If you can imagine an Andalusian trio of two mandolins and a guitar playing these folk songs in one of the old, moonlit gardens of southern Spain, you are in the proper mood for the enjoyment of this music. Although, as he himself has told us, the composer has followed a definite design as regards tonal, rhythmical, and thematic material, this design need not trouble us just now; it is sufficient for us to realize its presence, furnishing a unifying skeletal background for the whole. The end for which the music was written is that of "evoking the memory of certain places, sensations, and sentiments"—an end much more in accordance with the real province of the art than that of mere description. In the orchestration, although Falla uses no unusual instruments other than the piano, we hear many effects peculiar to the popular Andalusian mandolins and guitars.

The first number, "At Generalife," introduces us to those romantic gardens on a hillside overlooking the Alhambra—the most beautiful spot in Granada, if not in all Spain. When we first hear the music, it seems as if it had already been playing for some time, for no attempt is made at an introduction; the music simply starts. We are set down in the midst of this picturesque setting, and memories of the ancient courts of Moorish kingdoms in Spain float before us in the melodies and rhythms. Granada at the height of its glory has returned; under the long dynasty of the Nascides, greatest of the Moorish rulers in Spain, it has become the center of Spanish culture, patron of Arabic art and learning, proud possesser of the Alhambra, its royal castle which seems like a realized vision of *The Arabian Nights*. These Oriental melodies, with their tinkling, mandolin accompaniments, suggest that all about us are gardens with gushing fountains, dreamy patios, melancholy cypress thickets, and flowering pomegranates, much the same as they were when they belonged to the summer palace of the Moorish kings above us on the hill. Ghosts of the past are everywhere; here under a six-centuries-old cypress was, perhaps, the trysting place of the Sultana and Hamet, head of the noblest family of the kingdom—a tryst which, like that of Tristan and Isolde, was destined to cost the life of the King's trusted courtier.

The music comes to a pause, and we are transported to another garden for the second part of the suite—"Dance in the Distance." About us again are the orange trees, the myrtles, and the palms, the rushing and splashing of water. In the distance we hear the music which accompanies a series of dances, the mandolins sounding scraps of Oriental tunes. One dance follows another, the rhythmic figures changing in quick succession and whirling to an excited close.

Suddenly—this time without any break in the music—we are "In the Gardens of the Sierra at Cordova." The owners of the gardens are hosts to a gay party: gypsy musicians play a *zambra*, sing and dance. (It is interesting to recall the fact that the gypsies came into Spain from the East at about the time the Catholic sovereigns were trying to force out the Moors—the fifteenth century.) Happy shadows flit about under the trees; the wines, set out on the long tables, flow freely. There are wild rhythms, rude songs; a dancer steps out, her stamping feet and alluring gestures flash in the moon-light. Although very few of us have experienced a night like this, we are like the sleeper awakened in *The Arabian Nights*, for we hear and see things with other senses than our own, and yet with senses which we realize all the time to be our own.

It is a dream, and yet we know it to be real, brought to us by the magic of this composer who has made his music able to circumvent the barriers of time and space, and who has brought us directly into touch with the beauty of his own people, a beauty which will last as long as romance holds its spell.

ADDITIONAL EXAMPLES OF RAVEL'S AND FALLA'S STYLE

Gaspard de la nuit   RAVEL

We have already mentioned the first number, *Ondine*, of this fiendishly difficult pianistic excursion into the realm of the fantastic. Based on poems by Aloysius Bertrand, these pieces require not only an interpreter capable of brilliantly conquering Ravel's peculiar technical demands, but also an imagination that gives them their proper eerie quality. In the second, *Le Gibet* (The Gallows), a mournful one-toned bell sounds throughout, forming a central pivot point for Ravel's astonishing macabre fantasy. *Scarbo*, the third, is a grimacing will-o'-the-wisp, who is finally blown out like the flame of a wax taper.

L'Enfant et les sortilèges (The Child and the Sorcerers)   RAVEL

This peculiarly French ballet-opera telling the story of an evil-minded youngster, who delighted in torturing the animate and inanimate objects of the nonhuman world about him until they, in desperation, turn on him and force him to repent the evil of his ways, is characteristic of Ravel. Never entirely human, delighting in all sorts of depiction of mechanical details, cynical, fanciful, and witty by turn, this music is typical of Parisian artistic attitudes of the early decades of this century. Its most famous section is the fanciful love duet between two cats; its most imaginative the section descriptive of the sounds of the tiny night animals. It needs a good imagination on the part of both the interpreters and the hearers.

Three Cornered Hat: Dances   FALLA

Like most composers of ballet music, Falla has made use of the lively, exuberant music from his rather bawdy ballet, *Three-Cornered Hat*, for a concert suite. The three dances usually heard are: (1) *The Neighbors*, (2) *The Miller's Dance*, and (3) *Final Dance*. All are authentically Spanish in quality.

El Amor Brujo (Love the Magician): "Ritual Fire Dance"   FALLA

Another example of a composer's being known by a work of comparatively inferior quality, this, originally for orchestra, makes a fiery virtuoso piece for the piano, with plenty of percussive noises and strong rhythmic verve. Hence it is popular.

TOPICS FOR DISCUSSION

Compare, according to your knowledge of their works, the aims, styles, and values of the music of Debussy and Ravel. Which do you think most representative of French culture and of the French mind? Does one look forward and the other backward? Has either ceased, wholly or partially, to represent the artistic "movement" of his period?

What are the special attractions of the art of Falla? Are there, in your opinion, any weaknesses in his and other composers' cult of Spanish nationalism? Are these inherent in that country's folk music, or in the composers' treatment of it?

An English critic has said: "It matters not that we can transpose the titles of *Nuages* and *Fêtes* (two of the orchestral nocturnes), call each by the other's name and see in the magic fanfares of the second the pageant of cloud and sky or hear the echoes of rejoicing in the first." Discuss, in this connection, the value and meaning of attaching definite titles to such movements.

Why, after lingering in obscurity, did Spanish music so pleasingly excite nineteenth-century musicians?

Why is Falla's music so engaging? Does any other Spanish composer seem as pleasing to you?

CHAPTER 25

More About Nationalism

꧁ ꧂

MOUSSORGSKY'S MASTERPIECE

We left our earlier discussion of Russian nationalism with only a mention of the greatest of all the Russian Nationalists, Modest Moussorgsky (1835-1881). Working largely in dramatic and program styles, and in spite of a weakness of character which strewed his life with the "ruins of large enterprises abandoned at various stages of completion," he left behind one of the most vital and truly revolutionary compositions in the history of music in his opera *Boris Godunov*. This is true in spite of the fact that many of the most individual and expressive aspects of the original have undoubtedly been smoothed over and ironed out in the version most commonly used in the opera houses of the world—the revision and reorchestration by his friend Rimsky-Korsakov.

Moussorgsky wrote his own libretto based on a drama by Pushkin relating the most important episodes in the life of Boris Godunov, the regent who ruled Russia in the days immediately following the reign of Ivan the Terrible. Whether or not this sixteenth-century tyrant murdered the six-year-old czarevitch in order to gain the throne seems a debatable historical point, but Pushkin's treatment of the story and Moussorgsky's opera revolve around this incident and are filled with the remorse of the czar at the thoughts of his crime. A pretender appears in the form of a dissolute monk, Gregory, who claims to be the czarevitch grown to manhood; the Poles and the Cossacks follow him, and the Russian peasants revolt because of their sufferings under Boris. No longer able to face his adversaries, Boris is driven almost insane with remorse. Not a pretty story, but one filled with gloom and anguish and somehow strangely prophetic of the peculiar fate of the tortured Russian people. Out of it Moussorgsky wove a tremendous score in which the true hero is the chorus, representing the people in their struggle for freedom.

In the beginning of the opera the people cry to Boris for help:

> *To whom abandon us, Father,*
> *Unto whom dost leave thy people, O Provider?*
> *We are all poor orphans,*
> *Poor and defenseless!*
> *Yes, we entreat thee,*
> *Implore with tears,*
> *With hot, burning tears:*
> *Pity us, pity us, pity us!*
> *Master and Father!*

And later, at the coronation in the Red Square in Moscow, after one of the boyars shouts: "Long life to Czar Boris Feodorovitch!" they sing:

> *As the sun is resplendent in heaven with glory,*
> *Glory! Just so is Czar Boris in Russia.*
> *Glory! Glory!*
> *Long life and good health,*
> *Our Czar and Master,*
> *Sing, rejoice, ye people,*
> *Sing, rejoice, ye true believers!*
> *Let us extol our Czar Boris,*
> *Hail our Czar Boris Feodorovitch.*
> *Glory, Glory, Glory!*

The newly crowned Boris appears and addresses his people in one of the greatest bass arias in all opera, full of the spirit of foreboding and gloom so characteristic of the Russians:

> *My soul is rent!*
> *Against my will, ill-omened dark forebodings*
> *Oppress my heart.*
> *O blessed One!*
> *O Thou, my reigning Father!*
> *Thou seest in heaven faithful subjects' tears!*
> *Look down on me and send a blessing from on high*
> *Upon my kingdom,*

> *That I may be benign and just as you*
> *And with glory rule my people.*
> *Now let us go and kneel in prayer*
> *Before the tombs of Russia's sovereigns.*
> *And the people all shall feast,*
> *All from Boyar to lowliest beggar,*
> *All shall find room, all are welcome*
> *As my honored guests.*

> Chorus: *Glory! Glory! Glory!*
> *Long life and good health, our Master,*
> *As the sun is resplendent in heaven with glory,*
> *Glory! So is Czar Boris in Russia.*
> *Glory! Long may he reign,*
> *Glory! Glory! Glory!*

Another great bass solo number, giving some of the facts of Boris' ill-starred reign, is heard in Act II. Tormented by his guilty conscience, Boris pours out his soul in this monologue, which seems to foreshadow Russian history several centuries later:

> *I have attained the highest power,*
> *Six years I have reigned peacefully,*
> *But there is no happiness in my troubled soul.*
> *In vain the soothsayers promised*
> *Long life and long reign, unmolested.*
> *Nor life, nor power, nor illusion of glory,*
> *Nor mob acclaim can rejoice me.*
> *In my family I sought consolation,*
> *I prepared my daughter a marriage feast,*
> *For my Czarevna, my pure dove.*
> *As by a tempest, the bridegroom was carried off. . . .*
> *Thus the heavy hand of Justice*
> *Is dreadful on my guilty soul . . .*
> *Impenetrable darkness enfolds me,*
> *If only there were a ray of comforting light.*
> *My heart is full of sorrow, grieving,*
> *Beating in weariness.*
> *What is this palpitation?*
> *What does it anticipate?*
> *With fervent prayers I implored the Saints,*
> *I hoped to subdue the anguish of my soul.*
> *In all my glory and limitless power,*
> *I, the ruler of Russia, I begged in tears for solace.*

And then the reports:
The Boyars' sedition, Lithuanian plots
And underground intrigues;
Famine and plague, and perfidy and ruination.
Like wild beasts the people stalk through the land,
Hungry, helpless, Russia groans.
And in this bitter agony inflicted upon us by God
To test us for our grievous sins
For all the guilt, they name me
And curse on every square: Boris!
And even sleep brings no rest:
In the darkness of the night,
The blood-stained child arises, with eyes burning
And clenched little fists,
Begs for pity and there is no pity.
A ghastly wound gapes!
A last cry of death is heard.
Oh, my God!

In the last act Boris, full of remorse, dies surrounded by a crowd of his followers, including his young son, Feodore:

Farewell, my son, I am dying,
Forthwith thou wilt begin thy reign;
Seek not to know the path I took to become Czar,
For thee it matters not.
Thou wilt be Czar by thy own rights,
My lawful heir, my first-begotten son.
My son! Child of my flesh and blood,
Do not trust the slanders of the seditious boyars,
Watch with a hawk's eye
Their secret intrigues with Lithuania,
All treason wipe out mercilessly, without clemency!
Strictly examine the people's justice,
Judge without prejudice.
Stand on guard as Defender of the Faith,
Honor all the saints of God with devotion!
God, dispense from Thy unapproachable heights
Thy blessed heavenly light
Upon my innocent offspring,
Gentle and pure;
O guardian angels, shield with your luminous wings
My own, my dear son
From suffering, from evil and temptation.

(The sound of bells and choristers is heard.)
Hark, 'tis the funeral knell,
The funeral dirge!
(*FEODORE: Sovereign, be calm, God will help!*)
No! No, my son, my hour is come—
O God! Woe is me,
Vainly cannot I expiate a sin?
O evil Death! What torment is thy cruelty
Wait for a little . . . I am still Czar,
I am still Czar!
God! Death! (spoken) Forgive me,
Here is your Czar,
Forgive me, forgive me. . . .[1]

The last scene (sometimes these two scenes from Act IV are reversed in performance) shows a snowy forest clearing on the outskirts of Moscow. Full of revolutionary ardor, the people cry "Death to Boris" and welcome the Pretender, who appears and proclaims himself "Czarevitch of all the Russias, Prince of the blood and lawful ruler." As the scene ends, only the poor village simpleton remains on stage; seated on a stone and swaying from side to side, he wails: "Woe to Russia! Weep, weep, weep, ye starving Russian people!"

THE AGE OF TCHAIKOVSKY

Tchaikovsky, one of whose symphonies we shall study later, was not considered a true nationalist by the Kutchka because of his European training and background. With Anton Rubinstein and other followers in St. Petersburg, Tchaikovsky always remained outside the influence of the Moscow Kutchka group, although much of his music sounds very "Russian" to most ears. His great significance as a leading figure in the field of European symphonic music has somewhat overshadowed his importance as a nationalist. Yet there are many elements in his music suggestive of his Russian background: characteristic folk tunes; violent contrasts of mood and outbursts of emotion; materials from Russian sources for his operas. Following directly in his eclectic tradition of superimposing European training and influences on good Russian foundations were Arensky (1861-1906); Glazunov (1865-1936); Gretchaninov

[1] Translated by Alice Berezowsky.

(1864-1956), known for some of the finest Russian church music; Rachmaninoff (1873-1943), whose Romantic symphonies and piano concertos made him extremely popular and very widely copied; Scriabin (1872-1915), whose harmonic inventions, which attracted considerable attention around the turn of the century, no longer seem very important; Stravinsky (b. 1882), one of the leading spirits in twentieth-century music, a true cosmopolite whom we shall study at greater length; Medtner (1879-1951), who has written a number of large-scale works which mix some of the flavor of Brahms with his Russianism; Glière (1875-1956), who, although he composed a glittering program symphony on the life and adventures of the folk hero *Ilya Mourometz*, quite Wagnerian in character, became an important member of the Organizing Committee of the Soviet Composers in 1939; and Prokofiev (1891-1953), who wrote many important works outside Russia but returned there in 1934, simplifying and popularizing his style to be in fashion with the prevailing ideology of the Soviet authorities.

Continuing more in the Kutchka traditions were Liadoff (1855-1914), who wrote orchestral music based on Russian legends; Taneiev (1850-1915), who composed mostly chamber music; Ippolitov-Ivanov (1859-1935), whose researches at Tiflis, studying the native music, produced such picturesque scores as his Caucasian Sketches; Kalinnikov (1866-1901); and the present-day Soviet composers, among the most prominent of whom are Shostakovich (b. 1906), Khachaturian (b. 1903), and Kabalevsky (b. 1904).

Certainly the best known of the modern Russian composers is Shostakovich, a most enigmatic figure in Soviet music. Although he was brought up in the nationalist traditions, his *First Symphony* (1925) shows the influence of central European composers. His opera *Lady Macbeth of Mzensk*, which touched peasant life in pre-Soviet Russia with a fiery finger, created quite a sensation at its first performance in 1934 and was condemned by Pravda as a "leftish mess instead of human music." At various times in his career, Shostakovich, like others (among them Prokofiev, Khachaturian, Shebalov, and Miaskovsky), was considered by the authorities who control art affairs in the U.S.S.R. to have fallen short of the ideals of Dialectical Materialism, the theoretical basis of the policy formulated by Marx and Engels and adopted by the Bolshevik Party when it took power in 1917. According to this theory art, because it is a part of reality, must reflect "objective truth" as well as embody the ideals of social consciousness. In mirroring the reality of life as it is lived in the Soviet Union the composer can project new and powerful *avant garde* ideas only when they are expressed in a language intelligible to the masses of the people, and when they serve the progress of mankind.

This means that music, as well as the other arts, must be made to glorify the New Russia, extol the workman's role in the development of his native land, depict the country's tremendous progress, and express the people's joy and faith in its future. If a creator does this, he is an effective composer, painter, or writer and deserves the support of the state. If he does not, his works are condemned.

Shostakovich's maturity dates from his *Fifth Symphony* (1937) and is characterized by his growing ability to develop his musical apparatus on a large scale, rather than simply to juxtapose borrowed styles, as in his earlier works—the *First Symphony*, for example. In the later works there is a wide difference in quality. The best of them seem to be the *Tenth Symphony* (1953), an epic type of work which, according to one critic, contains his greatest achievement "in beauty of thematic ideas, their expansion, combination and development," and the *Concerto for Cello in E flat*, Op. 107.

Composers like Shostakovich and Prokofiev have managed to interest the world at large by their individual modes of expression. Prokofiev appears, in a suite of program music like *Peter and the Wolf*, to make the best of both worlds, pleasing his fellow Russians, both official and lay, as well as attracting the attention of a large outside audience. His resort in some works to older symphonic fashions (for example, the Classical Symphony), his amusing key-twists and avoidance of extreme dissonance, his rhythmic vim and tuneful style, and the dramatic zest of music like that which he wrote for the film *Alexander Nevsky*, make him a popular composer.

Aram Khachaturian is an Armenian who owes his present standing as much to the encouragement given to culture in the remote Russian republics as to the vivid color he has been able to inject into his music. Although virile, exotic, and engagingly different, such works as the *Gayne* and *Masquerade* suites do not hold up very well under repeated hearings.

The music of a whole host of younger Soviet composers is not very widely known outside Russia. These men, like the Soviet composers already mentioned, exist for the same end as all other individual citizens of the Communist State—the intensification of its power and the spread of its doctrines. The governments of the Communist countries lavish money and privileges on their composers and other artists in a way that seems incomprehensible to the citizens of the democracies. While this government support has yielded important artistic gains, especially in making art and music available to large masses of people, there are basic faults in this role of art in national life.

Everything the artists do, all the creative and interpretative activities of their lives, are directed toward the State. Such complete regimentation, subjugation to control, and consequent loss of the very freedom of thought without which art cannot exist are the prices the Communist artist must pay for the esteem and support given him by a bureaucratic and domineering government. We have always to remember that the creative imagination cannot tolerate ideological fetters without some loss of its vitality.

OTHER EUROPEAN NATIONALISTS

Illustrations of the music of the two best-known Czech Nationalists, Smetana (1824-1886) and Dvořák (1841-1904) have already been given. The particular melodic and rhythmic idioms of their music became widely accepted as part of the European nationalistic tradition and inspired a number of younger Czech composers, such as Joseph Suk (1874-1935), Vitězslav Novak (1870-1949), and Otakar Ostrčil (1879-1935). Leoš Janáček (1854-1928) was the most strongly nationalistic, having achieved, especially in his operas, one of the most convincingly civilized integrations of folk and art styles of all nationalist composers.

Edvard Grieg (1843-1907) was the most popular of the Scandinavian Nationals. His original harmonies, folk-like melodies, and distinctive dance rhythms established his fame far beyond the confines of his native Norway. But Finnish Jan Sibelius (1865-1957), a composer of first magnitude, completely dominated the field of Scandinavian music. The special characteristics of his music, as found, for example, in the *Second Symphony*, strongly suggest the character of his countrymen, as well as their historical and legendary backgrounds. There have been a few other important Finnish nationals: Merikanto (b. 1893), Klami (b. 1909), and Pylkkänen (b. 1918), for all of whom the national romantic tradition is still very much a reality.

Swedish Nationalists include such men as Wilhelm Peterson-Berger (1867-1942), Hugo Alfvén (b. 1872), and Ture Rangström (1884-1947), who enthusiastically declared, "How wonderful it would be if Swedish song, our deepest melodic nature, should try to permeate a Swedish instrumental style with its spirit!"

BRITISH NATIONALISM

If one asks, "What is *British* Nationalism?" the experienced critic in England replies, "Why, that of Elgar and Vaughan Williams—and Delius—and Holst—and, of course, on the Irish side, Bax—" And one has to cry, "Stop! What on earth have all these men in common? Surely they are all antipodal?" So they are, but so are the elements of British character. This is the first step towards understanding the British, if anyone wants to try that difficult exercise!

All these composers have *some* English traits strongly developed, and all differ widely. No British musician could mistake one for the other, or fail to "place" a piece by any of them. There is an essence of each, and few foreigners can distill it. Newman, in commenting on a performance by the famous Toscanini of the *Enigma Variations* by Elgar, said, "We were left with the puzzled feeling that in some curious unanalyzable way this was not Elgar, that something in the blood of the music had been left out of it." And again, writing of Menuhin's playing of the Elgar violin concerto, Newman said, "I feel that now and then the thing was not English, and therefore not ideal Elgar."

ELGAR's *Enigma Variations*

Of the group named above, Elgar, whom many British deem their greatest composer, is the easiest to understand as far as style of writing goes. He was a classical-romantic builder, a good link with Brahms, for instance, though his building material was often much

Sir Edward Elgar

more extensive than any former composer's, and he carried the use of leading themes further than anyone except Wagner. Elgar (1857–1934) stands as one of the few great English composers since Purcell —the first real world figure of British music. In many ways he was the typical nineteenth-century Englishman; in others he transcended typical British traits as far as Shakespeare did (and when we think of "typical" Englishmen, we have to remember Shakespeare as well as the florid John Bull of the cartoons, who really never did represent England particularly well). Elgar was the consummate craftsman, the reserved, proud, thorough gentleman. Underneath his reserve, however, there is a vein of deep and often noble sentiment— when he allows us to hear it. To a listener of another nation, this characteristic reserve and careful husbanding of emotional resources are among the most puzzling attributes in Elgar's music. The emotional motivation is so clearly present in all the best things he wrote, that a foreigner cannot but wish that he had sometimes infused a greater warmth and poignancy into his writing. It is worth emphasizing that he was (like more Englishmen than you might imagine) a character full of contradictions.

In hearing such a work as his *Enigma Variations*, we are convinced that, taking the personal and nationalistic traits for what they are worth, it is great music. Elgar's pride of workmanship stood him in good stead here, for he was largely concerned with a specifically musical problem—the writing of a number of variants of a single theme. The theme-and-variation form became unfortunately hackneyed and stylized during the eighteenth century. Elgar, writing in the latter part of the nineteenth century, did not hesitate to employ this old form, and he handled it with such consummate mastery that he produced an outstanding masterpiece. The interesting thing about his treatment is that, although the different variations present in some detail (as we know from Elgar's own program notes) musical portraits of various friends, the whole work is wonderfully effective as music per se. In writing this work Elgar achieved a fine combination of one of the most formal devices of absolute music and a detailed programmatic manner of treatment.

The theme which we hear at the beginning, with its slightly melancholy, serious, reserved character, is real Elgar; it was invented, in the words of the composer, to fit another and greater theme, the latter always remaining unheard—hence the title, *Enigma*. The variations are as different in substance as the idiosyncrasies of the friends they portray; but in all of them we can recognize the contour of the main theme shaping and molding the music, though at times its influence is felt rather than heard.

Here is an outline of the meaning of the variations as given by Elgar some time after the work was published:

1. C.A.E. (the composer's wife). Really a prolongation of the theme, with romantic and delicate additions.
2. H.D.S.-P. A friend who was an amateur pianist and player of chamber music; his characteristic run over the keys before beginning to play is here humorously travestied.
3. R.B.T. A friend who loved to take the part of an old man in amateur theatricals; note the low voice flying off occasionally into falsetto timbre.
4. W.M.B. Portrait of a very forceful squire, gentleman, and scholar.
5. R.P.A. Dedicated to Richard P. Arnold, son of the famous poet Matthew Arnold. "His serious conversation was continually broken up by whimsical and witty remarks."
6. Ysobel. To a feminine friend, an amateur viola player. Out of the

opening phrase, difficult for one beginning string playing, is built a pensive, romantic movement.

7. Troyte. Suggests the maladroit attempts of this friend to play the piano and the efforts of the instructor (Elgar himself) to make some order out of chaos. The final section records the efforts to have been in vain.

8. W.N. The characteristic laugh of a gracious friend, whose personality and beautiful old English home are here suggested.

9. Nimrod. The record of a long summer-evening talk when a friend (A. J. Jaeger) discoursed eloquently on the beauty of Beethoven's music. The opening suggests the slow movement of the Pathétique sonata.

10. Dorabella. An intermezzo of dance-like lightness.

11. G.R.S. To an organist friend: descriptive of his dog's falling down a steep bank into the river (measure 1), his paddling to find a landing place (2-3), and his rejoicing bark on landing (5). "G.R.S. said, 'Set that to music!' I did; here it is,' wrote Elgar.

12. B.G.N. To a serious and devoted friend, a cello player of distinction.

13. Romanza, dedicated to a friend who, at the time it was written, was on a sea voyage. The clarinet quotes a theme from Mendelssohn's overture, *Calm Sea and Prosperous Voyage*.

14. E.D.U. ("Edu," a nickname of the composer). Written at a time when friends were dubious and generally discouraging as to the composer's future. We must remember that he was then about forty; this expresses his determination to win through somehow. References to variations 1 and 9 are heard.

Elgar's other outstanding works are two magnificent symphonies, concertos for violin and cello, and one of the finest, most complex tone poems, *Falstaff*. These are among the greatest musical glories of nineteenth-century Britain.

Delius the Rhapsodist

Nothing could be further removed from the martial side of Elgar's spirit, with which the *Enigma* takes its leave, than the fragrant, delicate beauty of such a work as Delius' *On Hearing the First Cuckoo in Spring* or *The Walk to the Paradise Garden*, an extract from an opera. Here we are in the midst of natural loveliness, distilled into music. English people find that this composer and Vaughan Williams reflect aspects of their own countryside, but that the charm of Delius is universal. His music is emotionally reflective, suggestive of the poetic retrospection inherent in every sensitive person and of spiritual self-communion. As Heseltine, Delius' understanding biographer, put it, "One feels that all his music is evolved out of the emotions of a past that was never fully realized when it was present, emotions which only become real after they have ceased to be experienced. The message of his music is one of ultimate assurance and peace. It is full of a great kindliness which makes us feel akin to all things living, and gives us an almost conscious sense of our part in the great rhythm of the universe."[2]

The beautiful rhapsody *On Hearing the First Cuckoo in Spring* is one of Delius' finest achievements. The musician-poet needs only the title to suggest what evoked this mood in his creative consciousness, and we need no further program to respond immediately and fully to his haunting suggestions. There is no concern here over particularized events, details of thematic structure, or other exterior considerations; we are within the true domains of music. How marvelously its magic images are communicated! With the opening measures Delius evokes immediately the mood of early spring and, by the folkish character of the tune he sings, suggests a northern spring, loveliest of all seasons. The hedgerows are wet with early morning dew, glittering in the warm sunlight; we are greeted with the sweet smell of awakening earth, and from far in the distance comes the sound of the first cuckoo. By means of the constantly shifting harmonies which he supplies to the folk tune Delius works his spell, and we listen entranced, forgetting to be concerned with the minutiae of musical structure. A note of homesickness creeps into the music; these seem to be "home thoughts, from abroad," to use Browning's phrase. There is a suggestion of melancholy, too, as if the composer would hint, with a subtlety beyond the power of words, at that *memento mori* so peculiar to spring—the reminder, in the midst of all the growing strength, of the transitory nature of life. It is the melancholy reflected by Housman:

> *Loveliest of trees, the cherry now*
> *Is hung with bloom along the bough,*
> *And stands about the woodland ride*
> *Wearing white for Eastertide.*

[2] Philip Heseltine, *Delius*. London: 1923.

Now, of my threescore years and ten
Twenty will not come again,
And take from seventy springs a score,
It only leaves me fifty more.

And since to look at things in bloom
Fifty springs are little room,
About the woodlands I will go
To see the cherry hung with snow.[3]

This is a simple, haunting melody which, within its particular milieu, is unequaled. When we tire of the soul-stirring struggles and seek relief from the majestic utterances of the Titans of music, it is refreshing to walk for a while the quiet, dreamy ways with Delius and delight our souls with his fragile, tender beauty. Perhaps the only detail necessary to note is the surety of this composer's expression. Delius does not give the slightest feeling of hesitancy, either in the way he repeats his charming melody or in the way he makes it sing from the orchestra. All is carefully and competently ordered, though there is not the least sign of preoccupation with intellectual manipulation; here we have a happy blending of sensibility and intelligence—a perfect interpretation of the idyllic in terms of music.

CONTRASTED TYPES

Ralph Vaughan Williams (1872-1958) has often been compared to Wordsworth, but he might almost be likened to any poet of nature and philosophic leanings; in his music for the masque *Job* there is something of Miltonic power. *A London Symphony* has been well recorded; but the *Sea Symphony*, a choral and instrumental evocation of Whitman, and the *Pastoral Symphony*, consistently cast in reflective mood and therefore of delight to lovers of nature and of the kind of music that poses no problems, are not so often heard. The composer has not hesitated to carry his love for folk idioms over into the field of opera and has achieved considerable success with his interesting and bustling *Hugh the Drover*.

A friend of Vaughan Williams once said that the very pains this composer took to shed convention and express his innermost feelings tend to limit the appeal of his music to people of like feelings.

[3] *A Shropshire Lad* by A. E. Housman. New York: Holt, 1924.

This may be true of his work up to 1934; then there came a radical change in the *Fourth Symphony, in f minor*. This is a work of violence—harsh, bitter, with tremendous drive, as if the composer would repudiate everything he had written up to that period. Certainly the temper of the times had a great deal to do with its style; its fighting challenge seems part and parcel of the epoch that foisted Fascism and Nazism on an unwitting world.

After this ferocious piece he returned, in his *Fifth Symphony*, written during World War II, to his more peaceful, heart-easing style. Dedicated "without permission" to Sibelius, this work contains a number of high spots: the exquisite slow movement, the rather delicate scherzo, and finale in good Purcellian manner—a series of variations on a ground bass. The *Sixth Symphony*, written in 1947, although it has no program attached, seems definitely to have come out of the composer's war experiences. It has a rather unusual order of movements: a fast, violently agitated first, followed by a peaceful resolution in the second; another fast scherzo (altered after the symphony's publication); then a slow final movement which, in its imaginative conception, its deep emotion, and its strong restraint of expression, is certainly one of the most beautiful episodes in present-day music. Here is a splendid example of what a well-equipped composer can do in the blending of old and new technics to form a really personal means of expression.

Gustav Holst (1874-1934), British in spite of his name, is considered by a few enthusiasts the peer of Vaughan Williams, Bax, and Delius. His music is often austere, sometimes astringent, and, at his broadest, sounds a strongly tuneful British note. He was a lover of the Elizabethans, modeled his music on no very obvious plans of the past, and, at his best, combined austerity with wonderful spiritual insight, as in his choral work *Hymn of Jesus*. *The Planets*, a large-scale suite for orchestra, brought him fame. In his late years Holst wrote little, his austerity grew and so, in the eyes of some, did beauty. There have been many doubters of the permanence of this music, but no one could ever doubt the sincerity and high artistic integrity of the man.

A CELTIC TONE POET

Holst's contemporary, Arnold Bax (1883-1953) represents the Celtic side of the biggest modern British music. There is in him a

certain expansiveness, an efflorescence of subtly expressive ornamentation, a length of wind that sometimes seems excessive, but an
informing richness of spirit. He composed much chamber music
and several symphonies. Every now and then Bax can be gay, as
the jig finale of his *Oboe Quartet* and two of the movements in the
G Major Quartet (to name only a few examples) indicate.

A good idea of his style may be gained from the *Nonet* for flute,
bass clarinet, oboe, harp, and string quartet with bass, one of the
loveliest works in all chamber-music literature.

OTHER COMPOSERS

Mention should also be made of Frank Bridge (1879-1941), a
prolific writer of chamber music, and Arthur Bliss (b. 1891), a composer with ideas of his own. The latter was one of the first English
composers to write good music for the films, and his suite from the
music for H. G. Wells' famous film *Things to Come* is typical of
his vigorous style.

William Walton (b. 1902) was at one time a leader among the
younger English composers. A somewhat skittish, parodic earlier
style, of which *Façade* (1923) is typical, gave place to the deeper
power of such large-scale works as the *Viola Concerto* (1929),
the *First Symphony* (1932), the *Violin Concerto* (1939), and the
Second Symphony (1960). There is also the choral work *Belshaz-
zar's Feast*, a brilliant, even gaudy, evocation of his sharp-edged,
pungent style.

Ernest Moeran (1894-1950) combined a love for folk song with
an Irish background; his chamber music, direct and stylish, is paralleled by part songs owning affectionate allegiance to Elizabethan
feeling. His *Symphony* has a most striking slow movement. Edmund
Rubbra (b. 1901) has written symphonies and choral works with
something of the weight of Brahms, although he occasionally falls
into dourness. An earnest thinker rather than an easy charmer, he
is generally considered one of the most important British composers
of the mid-century. The music of Michael Tippett (b. 1905) is of
harder nature and a strong polyphonic texture. Elizabeth Maconchy
(b. 1907) is one of the few women composers to make a name after
the pioneer feminist Ethel Smyth (1858-1944). Maconchy has
cleverly handled a consistent multi-key style, reminding the listener,

in part, of Hindemith; in quartets she has been forceful, concise, even dramatic.

Benjamin Britten (b. 1913) has had the greatest success in getting his operas produced. *Peter Grimes*, his first big-scale work, based on a poem by the English poet George Crabbe (1754-1832), reflects something of the latter's dark, tragic feeling. *The Rape of Lucretia*, based on the classic Roman legend, remains a rather pallid crossing of oratorio and operatic styles. *Albert Herring*, a "lyrical comedy" of small-town County society in England, is naturally limited in appeal. *Billy Budd* and *The Turn of the Screw* have librettos taken from American authors, while *A Midsummer Night's Dream* is a rethinking of the Shakesperian play. If there are brittle parts in Britten's make-up, there are also indubitable invention and skill in swift evocation with small means—if also, as one feels so often in modern music, with small ideas. Britten's greatest weakness seems to be his inability to come to grips with stirring emotions—a fatal shortcoming in an opera composer!

There seems to be no striking "English" quality in the art of the mid-twentieth century. Of the older founts of inspiration, folk song and Tudor music, the former has trickled into the sands, and the latter has now much less force than the polyphony of the eighteenth century. The trend seems to be toward the mid-European fashions set by Stravinsky, Hindemith, Schönberg, and Bartók, and toward the fashionable atonality.

AMERICAN NATIONALISM

In concluding this chapter we may ask "How about American Nationalism? Is there such an expression in music, as there is in the other arts?" The answer, of course, is yes—decidedly. The particular influences that have helped shape American music are discussed in detail in Chapter 30.

LIST OF SUGGESTED MUSIC

Kamarinskaya   GLINKA

This illustrates what the earliest exponent of Russian nationalism could do in the way of manipulating folk songs.

Islamey, Oriental Fantasy (piano) BALAKIREV
A terrifically difficult piece, after Liszt, which shows the Oriental side of the Russian imagination.

Prince Igor, "Polovtsian Dances" BORODIN
Russian color and rhythmic effects have made this music popular everywhere.

Symphony No. 2 in b minor BORODIN
This is an indication of what this chemist-composer could do in the way of an extended piece of music.

Caucasian Sketches, Op. 10 IPPOLITOV-IVANOV
Easily assimilated program music, the sections are descriptive of Georgian life:
1. In a Mountain Pass
2. In the Village
3. In the Mosque
4. Procession of the Sirdar

Scheherazade
Russian Easter Festival, Op. 36 RIMSKY-KORSAKOV
The first is discussed in the text; the second is hardly more than a splotch of Russian color, but what a gorgeous splotch it is!

Symphony No. 6 (Pathétique) TCHAIKOVSKY
This is the most popular of all Russian compositions, although it is scarcely "nationalistic."

Pictures at an Exhibition MOUSSORGSKY
It is rather difficult to remember that this was originally a piano piece because it has achieved popularity largely through the orchestration which Ravel made of it. It is pure program music, descriptive of various pictures painted by an artist friend of the composer. Especially effective are *Bydlo*, a description of an old Polish oxcart; *Two Polish Jews*, one rich, one poor; and *The Great Gate at Kiev*.

Boris Godunov MOUSSORGSKY
The excerpts from this greatest of all Russian operas discussed in the text are enough to show the essential character of this music, but one should hear the whole in order to realize its cumulative power and unusual appeal.

Concerto for Piano and Orchestra   SCRIABIN
This piece exemplifies a *fin de siècle* type of lush romanticism on an original harmonic basis.

Concerto No. 4, in g minor (piano)   RACHMANINOFF
Here is real Russian nostalgia, deeply felt and wonderfully expressed; whether one likes it or not is a matter of taste. To have heard this work played by the composer was a great musical experience. Fortunately, the symphony and some of Rachmaninoff's other works have been preserved in fine recordings which are readily available.

Symphony No. 3, in b minor (Ilya Mourometz)   GLIÈRE
This is something else again; while based on the adventures of a Russian folk hero, it is largely Germanic in treatment, with resultant gorgeousness of tone and lushness of sentiment which marked the post-Wagnerian style. A rather queer mixture.

The Firebird
Petrouchka
The Rite of Spring (Le Sacre du printemps)   STRAVINSKY
These orchestral suites are all drawn from music originally written for the Russian Ballet, in itself a forceful and moving manifestation of the nationalist spirit. For many listeners these suites must always remain the most characteristic and significant of the great modernist's works. *Petrouchka* is discussed at some length in a later chapter. It contains a wealth of musical ideas, in strange contrast to the spareness of his later works, and a warmth that he later lost completely.

Symphony of Psalms (chorus and orchestra)
Symphony in Three Movements   STRAVINSKY
In these representative post-Rite of Spring works, the composer strives to reconstruct older styles as well as to indulge his late philosophy of composing music "without feeling." In listening to these it may pay to remember the admonition of another famous contemporary: "Artists who want to go back to a period, who try to obey the laws of an obsolete aesthetic or of a novel one, who enjoy themselves in eclecticism or in the imitation of a style, alienate themselves from nature. The product shows it—no such product

survives its time." (Schönberg in *Style and Idea*. New York: Philosophical Library.)

Peter and the Wolf   PROKOFIEV

Childish (in either the real or the sophisticated sense), entertaining, and educational—what more could one ask?

Ala and Lolly "Scythian Suite"   PROKOFIEV

Russian barbarism in the raw, this is a wonderfully effective thriller of about the vintage of Stravinsky's *Le Sacre du printemps* (see above), which latter must always remain the classic portrayal of pagan Russia.

Alexander Nevsky   PROKOFIEV

An example of what film music can be like if the composer really believes in what he writes; composed for Eisenstein's historical film dealing with the thirteenth-century defeat of the Teutonic Knights in their attempt to invade Russia, the descriptive power of this music is enormous. Especially effective are the Battle on the Ice and The Field of the Dead, a vocal lament for those fallen in battle.

Symphony No. 5   PROKOFIEV

One of the greatest achievements of Russian nationalism, although it is much more in the spirit of Western tradition than the Soviet authorities are considered to like. Difficult listening but worth all the time and effort it takes, which can hardly be said for most of its contemporaries. Written in 1944.

Symphony No. 1   SHOSTAKOVICH

Although this student work, written when the composer was only nineteen, shows definite influences of Hindemith, Mahler, Berg, and even Tchaikovsky, it is a striking composition.

Symphony No. 5   SHOSTAKOVICH

Discussed in detail in Chapter 34, this is his most popular work.

Symphony No. 10   SHOSTAKOVICH

This, perhaps his most closely knit work, is of epic quality.

Piano Concerto (1936)   KHACHATURIAN

An ingenious combination of Armenian local color and rhythms with a Tchaikovsky-like European base, and in spite of clever tricks and banalities this is a most effective piece, well-calculated to appeal in rather obvious ways.

Violin Concerto (1940)	KHACHATURIAN
Gayne (Ballet Suites Nos. 1 and 2)	KHACHATURIAN
Jenufa (Opera) (1904)	JANÁCEK
Taras Bulba (1918)	JANÁCEK
Kat'a Kabanova (Opera) (1921)	JANÁCEK
Midsommarvaka No. 1 (Swedish Rhapsody)	ALFVÉN
Enigma Variations	ELGAR
Dream of Gerontius (Oratorio)	ELGAR
Serenade in e minor for Strings	ELGAR
Symphony No. 2 ("London")	VAUGHAN WILLIAMS
Symphony No. 4, in f minor	VAUGHAN WILLIAMS
Symphony No. 5, in D Major	VAUGHAN WILLIAMS
Symphony No. 6, in e minor	VAUGHAN WILLIAMS
Symphony No. 9, in e minor	VAUGHAN WILLIAMS
On Wenlock Edge (tenor, string quartet, piano)	VAUGHAN WILLIAMS

The composer set this beautiful song cycle to poems of A. E. Housman.

On Hearing the First Cuckoo in Spring	DELIUS
Brigg Fair	DELIUS

This rhapsodic series of variations is based on an old English folk song.

In a Summer Garden	DELIUS

We find here as near an evocation of pure emotions as music can ever achieve.

Appalachia	DELIUS

Delius composed this long set of variations on an old slave song heard in Florida.

Sea Drift	DELIUS

Based on a poem by Walt Whitman, the last lines of this choral work seem to summarize Delius' aesthetic philosophy:

O troubled reflection in the sea!
Oh throat, oh throbbing heart!
And I singing uselessly, uselessly all the night.
Oh past! Oh happy life! Oh songs of joy!
In the air, in the woods, over fields!

Summer Night on the River	DELIUS
The Planets (Suite)	HOLST

This suite is made of the best four numbers from the complete set of seven.

Garden of Fand	BAX
Tintagel	BAX
Discourse for Orchestra	BLISS
Façade	WALTON

This setting of Edith Sitwell's expressionistic poems, a good example of the rather skittish art of the 1920's, holds up well, especially if heard with Dame Edith's reading.

Belshazzar's Feast	WALTON

Certainly, this is one of the best of modern choral works.

Concerto for Cello and Orchestra	WALTON
Peter Grimes, Four Sea Interludes	BRITTEN
Young Person's Guide to the Orchestra	BRITTEN
Serenade for Tenor, Horn, Strings	BRITTEN

TOPICS FOR DISCUSSION

What are the strengths of nationalistic art? Its weaknesses?

In these days of rapid communication, do you think a really nationalistic expression in art is possible?

Some people find that, after a time, music based on national idioms loses its interest. Why is this natural? If our own national idioms could be as well defined as the Spanish or Hungarian, should we expect to find them tiring? Is this a general weakness of nationalism?

Why did some countries become so prominent in this nineteenth-century movement? Which of the idioms most attracts you?

How does English music stand up to your impressions of English character? Can you feel the differences among the natures of the people who make up Great Britain—the English, Irish, Scotch, and Welsh?

A few people think Elgar's music is vulgar. Others have found it derivative from other European music. Many British people cherish it, finding in it a good expression of what they think are the British qualities of character. What would you say are the chief differences between listeners which account for these divergent estimates?

Do you consider it important for a nation's composers to make use of folk music?

CHAPTER 26

Beauty

WHAT IS BEAUTY?

Before we begin the study of some of the more "modern" pieces of music, it will be well to ask ourselves why this kind of music, beginning at the start of the century with the works of Stravinsky and coming down to most of the works of contemporary composers, sounds so strange to us. First of all we have to realize that the conceptions of melody, harmony, and rhythm which we hold today have changed throughout the course of the development of the art, and that those used by the more recent writers are entirely different from those with which we are generally familiar. We do not have to listen very long to a piece like the one we are about to consider— Stravinsky's *Petrouchka*—to realize how true this is. There may be formal order and reason here, but it is of a sort difficult for us to find. There is certainly harmony, but it is quite different from that to which we are accustomed; there is melody of an unusual kind, and a peculiar, explosive, complicated set of rhythms. It seems somehow difficult to feel sure that these combine to make music that is worthy of our attention. Is this music anything more than an intellectual exercise done for the gratification of some esoteric individual's sense of pride in his skill? Has it, after everything is said and done, real beauty?

This question, like the famous one propounded by Pilate nineteen hundred years ago, is one that has troubled man ever since he has been aware that "beauty" exists. "What is truth?" and "What is beauty?" are questions that have held a strange fascination for men throughout the centuries. From Aristotle to the Italian philosopher Benedetto Croce, these perplexing questions have intrigued the minds of men, perhaps the more because no real answer is possible. Only the Italians have been wise enough to realize that "truth is a mirage, while beauty, however subjective, is a possession and a reality." Schiller said that truth exists for the wise and beauty for the feeling heart, and Oliver Wendell Holmes said that "beauty is an index of a larger fact than wisdom."

How may we recognize beauty when we encounter it in art? How can it be measured, since it is difficult to find anything which some persons will not declare beautiful, and some—now more, now fewer—ugly? How can there be any hope in trying to ascertain whether or not there is beauty in the music we hear, when one of the greatest artists who ever lived, Anatole France, admits in his book, On Life and Letters: "I believe that we shall never know exactly why a thing is beautiful"? The bewildered amateur listener has every right to ask such questions. As sensitive and thoroughly equipped as critic as Lawrence Gilman tells us that there is no touchstone that will enable us to detect the presence or absence of beauty in a piece of music. No wonder, then, that it is difficult for less experienced individuals to know what attitude to take towards music that they are not inclined to like! A short résumé of the general conception of the philosophers on the whole subject may help clarify this problem.

Two Interpretations: Design or Ethics?

Roughly speaking, there have been two general schools of thought throughout the years as to the nature of beauty. One holds that the intangible quality of beauty in an object lies in the skillful arrangement of its parts in order and symmetry, in repetition of design— in a word, in its form. Kant (1724-1804) in his *Critique of Judgment* correlates design and beauty; the beautiful, he says, is that which shows symmetry and unity of structure "as if it had been designed by intelligence." Beethoven's *Fifth Symphony* to such a thinker would be a work of beauty because of its strongly knit design; its progressive and continuous development from its beginning to its inevitable conclusion; its manifest signs of having been wrought by a great "intelligence." The other great school of thought maintains that the beauty of a thing resides in the reactions which it arouses in the mind of the beholder. Beauty is not intrinsic in the object itself, but has rather an aesthetic existence in the observer's perception. Spinoza (1632-1677) considers "ugly" and "beautiful" to be two subjective terms: "Only in relation to our imagination can things be called beautiful or ugly, well-ordered or confused." E. F. Carritt of University College, Oxford, whose book *What Is Beauty?* contains a good summary of thought about this whole subject, holds as his own belief that beauty is to be found in what is "expressive of feeling . . . when an arrangement of sound, shape, or color seems the natural and not artificial embodiment of an experience." To thinkers of this school, Beethoven's *Fifth Symphony* would be beautiful because of its ability to suggest naturally to the hearer concepts of an experience which he can recognize in it—Fate challenging Man to come out and do battle with his destiny, or whatever else it may be.

There have been other teachings as to the nature of beauty. The Greeks identified it with what is good and often with what is useful. Some of the more poetic thinkers have asserted that beauty and truth are synonymous. Ruskin thought beauty to be a reflection or emanation of divine perfection and so insisted that it is correlated with goodness, a point of view hardly tenable today! Anatole France says that our feeling for the beautiful is our only guide in trying to determine what is or is not beautiful; this is not very helpful, unfortunately, since there are not many men so sensitively equipped as he was. Langfeld, in his *The Aesthetic Attitude*, tells us that beauty is a relationship between two variables: the human organism and the object. The conception which Gilman advises us to hold regarding beauty is that we should not try to speak of it as if it were an absolute detectable quality, "as positively present or absent as the property of roundness in a ball or sharpness in a needle." It can be neither subjective nor objective; neither the result of intellectual and emotional activity nor a value inherent in the object; not dependent entirely either on the person who experiences it or on the thing experienced.

WHAT IS THE MUSICIAN'S SOLUTION?

Although it negates the validity of the contentions of both great groups of thought, Gilman's practical way seems to be the only one

for the music lover to follow. We do not have to hear a great deal
of music to realize that our ideas of beauty can never coincide with
those of others, nor should we expect that they would. To some,
Schubert's music is supremely satisfying in its natural beauty; others
are not so enthusiastic about it. There is beauty in Tchaikovsky for
some, in Stravinsky for others, and there can be no real reason why
we should affirm or deny any of these "beauties." Only by adopting the point of view that whatever beauty there is in music is a
relationship between us as human individuals and the music which
the composer has left us can we proceed to discuss what we hear
intelligently and reasonably. Such a viewpoint clears up the seemingly inexplicable differences of opinion that are constantly arising
among music lovers and critics. A person may be sincerely convinced, for instance, that Debussy's *L'Après-midi d'un faune* is one
of the world's great masterpieces, full of a strange beauty belonging to a world entirely outside our ordinary existence. Another
person may strongly deny this and feel that the texture of the music
is thin, vapid, that its peculiar method of construction does not lead
us anywhere, even that its elusiveness and vagueness are pretenses
for hiding its essential poverty of ideas. At first we are inclined to
say, of course, that either the first man is right and the other so
obtuse that he cannot recognize beauty when it does not conform to
the usual models of Brahms, Beethoven, and Company; or that the
second is right and the first cannot recognize poor music when he
hears it. It is difficult, of course, to put aside these absolute ideas of
music's being either beautiful or not beautiful, for there are so
many times when we feel sure of beauty's presence as in the case of
the music of Bach and Mozart. Yet the wise listener knows that it
must be done; he has learned from experience that often for him
beauty fades out of music which he once thought would hold it to
the end of his days, and that it can come into music which he was
sure could never possess it. The more experienced the music lover,
the less dogmatic his opinions as to whether or not music is beautiful.

There are guides which will help a musical pilgrim through the
confusing thought of conflicting opinions and pillars of cloud and
fire that he can trustingly follow in his long journey. For it would
be ridiculous to suppose that a person's opinions on the beauty of
music are merely a matter of taste, like that in soups, dress, or other

matters of individual opinion. There is, however, one test that we may well apply to the music we hear: Is it alive—does it communicate to us a vividness of life, does it seem as if the creator had been "alive with it at the moment of creation"? As we become more and more familiar with music, we realize the value of such a test: for all the works that have survived the period which produced them certainly do possess this sense of freshness, vividness of life, and feeling of creative vigor. This creative breath exists, of course, in varying degrees; it must have blown with tremendous force when Bach wrote his *B Minor Mass*, or Beethoven his *Eroica Symphony*, or Wagner his *Tristan und Isolde*. It came more slowly and calmly to Brahms as he set down for us the majestic measures of his *First Symphony*, or to César Franck, lovable mystic in his organ loft, as he composed his mighty *Chorals*. We may think it to have become almost somnolent in Debussy as he depicts the pagan pleasures of *L'Après-midi d'un faune* or tells us the sad story of those shadowy, symbolic figures, *Pelléas and Mélisande*. Nonetheless, it breathes through all these works, as it does through the other great masterpieces of music.

MUSIC IN ITS OWN TERMS

There is another reasonable test the listener might make: Does the music keep within the limits of its own element, tone? Does it degenerate into noise or, on the other hand, appeal largely through the intellect? In either case, it is not great music. Apply this to *Le Sacre du printemps:* Does the composer descend to the level of mere noisemaking in his attempts to describe musically the rites of primitive man, or has he overstepped the natural boundaries of tonal possibilities and written music that is largely an intellectual tour de force? In either case, he would exceed the limitations of his material, and the result could not reasonably be called great art.

LIST OF SUGGESTED MUSIC

Le Sacre du printemps (The Rites of Spring)   STRAVINSKY

How are the elements of beauty expressed in this problem in musical aesthetics?

Tristan und Isolde, Prelude and Love Death   WAGNER

Whatever else may be said of it, this is music which certainly possesses the "sense of freshness, vividness of life, feeling of creative vigor."

TOPICS FOR DISCUSSION

Where do you conceive beauty to exist in the mind and intentions of the type of serious composer or artist broadly described as "extremist"?

How is it that lovers of classical or romantic music can definitely describe and account for the beauty they find in that music, while lovers of extremist music seem unable to do so? Is this ability a legitimate standard of beauty?

Can there be a type of beauty which only the composer might find in his work and which he does not expect others to find? How could this aspect of beauty be defined?

If modern artists eschew older standards of beauty, what do they offer in their place? In place of the old "melody," what is the contemporary composer offering?

Compare contemporary advanced music with sculpture and painting. Does the music of today hold the same place as the other artistic expressions?

CHAPTER 27

STRAVINSKY'S *Petrouchka*

૮ઠ ૢ૩ન

STRAVINSKY, A BORN BALLET COMPOSER

Musicians, like poets and novelists, have looked at life and wrought their philosophy in their art. In Beethoven's *Coriolanus Overture* or Brahms' *Tragic Overture* we feel, avowed or tacit, the drama of conflict. In Liszt's *Les Préludes* we have another view of life. It remained for some of the Russian composers in the last century to escape, in their music, into the puppet world of the folk tale and to draw after them the child that is in all of us, as the Pied Piper drew the children of Hamelin. Perhaps in our Western sophistication, we soon tire of some of this gaily colored music, but while its spell works, how delightful to forgo the realities of life and follow the Russian piper!

The music now to be considered, Stravinsky's *Petrouchka*, is a gorgeous specimen of this type of art, showing the composer at his best. It might be said of Stravinsky, as Newman said of Strauss, that he is a clever man who was once a genius. Those who may have disliked his later works, but missed *Petrouchka* and *The Firebird*, will have an altogether different idea of him after listening to these two works, masterpieces in their curious way. In *Petrouchka* Stravinsky identifies himself with the inventor of the folk tale in looking at life with the detached observation of the cynic, amusedly watching the futile, puppetlike activities of the human race. The composer, who wrote this music in 1912, is a typical artist of his time, as all great artists must be. Anti-romantic, realistic, his music is a product of the Machine Age in revolt against the emotional softness and intellectual haziness of its predecessors. Stravinsky, like the contemporary painters, sculptors, and writers, tried to produce an art as free as possible from emotion; an art which concerned itself chiefly with the delivery of its message in the most lucid way possible, adapting its style to the necessities of the occasion and paying little attention to older methods of expression.

This vignette from the hand of a master is a striking commentary on man and the machine, viewed from the vantage point of the twentieth century; no other time could possibly have produced it. It is engraved with real understanding of the human being's essential futility, full of laughter at his unconscious comedy, and tinged with pity at his inevitable fate. As we might expect, the music is as different in its sound from anything we have heard up to this point as the idea back of its conception is different from anything felt or expressed by the Romanticists or the Impressionists. The older ideas of harmonic and orchestral combination are entirely cast aside; new types of dissonant chords are often frantically and forcefully emphasized. Scrappy melodies that are terribly banal in their awkward simplicity (melodies which are in character in *Petrouchka*, but which are Stravinsky's outstanding weakness in some of his other large works); melodies and chords in different keys at the same time; pungent rhythms which, like the chords and melodies, are repeated and repeated—all are characteristic of Stravinsky's style and are used to suit his particular purpose here. There is seemingly no sense of continuity throughout the whole work—everything is reduced to the idea of the moment, without relation to what has preceded or what is to follow.

MUSIC FOR THE RUSSIAN BALLET

Like many of this composer's early works, *Petrouchka* was designed originally as music to accompany one of the colorful Russian ballets. The music is so picturesque and self-sufficient, however, that only a general idea of the ballet scenario is necessary for completely enjoying the work. Alexandre Benois, who was responsible for the development of the story, tells us that some of the music (the *Russian Dance* and *Petrouchka's Cry*) was written before any of

Photo by Merlyn Severn

THE BLACKAMOOR, COLUMBINE, AND PETROUCHKA

the detailed action had been decided on, and the program of the ballet was actually developed around this music.[1]

The story was conceived to represent the old Butter Week carnival held in St. Petersburg and to include a performance of Petrouchka, the Russian Punch and Judy show. It was fitted into four fairly short acts, without any intermissions; the first and last take place at the Carnival Fair, the two middle ones show the interior of the Showman's theater. There are three principals—the puppets commonly found in a Russian Punch and Judy performance: Petrouchka (or Punch), a sort of personification of the spiritual and suffering side of humanity; his lovely Columbine, the incarnation of the eternal feminine; and the gaudy and brilliant Blackamoor, the embodiment of everything senselessly attractive, powerfully masculine, and undeservingly triumphant. These puppets are brought to life at the command of the Showman, and the scenes which tell of their living, working, and dying are interspersed

---

[1] In his fascinating book *Reminiscences of the Russian Ballet*. London: Putnam. The motivation of the story as given here is taken from Benois.

with those which give the atmosphere of the Fair where their little tragi-comedy is played out.

Such a background was ideal for Stravinsky's particular genius, and it inspired him to one of his best efforts. His music tells the story vividly, realistically, with no superfluous touches, no unnecessary details. It has little grace or charm; all its hard, brittle details stand off sharply from one another, but they are nevertheless wonderfully effective. The whole makes a complete picture for those who are able to see the man-machine in all his comedy; the music, written to depict the scenes of an old Russian fair of some hundred years ago, fits just as well the scene of a contemporary amusement park. The essential crudeness of this music, a feeling of servant-girl grace and coachman ardor, a spirit of humanity unloosed from its fetters, make it timeless.

THE VARIOUS EPISODES OF *PETROUCHKA*[2]

The ballet begins with a realistic suggestion of the bustle and confusion attendant on the Fair. A constantly repeated figure suggests the pathetic tawdriness of it all:

From this undulating tonal background there stand out little whiffs of flute melody and a counter-tune on the cellos; the whole is finally crystallized into a real march tune of primitive, folky flavor:

Presently, in the midst of the excitement, there sound the first wheezes of an organ-grinder's tune, with the piccolo and the flute adding appropriate gasps. A danseuse comes tripping up, marking the rhythm of the organ-grinder's tune with a triangle.

Meno moso

Flutes *mf*

Soon another tune from the opposite side of the stage is heard on a music box, all three tunes joining in intermingling counterpoint. In spite of all this excitement, what a world of pathos there is in these cheap organ tunes!

The uproar recommences and continues until a drum roll introduces us to the Showman. Grunts from the bassoons and contra-bassoons, followed by some excruciating chords on the clarinets, horns, celesta, harp, and strings, place him on the scene. He stands in front of his little booth and plays some charming and quite ineffectual arpeggios on his flute. The harsh chords are again heard as he pulls up the curtain and reveals the inanimate forms of his three puppets. Three quirks on his flute summon them to life, and they immediately begin a terrific swirling dance, full of all sorts of ingenious rhythms.

Allegro

Winds, piano *f*

How mechanized the whole dance, the same little tune appearing over and over again, hard and percussive through all its brilliance! The pages of the score here are black with notes; two piccolos, two flutes, three oboes, English horn, three clarinets, three bassoons, four horns, two trumpets, two trombones, xylophone, bells, two harps, piano, in addition to the usual strings, are all kept busy in the mad whirls of this dance. Little scraps of a new tune are heard and reheard, the piano takes up the rhythm alone, and the whole thing suddenly ends in three outlandish chords.

The next scene represents the black room where the Showman imprisons his puppet, Petrouchka, now alive and fully conscious of his surroundings. It opens with a terribly dissonant chord (out of which the whole work originally grew) characterizing the grief, rage, and love, as well as the hopeless despair, of the poor chuckle-head:

A portrait of the Showman on the wall reminds him that he is in his master's power and arouses Petrouchka's indignation when he finds himself in solitary confinement; he shakes his fist at the picture and pours out his maledictions and curses.

The dainty Columbine minces in to the sort of inane melody so often associated with ballerinas:

Petrouchka makes timid advances and is, of course, repulsed—to the accompaniment of a clarinet cadenza. Then follows a section marked in the score, Petrouchka's Despair, amazingly effective and full of real feeling. The hopeless love of the imaginative poet is clearly suggested, with perfect understanding but no wasted sympathy.

This scene is followed by a third entitled *Chez le Maure* (At the Moor's), showing the passion awakened in the ballerina (Columbine) by the foolish Blackamoor. Benois invented a consciously absurd pantomime to start this scene: to a characteristic Oriental-like dance tune, the Moor idles away the time of his confinement within the blank walls of the theater by playing with a coconut:

The Ballerina appears (to a little trumpet melody with drum accompaniment) at the moment of the Moor's wildest ecstasy with the coconut:

She flirts with him, their love-making suggested by a waltz-like theme:

Petrouchka, mad with jealousy, rushes in but is pushed aside by the imperious Moor as the curtain falls.

The last scene contains the *dénouement* of this story of passion and jealousy within the walls of the little theater. We are again in the midst of the Fair. The familiar din has recommenced and grows even louder as the excitement reaches its height in a merry dance of the Nursemaids. The oboe, followed by a horn and then by the strings, plays the infectious tune; a trumpet is heard in another typical Stravinsky melody. At the climax of the merriment, a performing bear comes on (this incident is omitted in some versions) with a high tune for the clarinets answered by growls from the tuba. The festivities are resumed after this momentary interruption; there are other square-cut tunes and heavy peasant rhythms, cheap and tawdry as the rabble they delineate. The Grooms and the Coachmen dance a stolid rhythm, to which is later added the bright tune of the Nursemaids as they join in the fun:

The mirth grows more and more frenzied as a troupe of mummers joins the mad circle. Wild, whirling wood-wind and string figures suggest the antics of these new arrivals, and the concert version of the suite ends on this note. In the complete ballet version, Stravinsky does not have to maintain the fetish of the happy ending and proves himself a greater artist. He uses this frenzy of excitement as the prelude to the final tragedy; a sudden cry from a muted trumpet stops all the excitement. Petrouchka dashes out of the little theater followed by the angry Moor; there is a brief, terrible struggle, and the Blackamoor kills him with a blow from his sword. The final measures, in which Stravinsky expresses Petrouchka's agony and his piteous good-by to life, are among the composer's finest inspirations. We hear a kind of broken sob—produced by throwing a tambourine on the floor—as Petrouchka's soul departs to a better world. But in the end he proves to be immortal, for as the old showman drags the broken doll through the snow, the spirit of Petrouchka suddenly appears above the little theater (to a piercing trumpet melody), and the terrified old man throws down the doll and rushes off. The curtain falls to a suggestion by three horns of the repeated figure heard at the beginning.

Martin Johnson, in his penetrating series of historical studies *Art and Scientific Thought*, defines the central philosophy underlying this gay and tragic fantasy: "There are few modern people who do not occasionally suffer from the disease which Petrouchka symbolizes, the disease of possessing an oversensitive consciousness of ugliness and deficiency without the strength or the wit necessary for escape."

STRAVINSKY'S CAREER AND INFLUENCE

Something needs to be added about Stravinsky's tremendous influence as a composer; in this respect he stands directly in the great line of innovators that starts with Wagner and continues with Debussy. No other twentieth-century composer has exercised anything like the hold he has had on music during the first half of the twentieth century, and it may truly be said that he has changed, for better or worse, the whole course of its development through his influence on composers of recent times. His work divides itself naturally into three periods.

The first is characterized by a style he formed in his native Russia from his experience with Italian opera and the music of the Russian Nationalists (especially that of his teacher Rimsky-Korsakov). Beginning in 1908 with the *Fireworks* and ending with *Le Sacre du printemps* and *Les Noces*, this period contains works of tremendous originality and power, written, as one admirer has said, when Stravinsky was still more a musician than a theorist. There is a richness of musical ideas in these works that he did not permit himself later in his career, as well as a human warmth that he later lost. Although the period includes a variety of styles, the music holds together because it is suggested by life itself rather than by speculations about aesthetics. Some of the most important works of this period are ballets—pure program music. Strikingly original were the polytonal dissonances and the strongly emphasized accents displaced from their usual place in the music's rhythmical structure. New sounds and effects were often introduced, ranging from the delicate sonorities of Impressionism (*The Firebird*, for example) to effects of primitive power and barbaric violence (*Le Sacre du printemps* and *Les Noces*). These works were written for a huge orchestra, with a doubling of the conventional number of woodwind, brass, and percussion instruments, and the introduction of other, rarely used instruments. One feels that the composer wanted to use the massive resources of his huge orchestra to accentuate rhythmic interest, harmonic dissonances, and coloristic possibilities, as well as to communicate Romantic expressiveness.

During the time he was engaged with these tremendous program-style works, Stravinsky began to speculate on the nature of the art of music and came to some rather startling conclusions, which caused a complete change in his style. In this he was unquestionably influenced by the aesthetic atmosphere of the time and place (Paris, 1909-1913) and the ideas of such workers in the other arts as Picasso and Cocteau. He concluded that "music is by its very nature essentially powerless to express anything at all, whether a feeling, an attitude of mind, a psychological mood, a phenomenon of nature. Expression has never been an inherent property of music. It is simply an additional attribute which, unconsciously, only by force of habit we have come to confuse with its essential being."

So this has come to be known as his "neoclassic" period. All sorts of experiments with distinctively dissonant tonalities, "homages" to the styles of composers of other periods, simplification and reduction of performing media, economy of texture in an attempt to make music more purely musical have not endeared most of the music of this period to the average listener. Although he is able to recognize several outstanding works, he is apt to feel that Stravinsky's genius during this time no longer possessed the dazzling glow of his earlier period and that, in general, experimentation often took the place of inspiration and reduced composition to a process of musical essays in pattern, form, and tonality.

In Stravinsky's most recent works his admirers see a third period of his influence, one which brings this attitude of experimentation to bear on forms of the widest range, from ballet to church music, from symphony to opera. Although in general Stravinsky's works may be said to rest solidly on the stability of tonal centers, his latest compositions in this period have embraced the technique of twelve-note tone-row composition employed in the music of Schönberg and his followers. In employing this style, to which hitherto he had been antagonistic, Stravinsky may have come to realize that his "neo" tendencies, insofar as they influence present-day writing, have run their natural course and exhausted their general usefulness.

In the face of so many style changes and different viewpoints in Stravinsky's creative career, it is difficult to come to a definite conclusion as to what the final status of this non-academic, unforseeable, unmistakably original composer will be. Roy Harris has said[3] that many of Stravinsky's admirers have come to wonder whether he will ever find *terra firma*. His various aesthetic attitudes remain as signs of a house badly divided against itself: Super-Expressionism, Neo-Paganism, Neo-Classicism, Neo-Romanticism, Neo-Jazz, Neo-Ecclesiasticism, and most recently, Neo-Serialism—all competing with each other within one artist. What a patchwork of proclamations and renunciations! André Hodeir feels that Stravinsky is one of those exceptional creators who, born during the last stages of an epoch, are responsible for hastening its downfall.[4] Having helped burst the bonds of the older traditions, these "creative destroyers" seem destined to retrace their steps and rehash their own works as well as those of their predecessors. This seems a reasonable explanation of the careers of a number of important contemporary artists, including Bartók and Picasso.

LIST OF SUGGESTED MUSIC

This list of representative Stravinsky compositions, all of them well recorded, will help the amateur listener form his own opinions.

FIRST PERIOD

1908 *Fireworks*

[3] In *Musical America*, May, 1961.
[4] *Since Debussy*. New York: Grove Press, 1960.

1910 *The Firebird (L'Oiseau de feu)*
Either the complete ballet or selections comprising the orchestral suite may be chosen.

1912 *Petrouchka*
Choose the complete ballet rather than the orchestral suite.

1913 *Le Sacre du printemps* (The Rite of Spring)

1918 *L'Histoire du Soldat* (The Soldier's Tale)
This is ballet with speaking parts.

1923 *Les Noces* (The Wedding)
This ballet has a chorus and songs.

Second Period

1920 *Pulcinella*
The composer based this ballet on music by **Pergolesi.**

1920 *Symphonies of Wind Instruments*

1922-1923 *Octet for Wind Instruments*

1923-1924 *Concerto for Piano and Wind Orchestra*

1924 *Piano Sonata*

1927 *Oedipus Rex*

1927-1928 *Apollon Musagête*

1930 *Symphonie des psaumes* (Symphony of Psalms)

1931 *Concerto in D Major for Violin and Orchestra*

Third Period

1945 *Symphony in Three Movements*

1946 *Concerto Grosso in D Major*

1948 *Mass*

1951 *The Rake's Progress*
This late Stravinsky opera was composed after Hogarth.

1954 *In Memoriam, Dylan Thomas* (tenor, string quartet and **four** trombones)

1956 *Canticum Sacrum ad Honorem Sancti Marci Nominis*

1954-1957 *Agon* (ballet)

1957-1958 *Threni id est Lamentationes Jereminae*

TOPICS FOR DISCUSSION

If you have heard other music by Stravinsky, discuss the statement by an English critic that his nickname might well be "What-shall-I-do-to-be-saved?"

What do you think of Stravinsky's philosophy about emotion in music? Discuss his mastery of the technic of composition.

Designate the various types of Russian music developed in the nineteenth century. Do you consider Stravinsky dominant in any one of these?

Note the parallels and differences between *Petrouchka* and *Scheherazade*. Is there a different type of imagination in the two works? Which do you consider the richer from this point of view?

Has Stravinsky's later music proved as interesting as the music of his youth? Has he grown, declined, or just faded? Does he represent strong, persistent Russian traits? Has he persisted in nationalistic expression?

What have been the best and worst influences of Stravinsky on the contemporary world of music? Are they the essence of the spirit of the twentieth century?

CHAPTER 28

Modern Trends in Art

❦

WHITHER, AND WHY?

The works of Igor Stravinsky (born in Russia in 1882) and his most important contemporary, Arnold Schönberg (Vienna, 1874, d. 1951), are important landmarks in music. These men may be said to stand at the parting of the ways. They are the last representatives of a long line which stretches back into the past and contains most of what we consider great in music. Ahead of them is a line which stretches out into the future, tenuous but holding tremendous possibilities of developments as yet undreamed of.

The early works of these composers—things like Stravinsky's *Firebird* Suite and Schönberg's *Verklärte Nacht*—present no difficulties to the average listener. Their later works, however (such things as Stravinsky's *Oedipus Rex* and Schönberg's *Pierrot lunaire*), seem to belong to another and much more perplexing era. We are coming to realize that they represent in time, although certainly not in importance, the culminating point of all the developments of the past.

The listener trying to familiarize himself with the masterpieces of music is apt to halt abruptly and become hesitant about trying to go further when confronted with some of this newer work. He realizes that he has to grow into music and learn to appreciate its qualities and beauties gradually. But, as we have said earlier in this book, there is nothing in the music of Richard Strauss, Wagner, Beethoven, Mozart, Haydn, or Bach that will not yield to such prac-

Courtesy, Museum of Modern Art, New York

PICASSO: THREE MUSICIANS
A cubist style that became more and more overtly neo-classic.

tice and experience. Much of the music written within the first half of our own century, however, is likely to baffle the amateur listener; he senses that he is somehow at a disadvantage with it, like a person lost in a fog without any tangible means of communication with familiar surroundings. And he is right! This figure of his being lost in a fog is an apt, if crude, description of most listeners' reaction to the music produced in the period beginning with the works of Schönberg and Stravinsky, the composers who broke so strongly with past tradition at the start of the century. In our attempt to find out why this is true and what the listener may do to rid himself of this sense of puzzlement, we should first of all realize that modern music has but followed the general trend of the arts of this time in turning away from things connected with the past. In experimenting with new devices, many of them so radically different that they have inaugurated a revolution in artistic expression, the twentieth-century artist, like all his predecessors, has shown himself an individual unusually sensitive to the times in which he lives, and often prophetic of the times to come. Since the half century has been dark and troublous, its mirror in art has often been dim and disturbed.

As a curator of the Metropolitan Museum has said:

> If we understand history fully we should understand the art of our times; for it is still, as it always has been, the mirror of ourselves. If our art seems violent, it is because we have perpetrated more violence than any other generation. If it deals with weird dreams, it is because we have opened up the caverns of the mind and let such phantoms loose. If it is filled with broken shapes, it is because we have watched the order of our fathers break and fall to pieces at our feet.[1]

TWENTIETH-CENTURY CHANGES

No one can understand the fundamental reason for so much of the insecurity, the experimentation, the dehumanization, and the increasing unintelligibility that we feel in twentieth-century literature, painting, and music without realizing the great breach which the First World War (1914-1918) made in our way of thinking and responding. While we go on living in much the same exterior way, with many of the visible monuments of the nineteenth century still about us, all our invisible landmarks have been debased, distorted, or destroyed.

The nineteenth century was a period of confidence, poetically expressed by Browning's essentially Romantic outburst:

> *God's in His heaven—*
> *All's right with the world.*

The belief was that the Law of Progress (with a capital P) held everywhere. Just as the technical achievements of modern culture were thought to be advanced and enriched, so its spiritual achieve-

[1] Robert Beverly Hale, *One Hundred American Painters of the 20th Century.* Cambridge: Harvard University Press, 1950.

MIRO: CATALAN LANDSCAPE

The Surrealists gave dreams and hallucinations a place in their poems and pictures. Under Surrealist influences, this Spanish artist concluded that "in painting one must go beyond form to achieve poetry." In this picture he tries to produce a poem as well as a composition in form and color.

ments—its literature and art and philosophy—were thought to be better and richer than those of times past. Degeneration of any kind was thought impossible in what was bravely called a Century of Progress. Thus nineteenth-century artists were inclined to be buoyant, confident, secure, and more or less complacent; Utopia was just around the corner, and those who thought otherwise were looked on as neurotic prophets of degeneration. As a modern historian has put it: "Under the influence of the new ideology that had grown up with capitalism and mechanical invention, the leading minds of this period thought that mankind had found the secret of happiness by turning his attention to burying his doubts under the quantitative solution of its problems."[2]

All this changed under the impact of thirty terrible years, years that included two World Wars and the dreadful suffering inflicted

[2] Lewis Mumford, "Mirror of a Violent Half-Century," *New York Times Book Review*, Jan. 15, 1950.

on the world by the restoration of institutions reminiscent of the Dark Ages—slavery, torture, and the mass destruction of human beings. Then too, in view of what he has learned in the twentieth century, man is no longer sure of himself or his capabilities, or even of his ultimate destination. The revelations of Freud, in an attempt to establish a system of psychology not based on mere external evidence, have shown man that the world is full of "instinctual urges and explosive emotions." He no longer is able to feel under him any base of steadiness such as the belief in progress which sustained the nineteenth century, the power of reason in which the eighteenth century so firmly believed, or the light of religious faith which illumined some of the darkest stretches of human existence during the Middle Ages. For most men today, and especially for the artists such buttresses of existence simply do not exist.

Is it any wonder, then, that the art of the twentieth century turned experimental, objective, abstract, ugly, and often brutal in its violent revolt against the Romantic cultivation of emotion and the Impressionistic fostering of sensation for their own sake? In addition, there was the reaction against the smug, storytelling kind of art that had developed during the nineteenth century to meet the needs of an industrialized, largely unimaginative civilization, one which fundamentally cared little about art but was sure that it knew what it liked. A general spirit of revolt spread through all the arts. Painting, especially, constituted the battleground on which most of the concepts concerning what has come to be known as "modern art" were determined.

In the second half of the twentieth century the term *modernism* no longer has the connotation of revolutionary significance it once possessed; it is used to describe a well-established tradition which produced a certain type of art—some good, some bad—between about 1890 and 1950. This period had its significant triumphs, especially in painting and functional architecture, and the art it produced (as well as the theories that went with it) no longer seems iconoclastic. Today critics are more inclined to ask "Is this art good?" than "Is it modern?" The passage of time has enabled us to realize that many of the ideas and ideals which seemed so fresh and individual at the beginning of the era have themselves become fixed ideas and rigid formulas that tend to be as destructive of creativity

AMERICAN CUBISM:
MY EGYPT
An oil painting by Charles Demuth (1833-1935).

Collection of Whitney Museum of American Art

as any influence from the past. "Modern" as a synonym of "contemporary" is not necessarily a laudatory adjective.

The art produced from 1890 to 1950 is an entirely different kind of art from anything that had been seen before. We have said that the Romantic artists, in order to stimulate their visions of life and reality, turned nostalgically to the past, to the great legends of various peoples, and to the patriotic spirit of the different countries. As the scientists of the era began to explore the mysteries of the physical universe, however, intelligent men, especially the artists, began to wonder more and more about the reality of their own being. Just what was man? Was he a creature so completely determined by evolutionary processes as to make it impossible for him to control his own thoughts and actions, or could he determine his own relationship to the past and chart his own course into the future? The necessity of affirming man's reality, of triumphing over time and history, began to be argued by thinkers of the late nineteenth century. Freud crystallized the thinking when his psychological inves-

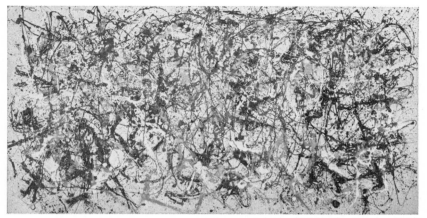

JACKSON POLLACK: AUTUMN RHYTHM
A fine example of contemporary abstractionism.

tigations led him to conclude that the "one positive means of controlling man's brief span lies within himself."

The desire to assert his own personality, to conquer the difficulties of time and space, stimulated the artist of the late-nineteenth and early-twentieth century to devise new ways of expressing his visions of life and his ideas of reality. To the writer Marcel Proust (1871-1922), this was done through "remembrance of things past." Understanding that anything like complete reality is incapable of being grasped because observation itself changes the things observed, Proust portrayed the past as a series of approximations, each of which presented it in different aspects, felt differently at different times, by different people, and under different circumstances. He believed that only a complete evocation of the past can give us the content of any moment; since this is difficult, in fact, impossible, reality eludes us and life becomes completely unintelligible.

The artist Claude Monet (1840-1926) presented his landscapes as new conceptions of the relationship between space and time. For him reality was achieved through the presentation of transient, enchantingly colored moments each illustrating the adage, "All things flow: the same water never flows beneath the bridge twice." For James Joyce (1882-1941) reality consisted in apprehending the existence of different levels of human experience. His *Ulysses* traces the simultaneous thoughts and actions of a number of persons in Dublin during the course of a single day and night. In order to do this as completely as possible, he did not hesitate to invent and use new technics—interior monologues, parodies of all sorts, portmanteau words coined in various ways, puns, dream sequences, streams of consciousness and so on. Pablo Picasso (b. 1881) attempts to state reality by viewing an object from all sides at the same time and distorting visual appearances to emphasize certain ideas he wishes to communicate. Arnold Schönberg (1874-1951), greatly affected by Freud's analysis of the great role played by the unconscious (the Id) in the soul-life of man, invented new technics to depict in music the dark, inaccessible part of man's personality.

The development and adaptation of all sorts of technics, styles, and forms, some of them going back to the earliest periods of human existence, is an integral aspect of modern art. The modern artist sometimes uses forms and technics from the past with very slight changes, assembling details from different sources in entirely new combinations; sometimes, on the other hand, he develops entirely new forms and technics to suit his particular purposes. Aware that the technical resources of a period are quickly exhausted, the modern painter, musician, or sculptor continuously seeks new ways of expressing himself. Men like Picasso and Stravinsky worked in different styles at different stages of their careers, turning quickly and easily from one to another without hesitating to cultivate some of the different idioms simultaneously.

The development of a huge audience through mass communications—radio, television, phonograph, movies—has strongly affected modern art. Feeling that this mass audience has only the most casual understanding of, and sympathy for, their art and is interested only in the obvious and familiar, modern artists have intuitively withdrawn from contact with the outside world. They have produced things for an "ideal" audience, which often consists largely of other artists with kindred tastes. Freed from the demands and dictates of popular taste, their experiments have been guided largely by their own desires. This is certainly not an altogether healthy situation!

There have been a great number of subdivisions and "ism-revolts" within the general period we are considering. Usually these move-

MUNCH: THE SHRIEK
*The intense emotion in this picture
is indicative of the Expressionist
movement.*

Courtesy, Museum of Modern Art

ments have started in the art of painting and later spread to the other
arts. Following the lead and embracing ideas of three important post-
impressionist painters, Cézanne, Van Gogh, and Gauguin, there
developed the following: *Fauvism* ("Wild Beasts"), which believes
in laying-on of color to the exclusion of almost everything else;
Cubism, which treats nature by reducing all objects to their geo-
metrical forms and re-assembling them into new designs which did
not necessarily suggest natural appearances or literary meanings;
Expressionism, which conceives of man as imposing himself on
nature, events and himself "from the inside," thus projecting the
artist's state of mind, his emotions and feelings without being particularly concerned with technical processes; *Dadism*, which, arising out of a universal disgust following on the First World War,
negates beauty; *Surrealism*, which, influenced by Freud, is concerned with what is dictated by the unconscious mind of the artist
and believes in creation without the control of reason and restraint of
aesthetic and moral considerations; *Abstractionism*, which treats the
representational element so that it is unrecognizable or deliberately
avoided; *Abstract Expressionism*, which is concerned with opening

up a new world of "psychological space" by a sort of dream-thinking, without making any use of representation, supercharging its creations with interior significance and assurance as to the psychological meaning of line and color.

An improvisatory element has become important in mid-century art: painters leave their technical processes to chance and often seem surprised at the results; musicians do not hesitate to improvise performances so that the outcome is different each time they play; and painters and writers, swayed by the spirit of the moment, are never entirely sure just what they mean.

While we who believe in progress and desire to become *au courant* with the various developments in the contemporary arts must cultivate wide sympathies for all experiments which seem to promise worthwhile and profitable results, we must be careful to guard against those experimenters, unfortunately only too common, who seek merely to exploit current fashions or to associate themselves with reputable innovators. Spuriousness is easily cultivated; a distinguished painter-teacher has declared that he could take "any susceptible and reasonably talented student and in a year get him or her into an up-to-date, abstract show, and discussed. That never could have happened in the past!" Without doubt, the same thing could be said about composers.

A MODERN CREDO

Underlying all these "isms" are certain general aesthetic principles which help explain the particular quality of modern art. The first and most important of these is the right of the artist to express his own individualism, regardless of tradition or officialdom. This has been a fundamental belief of artists in all ages, of course, but it has never been held more strongly or with such utter disregard for the consequences. André Malraux has put it well:

> The longdrawn struggle between officialdom and the pioneers draws to a close. Everywhere, except in Soviet Russia, the moderns are triumphant. Modern art has become a law unto itself which has replaced traditional art with a system of research and exploration. In this quest the artist (and perhaps, modern man in general) knows only his starting point, his methods and his bearings—no more than these—and follows in the steps of the great sea adventures.[3]

[3] André Malraux, *Psychology of Art*. New York: Pantheon Books, Inc.

Whether or not the artist has ventured too far and has been stranded on the sands of his own impotence is a question that only time can answer. There is little doubt, however, that this struggle and determination of the artist to be himself has resulted in beneficial broadenings of the horizons of art, which, especially during the nineteenth century, had become rather painfully constricted.

A second general principle underlying modern art is that nature is not merely a subject to be imitated on canvas or in marble or clay, or which has a meaning to be conveyed through the use of words, but that it is rather a jumping-off place for whatever the artist thinks or feels. This principle is naturally a corollary of the first, and it is the basis for the reasoning in what has come to be known as abstract or nonrepresentative art. This is art that is responsive to its own laws of aesthetic and structure, an absolute in itself rather than a means for transmitting experiences or feelings, suggesting ideas, or picturing definite objects. The average person likes to get pleasure from what he can recognize in a picture or a book. Modern artists are inclined to deny him his pleasure, at the same time offering him other, sometimes quite shocking, pleasures which tend to "feed the imagination with new fires of experience." These contemporary artists are asking, as Walt Whitman did: "Who are you that needs to be told what you already know?"

In this respect, as Pater has reminded us, the other arts tend toward the condition of music, the one art in which this state of abstraction is completely natural. As we have already said, since music does not have to mean anything, it can mean everything; it is this happy state that the modern creators in the other arts have envied and have tried to attain.

Still a third general characteristic of modern art is the absence of what may be called rhetoric—that is, doing a thing supremely well for the joy and pleasure that can result from the achievement. This is the sort of satisfaction we get from the realization of the development of musical ideas in the Beethoven symphonies or the rich ornamentation in Baroque architecture or the lifelike depiction and coloration in the works of the great Dutch genre painters. The modernists demand simplicity, terseness, sometimes even brutality of expression, such as that in the drawings of Picasso.

In this again they have had a salutary influence on artistic creation, which during the preceding century had inclined toward

LE CORBUSIER: HIGH COURT IN CHANDIGARH, INDIA

grandiose, rather elephantine dimensions. Milhaud's (b. 1892) *Opéras-minutes* (lasting from five to ten minutes) are in strange contrast to Wagner's great five-hour operas; whether they are as effective is another question. Schönberg's little piano and orchestral pieces written in his later, more modern, style stand in vivid contrast to his romantically conceived cantata *Gurrelieder*, written under the older ideals and demanding five soloists, three separate male choirs, and eight-part mixed choir, and a larger and more complicated orchestra than had even been used up to that time (1900).

But all this can be overdone; brevity and terseness and essentiality can be tiresome as well as useful. The experienced listener, observer, or reader is often inclined to miss some of the leisurely treatment given their subjects by older artists, a treatment that is an essential part of the results they achieved. As Voltaire said, "The superfluous are sometimes the necessary things."

CONTEMPORARY PARALLELS

In the pursuit of their search for reality, artists of the modern period have produced some startling as well as effective works which show both the uncertainty of the first half of the twentieth century and its creative inventiveness. We are beginning to wonder, however, how large they will loom in the uncertain future. This revolution has affected the various arts differently. In painting, where it had plenty of active precursors, it has been a movement of liberation, enabling us to see the world and ourselves in a new way. In literature it has been less influential, although it has produced a number of interesting stylistic experiments and a few masterworks. In architecture its accent has been on function rather than form, with the result that the world has become covered with rather austere, very useful, and honestly constructed buildings which do not strike the average observer as having any great beauty. In music the influence has been generally a confining rather than a liberating one, although there have been a few composers who have attained creative excellence and extended the bounds of technical resources.

Insofar as the opinion of the public is concerned, the long history of Central European experimentation in the arts during this century has resulted in a disregard for the values of ordinary human beings—a sort of dehumanization that has affected all the arts. Perhaps this is inevitable in an era such as ours, devoted as it has been to an increasing mechanization of life and vulgarization of thought. There are many who hope that this whole period will be considered one of gestation rather than of accomplishment, and that it will lead to an era of more stable artistic achievement and consequential artistic results.

TOPICS FOR FURTHER DISCUSSION

What is Art going to look and sound like in the future?

Discuss the following statements made at a discussion of experts on "Whither Art?"

> Dollars and art shouldn't mix but they do today; since you cannot destroy money, money is destroying art. Art is now a commodity, like soap or securities. The great artist of tomorrow will go underground.

CHAPTER 29

"This Modern Stuff"

ক্ষী ই্থ

Perhaps to no other art has the expression "this modern stuff" been applied so frequently as it has been to music. Before considering the reasons, it will be necessary to consider some matters of technical procedure which lie at the very root of modern composing practices and which, even more than the aesthetic considerations we have just discussed, account for the difficulties of apprehending contemporary music.

TONALITY AS FOUNDATION

Because he is so largely unaware of the technical changes undergone by the art during the twentieth century, the average listener becomes confused and sometimes angrily bewildered when he listens to modern music. He has lost one of the compasses that formerly had kept him fixed in his listening course, no matter how strongly the dissonantal winds might blow or how thickly the key-changing fogs might settle down about him.

This is a matter of losing the sense of what we call tonality—that is, the awareness of certain foundational centers of rest and finality about which music written from Bach to Wagner evolved. This earlier music had as its grammatical foundations the major and minor scales, the common chords built out of them, and the sense of key relationship which they gave. Bach established this sense of tonality very firmly in his music, and most of the composers of the music of the eighteenth and nineteenth centuries built on his foundations. One of the most famous of his works is a collection of compositions (preludes and fugues) comprising a complete cycle in all the major and minor keys. In these, and in everything else he wrote (for there is a great deal of his music which can be thought of as "modern"), the whole composition revolves around a key center, starting from it and—no matter how far removed it may get from it—returning to it at the end. This can be heard in an example we have already quoted, the *Prelude and Fugue in C Major*, from this famous collection—*The Well-Tempered Clavier*. Throughout these two pieces the key center is firmly fixed and constantly referred to.

The same is true in the symphonies of Mozart, Beethoven, and Brahms. Take any single movement from their works—for instance, the first from Beethoven's *Fifth Symphony*. It starts with strong marking of the tonality of C minor and finishes, after wandering through other key centers, firmly in the same key. So it is with Brahms and even with Richard Strauss who, in spite of his contemporaneousness (he died in 1949) and his strong, pungent dissonances, cannot be called modern in this technical sense. We can say specifically that the proportion of music that can be referred to common chords and keys—that is, music with this sense of fixed tonality—is proportionately little less in such a work as Strauss' *Domestic Symphony* than in Bach's *St. Matthew Passion*, which are one hundred seventy-five years apart. In this sense the two works have a common grammatical foundation that is not modern at all.

CHROMATIC UNHINGING

It was the old magician Wagner who was responsible for the concept of unhinging the sense of fixed tonality prevalent in music up to his time. His late, mature works are characterized by an increasing use of dissonance—that is, by chords which are not immediately and pleasantly satisfying to the ear because they are incomplete in themselves and not restful as tonal entities. Wagner provided the basis for the modern idea of "atonality" when he absorbed into his fundamental system of harmony what before his time had been ornamental, incidental notes—*appoggiature* is the technical term for them. The Prelude to *Tristan und Isolde* shows this clearly; in fact, the whole opera is the climax of this use of the *appoggiatura* as a means of music expression and musical continuity. Listen to the way it starts; there is much emphasis, in both melody and harmony, on those notes (marked in this excerpt with circles) which in the older system would have been incidental and which Wagner here makes fundamental. You cannot but realize immediately that in this we are already removed from the sense of tonality as expressed by Bach; each of the twelve half-steps making up the octave is of equal significance and importance:

Thus was established a new tyranny of chromatic or half-tone harmony and melody, based on these steps and without any of the sense of finality expressed in the older system. Succeeding composers revolted in turn against this new, restless harmony; we have seen how the Impressionists, led by Debussy, added floating chords based partly on the whole-tone scale and parallel chords made up of unusual intervals. There resulted in still vaguer and less fixed tonalities, such as those to be heard in Debussy's *Nuages* or Ravel's *Daphnis and Chloe* suite. All these innovations made for more and more unhinging of the feeling of tonality that is fundamental to the older style.

POLYTONALITY

Stravinsky, in a work such as his ballet *Petrouchka*, employed still another freeing and unhinging device, polytonality—the simultaneous use of two tonalities, one superimposed on the other, which results in a very unorthodox combination of sounds, with little sense of finality. A great deal of the puzzlement which arises in hearing this work for the first time is due to this superimposition of key planes upon one another, but the initial shock experienced by the listeners of 1912 has long since passed, and we accept polytonality without question as a standard technical device of the modern composer.

If you refer to the discussion of *Petrouchka* on page 308, you will find that the so-called Petrouchka chord, the kernel of the whole work, is made up of two arpeggios, one in C Major super-imposed upon one in F sharp Major. Their conjunction produces a strikingly original example of polytonality. This same device is even more apparent in Stravinsky's next work (his great Declaration of Independence of Modernism, as it has been well called), *Le Sacre du printemps*.[1] Its pitiless polytonal dissonances and its furious rhythmic changes, caused by the bold displacement of usual accents, resulted in a tremendous demonstration of disapproval when it was first produced in Paris in 1913. Notice how the dissonances are often created by the superimposition of ordinary chords placed in entirely different tonalities:

Today *The Rite of Spring* is looked on as one of the great classics of music, and there are no disturbances in concert halls when it is played. Jean Cocteau, one of Stravinky's contemporaries in Paris— a poet, playwright and general propagandist for modern art—has thus described the simple story of this ballet, a story inspired largely by the enthusiasm of the period for primitive art.

[1] Excerpts from *Le Sacre du printemps* are reprinted by permission. Copyright 1921 by Edition Russe de Musique; assigned to Boosey & Hawkes Ltd.

FIRST TABLEAU:

The prehistoric youth of Russia is reveling in the game and dances of
Spring (Dance of the Youth and Maidens—Dance of Abduction—
Spring Rounds—Games of the Rival Towns); they adore the earth and
the Sage who reminds them of the Sacred Rite (Entrance of the Cele-
brant—The Kiss to the Earth—Dance to the Earth). Notice the brusque
shifting of accents and the rough polytonal chords of these sections.

Between the two parts of the ballet is the Interlude of the Pagan
Night, full of the strange stirrings and the mysterious questionings of
a primitive world as darkness settles upon it.

SECOND TABLEAU:

For Spring to return, these primitive and credulous people believe it
necessary to sacrifice a young girl, a Chosen One. (The Mystic Circle
of the Adolescents—Dance to the Glorified One). She is left alone in
the forest; the ancestors come out of the shadows and form a circle
(Evocation of the Ancestors). Inspired by them, the Chosen One dances
in rhythms marked by long syncopations (Sacrificial Dance). When she
falls dead, the ancestors approach and, picking her up, lift her toward
the skies . . .

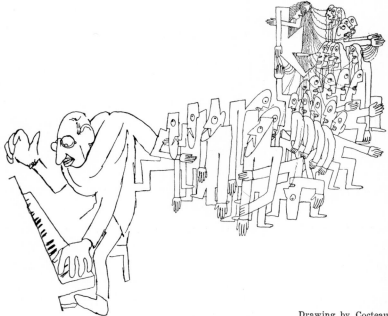

Drawing by Cocteau

STRAVINSKY REHEARSING LE SACRE DU PRINTEMPS

Each tableau contains an introduction and a series of dances which follow each other without break, so that there is a gradual build-up toward the dynamic climax. While each dance has its own character, the short, brittle chords, rhythmic patterns, and structural themes of all are much alike and so give a sense of concentrated unity to the whole. The theme with which the first introduction starts is typical:

ATONALITY

From this device of polytonality it was but a step further to the use of atonality—that is, music without any sense of key at all or, as its greatest exponent preferred to call it, the *Method of Composing with Twelve Tones* (Dodecaphony). Thus the fullest possible freedom, with every conceivable combination and progression within the chromatic, or twelve-tone, scale, was attained. The full unhinging of the older tonality concept was completely and consciously achieved by the end of the second decade of this century. With this dissolution of the classical system came the need for a new one that could give some sort of order and stability to what was written and supply new theories to account for the materials used.

This was provided in the works and theoretical treatises of Arnold Schönberg and his two pupils, Alban Berg and Anton Webern. We have here a close parallel to developments in other fields. Like the Newtonian system in physics, the older Bach-Wagner classical system of tonality seemed perfectly satisfactory in view of the facts known and recognized at the time, but it appears inadequate in the light of recent discoveries. New theories have had to be evolved (which, of course, in time may again be displaced) in order to interpret for us the whole universe of musical sounds as it is now conceived, contained in the twelve notes of the chromatic scale.

Beginning in a style strongly reminiscent of Wagner and endowed with an extraordinarily facile technical equipment, Schönberg wrote such things are *Verklärte Nacht* and *Gurrelieder*, pieces that are strongly communicative, highly romantic, and thoroughly enjoyable from the older viewpoint. But style in art, as Schönberg himself said, changes approximately every ten to fifteen years. Feeling the necessity for developing a style that would take advantage of the emancipation of the dissonance which had gradually been taking place since the time of Wagner, he began, around 1908, with his Op. 10, writing compositions that differ not only harmonically but also "melodically, thematically, and motivally" (his own words) from anything that had been done up to that time.

PIERROT LUNAIRE

The outstanding work of this period of change is *Pierrot Lunaire*[2] (Moonstruck Pierrot), written in 1912. Set to twenty-one poems by Albert Giraud (translated into German by Hartleben) it treats in a highly expressionistic manner a figure from the early pantomimes, a pathetic figure who hides his real feelings behind a mask of fantasy. The score calls for only a small complement of interpreters: a vocalist who neither sings nor declaims but "recites in song-speech"; a violin or viola, a cello, a piano, a flute or piccolo, and a clarinet or bass clarinet. From this rather meager combination of instruments, Schönberg has wrought an expressionistic score which stabs with color, sears with dissonance, but which lingers in our memory. We may or may not "like" it, but we have to acknowledge that it communicates something which is part and parcel of its time, and that in it Schönberg mirrors his own inner feelings about that time, quite in defiance of set theories or usual connotations.

A good idea of the nature of this work may be gained from its first four numbers, each of them typically *expressionistic*—striving to convey to the listener inner experiences rather than outer impressions and always inspired by the possibilities of the materials of music to awaken and increase feeling. Here is an approximate translation of the German poems and a few measures of the score to show how the composer, in spite of his intellectual theories, evolved his

[2] Excerpts from Pierrot Lunaire reprinted by permission of Associated Music Publishers, Inc., New York.

musical setting, a wave-like series of tones, out of the sentiment of the text.

1. Moonstruck

The wine that you drink with your eyes
The moon of the night pours down in waves,
And a springtide flood o'erflows the still horizon.

Desires, ghostly and sweet,
Swim numberlessly through the flutes!
The wine that you drink with your eyes,
The moon of the night pours down in waves.

The poet, whom devotion drives
Intoxicated by the holy potion,
Turns toward heaven, enraptured,
Reeling, sucks and sips
The wine that you drink with your eyes.

2. Colombine

Pale blossoms of the moonlight,
White wonder roses,
Bloom in the July night—
How I would like only one!

To quell my anxious grief,
I seek in the dark streams
Pale blossoms of the moonlight,
White wonder roses.

Were all my longings silenced,
Were I allowed fabulously,
So blissfully, gently to shed
On thy brown hair,
Pale blossoms of the moonlight!

The Dandy

With a fantastic beam of light
The moon illumines the crystal flakes
On the black, most holy wash-stand
Of the tranquil dandy of Bergamo.

In singing, bronze scales
The fountain laughs with light metallic sound,
With a fantastic beam of light
The moon illumes the crystal flakes.

Pierrot with a waxy countenance
Stands musing and thinks how to paint himself today.
He casts aside the oriental red and green
And paints his face in exalted style
With a fantastic moonbeam.

A Pale Washerwoman

A pale washerwoman
Washes faded clothing at night.
Bare, silver white arms
She stretches deep in the water.

Breezes creep in through the lighting
And softly move the stream.
A pale washerwoman
Washes faded clothing at night.

And the gentle maid of heaven,
Lightly flattered by the branches,
Lays out on the dark meadows
Her lightly woven linen—
A pale washerwoman.[3]

[3] Translated by Richard Boswell.

A NEW MUSICAL ORDER

After writing this revolutionary work, Schönberg composed nothing for ten years. During this period he devoted his time to formulating a new musical order, which would bring the anarchism produced by his dissolution of the ideas of functional harmony into some sort of coherence. Around 1921 he formulated his principle of "composing with twelve tones related only with one another." The basis of both melodies and chords in this system is a fixed arrangement of the twelve notes of the chromatic scale in a particular order, called a tone-row. Only the notes of this basic series can be used in any one composition, and they comprise, in various combinations, what he called the *gestalt*, or essence, of the work. In one of the earliest compositions written according to this dodecaphonic (twelve-note system), the *Five Piano Pieces*, Op. 23,[4] we find these measures:

[4] © Copyright 1923 and 1951 by Wilhelm Hansen, Copenhagen.

These are derived from this tone-row:

Since every detail of a piece's construction is derived from its tone-row, this may be turned upside down, backwards, or upside down *and* backwards; four fundamental versions of the row are possible, and each version may begin on any one of the twelve tones of the scale (forty-eight possibilities). Thus, since the tones of the row may be duplicated in any octave, distributed among the various instruments, combined into chords, and presented in an infinite number of rhythmic patterns, there are countless combinations of the twelve tones available to the composer before he exhausts the limitations of this system. Like all new possibilities in the field of artistic construction, the system offers a fresh challenge to the composer's creative ingenuity.

It is this arbitrary, mathematical type of writing which so strongly irritates listeners who feel that modern composers are trying to make technical innovations take the place of musical ideas. The test of music, they say, is not the constructive system behind it, but how it sounds. This twelve-tone system does not "sound" to them, does not communicate anything beyond a pedantic interest in something different. Schönberg's disciples would probably reply that, since it enables the composer to express himself and his time more characteristically than does the older tonal music, it is a valid technic for present-day use.

SCHÖNBERG'S FOLLOWERS

Alban Berg, the outstanding disciple of Schönberg, outstripped his teacher and founded a school of his own. While employing Schönberg's tone-row system Berg's music is by no means confined to it, and such works as *Wozzeck*, the only major opera written since Debussy's *Pélleas et Mélisande*, show him to be one of the last great representatives of the Romantic tradition. Anton Webern, another Schönberg pupil, used his master's ideas in order to secure special sensibilities of organization and tone-color. His *Six Pieces for Orchestra*, Op. 6, shows his exaggerated desire for conciseness, as well as his fascinating love of color for its own sake.

We are only now beginning to realize that Schönberg and Berg, who for so long have been considered the destroyers of the old tradition, extended it. They tried to intensify human emotion in a new, introverted manner by all the tremendous musical powers at their command. Anton Webern, on the other hand, although he used the same techniques, was the forerunner of an abstract type of music which, with its insistence on new forms, its rigorous concentration on organization, and its rejection of any kind of emotional content, marks a definite break with the past. He was really a "musical Columbus" showing the way to such men as Boulez, Barraqué, and Stockhausen, whose music, whether we like it or not, can actually be thought of as belonging to a new era.

After the Second World War, the practice of composing in tone-rows languished throughout the whole musical world. It has been revived in Paris by these new atonalists in an attempt to challenge the apparent victory of the neoclassical reaction set in motion by Stravinsky and followed by many other composers of this century. For a long time the influence of *Les Six*, a group of composers founded there in 1919, was dominant in Paris. In general, these men wrote music whose displaced accents, polytonal harmonies, and distorted melodies provided only a veneer to works "classical" in style and structure. This was a rather lighthearted way of achieving what Hodeir has called the sole ambition of every contemporary composer—"to find his way out of the musical world created by his forefathers."

This struggle has given us a great variety of attempted solutions (in addition to the antics of *Les Six* and the brilliant facility of Prokofiev): the widespread revival of neoclassical academism; Hindemith's attempts to uncover fundamental laws of composition by analyzing the acoustical properties and physical laws of sound; Bartók's attempt to stamp the personal marks of his genius on material borrowed largely from the past; the important school of English composers who rose to prominence between the First and Second World Wars; and the important Americans, including such men as Piston, Copland, Harris, and Schuman, schooled in the Stravinskian "neoclassic" traditions.

OTHER PUZZLING PROBLEMS

In addition to the emancipation of dissonance, other new features of contemporary music tend to bother the listener. Composers of this music are more and more preoccupied with a rhythmical system which shifts the metrical flow constantly, sometimes with each measure, as this excerpt from Stravinsky's *Le Sacre du printemps* shows clearly enough:

We may say that in modern music the sense of rhythmic pulse has become as unhinged as the sense of tonality. This provides a freedom and spontaneity unknown in music in which a single meter prevails throughout an entire movement or section and suggests the free meters of the earliest music of the Christian Era and the complexity and flexibility of Asiatic and African music. Often several of these free rhythmical patterns are piled on top of each other, so that they unfold simultaneously, in what is called polyrhythm.

Melody follows rhythm and tonality in assuming different shapes in contemporary music; no longer do composers strive for expressive tunes of four to eight measures in length, each marked by distinctive cadences. The aim now is to drive forward at almost any cost, cutting out all superfluous notes, no matter what difficulties may result for the performer or the listener. Present-day melodies strive to avoid all romantic tendencies; they no longer try to be vocal in character (that is, possible of being sung); they do not have to make sense to the human ear, but may contain as wide leaps and dissonant intervals as the composers desire. In their attempt to avoid the obvious they often border on what seems to be complete musical unintelligibility, but experience has shown that familiarity can increase their recognizability, even in such a theme as Schönberg uses for his variations in *Serenade*, Op. 24.[5]

[5] © Copyright 1924 and 1952 by Wilhelm Hansen, Copenhagen.

Orchestration in the twentieth century has followed the same general anti-Romantic tendencies as those prevailing in the other arts. No longer used are the lush sonorities made popular by such Romantic composers as Wagner, Mahler, and the early Schönberg. The present trend is toward lean, sparse, bright sound conveyed largely through linear, contrapuntal texture rather than through colorful chords or enchanting melodies. This is quite in keeping with the general non-expressive, impersonal, intellectual character of most of the art being produced today—functional architecture, non-objective painting, starved prose, and so on.

The plan to substitute new forms or constructional schemes for those that have been used for centuries does not make listening any easier. Having become somewhat familiar with the older, classical forms, the listener may become confused with the way a modern composer often shapes traditional schemes, such as the sonata-form, the fugue, the variation, the suite, and the concerto, to suit his particular constructive needs. In addition, the atonalists, since they renounce all devices peculiar to tonality, have had to devise new principles of structure. Contrasts of themes, changes of dynamics, variance of textures, and new vocal and instrumental sonorities, rather than development of thematic materials, are used as foundations. The opera has been subject to unique experimentation, not only in the type of subjects used for librettos (Berg's *Wozzeck* or Stravinky's *Rake's Progress*, for instance), but also in their length (Milhaud's *Minute Operas*) and social content (Blitzstein's *The Cradle Will Rock*).

At one time during the century there seemed to be considerable interest in smaller divisions of the tone than the one used as the basis for all European music—the half-tone. Microtonal music, employing quarter, eighth, and sixteenth tones, was tried, but so many new combinations have been shown to be possible with the use of the present divisions of the scale—half and whole tones—that these experiments seem to have been largely abandoned.

New Instruments

Still another puzzling factor for the listener of today is the fact that new instruments for the production of music have been evolved and, as always, composers are striving to evolve new kinds of music peculiarly suited to their demands. The technology of acoustics and radio engineering has reached a point which makes it practicable to produce synthetic tone by electronic means. We have electronic pianos and organs, steel guitars, and the Theremin and Ondes Martenot (the last two oscillating-tube instruments in which the pitch is infinitely variable). The latest engineering triumph is an instrument which parallels the electric computer, whereby the composer may produce single or composite tones directly, without having to go through the previously used laborious process of committing his ideas to paper and then having someone else reproduce them. We have what is called *electronic music*, made by transforming and manipulating purely electronic sounds in any manner suggested by the mechanical ingenuity or the musical imagination of the manipulator. *Musique concrète*, on the other hand, consists of electronically modified natural sounds. Many composers use mixtures of both these types of engineered music and also combine electronic with the older type of instrumental and vocal music.

OUR ATTITUDE

What should be our attitude toward these changes and experiments? Realizing that there has been and will be faking by innovators who wish to attract attention to themselves by producing something "new," we must nevertheless keep an open mind on the whole question, especially since the use of so many new and partly unproved resources makes the truth hard to perceive. Buck's admonition, in his admirable little *History of Music*, needs to be kept always in mind: "We must remember that what we call 'ugliness' is merely a convenient name for things at the moment outside the cluster of the things we are accustomed to call 'beautiful' and that the life of music depends upon our keeping that cluster elastic."

The final factor in every judgment of contemporary art is the natural unwillingness of the public mind to accept aesthetic ideas strongly at variance with those with which it is familiar. For those concerned with its propagandism, the cause of modern music is no longer a cause célèbre; it has already been won. But the average listener is still unwilling to accept many of its ideals. This seems the great weakness of modern art, this inability of the artist and his public to meet on anything like a common ground—what might be called the ivory-towerism of the creative artist, who remains quite unconcerned with the opinion of his contemporary listeners or observers or readers. In fact, he is rather inclined to treat such opinion with contempt, and much of the music originating in this period has failed to obtain a permanent hold on the affections of contemporary audiences. In spite of the fact that the average listener probably absorbs more good music in a week than his ancestors did in a year and has a correspondingly greater acquaintance with music of all types than had his predecessors, there is no great demand for the work of contemporary composers.

Audiences will listen to modern music politely and even complacently, but without any great enthusiasm. We are speaking now of average, cross-section audiences, even those of the quality attending good symphony concerts, and not of cult-audiences. Although a tremendous amount of contemporary music has been made available on recordings, these tend to be short lived and are often cut from the catalogs. Contemporary music, to an extent not equaled by modern painting or literature, has become a thing apart from what the public thinks of as music. Winthrop Sargent calls it "something that aesthetes and professors discuss, that composers argue about, that foundations support with fellowships and avant garde societies are formed to propagate. But it still remains outside the general consciousness, despite a generation and more of feverish and enthusiastic societies, leagues, and guilds."

Part of this difficulty is the fault of listeners who are not inclined to realize the significance of the inevitable changes brought about by the nature of art itself. Too many modernistic composers have considered their craft a complex problem in musical structure or an art of arranging sounds in an intriguing, provocative manner rather than a means of communication. No genuine, lasting art can ever be produced under these circumstances. It is absolutely true, as the Dean of Fine Arts in a great American university has said, that to succeed, art must be understood by the great masses of the people. If only the artist or the initiated coteries can understand and appreciate a type of art, then performance in the name of art with such limited appeal fails to meet the test of primary definition of art and thus fails to perform its primary function.

This remains the real failure of modern music. How the problem can be resolved remains to be seen, but somehow it must be if our contemporary expression in music is to have any permanent validity.

PAUL HINDEMITH

There are several important twentieth-century composers who, while they have been in the forefront of this revolution which looks to the future, have received their main sustenance from the past. One of the most important of these is Paul Hindemith, a German who settled in the United States when the Nazis came to power in his native country and afterward returned to Europe. An excellent craftsman, familiar with all styles, the early medieval and the latest dodecuple, he has written an enormous number of works—operas, chamber music, orchestral works, piano and choral pieces.

Around 1920, along with other composers of the time, Hindemith produced a type of music called *Gebrauchsmusik* ("Utility Music"). Written in a modern anti-Romantic style, it was simple enough even for amateur musicians to play and sing. In his music, contrary to the ideals of many modernists, he tried to make himself intelligible to the average person. Although many of his works are complex enough in texture, their tonality is clearly defined; Hindemith believed that "tonality is fundamental to music just as gravity is a fundamental force in the natural world." His tendency to look backward to the medieval style is shown in two of his best works: the *Mathis der Maler* symphony, extracted from his opera on the subject of Matthias Grünewald's wonderful altar piece painted with the intensity and angularity of medieval style; and the ballet music, *Nobilissima Visione*, written around the life of St. Francis of Assisi. A later opera, *Die Harmonie der Welt* (The Harmony of the World), based on the life of the German scientist of the Baroque period, Johannes Kepler, does not seem to have been similarly successful.

As is true when any composer writes a great deal, Hindemith has produced works that are interesting only from the viewpoint of technical resource and interpretative facility. At his best, however, he stands as the last representative of the German line stretching back through Beethoven and Bach to Heinrich Schütz in the seventeenth century. In addition, Hindemith is perhaps the finest all-around musician of our time, creatively active as a theorist, teacher, player, and conductor, as well as composer.

BÉLA BARTÓK

A significant composer, whose works have come very much into their own since his death as an exile in New York in 1945, is Béla Bartók. Originally a folklorist, he was interested chiefly in establishing the true character of the native songs of Hungary as distinct from the *ersatz* gypsy product that had been foisted off on the world by such important composers as Liszt (in his *Hungarian Rhapsodies*) and Brahms (in his *Hungarian Dances*). Using his extensive knowledge of this folk material as a basis, Bartók drew on all the new harmonic, rhythmic, microtonal resources of his time to evolve a distinctive and unusual personal expression, one which many feel to be the most significant in present-day music.

Like Dvořák, Bartók was essentially a peasant, and his music is direct and down to earth, no matter how bewildered or troubled it may seem. His was a typical artist's mind reacting to the violence and insecurity of his time; yet it never produced, as did Stravinsky's, merely witty or superficial music, nor did it lose itself in introspective lamentation, as did Schönberg's. He wrote a set of six string quartets, which may well be the major contribution to this medium during the twentieth century; three concertos for piano and orchestra; a violin concerto; two violin sonatas; and a set of 153 piano pieces, called *Mikrokosmos*, carefully graded for educational purposes from the simplest to the most technically advanced styles.

In many ways, his most popular work is the *Concerto for Orchestra*. Written in 1943, it is a dramatic and ingratiating composition, admired by musicians and the general public alike. His last work (left unfinished at his death and later orchestrated and prepared for performance by Tibor Serly) was a *Viola Concerto*, commissioned by William Primrose in 1945. In all these later works, Bartók seemed to have become acutely aware of the fundamental problem of the twentieth-century composer (discussed in this chapter)— the communication of new musical ideas in terms that are intelligible to the general public. He was one of the few modern writers not afraid to face this problem squarely, and in all of the music written during the last ten years of his life he sought a progressive clarification and simplification of style. He abandoned whatever was meaningless and merely fashionable in his earlier writing and developed what seems to be the most powerful and meaningful expression to be found in the music of his time.

THE NEW AND THE OLD

As a final summation of the technical achievements of the modern composers, we should try to compare the older and newer systems at a point where they approach the same sort of problem. This can be done quite easily and neatly. Bach, as we have said, exploited the tonal universe as fully as the classical system of tonality would allow; while able to use every key, he had to be fundamentally diatonic in each, as is shown by the example already quoted from his *Well-Tempered Clavier*, the *Prelude and Fugue No. 1 in C Major*. Hindemith, over two hundred years later, approached the same problem from the modern standpoint in his *Ludus Tonalis*, a collection of interludes and fugues in all the different keys. We can hear the difference if we compare Bach's fugue with that of Hindemith in the same key; the latter is fully chromatic and freely uses all the intervals and harmonic combinations possible in the new system. It is, therefore, simply a measure of the extension of musical materials since Bach's time; whether or not these are the materials from which our future music will be formed remains an open question. Close at hand is some sort of fundamental reorientation in which music is doomed to surrender its affinity with humanity and its tremendous power of spiritual communication to a rational integration and collectivization where mechanical robots will be supreme, and such instruments as the tone synthesizer, the electric computer and the tape recorder will become the means of producing sound. Then—and this is by no means an arbitrary statement but one unfortunately warranted by historical developments—new materials will have to be discovered to fit the new trends.

LIST OF SUGGESTED MUSIC

Arnold Schönberg

1899 *Verklärte Nacht*, Op. 4 (string orchestra)

1900-1911 *Gurrelieder*

1906 *Chamber Symphony, in E flat Major*, Op. 9
These may be said to represent a first period during which Schönberg was strongly influenced by the works of German Romanticism.

1907 *Book of the Hanging Gardens*, Op. 15 (songs with piano)

1908 *Five Pieces for Orchestra*, Op. 16

1911 *Six Little Pieces for Piano*, Op. 19

1912 *Pierrot Lunaire*, Op. 21
These show the composer's tendency toward writing works free of a felt tonality.

1924 *Suite for Piano*, Op. 25

1924 *Quintet for Wind Instruments*, Op. 26

1926 *Quartet No. 3*, Op. 30 (strings)

1927-1928 *Variations for Orchestra*, Op. 31
Written according to his principle of "composition with twelve notes," these illustrate very free forms and meters.

1936 *Concerto for Violin and Orchestra*, Op. 36

1943 *Concerto for Piano and Orchestra*, Op. 42

1943 *Theme and Variations for Band*, Op. 43a

1947 *Survivor from Warsaw*, Op. 46

1932-1951 *Moses and Aaron* (opera)
These represent a blend of styles, with more attention paid to traditional principles of form and tonality.

Alban Berg

Sonata for Piano, Op. 1
One of Berg's few tonal pieces.

1910 *Quartet,* Op. 3 (strings)

1914-1921 *Wozzeck* (opera)

1928-1934 *Lulu* (opera)

1935 *Concerto for Violin and Orchestra*

ANTON WEBERN

1909 *Five Movements for String Quartet,* Op. 5

1910 *Six Pieces for Orchestra,* Op. 6

1928 *Symphony,* Op. 21

All of these show the composer particularly concerned with economical, cohesive, and condensed expression, with great attention to gradations of tone color.

PAUL HINDEMITH

1922 *Kleine Kammermusik,* Op. 24, No. 2

1934 *Mathis der Maler* (opera)

1935 *Sonata No. 3 in E Major for Violin and Piano*

1943 *Symphonic Metamorphoses on Themes by Weber*

1951 *Symphony Harmonie der Welt*

BÉLA BARTÓK

1912-1930-1933 *Hungarian Folk Songs*

1911 *Blue Beard's Castle* (opera)

1936 *Music for Strings, Percussion and Celesta*

1938 *Concerto for Violin and Orchestra*

Quartets:

   1908 *No. 1,* Op. 7

   1917 *No. 2,* Op. 17

   1934 *No. 5*

   1939 *No. 6*

1943 *Concerto for Orchestra*

ZOLTÁN KODÁLY

Originally a co-worker in the folklore field with Bartók, Kodály soon developed a style of his own, which incorporates passionate Romantic expression with a tendency towards folk-song simplicity and flavor.

1926 *Háry János Suite*

1923 *Psalmus Hungaricus*, Op. 13
One of the noblest of modern choral works.

ERIK SATIE

More imaginatively than technically equipped, Satie was a strikingly original composer. He had some influence on the style of Debussy, and although he is best known for the ironically humorous character of his music, he knew exactly what he wanted to say and how best to make it effective.

1888 *Trois Gymnopédies*

1903 *Pièces en forme de poire* (Pieces in the shape of a Pear) (piano)

1919 *Socrate* (symphonic drama)

In Paris in 1919 a group of composers—Auric, Durey, Honegger, Milhaud, Poulenc, and Tailleferre—became known as *Les Six*.

DARIUS MILHAUD

Perhaps the most prolific member of *Les Six*, Milhaud has written in a wide variety of styles. Cheerfully modish and witty, his two best known works are characteristic:

1919 *Le Boeuf sur le Toit* (The Bull on the Roof)
This is a fantasy on South American airs.

1923 *Creation du monde* (The Creation of the World)
This ballet was one of the first and most successful applications of jazz to serious forms.

FRANCIS POULENC

While no recent French composer has so captured the taste of an international audience as has Poulenc, it is as vocal composer that he has his surest claim to fame. His song cycles are distinguished by a seriousness quite different from the many tongue-in-cheek works he wrote along with other members of *Les Six*.

1932 *Le Bal Masqué* (The Masked Ball) (orchestra)

Dialogues des Carmelites
This is a most effective opera on a religious theme.

ARTHUR HONEGGER

A Swiss member of *Les Six*, Honegger's fame began with

1923 *Pacific 231*.
This symphonic piece is based on the sounds of a steam locomotive.

1926 *Le Roi David* (King David)

1935 *Jeanne d'Arc au Bûcher* (Joan of Arc at the Stake)
These are his two best dramatic oratorios.

GEORGES AURIC

Another member of *Les Six* concerned principally with the "wrong-note" type of dissonance popular in the twenties, Auric wrote a great deal of film music.

1950 *Phèdre* (ballet suite)

FRANK MARTIN

A Swiss composer whose music is played a great deal in Europe, Martin is one of the many composers interested in the tone-row serial technique of Schönberg.

1945 *Petite Symphonie Concertante*

JEAN FRANÇAIX

A Frenchman writing in the neoclassic style, Françaix has been called a "will-o'-the-wisp talent."

1932 *Concertino for Piano and Orchestra*

JEAN LANGLAIS

A French organist who is making his instrument a powerful force in contemporary music, Langlais' music is full of lovely color.

1949 *Incantation for a Holy Day*

OLIVIER MESSIAEN

This devout composer's ideal is, in his words, "a true music, that is a spiritual music, one which is an act of faith, a music which touches on every subject and yet remains in constant touch with God; then, too, an original music, whose language may open a few new doors and pluck off a few, still distant stars."

Complete Organ Works (Recorded by the composer)

ANDRE JOLIVET

1955 *Suite Transocéane*

PIERRE BOULEZ

One of the leaders of a new, constructive idiom, pupil of Messiaen and René Leibowitz (who was a pupil of Schönberg and Webern), Boulez may be said to be the leader of today's most characteristic *avant garde* school. As yet his music is little known outside France.

1955 *Marteau sans Maitre* (cantata)

1957 *Improvisation sur Mallarmé No. 2*

GOFFREDO PETRASSI

This Italian composer has written in both the neoclassic, out-of-tonality style and that of serial construction. This is one of his earlier works:

1934 *Concerto for Orchestra*

LUIGI DALLAPICCOLA

Chief of the Italian dodecaphonists, or twelve-tone writers, Dallapiccola has cultivated a characteristic Italian lyricism in his writing.

1954 *Variazoni per Orchestra*

Because of fortuitous circumstances, Germany has become a sort of microcosm of the varied European contemporary compositional techniques. More than in any other country, opera writing has flourished here because of the multiple opportunities for stage productions.

CARL ORFF

This much-played composer has written a number of operas and opera-cantatas in a distinctive style stripped of all harmonic complexities.

1935-1936 *Carmina Burana* (scenic cantata)
This work of real charm and great rhythmic power is based on poems by the thirteenth century Goliards, wandering students and young ecclesiastical outcasts.

1949 *Antigonae* (opera)
Based on Greek mythology, this is Orff's most ambitious work. It is scored for a wind and percussion orchestra.

WARNER EGK

Egk is the natural follower of the great German Romantic, Richard Strauss.

1949 *French Suite After Rameau*

BORIS BLACHER

Variations on a Theme by Paganini, Op. 26

1954 *Studie in Pianissimo*, Op. 45

KARL AMADEUS HARTMANN

This composer belongs to the older Romantic symphonic tradition.

Symphony No. 6 for Large Orchestra

HANS WERNER HENZE

Prinz vom Homburg (opera)

KARLHEINZ STOCKHAUSEN

This young experimenter is the borderline between the extension of the older system as found in Webern and the unchartered music of the future—*musique concrète* and the world of electronic sound.

Gesang der Jünglinge
One of the most famous pieces of electronic music to date.

1956 *Zeitmasse for Woodwind Quintet*

This piece introduces the notion of controlled chance: it deliberately gives the performers a freedom to interpret certain passages as they like.

TOPICS FOR DISCUSSION

Do you agree that the older means of expression have been exhausted and that modern composers must employ different ones?

How do these innovations and experiments affect you and your pleasure in music?

Can you suggest any means of determining whether new music is positive, affirmative, the music of life, or merely negative and antithetical?

How would you define *musique concrète* for someone who had never heard it? What are its best and worst points?

CHAPTER 30

Music in the Americas,
North and South

৵৽ ৡৄ

> *"Culturally, it is true that America, which had
> begun with the inheritance of the whole European
> past, had never known infancy; it is equally clear
> that she is not decadent. Between these two extremes
> it is difficult to generalize."*
> HENRY STEELE COMMAGER in *The American Mind.*

John Tasker Howard has written a book on American music that
should be consulted by all those interested in the details of the
development of music within the United States of America.[1] In the
course of its seven hundred pages Howard does not succeed in
answering, however, the two questions which have always con-
founded writers on this subject: "Who are the American composers, and why?" and "What can legitimately be called *American*
music?" Probably no definite answer to these can be given, but some
consideration of them is necessary if we are to come to a conclusion
regarding the present status and the expectations of music in
America.

In any such consideration the word American will be used in its
usual connotation, pertaining to the inhabitants of the United States,
although such a nomenclature is obviously faulty and unfair. For
there are other Americans of importance, who should be included

[1] *Our American Music.* New York: Crowell, 1955.

in such a term—the peoples of Mexico and Central America and those inhabiting the South American continent. We will have something to say later about music in these lands, which had developed important musical systems long before European settlers arrived, and where European music was extensively cultivated even before it secured a foothold in the northern part of North America.

AMERICAN MUSICAL HISTORY

The history of music in the United States is, of course, comparatively brief, covering only three hundred years. When Elizabethan England was a "nest of singing birds," when Palestrina and Di Lasso were carrying Italian music to its greatest heights, and when Schütz was laying the foundations for the future greatness of German music, America had not yet even been settled. New Amsterdam, the Dutch colony, became New York, the English possession, at about the time two of the greatest German composers, Handel and Bach, were born. The embattled farmers at Lexington fired their famous shot when Haydn and Mozart were at the height of their brilliant careers and Beethoven was just starting his stormy life. The end of the first decade of the nineteenth century witnessed the birth of the great men of the German Romantic movement—Chopin in 1810, Liszt in 1811, Schumann in 1810, and Wagner in 1813, as well as that of the man responsible for the establishment of the permanent American union—Abraham Lincoln, in 1809. During the great years of the flowering of European music, the United States was largely concerned with the basic work of pioneering and economic expansion, and it is little wonder that music had rather a pitiful and meager existence during that time.

Howard divides musical history in the United States into the conventional three periods: (1) from 1620 to 1800, when "Euterpe came to the wilderness" and made the best of a rather bad situation; (2) 1800 to 1860, when "Euterpe made up her mind to stay" and the alien tides of immigration, particularly that from Germany, gave a tremendous stimulus to the arts; (3) from 1860 to the present day, during which time "Euterpe makes a home in America"; native-born composers have received encouragement, and an attempt has been made to determine just what the "American idiom" should be.

Edward MacDowell
The first American composer of note.

SEEKING A DEFINITION

The definition of the term "American composer" is difficult. Some writers insist that any man, whether born in the United States or coming from abroad, who is trying to express in his music what he feels to be the spirit of the country and using materials that are largely indigenous, is a real American composer. Others feel that native-born composers, whether or not they pay homage to the national spirit, have sole right to this title but only as long as they follow modern tendencies. It has been maintained that the composer, whether born in the United States or elsewhere, who takes the materials he finds at hand (Indian or Negro folk music, jazz, and so on) and adapts these to suit his purpose is an American composer. The view of the conservatives is that any resident composer who writes good music may be called an American composer, though his work be based on the conventional European types without attempting to be new or startlingly national in spirit.

What determines the characteristics of American music? Should it be based on the native folk idioms? Is it American simply because the composer has passed part of his physical existence within the country? Must it express some phase of life, some aspect of feeling that can be definitely recognized as American? Or is music American because it contains new ideas created by an American resident or peculiar to the American people? Can the men who have infused native feeling into the conservative idioms be called American composers?

Howard's definitions of American composer and American music are helpful in trying to answer such perplexing questions. He says that a composer is an American if by birth or choice of residence he becomes identified with our life and institutions *before his talents have had their greatest outlet*; the music he writes is American if it makes a genuine contribution to the country's cultural development. This will not do for Roy Harris, however, who, in an essay on "The Problems of the American Composer," insists that an American composer must be able to be recognized as belonging to that culture which the peculiar climatic, social, political, and economic conditions of the United States have produced. His moods must not be the warmed-over ones of eighteenth-century and nineteenth-century European society, nor his material merely the rearranged formulas of the conventional type. Still another writer on the subject, Lazare Saminsky, says that any music that is born of the creator's conviction that America is his native soil is American music.

THE INDIVIDUAL AMERICAN QUALITY GROWS

It is difficult for the European to envisage Americans as anything but transplanted Europeans of various types and differing qualities and thus incapable of producing anything in the way of an indigenous art. It is almost impossible for anyone not on the immediate scene to realize that there is gradually coming into being in the United States a population which, because of its past and present experiences, its geographical surroundings, and its future hopes, is sharply different from that of any European country. Frank Ernest Hill in *What Is American?* states this clearly: "We have thought of the American quality as a modification of the European. If we are

AUGUSTUS SAINT-GAUDENS:
THE PURITAN

Courtesy, Metropolitan Museum of Art

to realize it fully we shall perhaps give it as definite and separate a place as we give to 'African' or 'Oriental.' " If this is the case, why should it not lead eventually to the production of a really national art?

There are a number of factors that have contributed to forming the background of this American race. Prominent among them has been the constant absorption with the problems of the frontier, a factor which we have already mentioned. The tremendously pressing business of gaining a living left little time for any consideration of art. Thus the American has no ripened and matured civilization to serve as a ready soil from which his art can flower. As Hill puts it, the frontier has no place for a Michelangelo or a Shakespeare (or for a Bach!), although it can produce a Lincoln. And unfortunately, the Puritan attitude, which has dominated much of our intellectual history, is that cultivation of the arts is a ministration to pleasure, which should not take up much of man's time. Then too, the dominance of the Machine Age, which seems to be able so effectively to outlaw beauty and romance as well as that "priceless thing, true individuality," has had a strong influence on the art life of America. These, together with the generally unstable influence of contemporary existence, have been largely responsible for the fact that the Americans as a people have as yet produced no great art.

Yet there are elements in the American character at present which give promise of a richer future. The dominating moralistic influences which so long played havoc with the country's artistic possibilities have been strikingly mitigated. The American melting pot has integrated bloods of a widely differing character, and the science of genetics teaches that the hybrid is likely to be stronger than the descendant sprung from a pure strain. The courage, resourcefulness, and energy of the people, features which always impress Europeans, have been healthfully tempered by a forced realization that the material aspect of life is not necessarily all-important. The very wealth and leisure which the machine has made possible have given a wider and more understanding interest in art, an interest that has dynamic possibilities for the future. When the American has learned, as Hill says, to integrate art and life, to blend practical life with imaginative creation, there are good reasons for thinking that he will be able to produce native art that can be called great.

A treatment of American music, no matter how brief, naturally involves a discussion of three of its aspects—folk music, popular (composed) music, and what, for want of a better term, may be called art music. Folk music in America means just what it means in Europe and elsewhere: music of indeterminate antiquity, unknown origins, and traditionally handed down from one generation to another, often in several different versions. Such songs and dances flourished among the families in pioneer communities, where this sort of music provided the only pleasures. This simple entertainment is a far cry from the modern urban "civilization," which depends largely on others for its amusement. (Perhaps this is one reason why the appeal of folk music has returned so strongly to the country as a whole.)

Popular (composed) music has an existence quite apart from both folk and art music; its more formal verses and music, although influenced by folk music, are consciously created for different purposes—patriotic, social, and entertainment—and have secured a wide recognition throughout the world as being characteristically American. Evidence is accumulating that art music—that is, music written by an individual artist in order to communicate his experience and feelings, and therefore taking on a fixed, completed form —has entered a new and important phase in the United States within the last twenty-five years. Given the political, economic, and social conditions of the present-day world, it would seem that the future of this type of music, for a great many years at least, may lie largely in this country.

AMERICAN FOLK MUSIC

Anton Dvořák, who came to New York in 1892, was the first well-known composer to recognize the individual character and importance of American folk music. He believed, and there are students of the subject who agree with him, that the so-called American Negro music is in reality a representative American folk music, a mixture of the musics of the white, black, and Amerind races that is entirely indigenous to this continent.[2] Most authorities agree that the Negro spirituals and plantation songs as they are used today, are an adaptation by the Negro of the familiar traditional hymns and songs of the whites; in fitting this music to his idiom, the melodic and rhythmic peculiarities of his race, perhaps brought with him from Africa, played an important role. The result, including some characteristics taken from the music of the American Indian, is a folk music different from that of any other country. Whether or not it is representatively American, it has become so known the world over and was the prototype for the characteristic composed songs of Stephen Foster, which were written originally for the troupes of Negro minstrels popular in the second half of the nineteenth century.[3] These Foster songs have become so integral a part of American tradition that "My Old Kentucky Home" and

[2] See an article which was published by Dvořák in 1895 in *Harper's Magazine*.

[3] According to tradition, it was "Daddy Rice" who first started the minstrel vogue in Louisville, Kentucky, when he put on a "Jump Jim Crow" act there in 1830. The most famous of all the troupes was the Christy Minstrels, for whom Foster wrote his best songs. When these were first published they were attributed, with Foster's consent, to Christy. But in 1852 Foster asked the band leader that he be given proper credit in the future: "I find I cannot write at all unless I write for public approbation and get credit for what I write."

Collection of Whitney Museum of American Art

EDWARD HOPPER: EARLY SUNDAY MORNING

"Old Folks at Home" are considered the world over to be American "folk" songs.

Another source of American folk music, the richness of which is only now beginning to be realized, is the music brought here by immigrants to this huge continent and preserved by them, with or without alteration, from generation to generation. Sometimes this traditional music has survived almost intact, as in the case of the Irish settlers who, coming to the South and finding the best of the land already occupied, moved into the hills of Kentucky and Tennessee. Their descendants, isolated for more than a century from the rest of the continent, still sing the old-country songs with much of their pristine quality after the original forms have vanished from the land which gave them birth.

Most of the transplanted European folk songs have been altered to suit local conditions and American customs; often their form and subject matter are so changed that it is difficult to recognize their original source.[4] Thus there has emerged a great body of ballads,

[4] John Lomax, who has collected hundreds of American folk songs and preserved them in the Library of Congress, Washington, tells of recognizing the lovely ballad "Barbara Allen" in the Negro convict song "Bobby," the subject of which the Negro ships as a corpse out of the railway depot at Dallas, Texas, leaving her relations "squallin' an' holl'rin' with grief."

pioneer songs, sea chanteys, drinking songs, and the like, songs that are American in the real sense. No matter what their origins, these folk songs have so assimilated the American spirit that they are expressive of a whole culture; they so perfectly reflect a democratic community of thought that they are adaptable to every type of citizen and singable by every sort of people. In this way they are unique.

Americans have always been hard-working people and as such have always sung; each new frontier has created its own music. The cowboys on the prairie,[5] the roustabouts on the rivers, the workers on the canals and railroads, the soldiers fighting the country's wars, the backwoods pioneers bent on relaxation, all have made original and unique contributions to American folk song, contributions that are as native as corn pone, chewing tobacco, or Boston baked beans. Recent research has shown that these native songs, instead of being confined to a few types such as hillbilly ballads or cowboy songs, have been produced everywhere, from Vermont to Florida, from Michigan to Texas. The Library of Congress has many thousands of recordings of these native songs—play, party, and square dances, prison wails, work songs, folk hymns, and the like. These embody the very spirit of the country, a youthfulness, gaiety, crudity, sentimentality, cocksure braggadocio, and homespun sincerity that is far more genuine than most of the intellectual and serious music as yet produced in America.

An interesting fact in the development of folk music has been the increase in its popularity following World War II. Whatever the reasons—the acceptance of folk singers on the radio and television or the do-it-yourself craze which gives people an excuse for participating in music they admire—the United States found itself in the middle of a folk-song boom at the middle of this century. There are many varieties of singers who have helped make this music

---

[5] Illustrating the fact that there can be a modern growth of folk song, Lomax describes the origin of cowboy songs:

"Not only were sharp, rhythmic yells (sometimes beaten into verse) employed to stir up lagging cattle, but also during the long watches the nightguards, as they rode round and round the herd, improvised cattle lullabies which quieted the animals and soothed them to sleep. Some of the best of the so-called 'dogie songs' seem to have been created for the purpose of preventing cattle stampedes—such songs coming straight from the heart of the cowboy, speaking familiarly to his herd in the stillness of the night."

popular: the genuine folk singers, the "city-billies" who gather their materials decidedly at second hand, the "art singers" who transform these wild flowers of music into a carefully cultivated garden, and the frankly commercial groups who shape folk lyrics and tunes into any format with a popular appeal. All of these are helping develop the folk-song as an important and significant part of American musical life.

LIGHT MUSIC

Like most other music, popular music in America has had various origins. The early settlers had little time for what they called "amusements"; life with them was grim and serious, and the use of music was largely confined to occasions of religious worship or social intercourse. The first native form of amusement music to thrive in the United States was connected with the Negro minstrel show (already mentioned in connection with Foster's songs); this was popular throughout the country for over sixty years. Then followed the more sophisticated variety and burlesque shows, patterned after continental models and flourishing in the larger seaboard towns. The Gilbert and Sullivan comic operas became almost as well liked here as they were in England, and native composers imitated them as well as their French and Viennese counterparts. Victor Herbert's graceful works in this genre, while based on European types, are definitely American in the lilt of their melodies, the verve of their rhythms, and the sparkle of their wit. Even more nationalistic are the marches of John Philip Sousa, known the world over; nothing better characterizes the youthful spirit, optimism, and patriotic fervor of the United States of their day.

The heyday of the Herbert operettas and the Sousa marches witnessed the development of the peculiarly American ragtime, music marked by a strongly accented melody superimposed on a regularly accented accompaniment. This is an African characteristic brought to America by the slaves and used by their descendants in their dance music; during the latter part of the nineteenth century it was imitated by white composers because of its happy, infectious rhythm, and developed, through the infusion of other folk elements, into jazz and then into swing.

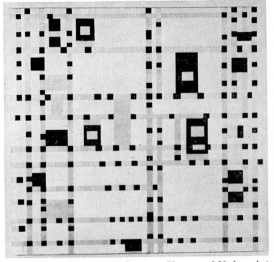

PIET MONDRIAN:
BROADWAY BOOGIE
WOOGIE

Courtesy, Museum of Modern Art

There have been a number of factors which contributed to this evolution. Among them may be mentioned the intensely felt, every-day, worldly, disillusioned songs of the Negro, the spiritual and the blues, with their familiar rhythmic inheritance from African dances;[6] the particular social background of the city of the birth of this music—New Orleans—at the turn of the century; the spread of the jazz style by its enthusiasts, both Negro and white dance musicians, up the Mississippi Valley and into the great metropolitan centers—Chicago, San Francisco, and finally New York; the effec-tive attempt to popularize it by composers steeped in these metro-politan traditions—such as Irving Berlin[7] and George Gershwin; the fabulously successful efforts of the "arrangers" who prepared the jazz scores for Hollywood and New York.[8]

[6] The difference between the religious spirituals and the secular blues has thus been characterized by a Negro writer: "To the spiritual writers, a great flood would have been considered as a visitation of a wrathful God upon a sinful people; the blues singer would simply have raised the question, 'Where can a po' girl go?'"

It was W. C. Handy who first caught the spirit of this Negro form and who made it a vital part of American dance music with his "Memphis Blues" (1912) and the even more famous "St. Louis Blues" (1914).

[7] An early writer on jazz called Berlin the "Bach, Haydn, Mozart, and Beethoven of jazz—all the old masters in one."

[8] None of the authorities on the subject seem to be clear as to the exact differences between jazz and swing; all agree, however, that swing's outstanding characteristic

It was Paul Whiteman who first tried to popularize what he called "symphonic jazz"—music written for the theater and concert hall rather than for the dance band. As late as 1926 Whiteman was given first and Beethoven second place in a poll taken of the students in an American university to determine the identity of the world's greatest musician. Such fame came from his commissioning and playing Gershwin's famous *Rhapsody in Blue*, a work which certainly owed some of its success to its scoring by other men. In addition to this work, Gershwin made other experiments in symphonic jazz, several of them quite successful, especially when interpreted by sympathetic exponents. Of all the orchestral pieces left by Gershwin at his death in 1937, undoubtedly the best and most typical is *An American in Paris* (1928), with its highly imaginative development of its non-show music materials. Gershwin was not, as so many of his countrymen like to believe, a great composer, for he was not able to integrate his rhythmic and melodic ideas into a coherent whole. But he was a natural one, writing fluently and spontaneously, and therefore his music has a greater appeal than that of the more intellectual American composers. In spite of the fact that it does not blend its elements very well—a southern Negro story, a slangy musical vernacular, and materials borrowed from Italian opera—his popular opera *Porgy and Bess* has had tremendous success, especially in those countries not familiar with the Gershwin idiom. For the real admirer of this American composer, however, his numerous Broadway hits will always represent Gershwin at his inimitable best.

THE SWAY OF JAZZ

American and European composers (for jazz is popular not only in America but all over the world) who have been influenced by the ragtime and jazz idiom include Debussy, Stravinsky, Hindemith, Milhaud, Gruenberg, Křenek, Lambert, Carpenter, Weill, and Cop-

---

is its driving rhythm over which soloists improvise as they play. The terms "straight" (or sweet) jazz and "hot" jazz are generally used to designate the difference between jazz played as written and jazz that is largely improvised. Louis Armstrong puts it this way: "There'll probably be new names for the same music. There have been several names since I remember the good old days in New Orleans, when hot music was called 'ragtime music.' So you see instead of dying out it only gets new names."

land. But with the possible exception of Milhaud in his *Creation of the World*, they have always seemed too hampered by the essential characteristics of this medium to feel at home in it. Perhaps the chief contribution which this style of American writing can make to the general idiom lies in the new methods of exploring musical instruments and producing new tone colors through different orchestral combinations.

The serious study of jazz and its various periods as a development of American music has come into considerable prominence in recent years. Each of the specific developments has revolved around a certain instrumental combination, typical of its time and characteristic of a definite type of expression. In the earliest period (call it New Orleans, Dixieland, or Chicago) small bands were the rule; these were usually made up of a cornet or trumpet, trombone, and clarinet (sometimes a saxophone), backed by a rhythm section of piano and drums, with a banjo or string bass sometimes added. Such a combination gave lightness, flexibility, speed; its natural blend encouraged spontaneous improvisatory flights, for both solo instruments and the whole band. The next period (Swing) called for larger ensembles of twenty or so instrumentalists, all of them driving for mass effects rather than for individual flexibility or spontaneity of expression. There has been a strong revolt against these blasting groups, and now there seems to be a desire for exploring the more musical possibilities of the medium, especially those developed by the modern serious composers. Chromaticism, polytonality and highly developed rhythmic complexity are all part of Modern Jazz, which places a premium on subtlety of expression and variety of effects. Small bands are again the rule and these allow a more intimate musical intercourse among the players, although group improvisation in its older forms has not returned.

There are differing opinions as to the origins of this mighty American musical river and the relative importance of its many tributaries. Some trace jazz back to the arrival of the slaves, who brought African music to this continent. They trace its evolution through ragtime and the activities of the Negro musicians (mixed with those of other players of French, Italian, Spanish, or Portuguese extraction) in New Orleans at the turn of the century. From this fountainhead, they hold, jazz spread northward up the Mississippi

Courtesy, The Corcoran Gallery of Art, Washington, D. C.

GEORGE BELLOWS: FORTY-TWO KIDS

Valley and from there throughout the United States and the world.

Another school of thought, while agreeing on the importance of the early Negro musicians, is inclined to locate the source of jazz in the style that was defined by and perfected from Negro-oriented ragtime and blues by the all-white Original Dixieland Jazz Band, which arrived in New York from New Orleans and Chicago in 1917.

There are arguments between the *traditionalists*, who say that it is only important to play jazz with as much authenticity as possible in the style of its original backgrounds, and the *modernists*, who feel that, because of the rapidly changing, transitory nature of this music, the only true jazz is that which represents its most recent stage of development, even when it is influenced, as it is today, by "long-haired musicians." All jazz musicians, however, seem to agree that the mostly-written-down-rather-than-improvised jazz moves away from the essential spirit which is best represented by the freely improvised performances common to the earlier periods.

A great number of prominent personalities have taken part in the development of jazz, each of them attracting a large group of followers and making a definite contribution to the style. For the real enthusiasts, jazz is a serious form of music, containing sincere artistic qualities that are all the more powerful because they are largely spontaneous. Thus they feel that jazz deserves attention as an art and not merely as a nationalistic manifestation or as commercialized business. Unfortunately, in their eagerness to attract what they feel to be long overdue recognition, its devotees have attached to jazz certain personal, social and even ethnic values which have nothing to do with its quality as artistic expression. Because its manifestations do represent a certain degree of revolt against the established musical order and because it has been so closely associated with what some consider oppressed minorities, jazz is sometimes looked on as a necessary accessory of the "beat" generation. It can readily be seized as a symbol of the beatnik's hostility to society and his desire for ugliness and violence—qualities which he raises in his own mind to noble personal and social ideals. This, combined with the fact that jazz appeals naturally to young people, gives it a social significance entirely independent of its musical or artistic qualities.

American Show Music

In no other field of American musical endeavor have composers been so genuinely successful and so widely recognized as in the musical shows that have been presented on Broadway during the last few decades. Both the music and the lyrics of these shows have a dynamic force and an infectious appeal which attract attention the world over; they are the more attractive because they are so characteristic. No one but an American could have written George Gershwin's *Lady Be Good*, *Of Thee I Sing*, or *Oh Kay!*, Jerome Kern's *Show Boat*, Irving Berlin's *Annie, Get Your Gun*, or Richard Rogers' *Oklahoma*. In fact, Rogers, in conjunction with the late Oscar Hammerstein II, inaugurated a whole series of show classics that probably will go down in history as paralleling the earlier Gilbert and Sullivan operettas in significance. Clever adaptations of literary classics have resulted in such endearing scores as *Kiss Me Kate* (from Shakespeare) and *My Fair Lady* (from George Bernard

Shaw); topical themes, such as *West Side Story*, a powerful adaptation of the Romeo and Juliet theme, are wonderfully suited to modern music. Kurt Weill, whose socially significant European theater piece, *Three Penny Opera* (1928), is a classic in its own right, settled in the United States in 1935. Here he produced a number of works which combine the usages of Broadway with the best traditions of opera: *Street Scene*, a deft handling of the melodramatic incidents of tenement life in our great cities; *Lost in the Stars*, a portrayal of the difficult race problems characteristic of our times; and *Down in the Valley*, a native folk opera especially designed for amateurs.

"Popular" Music

In conclusion, a word needs to be said about another variety of light music—the type which, for want of a better name, is called popular and which is heard everywhere today in juke boxes, broadcasts, and so on. This is quite different from the kind of entertainment music we have just been considering. It is music that can captivate the senses without the active mental effort required in listening to serious music.[9] Popular music is a purely manufactured product, constructed, according to ready-made forms, out of the cheapest of materials. It consists of clichés from serious works, derivations of fake folk songs (hillbilly), and borrowings from Romantic composers. Its obvious rhythmic patterns are monotonously maintained and its lyrics are unabashedly sentimental and very poorly suited to the music they accompany. As Paul Henry Lang, a noted New York music critic, has said:

> This music does not come under the most liberal interpretation of the meaning of entertainment music. It is rather like cheap gum drops, manufactured from unknown and questionable ingredients with artificial flavor and color added. It is hard to believe that such musical obscenities constitute an answer to the American public's musical demands for entertainment.

The contemporary practice of providing a background for every activity—working, eating, studying, and so on—constantly subjects

[9] Entertainment art, be it music, literature, or painting, need not be trite, vulgar, or obvious. To be effective, it must be well put together; its ability to shape its matter must correspond to the result desired. The wonderful Viennese waltzes of the Strausses are good examples.

the modern citizen to this synthetic musical product. For the listener whose taste has been seasoned by exposure to original, well-constructed music, this is irritating and painful, to say the least; for the neophyte, it is absolutely poisonous. It places in jeopardy his whole musical future and his receptivity to good art. Dulling his appetite for what is original it pollutes his taste for what is good.

It must not be assumed, however, that all light or popular music is poor, or that all serious music is good. It is perfectly possible for well-constructed show music to be more artistic and entertaining than bona fide opera; some light music is more effective than labored symphonic music. The essential aim of the listener should be to seek out the best of each type. As the urbane Benny Goodman once said: "Music is music—only a snob turns his back on any of it that is first rate." But the emphasis must always be on the last two words of this wise observation!

CHAPTER 31

Music in the Americas (continued)

❧ § ❧

AMERICAN ART MUSIC

The American composers able to stand on their own feet in comparison with contemporary Europeans can conveniently be classified into "generations." The earliest of these centered largely in New England, and its prominent names were John K. Paine, Edward MacDowell, Arthur Foote, George W. Chadwick, and Horatio Parker. Of these only the music of MacDowell can be said to have any real vitality; it has a characteristic, refreshing quality that keeps it alive, though it can by no means be called original or great. Nor does it echo any strikingly individual or national idiom, what MacDowell himself suggested he would like to feel in American music—"the youthful, optimistic vitality and the undaunted tenacity of spirit that characterizes the American." The other men of this period wrote good music, but, unfortunately it was unoriginal.

A SECOND GENERATION

Later writers in the larger forms (symphonies, operas, quartets, and so on) who would meet Howard's requirement but hardly Harris', include Edgar Stillman Kelley, Daniel Gregory Mason, John Alden Carpenter, and Deems Taylor, whose two operas were the most successful of a long line of native works produced by the Metropolitan Opera in New York. Writers who have employed folk idioms in their compositions include Henry F. Gilbert, Harvey

ERNEST
BLOCH
(1950)

Photo by V. Hirsch-Hess

W. Loomis, Charles W. Cadman, and John Powell. Charles W. Griffes was a young composer who at his death in 1920 showed unusual promise. Whether or not Ernest Bloch can be called an American composer is a question, but there is little doubt that he has produced some of the most significant music of all those who have lived and worked in America. A Swiss, Bloch did not come to the United States until 1916 and although some of his most important works were written before this, Americans gave him a great deal of encouragement. He had a number of important teaching positions and guided the training of some of the most important American composers of our day. After retiring, he worked at his very individual type of composition until his death in 1959. His style never followed the fads and fancies of the day, although he did not hesitate to use dissonance and radical harmonies as they were needed for a particular purpose. It would certainly seem, as one of his critics has said, that Bloch's best works have more chance of enduring than the music of some of the more publicized mid-century composers.

Another gifted, though not very original, foreign-born composer who spent his best creative years in the United States was Charles M. Loeffler. The most individual composer of this generation was the native American, Charles Ives (1874-1954). His compositions have been felicitously compared to the "barbaric yawp" of Walt

Whitman—a strange mixture comprised of undigested eclectic elements, predated experiments in polyrhythms and harmonies, and a sprinkling of naïve Americanisms such as cowboy tunes, hymn melodies and ragtime. This gives his music a peculiarly capricious and eccentric character which has not recommended it widely. In the same vein, but on a much smaller scale, is the music of another New Englander, Carl Ruggles.

MEN OF THE 1920's

The next generation comprises men active in the 1920's, of more striking musical physiognony, coming from various backgrounds, and showing different tendencies. Most of them, like their conferes, the painters and writers, reflect contemporary European tendencies in art. A few were conservatives, others rebelled strongly against European backgrounds; some were romantics, others neoclassics[1] in their predilections; some were frankly nationalistic, others made no attempt to be American in content.

Without attempting anything in the way of a complete list, the following significant composers of this generation may be mentioned: Louis Gruenberg; Edgar Varese (a naturalized American born in Paris), whose *Music for Percussion and Winds* includes such characteristic titles as *Ionization, Density, Integrales,* and *Octandre;* Wallingford Riegger who, until his death in 1961, was looked upon as the titular dean of this group; and Aaron Copland, whose music, in its characteristic harmonic features, the slowness of so much of its rhythmic design, and the melancholy sparseness of its melodic patterns, suggests to a foreign observer the loneliness of great American cities "merging into the vast stillness and timelessness of the prairie."

Copland's works divide themselves readily into various groups: the first, showing stridency and drive characteristic of the day, includes the engaging *Music for the Theater* (1925), *El Salón México*

---

[1] Roger Sessions summed up the ideals of this group as he saw them:

"Younger men are dreaming of an entirely different kind of music—a music which derives its power from forms beautiful and significant by virtue of inherent musical weight rather than intensity of utterance; a music whose impersonality and self-sufficiency preclude the exotic, which takes its impulse from the realities of a passionate logic; which in the authentic freshness of its moods, is the reverse of ironic and, in its very aloofness from the concrete preoccupations of life, strives rather to contribute form, design, a vision of order and harmony." (Reprinted by permission of the quarterly review *Modern Music,* November-December, 1927.)

(1936); the second, comparatively inaccessible and austere, includes the *Piano Variations* (1930), *Sonata for Piano* (1939-1941), and *Orchestra Variations* (1957); the third includes music which makes an appeal to the general public, the ballet *Billy the Kid* (1938), *Appalachian Spring* (1944), *A Lincoln Portrait* (written as a radio piece), an opera, *The Tender Land*, and the *Third Symphony* (1946).

Henry Cowell's innovations of tone clusters and the like have not proved very significant. Howard Hanson's symphonies show a curious predilection for overstatement and bombast, considering the rather meager quality of their northern-hued musical content. Roy Harris, who above all other American composers has had opportunity to hear his works played, does not seem in his later compositions to have been able to sustain the level of his *Third Symphony* (1933), which has justly been called the most distinguished work in this form yet produced by a native American. With its awkward angularity, its powerful rhythmic effects, its sprawling form, it suggests the vast and curiously empty quality of so much American life. (An analysis will be found on page 436.)

Roger Sessions, a composer of music difficult for the average listener to apprehend, is, as one of his friends has described him, a man of "profound culture and granitic intellectual powers—essentially a thinker." Unfortunately, his music often sounds that way; it thinks for measures on end, and this seems a rather questionable asset. Walter Piston's works are also rather meager in expressive content, although this composer's skill and sincerity are evident enough; he appears to have attempted to remove some of this obscurity in his *Third Symphony* (1947). Randall Thompson's music is more in the European late-nineteenth-century idiom than is that of his contemporary, Virgil Thomson. The latter's operas, *Four Saints in Three Acts* and *Mother of Us All* (1947), with librettos by Gertrude Stein, show the characteristics of the milieu from which they sprang, Paris in the 1920's. He has written some excellent music for the films, particularly *The Plow That Broke the Plains* and *Louisiana Story*. He can be looked on as a neo-Romantic; his wish, as he has expressed it, is to communicate sincere personal sentiments with a maximum of directness. Douglas Moore's best attainments have been in the field of opera, especially his *The Devil and Daniel Webster*, *The Ballad of Baby Doe*, and the *Wings of the Dove*.

MORE RECENT COMPOSERS

A still younger generation includes Samuel Barber, whose earlier works, such as an *Essay for Orchestra* and his *First Symphony*, were conservative in their insistence on architectural details and romantic communication. In his later compositions he has seemed determined to come to grips with a more "advanced" style. Another important figure is Marc Blitzstein, whose most distinctive works, *The Cradle Will Rock* and *No for an Answer*, are theatrical hybrids combining the characteristics of social drama, revue, and opera, all with political implications. He was even rash enough to use the debated issues of a famous American murder trial as a theme for one of his operas. Paul Creston, a composer of Italian backgrounds and Catholic Church music training, has written a large amount of music in various forms. William Schuman has doubled in the fields of composing and educational administration; typical of his sharply dissonant, rather eclectic style are his ballet *Undertow* (1945) and his *Sixth Symphony* (1948). Gian-Carlo Menotti (born in Italy and a naturalized American) has given the present-day stage some skillfully concocted pieces in the Italian *buffa* tradition: *Amelia Goes to the Ball*, *The Old Maid and the Thief*, and *The Telephone*. His attempts at *verismo*, *The Medium*, *The Consul*, *Maria Golovin*, and *The Saint of Bleecker Street*, are sterner stuff which, in spite of obvious theatrical mannerisms and dramatic clichés, powerfully engage an audience's emotions, especially those opera-goers acclimated to Mascagni and Puccini. One of the boldest and most original composers of this generation is the meticulous workman Elliott Carter.

THE YOUNGER GENERATION

Among the younger men there are many who are able to write music that is fluent and well put together but few who have really distinctive things to say. These include Robert Palmer; Alexander Haieff, who combines Eastern traditions with modern technics; David Diamond, whose music unites, in his own words, "certain events and situations with purely abstract conceptions and manipulation of material"; Harold Shapiro, an assured master of modern craftsmanship, whose music seems to have more evocative power than that of many of his contemporaries; Leonard Bernstein, whose activities in so many fields have precluded the composition of much serious music; Ben Weber, who, although he belongs to no particular school, has evolved a style that is quite his own, traditional in sound although organized in serial technique; Norman Dello Joio, whose multifarious backgrounds—church music, Italian opera, American jazz, and modern ballet—have given him an eclectic style well-suited to mass communication; Peter Menin; Lucas Foss; John Cage, who in his belief that modern science has opened paths that the musician should follow, uses sounds as entities in themselves and not as "vehicles for man-made theories or expressions of human sentiment"; and Easley Blackwood, who seems to be typical of his time in that he is eclectic and an extremely skillful technician, flirts with tone-row composition without adopting it wholeheartedly, and is proficient in all contemporary clichés without having very much to communicate. Otto Luening and Vladimir Ussachevsky are the best known American exponents of tape-recorder and electronic music.

The fact that almost all these composers are native born and trained shows that tremendous advances have been made in the United States in professional musical training.

World War II peculiarly accelerated the growth of the country as a musical nation, for all of Europe's outstanding composers, performers, conductors, critics, and scholars who could get away came to the United States and became integral parts of American musical life. What will come of this new amalgamation of cultural influences only time can tell; there can be little doubt, however, that the center of the world's creative activity in music moved from Europe to the Western Hemisphere, and that the future of the art will be closely identified with whatever is accomplished in the United States. It is this fact that makes American music of unusual significance today.

MUSIC IN THE AMERICAS SOUTH OF THE UNITED STATES

In pre-Columbian days there flourished in Mexico several civilizations which cultivated the arts extensively. Recent archaeological research has shown the degrees of progress achieved by these cultures; and there are irrefutable proofs that music played a role of real importance in government, religion, and war, and that it was the object of special study and cultivation by the state.

Basing his materials not on archaeological melodies or quotations from pre-Conquest music, for no such records exist, but on a study of Aztec instruments and the way they must have sounded, Carlos Chávez, a modern Mexican composer, has given us, in his *Sinfonia India*, music which makes use of Indian motives and instrumental effects in order to evoke the spirit of pre-Cortezian Mexico.

In addition to the influence of these ancient American cultures, present-day Mexican and South American folk music, the more popular topical urban music of the streets, cafés, and ballrooms, and the serious art music of Central and South America are the result of a peculiar admixture of three components:

(1) Music which survived from the original Indian inhabitants of the continent.

(2) Music brought from Africa by the Negroes and developed by their peculiarly imaginative powers and strong rhythmic sense.

(3) Music imported by the European colonists, chiefly Spanish and Portuguese.

The particular social and geographic conditions of Central and South America have blended these components into a style of music that is strikingly original, rhythmically fascinating, melodically pleasing, and thoroughly alive.

Thanks to the enterprise of the Folklore Section of the Library of Congress and a few of the smaller recording companies, a great deal of this ethnic folk music from Latin-American countries is available for study and enjoyment. Their recordings, actually made in the field, give the listener that fragile and intimate spirit of "unawareness in music making" that is the exact opposite of the rather glamorous sophistication induced by the broadcast studio's interpretation of folk music. The backgrounds of Equatorial Africa, from which American Negro music sprang; the Afro-Bahian religious songs of Brazil, as well as many of the other folk songs of that country; West Indian songs and dances of all sorts; the folk music of Venezuela, Mexico, Peru—these are but some of the riches avail-

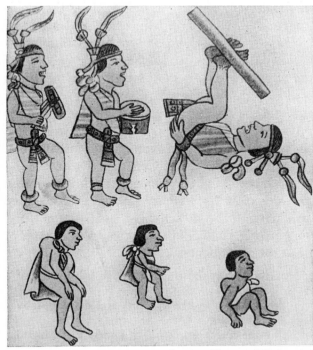

ANCIENT
AZTEC
MUSICIANS
*From The Codex
Florentinus.*

Courtesy, Museum of Modern Art

able in this treasure chest of Latin-American folk music. As one
lover of this music has well said, without falling into the trap of the
superficially intellectual or into one of the many cults of snobbism,
this music should be cultivated by any listener who wishes to enlarge
his taste and deepen his understanding of music in general.

There has been a wide exportation of the popular, topical music
of this region in recent years. Such native songs and dances as the
calypso, habanera, tango, rhumba, cha-cha, and meringué have become favorites in European and North American circles. These are
only some of the more obvious of these fascinating Latin-American
musical products; there are many more which, in their mixing of
exotic and colorful elements, are worth knowing. Unfortunately,
because of the influences of popular taste and the necessity of
streamlining it for commercial consumption, what we hear in North
American and European performances of this music is often quite
different from the original.

ANCIENT AZTEC MUSICIANS
From The Codex Florentinus.

IN MEXICO

The most important figure on the modern Mexican scene is Carlos Chávez, conductor and composer, whose music achieves a true, indigenous blend of the influences that have gone into the folk music of his country. This music, however, has been affected by the developments of the composer's generation, as is evident in its linear contrapuntal lines and its stark objectivity. At one moment it seems to express a primitive barbarism, in the next a machine-age spirit.

The list of other Mexican composers of serious music includes Silvestre Revueltas (who based his work on the popular music of his country's fairs and taverns and whose tragic death in 1940 robbed Latin-American music of one of its finest and most individual talents),[2] Candelario Huizar, Daniel Ayala Salvador Contreras, and Blas Galindo.

[2] Mayer-Serra, in his *Panorama de la Música Mexicana—desde la Independencia hasta La Actualidad* (published by El Colegio de México in 1941) makes this distinction between the two leading Mexican composers:

"For Chávez the aboriginal musical culture is the most important in the history of Mexican music; he tries to reconstruct musically this atmosphere of primitive purity, thinking to find in it the true Mexican character; for Revueltas, on the other hand, Mexico is genuinely represented by the remains of primitive cultures as well as by the surprising results of that mixture of races and civilizations that is so characteristic of modern Mexico."

SOUTH AMERICAN CREATORS

Small but active groups of composers have been working in the South American countries of Brazil, Chile, Argentina, and Uruguay. Here, as in Mexico, there has been a peculiar blending of many diverse elements and resources—chiefly Portuguese, Indian, and African. Of all these countries, Brazil has had the richest and most important musical development; by the middle of the nineteenth century its greatest city, Rio de Janeiro, had a cosmopolitan music culture comparable to that of the great European centers, supporting first-class operatic and concert performances and a good national conservatory. The first renowned Brazilian composer was the nineteenth-century Carlos Gomes, who was, indeed, the first opera composer of the Americas to win European recognition. Alberto Nepomuceno was a strong nationalist and sponsor of Brazil's greatest composer to date, Hector Villa-Lobos (1887-1960). A genius with an insatiable curiosity and seemingly inexhaustible energy, Villa-Lobos was almost entirely self-taught. He wrote over fourteen hundred works in every musical idiom; the best of these show great ingenuity, strong individuality, and originality. His major chamber-music work, the *Nonetto* for chamber orchestra and chorus, could have been written by no other composer. His great suites, the *Bachianas Brasilieras*, attempt to "transmit the spirit of Bach—a universal spirit, source, and end in itself" into the soul of Brazil, and are worth careful study.

Other leading Brazilian composers who are trying to build a contemporary national school are Oscar Lorenzo Fernandez, Francisco Mignone, and M. Carmargo Guarnieri.

In Argentina the best-known name seems to be Juan José Castro, conductor of the Colón opera of Buenos Aires, a brilliant and very successful composer as well as conductor; his older brother, a composer of even greater talent, José Mario Castro, is not so well known outside his native country. Belonging to the same *Grupo Renovacion* is Jacobo Ficher, composer of many symphonic and chamber works. Juan Carlos Paz seems to have become enamored of Schönbergian twelve-tone ideals, while the young Alberto Ginastera is looked upon by the Argentine musicians as their most promising composer. Prominent progressives in Uruguay include Carlos Estrada and Vincente Ascone.

In general it must be stated that, with one or two outstanding exceptions, these South and Central American composers, like so many of their contemporary brothers to the north, have shown a tendency to ignore their own birthright and imitate European music that was modern some years ago. The resulting music is both unfertile and unrepresentative.

In most of the South American countries there are folklorists who conduct important research work along the line of native songs and dances, as well as scholars who try to piece together these valuable finds in pre-Columbian music. Chief among these are Carlos Vega of Argentina and Luiz de Azevedo of Brazil.

It seems strange that a world war was needed to awaken the curiosity of the people of the United States to the activities of their neighbors to the south. All signs point to an increasingly active and profitable interchange of ideas between the countries of the American hemisphere in the years that lie ahead. In this, music is bound to play an important part.

LIST OF SUGGESTED MUSIC

RECORDED AMERICAN MUSIC

All lists of recorded music become dated as soon as they are written, since new recordings are constantly being issued and old ones are dropped. The reference for this list is the monthly *Schwann Catalog*, the standard guide to all monaural and stereophonic records currently available. Although it contains most of musical Americana, it does not list the valuable recordings of folk music available directly from the Library of Congress, Washington, D. C.: *Arias, Anthems, and Chorales from the American Moravians*, Vol. I.

1890	*Concerto No. 2, in d minor for Piano*	MAC DOWELL
1896	*Woodland Sketches* (piano)	MAC DOWELL
1897	*Symphony No. 2*	IVES
1906	*Pagan Poem*, Op. 14	LOEFFLER
1907	*Symphonic Sketches*	CHADWICK
1910	*Suite in E Major for Strings*	FOOTE
1915	*Adventures in a Perambulator*	CARPENTER

1920	*Pleasure Dome of Kubla Khan*	GRIFFES
1922	*Through the Looking Glass*	TAYLOR
1925	*Concerto Grosso No. 1*	BLOCH
1925	*Integrales*	VARÈSE
1926	*America, An Epic Rhapsody*	BLOCH
1928	*An American in Paris*	GERSHWIN
1930	*Symphony No. 2* ("Romantic")	HANSON
1935	*Density*	VARÈSE
1935	*Sinfonia India*	CHÁVEZ
1936	*El Salón México*	COPLAND
1937	*Symphony No. 2*	SESSIONS
1938	*Symphony No. 3*	HARRIS
1938	*The Incredible Flutist* (ballet)	PISTON
1940	*Symphony No. 4* ("Folksong")	HARRIS
1942	*Essay No. 2 for Orchestra*	BARBER
1943	*Symphony No. 2, Op. 19*	BARBER
1944	*Symphony No. 2, Op. 35*	CRESTON
1944	*Appalachian Spring*	COPLAND
1945	*Quartet No. 2*	BLOCH
1946-47	*Symphony No. 3*	RIEGGER
1947	*Mother of Us All*	THOMSON
1947	*Variations, Chaconne, and Finale*	DELLO JOIO
1948	*Symphony No. 6*	SCHUMAN
1948	*Quartet for Piano and Strings*	PALMER
1948	*Symphony No. 4*	DIAMOND
1949	*Organum for Orchestra*	RUGGLES
1950	*The Consul* (opera)	MENOTTI
1951	*Quartet*	CARTER
1953	*Symphony No. 6*	MENNIN

1954	*Piece for Tape Recorder*	LUENING AND USSACHEVSKY
1955	*Symphony No. 6*	PISTON
1956	*Ballad of Baby Doe* (opera)	MOORE
1957	*Orchestral Variations*	COPLAND
1957	*Music 1957*	COWELL
1958	*Poeme Électronique*	VARÈSE
1958	*Four Fragments from Canterbury Tales*	TRIMBLE
1960	*Symphony No. 2*	BLACKWOOD

TOPICS FOR DISCUSSION

Why do you think that, although a large number of American works have been recorded, they are so little known today?

In the list of recorded works given above, how many do you think have American characteristics?

CHAPTER 32

BEETHOVEN'S *Fifth Symphony*

࿊

BEETHOVEN'S EXCITING BACKGROUND

A shift from the study of modern trends to a consideration of the Fifth Symphony of Beethoven is not so abrupt as it first seems. We have suggested that the leaders of musical thought of the first two decades of the twentieth century have been looking for a new freedom from the older conventions. During a period marked by violent changes—physical, spiritual, and economic—these composers have demanded that music be permitted to cast off the fetters of the past and develop along the abstract lines of musical design. We have likewise suggested that the process of experimentation in these new fields, even though it has not yet produced figures which approximate the great masters of the past, deserves our attention. The results that have followed the practice of these modern ideals show up in rather unfortunate relief against the striking work of the Titan who lived and composed in a period of upheaval almost exactly like that which has given us our present-day conditions.

Ludwig van Beethoven wrote during the period of unsettlement and doubt that followed the French Revolution; he was born in 1770 and died in 1827. (The fall of the Bastile occurred, you remember, in 1789.) It was Beethoven who voiced the thoughts and emotions of that great time as did no other, raising himself and his music into the very "realms of the sunlight itself." His music is the incarnation of Taine's description of the period; it is filled with discontent with the present, a vague desire for a higher beauty and a more ideal happiness, the painful aspiration for the infinite. It is because of the manner in which he sang of these desires and aspirations that we listen to him today; he spoke a universal language and his message has reached the whole cultured world. He was not content merely with a garrulous protest against things as they existed. The music of the time had reached heights, under the genius of Haydn and Mozart, that seemed to make any further progress difficult, if not impossible. But, building firmly on the past, realizing that ideas are best communicated through music that follows fundamentals of design, Beethoven gathered up the surging discontents, strivings, and aspirations of his time and voiced them through a universally understood medium, charging them with a vitality and emotional power that is as strong today as it was in the early part of the nineteenth century. Thus he remains a man, not of historical yesterdays, but of today, and for all time. Shall we be able to say the same of the Stravinskys, Schönbergs, and their like a hundred years hence?

Some of the music that Beethoven wrote has become dated and old-fashioned. The quality of his work is uneven, for he had to live from the practice of his art and sometimes wrote things that were obviously designed for immediate consumption. While all of his work is filled with what one writer has called "moral intensity"— that is, a struggle to express the infinite—this intention is not always realized, and we have music that is grandiose and impressive rather than great. But in his best works, the *Eroica Symphony*, the *Fifth Symphony*, the *Ninth Symphony*, and the last string quartets, he stands unequaled both in the force of his thought and in the quality of its expression.

THE *C MINOR SYMPHONY*: A DRAMA IN PURE MUSIC

It is unfortunate, but perhaps inevitable, that the *Fifth* (*c minor*) *Symphony* of Beethoven, one of the most epochal of his works, suffered from overplaying almost from the day of its first performance. Sir George Grove tells us that the conductor who first introduced orchestral music into England played this symphony week after week. It was Grove's opinion that the tremendous hold which this work had on audiences was due to its "prodigious originality,

Courtesy, Steinway and Sons, New York

N. C. WYETH: BEETHOVEN AND NATURE

The composer's close contact with the beauties of nature was the source of some of his finest music. The painter has depicted him here in the mood of the Pastoral (Sixth) Symphony.

form, and conciseness." The very qualifications that have made it popular have given it staying power. Present-day writers might well ponder these two characteristics, popularity and staying power!

This work stands above all others as a triumphant demonstration of the eternal necessity of shaping expressive materials according to fundamental laws of design. It proves, as does no other single piece of music, that only if various elements at the disposal of the composer are combined according to organized plan will the final appeal of the whole be realized. No one knew better than Beethoven that the formal principles of music are not arbitrary rules laid down by authoritative fiat. Rather they were the result of continued experimentation from the early unidentified writers of simple songs down to the composers of his own day. The final object of experimentation was to find the best method of composing music so that it could give the hearer a feeling of definiteness, clarity, and unity of expression.

BEETHOVEN'S SHAPING OF FORM

We have already said what the most usual forms available to the composer of Beethoven's day were; it will be no surprise to find that he employed them all. As Grove says: "The *C Minor Symphony* is from the beginning to the end as strictly in accordance with the rules that govern the structure of musical composition as any symphony of Haydn." While the symphonic form as Beethoven used it was rigid in outline, his method permitted the widest liberties of style and idiom. Though the music is conceived in the most stringent of intellectual methods, it nevertheless is incandescent with fiery emotion. In this *Fifth Symphony* Beethoven brought the organization of form to a state of perfection, but he was "no theorist endeavoring to demonstrate the validity of his innovations. He was working in obedience to the dictates of his artistic soul" (Henderson in the *New York Sun*).

This work is a most significant example of the necessary interrelationship of form and substance. It is perfectly easy to dissect the first movement, for example, and show that it is written almost exactly according to the strictest pattern of sonata form. This is interesting and helpful, if we are trying to arrive at an understanding of the demands that this form makes on the composer. What is significant is that the substance of this music grows inexorably out of the formal design—one would be unthinkable without the other. Beethoven could have produced neither the logical coherence nor the dramatic intensity of this movement if he had not observed the necessities of formal design. On the other hand, the obedience to all the laws of structure known to artists would have been of little avail if Beethoven's thoughts had not been so original and the glow of their emotional power had not been so intense.

THE FIRST MOVEMENT

The first movement, as in every great symphony, gives the clue for the whole work. It is tensely dramatic—one of the few movements in all music, as a great contemporary composer has said, that we feel to be absolutely perfect. The gist of the movement, and for that matter of the whole symphony, lies in the first theme—the whole orchestra forcefully depicts Fate knocking at the door.

Noteworthy and delightful is the passage which immediately grows out of this opening summons, the bridge passage leading from the first to the second theme. This was a master stroke in 1808, and no one has yet produced a finer growth from a tiny seed. During it all, the first theme is driven home, and its rhythm and mood pushed onward for some sixty measures. Just as we are ready for the second theme, we hear the first once more on the horns (59-62). While the second theme is being given by the strings and the wood winds, in a sudden change of key and mood, we hear the first softly reflected by the basses (63-76).

There is a short third theme,

and then Beethoven rushes impetuously to finish the first section (the statement, or exposition) of 124 measures. In the old-fashioned, leisurely, eighteenth-century manner, Beethoven there draws a double bar and marks the measures for repetition. The chief object of that procedure was to enable the hearer to get the themes well in mind, but in the quickened tempo of modern life, this repetition is not often carried out.

The development, or "working-out," is short, only 123 measures. The perhaps overenthusiastic Berlioz suggested that in it Beethoven revealed all the secrets of his being—his private griefs, his lonely meditations, his bursts of enthusiasm, his anxious search for love. The gentle second theme has no place in this emotional display; practically all the material is drawn from the first theme, even the dramatic series of alternating high and low chords between the strings and the wood winds. The development section ends with an insistent hammering out of the rhythm of the opening, leading directly into the restatement, or recapitulation, with a typically Beethoven turn just after the first theme is heard again. At the moment when we are ready for the bridge passage that will lead us from the first to the second theme, a curious little oboe cadenza is interpolated (269), the sort of surprise that Beethoven often uses to give added piquancy. It lasts for just a moment, and then we are off again. The restatement is almost an exact replica of the statement (there are 126 measures), but instead of ending it abruptly as he did the first time, Beethoven adds a long coda of 129 measures to build up a bigger and more impressive climax. This is almost like another development; it seems as if Beethoven felt that he had more material at hand than he could logically crowd into his development section; the motto theme is again the predominating feature, but there is also a new theme (424). The coda is as well built as the rest; indeed, we may well ask whether there is a more keenly knit half-a-thousand bars in all music. It moves as an organic whole, bound together by the masterful motto theme, and drawn to its logical end with inexorable force.

The Second Movement

The second movement, in major, is necessarily a relief; after the somber minor of the first movement it sounds a note of quiet resignation and strength. Following the general scheme of theme and variations, Beethoven here uses two themes instead of one and adds some passages developed from the main theme instead of merely variants of it. This peculiar freedom displayed in the treatment of accepted and traditional formal schemes is characteristic of Beethoven.

The first theme is gracious, leisurely, kindly:

This is followed by the second, soaring in hope and aspiration:

Variations of these follow. The general scheme employed is the use of an accompaniment with notes twice as quick as those used in the original statement. The pattern is:

Variation 1 (Theme I) using sixteenth notes
         Theme II
Variation 2 (Theme I) using thirty-second notes
         Some development of Theme I and augmentation of
         Theme II
Variation 3 (Theme I) in minor
         Restatement and Extension of Theme I
Coda based largely on Theme I

THE THIRD MOVEMENT

It is important to note that Beethoven did not label the third movement a *scherzo*; he merely marked it *allegro*. This is not a joking movement, nor a humorous interlude; we feel rather that Fate's grim pursuit has again begun. The first whisperings of the basses are sinister; the upper strings take up the same figure and pause:

Then we become aware of the composer's purpose; the main motto theme is heard again as the second theme, but now it is in a rhythmic pattern of threes:

Notice the difference in effect. These two themes are alternated and somewhat developed for the remainder of the first part of the movement. The second section (the *trio*) is, in contrast to the first, in major, and we feel that Beethoven has indulged in the kind of writing more in the usual mood of his third movements. The opening section, quick and staccato, is given to the double basses, the instruments least fitted by nature to deal with this type of music, but they manage it.

Then the violas, second violins and finally the firsts have a try at the same theme, as if to show how easy it really is. The whole section is repeated, and the second part of the trio appears. It is introduced by several false starts on the part of the basses; they finally dash off, inviting the rest of the orchestra to join them. Instead of going back, as was customary, to the opening section of the trio, Beethoven repeats the second part and then leads us directly back to the beginning mood of the movement—but this time with what a difference! Now it is more eerie than ever; the wood winds alternate with plucked strings and everything is rushed along, faster and faster. Suddenly there is an interruption—everything stops, the rhythm is continued only by a kettledrum beating against a strange low note held by the strings. Gradually this astonishing interlude gathers pace, increases in volume, and before we realize what is really happening, there come those three glorious crashes that usher in the greatest finale devised up to that time, one that has hardly been equaled since.

The Triumph of the Last Movement

What strength and conviction and everlasting ardor breathe through this last movement! There is no doubt here of the composer's intent; this is triumph—"Oh, life is so beautiful, let me live,

live!" Even if one has had many years' experience in listening, this music, if properly interpreted, never seems to lose the thrill which can lift one out of one's seat.

The first theme is one of exulting triumph:

At measure 26 a subsidiary theme is introduced:

which leads to the second theme.

In measures 64-67 a final, concluding theme is heard:

Shortly after, the exposition comes to a close; again as in the first movement, this is marked for repetition, but is rarely so played. The development makes use of the second main theme almost entirely, again showing Beethoven's unconventional freedom of treatment when he finds it will suit his purpose. In this last movement a piccolo, three trombones, and a double bassoon are added to the orchestra, and their weight tells. At the climax of the development comes a dramatic pause, a change of time from two's to three's, and an astonishing appearance of the ghost of the motto theme:

It is as if the composer would suggest that even in the midst of joyful triumph the specter of man's inevitable fate lurks in the background. This "flashback," played by strings and wood winds, is also a most effective dramatic device for providing contrast before the return of the first theme in the restatement section. It quickly fades into the background; there is a short, sharp crescendo, and we are back again at the opening theme of the movement, all the more brilliant now for coming like the sun bursting from behind a cloud. The themes we have heard are again presented, now in the key unity of C Major. When we are more than a hundred bars from the end, the grand coda begins (318) with an exultant little fanfare. More and more intense, faster and faster, higher and higher grows the music; Beethoven builds up the excitement until the final chord, which he hammers almost as if demented. But the cool head is in command of the warm heart all the way, and this glorious rampage is carefully calculated and controlled down to the smallest detail. In the manner of a great artist, every detail is closely watched and designed, even when the music seems most free, and the effects are sure. Here, as in almost everything he did, Beethoven was absolutely individual, unlike anyone before or since. Here indeed "God rests in reason and moves in passion."

This symphony piles up, as all great works should. It begins with astonishing freedom of expression, achieved through strictness of structural detail, goes on to variations with spacious freedom and emotion in them, something quite different from the brief, rather stilted variations written by the older composers. Then there is the third movement, with its touch of the demonic, running without interruption into the magnificent finale. Masterful construction, magnificent tunes which everyone can remember, and the authentic thrill of music that cumulates in power and repose—no wonder the *Fifth Symphony* stands, a world's masterpiece for all time!

Because of its universality and the fact that it is an almost perfect model of symphonic construction, a line score of the whole work is given on pages 397-416, so that you may follow every detail.

TOPICS FOR DISCUSSION

Do you seek for meaning in the *Fifth Symphony*? Do you find a meaning? Do you habitually seek meanings in other program music? Do you approve of this tendency?

Sir John McEwen once said, "While language seeks to express a meaning, *music is itself the meaning*." Discuss this. Do you find it a bleak or comforting piece of philosophy?

A recent writer, in commenting on the remark "Thus Fate knocks at the door," which Beethoven is supposed to have made in answer to an inquiry about the meaning of the four-note motive which opens the *Fifth Symphony*, says, "In the philosophical sense, I submit that there is no purpose to music; that it is not 'for' anything. . . . Beethoven's Fifth Symphony may be Fate—or Kate—knocking at the door. That is up to you." What did he mean, and do you agree?

SYMPHONY NO. 5 IN C MINOR, OPUS 67

LUDWIG VAN BEETHOVEN

First Movement

Second Movement.

Fourth Movement.

BRAHMS' *First Symphony*

وهۆۇۆ

MAKING THE BEST OF BOTH WORLDS

Johannes Brahms (1833-1897) has of late years become popular because he made the best of the Classic and the Romantic worlds. And so, when people want to go back to something satisfying, they find that Brahms enriches both the mental and the emotional life. In early days he foolishly signed a manifesto against the sort of "new music" that Wagner was supposed to have introduced. As a result, he was thought of as a stern defender of the classics and was labeled for life. At heart he really was a Romantic, and a rather wild one, as his first *Piano Concerto* shows. He was a superb lyricist, as his songs prove, and he could build on the big forty-minute-symphony scale. Some think that he lacked passion; he had it, and occasionally it appears, all the stronger and sweeter because it is not thrown about all over his music. There is no lack of deep feeling in Brahms' music, even if he keeps "passion" undercover most of the time; music lovers cherish his pages as the quintessence of German Romanticism. The *First Symphony* shall stand for brief analysis as our example of Brahms. Although this was the first big work he wrote for orchestra alone, he was forty-three when it appeared and was thus finely mature.

SYMPHONY NO. 1, IN C MINOR

A slow introduction sets the scene—for what? Everyone can make his own background if he remembers that the composer meant

BRAHMS AS
PIANIST

his work to be listened to as an example of the dramatic life of music itself, not of the other arts. If we like to think again of life versus Destiny, well and good, but it is music's life, not just man's. The bass throbs, it binds the music—perhaps to earth. The first theme of the main movement (42, hinted at in measure 21 of the introduction) soars in arpeggio, as do many of Brahms' tunes:

This and the second theme, given to the oboe (121) and also evolved from the introduction, form the chief material from which the movement grows:

It never loses the cast of melancholy or pathos; indeed, that mood is never altogether absent, in some form or other, from the next two movements. Brahms has lovely taste in allowing the varying shades of musical feeling to follow each other with maximum emotional effect and, in the meantime, sustaining the flow of the music and its argument and interest. One feels each mood transition to be at once refreshing, since it comes at just the right moment, and vital to the continuity of the work—woven into its texture. Therein, of course, lies one of the greatest qualities of any composer. In this movement he may be said to attain even a tragic mood, but restrained, reflective pathos (suggested by the descending chromatic harmony he so often uses) is perhaps the emotional keynote.

Second Movement

The second movement is a fine example of Brahms' power of varying his emotional stresses while maintaining something of the same atmosphere as in the first movement. Here we have lyrical expansion instead of the keen, close development of seminal motives. There is something of Beethoven's breadth of spirit too, in the themes, as a few notes of each will show:

Notice how the oboe (17), in replying to the strings' enunciation of the first idea, is taken up by the strings before it has had the opportunity to finish its theme (22), as if they were eager to add sweet strength to the tranquillity of the oboe theme. After a section in which the solo parts for both oboe and clarinet predominate—very typical of Brahms' manner of writing for the orchestra—comes the repetition, freshly scored, of the original theme, followed by a leisurely, gently pathetic coda, with a final cadence. This is reminiscent of the opening of the first movement, but uses a flattened sixth of the scale, a device only too well known in vulgarized forms at the tail end of cheap ballads.

THIRD MOVEMENT

Brahms' scherzos are much meatier, more solid in style, and a bit slower in tempo than those of the other writers of symphonies. This one shows a feeling of German hominess most charmingly interpreted as art music. The general structural scheme of the scherzo-trio-scherzo is carried out. There are three main themes in the scherzo section: the one on the clarinets at the very beginning:

the one heard on the combined wood winds which follows shortly after (11) gracefully descending its melodic way:

and the clarinet tune which comes shortly before the trio section is introduced (45):

Brahms loved the warm, rich quality of the clarinet and used it frequently in solo parts. The trio has a 6/8 swing, is a bit faster, and is almost entirely given over to discussions between the wood winds and the strings. When the first section returns, the themes have a little more elaborate accompaniment, some of them borrowed from the trio; Brahms never wastes material, but loves to tie his whole structure by interrelating materials in this fashion.

FOURTH MOVEMENT

Brahms followed Beethoven's example (in his *Fifth Symphony*) in using the trombones in the last movement for the first time. Again we hear a slow introduction that is deeply dramatic. The violins and the horn (1) hint at the great tune that is to follow; the chromatic element, so prominent in the first movement, is again noticed. The exciting plucked-string work-up that begins at (5) is ex-

tremely brief; it leads, with greater agitation (29), into a magnificent horn theme, which Brahms tells us he heard first from the
alpine-horn players in Switzerland:

In this introduction we might figure a giant's heavy sigh as he strives
to throw off a mood of depression; then comes the horn's peaceful
entry. One could not wish a more beautiful example of this composer's evoking, with serene surety, a new mood at a vital moment;
this is a true stroke of fine art in its swaying of the balance of emotion. We realize again, as David Stanley Smith succinctly put it,
that "technical subtlety is the prime quality of great music," and we
understand more deeply how worthwhile is the closest study we
can make of the thousand subtleties of a great composer's technic.
After the horn theme there is a short, hymn-like section on the brass,
one of the finest bits of the whole work:

This leads to the entrance of the *allegro* (60), with one of the
world's great tunes, bracing the nerve and warming the heart:

This and succeeding passages, sustaining the feeling of exhilaration,
form a splendid foundation for the movement. Although fairly complex, it carries us along in a tide of powerful rhythms and glorious
harmonies. The second subject (117)

and another theme (148)

build up the movement's life.

Then a surprise—Brahms starts the development section with a full statement of the great swinging first theme before beginning the real development at measure 220. Based on material drawn from both main themes, this development section reaches a tremendous climax in the glorious proclamation of the Alpine horn theme from the introduction (beginning at 285). The second and third themes enter to round out the restatement, which ends at measure 367. A long coda begins, culminating in a galloping passage derived from the first main theme and presenting in a final stretto the chorale-like passage from the introduction (407). The whole builds up logically and inevitably in a triumphant paean of confident vitality.

The man who is fit for big music does not come out from hearing the best of Brahms at the same door of the spirit in which he went. Few of us win at once to the heart of this composer; we have to grow up to him, and that means work and time; but how often will equal labor give greater joy, and expense of time so great a satisfaction? The biggest, broadest art seeks for its service devotion and the refreshment of one's faculties. The man who makes music such as this symphony one of the broad bases of his experience and one of the touchstones of his taste wins something that he will never willingly let go, something that in the truest and deepest sense will gladden and enrich the rest of his life.

TOPICS FOR DISCUSSION

The *First Symphony* of Brahms has been referred to as the tenth, meaning that it is a logical successor to Beethoven's nine symphonies. Do you think this appropriate?

Compare this Brahms symphony with any others of his with which you are familiar. How would you rate it among his four works in this form?

Does Brahms or Beethoven make the most immediate appeal in this form? Which quality—ripeness of thought, power of sentiment, or management of form—stands out most in the works of each man?

In what does immediacy of appeal of music generally consist? Can the appeal differ for individual listeners?

Do you think that great music appeals immediately to people? Is true appreciation likely to come slowly for all great art? How does one know what makes art great?

CHAPTER 34

Five Later Symphonic Works

❦

After two of the great masterworks of symphonic literature have been studied, it is important to see what later composers did with the form. Although they may have followed in general the formal schemes of Beethoven and Brahms, we should realize that these men made contributions that mark their works as distinctly individual and as characteristic of the periods in which they lived. We have seen that Beethoven used the fundamental structural ideas of his predecessors in such a way as to make them his own; and that Brahms' intense preoccupation with the problems of symphonic form was due to a realization of his debt, as he expressed it, to the "giant whose steps he always heard behind himself"—Beethoven. So too, the works of the best symphonists of the latter part of the nineteenth and early years of the twentieth century owe much to the towering structures which preceded them. Yet even a brief study of such representative works as Tchaikovsky's *Fifth Symphony*, Sibelius' *Second*, Shostakovich's *Fifth;* Harris' *Third*, and Bartók's *Concerto for Orchestra* will show how the form changed and adapted itself to the needs of later composers.

TCHAIKOVSKY'S *FIFTH SYMPHONY*

In this symphony, written twelve years after Brahms' *First Symphony*, we find the Russian composer achieving a unique uniformity of mood and structure through the employment of a theme common to all four movements, what he called a "motto theme." It is almost as though Tchaikovsky had said to himself: "In this symphony at least I will rid myself of my tendency to rhapsodize [this composer was a severe self-critic] and will choose one theme around which my whole work can revolve. This symphony must and shall be homogenous." The motto theme is:

In carrying out his plans, Tchaikovsky employs the usual four movements, through which this theme runs like a dark thread in a gorgeous tapestry.

In the first movement there are two main subjects; the first (42-48), obviously influenced by the character of the motto theme, is sad and reflective:

The second, in contrast, is full of brightness and vitality (116-120):

Two subsidiary themes are immediately introduced, the first (154-157):

the second (170-174):

The composer, in his development section, considers these as important as his main subjects (in fact, the introduction of so much

thematic material robs the development of the particular importance
it possesses in the Beethoven and Brahms works), and we hear much
brilliance and animation, with plenty of repetition of themes and
those peculiar rushing passages so characteristic of this artist. The
main and subsidiary themes are restated, the first in rather shortened
form. Suddenly, in the midst of the brilliant coda (which begins at
471), the first theme reappears, the mood of the music grows somber
and dies away in Tchaikovsky's mournful manner, down and down
to lower strings and bassoon.

The second movement—*Andante cantabile, con alcuna licenza*
(slowly, in a singing manner, with some licence)—takes the form
of a songlike romanza. The first section (1-65) is based on a lovely
horn theme with string accompaniment (8-12):

Then follows a secondary theme, which is strongly worked up
during the rest of the section:

The middle section is of a quicker character (66-107); the theme
is given to the clarinet and answered by the bassoon:

The movement mounts to a climax, and then the challenging
motto theme appears briefly before the third section (108-157)
begins. The first theme, assigned to the strings, has a charming
wood-wind embroidery; the secondary theme returns with more
dramatic excitement. Everything is quickened and strengthened
until the coda, when suddenly the motto theme is heard again *fff*
(159), breaking in upon the prevailing happy mood of the movement. From this point there is a decrescendo until the pensive end,
marked *ppp*.

The third movement is a graceful 3/4 one to which the composer has given the name valse. It is based on this theme:

A sprightly, trio-like middle portion (73-144) stands out in fine contrast. After a restatement of almost exactly the same length as the first section, there follows a short coda of 52 measures. At the end occurs a weak citation of the motto theme in 3/4 time, its only appearance in the whole symphony which does not seem spontaneous.

In the finale the motto theme comes into its own; the impressive introduction to this last movement (1-57) is based entirely on it, in major, and we feel that this must have been the form of the origin of the theme. The movement grows clearer as it proceeds, as though "the heart had cast off a load of suffering and God's world shone out bright once more." The exposition is based on the following themes:

There is a development of some 120 measures and a restatement of approximately the same length as the exposition. The coda (426-565), the most important factor in the whole movement, heralds the final entry of the motto theme against a whirling wood-wind background; the clouds lift, the skies clear in this grandiose setting. Here is a fine example of this composer's Byronic power of becoming momentous and eloquent with small provocation. Like the popular Romantic poet, Tchaikovsky assumes on an insignificant occasion a more tragic mien than the average Englishman does (to use Bernard Shaw's words) when he is going to be executed. Here the composer whips himself into frenzy and proclaims this last utterance of his generative theme with tremendous power and impressiveness. Yet all the frenetic energy does not impress or move us as do the finales of the Beethoven and Brahms symphonies; in comparison Tchaikovsky's seems too obvious and unmotivated.

One need not pretend that this work is Jovian in order to enjoy it. It has its own color, due to consummate orchestral draftsmanship; it alternates romance and revelry; it delights in melancholy; yet in the end hope triumphs over despair. Tchaikovsky did not need to indulge in bizarre effects or violate accepted canons of form to make his work distinctive, but he did not hesitate to use whatever means his muse seemed to require to secure the effect desired. This stirring work is bound to occupy an important place among late Romantic compositions.

SIBELIUS' *SECOND SYMPHONY*[1]

It is natural that a composer who wrote almost a century later than Beethoven should display a tendency to rebel against many of the conventions and clichés that had become an essential part of Romantic expression. In many ways the seven symphonies of Sibelius are the record of such a revolt. In them Sibelius, a composer who kept himself isolated from the many fads and poses of his time, a man of incorrigible sincerity and true genius, gradually freed himself from what he felt to be German dominance in music. The later symphonies, particularly the *Fourth*, *Sixth* and *Seventh*, reveal this composer at the height of his individualistic expressive powers; the *Second*, written during his exuberant thirties, is a full, rounded expression of his virile talent, although it contains obvious connections with the past. During that early period one of his ardent admirers, with an enthusiasm which has not always been maintained by most critics, hailed Sibelius as a giant among men, composing with a seven-league stride that his fellows never knew or conceived, gifted with a fresh, northern sense of beauty.

The name of this composer has become inseparably connected with Finnish nationalism, and quite rightly. His music is full of the spirit of the north, colored with an austere, often ascetic, hue, shot

[1] Excerpts reprinted by permission of Associated Music Publishers, Inc., New York.

JEAN SIBELIUS

Photo, Davart

through with faërie fantasy, born of the same blood as the stirring northern sagas. There is a dark and somber character to much of the music Sibelius has written, a certain powerful, granitic strength and uncompromising austerity; with it all, however, there is a sincerity and spontaneity not excelled by any of his contemporaries, a warmth of emotion all the more moving because it is so well controlled.

This *Second Symphony* corresponds in its composer's career to the *Eroica* in Beethoven's or the *Fourth* in Tchaikovsky's; all three show their creators as young men girding their loins for the race ahead of them, fully conscious of their irrepressible genius and teeming with ideas. It shows many of the most characteristic traits of Sibelius' symphonic style: his molding of short, fertile, melodic fragments into a full-sized theme that finally arrives as a supreme climax, rather than working them out on principles of exposition, development, and recapitulation; his use of peculiarly built, whirring accompanimental passages, from which coherent ideas suddenly crystallize; and his repetition of melodic ideas and rhythmic patterns, sometimes almost to the point of satiety.

Even in such an early work as this *Second Symphony*, we should
not try to look for the ordinary structural patterns. Although
Sibelius follows the general ideals of symphonic form, the first movement is based on the following generative fragments, without any
hint of a first and second theme in the accepted manner.

1. A series of detached chords for the strings

2. A six-measure melody for the wood winds over a detached string
accompaniment

3. A theme given out by the bassoons

4. An epic-like proclamation by the violins alone, as virile as one
of the heroes in the *Kalevala*, Finland's great national poem

5. The most potent phrase of all, consisting largely of one high,
long-held note for the wood winds, followed by a sort of shake,
and a sudden drop of a fifth

These fragments succeed each other simply, with no transitions or connecting materials; they are gradually combined and gather meaning, the whole musical fabric unfolding without break and mounting toward inevitable climax. Sibelius' constructive process here is one of gradual fusion of material, rather than the usual dissection and reassembling of themes; it can be felt more easily than analyzed and "bespeaks a full heart, magnificent fertility, an absorption which pervades all things and directs them to a single end."

Again in the second movement, thematic snatches follow one another with poignant effect; they are dramatically contrasted and presented with a skill which never deviates from a single purpose, that of arousing expectation and of slow shaping toward a climax. Here are the materials out of which the movement is made:

1. A sad tune for the bassoons

2. An intense dramatic bit in accelerated pace

3. A lovely lyric string theme

4. Another lyric bit, this time played by oboes and clarinets

The two large contrasting sections which make up the third movement can be considered in the light of a scherzo and trio movement. The pace of the scherzo is swift—*vivacissimo*—the time, 6/8. A soft series of drum taps introduces the lovely trio, built on this simple oboe melody:

Both sections are repeated with a change of orchestration, and then a dramatic transition leads into the *Finale*, in which Sibelius yields to orthodoxy, for there are two principal theme groups:

Development, with plenty of spinning, whirring accompanimental figures, follows: Leading back to the restatement is a long-breathed, wonderfully sustained crescendo of 91 measures, after which the themes are dramatically restated, with magnificent accretion of instrumental power and color. A triumphant coda over a throbbing kettledrum bass brings the work to a clarion conclusion.

Coming from the composer's early period, this symphony is surprisingly effective and moving today, half a century after it was written, in spite of certain conventional idioms and derivations and a few close approaches to banality. It speaks of things that eternally matter with a greatness of manner and a sincerity of utterance that raise it high above so much of the music that has been written since. Its composer has shown himself to be completely independent of the cliques and schools that grew up all about him in the early decades of the twentieth century, cliques and schools that have sunk deeper and deeper into a morass of "chauvinism, self-deception, and evasion of emotional reality." Built firmly on the past, with no aim of overthrowing the great traditions of art, this music nevertheless points steadfastly toward the future; its composer, like Dante, is a revolutionary by temperament but a conservative by opinion. Above all else, he is a man, at least in this work, who thinks clearly and feels deeply, who does not hesitate to say elementary and sometimes obvious things in a simple and direct way. We may well leave the judgment of the result to the future.

SHOSTAKOVICH'S *FIFTH SYMPHONY*, Op. 47[2]

Written for performance in celebration of the twentieth anniversary of the Republic of Soviet Russia, this important work was first heard in Leningrad on November 21, 1937. At that time its composer was thirty-one and had a formidable number of compositions to his credit. He had come to the conclusion, "not acquired without travail, that music is not merely a combination of sounds arranged in a certain order, but an art capable of expressing by its own means the most diverse ideas or sentiments," as he himself put it in an article written just before the performance of this symphony.[3]

[3] *La Revue Musicale*, December, 1936.

KUKRINIKSI: CARI-
CATURE OF
SHOSTAKOVICH

Musical Quarterly, G. Schirmer

He goes on to say,

> Working ceaselessly to master my art, I am endeavoring to create my
> own musical style, which I am seeking to make simple and expressive.
> I cannot think of my further progress apart from our socialist structure,
> and the end which I set to my work is to contribute at every point
> toward the growth of our remarkable country. There can be no greater
> joy for a composer than the inner assurance of having assisted by his
> works in the elevation of Soviet musical culture, of having been called
> upon to play a leading role in the recasting of human perception.

This, perhaps, accounts for the directness and simplicity of the
symphony; Shostakovich does not hesitate to use, in the broadest
of ways, the abstract historical forms hallowed by the past, nor does
he hesitate to use, and very effectively, some of the newer devices
of "modernism." The point is that, however he writes, he says
something—he is a man with life and imagination and real musical
consciousness, not a mere conjurer of notes or designer of tonal pat-

terns. The design of this symphony is strikingly uncomplicated and unaffected; there is nothing here that need bother anyone who is willing to concede the prolonged use of dissonance as an effective means of musical communication. In contradistinction to so many of his contemporaries, Shostakovich has been wise enough to simplify and clarify his style to meet the needs of the large mass public for which he writes. The result is striking and impressive, if the hearer is not too far removed from life to appreciate the earthy, bourgeois tang of this music.

The first movement opens with a wide-jumping theme, stated antiphonally between the high and low strings:

The second theme is lyric and expressive and is a fine example of this composer's ability to write a tune of sustained melodic power:

There follows an extended development in which the tempo is quickened, the rhythms are tightened and the melodies made even more eloquent. With the restatement, the *largamente* mood of the opening theme is restored; the second theme is beautifully exploited by the wood winds over a throbbing string accompaniment. The end comes peacefully. The whole movement is taut and clear—there are only 305 measures in it—with little waste in thematic material or instrumental sonorities.

There is an ironic, gamin-like spirit to the second movement which has made it seem cheap to some ears. It is in the traditional scherzo form, all the elements of which are clearly discernible: after the opening allegretto section based on two themes, there comes a contrasting trio, and then the first part is repeated *da capo*. This vivacious dance movement serves as a perfect link between, and a necessary contrast to, the sustained mood of the first and third movements.

The third movement, marked largo, is one of slow melodic growth from simple beginnings that are again announced by the strings:

The mood of the whole movement is dark and brooding, as if the composer would reveal the melancholy searchings of his Russian soul. Gradually more and more voices enter; the tension increases and then subsides as the ecstatic melodies are sung once more muted and in high register. A stab of harp and celesta color brings the movement to a close.

The theme of the last movement, a rondo in buoyant march rhythm, is strongly Russian in flavor:

There is a slower section during which the lyric qualities of the earlier movements are recalled, and the whole is completed by an impressive and broadened reappearance of the rondo theme.

ROY HARRIS' *THIRD SYMPHONY*[4]

Roy Harris' *Third Symphony*, written in 1938, has already been mentioned as one of the best pieces yet produced by an American composer. It is interesting not only because it seems to express, in a spontaneous but rather awkward way, the essential buoyancy and self-assurance of the American spirit, but also because of its unusual form. It is one long continuous movement, with five sections to provide contrast and dramatic interest. The following description of its structural scheme is based on an analysis by the composer, who has never hesitated to talk about himself and his music.

[4] Excerpts reprinted by permission of G. Schirmer, Inc., New York. Copyright 1939.

The opening "arched," continuous melody consists of 118 measures; the first 55 form the left curve of the arch, the next 9 its climax, and the remaining 54 its right curve. It starts low in the strings

and expands into the *First Section,* described as "Tragic." The *Second* ("Lyric") *Section* continues the mood of the first, as well as its steadily evolving, continuous texture. It is written largely for strings, horns, and wood winds. The *Third Section* ("Pastoral") emphasizes wood-wind color and reveals the composer as a poet of nature; but the nature suggested by the music, with its harmonies based on fifths and fourths, is that of the wide open spaces of the great American plains, rather than the clipped, formal nature of the eighteenth century, or the wild, tempestuous nature of the nineteenth. The *Fourth Section* ("Fugue-Dramatic") is based on a sharp, biting subject, with plenty of possibilities for fugal development and brass treatment:

This fugal treatment gradually broadens into a spacious *Fifth Section* ("Dramatic-Tragic") marked by a steady drum dirge underlying an epic melody taken from the first section.

More than anything else Harris has done, this last part of the *Third Symphony* justifies the claim of his admirers that his music "echoes the dark fastness of the American soul, its despair, its courage, its defeat, and its triumph." None of his other symphonies seems to have the arresting qualities or the staying powers of this *Third.* This single work may well become Harris' musical monument.

BARTÓK'S *CONCERTO FOR ORCHESTRA*[5]

Commissioned by the Koussevitsky Foundation in 1943, while the composer was living in the United States, this work may be said to represent mature experience gained from a long career of music-

[5] Excerpts reprinted by permission. Copyright 1946 by Hawkes & Son (London) Ltd.

making, as well as Bartók's very fresh and individual use of materials and forms taken from the past. He described its general mood
as representing (apart from the jesting second movement) a gradual
transition from the seriousness of the first movement through the
lugubrious death song of the third to the confident assertion of the
last—the same sort of dramatic sequence we found in the symphonies of Beethoven, Brahms, Tchaikovsky, and Sibelius.

The title of the piece, the composer explained, is suggestive of
its tendency to use single instruments or instrumental groups in a
concertante or soloistic manner, following eighteenth-century usage.
In this case, however, the soloist is the whole orchestra—the various
solo players are called on to perform singly as well as to accompany
the others. In general it may be thought of as a symphony in five
movements, including two scherzos.

Bartók describes the first movement as being "more or less in
sonata form." Its slow introduction suggests the characteristics of
the principal thematic material of the whole work—a movement by
leaps (especially in intervals of fourths), in contrast to movement
by tone or half-tone steps. Notice this in the opening passage:

Hints of the other themes are suggested before they actually
appear. In the lively first theme of the main body of the movement,
fourths are again prominent:

A subsidiary theme, again making use of fourths, is heard on the
trombones just before the introduction of the second theme, built
on two notes heard in step movement on the oboe.
Subsidiary theme:

Second theme:

As the development proceeds, all sorts of contrapuntal imitations of the themes are heard. The restatement makes only brief mention of the first theme, but it dwells at some length on the second, presenting it with some striking effects. Toward the end comes a brass fugal section based on the subsidiary theme and then a coda with flashes of wood-wind sonorities.

The second, "jesting" movement, as Bartók called it, is concerned with pairing the wind instruments in specific intervals. Five short tuneful sections are introduced by a short-short-long drum rhythm which is echoed in the rhythmic pattern of each. The bassoons play their section in sixths, the oboes in thirds, the clarinets in sevenths, the flutes in fifths, and the trumpets in seconds. In the middle there is a short, chorale-like trio section for brass, starting:

and then the five sections are repeated with added instrumentation.

The third section, called a "lugubrious death song," may well have been prompted by the serious illness from which Bartók was recovering when he wrote it. It is rhapsodic in character, with typical Bartókian flashes of unusual and unorthodox sonorities, and is based largely on material from the introduction. There are two main themes, repeated in reverse order.

The *Interrupted Interlude* is an amusing concept which provides the work with its second scherzo. The smooth, flowing intermezzo consists of two contrasted themes with irregular meters, one a rather plaintive tune for the oboe:

and the other a broad, lyric theme for the strings:

This is suddenly interrupted by a sophisticated sort of café tune:

When this, in turn, fades away, the two intermezzo themes are heard again in reverse order, giving a charming and graceful finish to the movement.

The finale, marked *presto*, is another sonata-form movement, preceded by a rather heavy introduction on the horns. Then we hear the first main theme (obviously devised to display the virtuosity of any orchestra playing the piece) in a sort of *moto perpetuo* (perpetual motion).

The second theme makes its appearance on the bassoon, followed by contrapuntal entries for winds:

A third theme, again emphasizing fourths, is played by the trumpet and immediately inverted by another trumpet. It becomes the subject of a highly developed fugue, which forms the middle part of the movement.

In the restatement, a fanfare reminiscent of the one in the first movement is introduced. The coda ends in a mood of exultant, positive affirmation that makes this one of the most appealing works of its period.

Bartók has been accused of using his tremendous skill as an orchestrator to convey rather commonplace musical ideas and outmoded forms in this *Concerto,* one of his last works. Nonetheless, while not as aesthetically unified or as structurally advanced as some of his other works, it will be the *Concerto for Orchestra* (and perhaps his *Violin Concerto*) that will remain for most listeners Bartók's most appealing composition.

LIST OF SUGGESTED MUSIC

1888 *Symphony No. 5 in e minor*	TCHAIKOVSKY
1901 *Symphony No. 2, in D Major,* Op. 43	SIBELIUS
1937 *Symphony No. 5,* Op. 47	SHOSTAKOVICH
1938 *Symphony No. 3*	HARRIS
1935 *Music for Strings, Percussion and Celesta*	BARTÓK

TOPICS FOR DISCUSSION

Which of the five works discussed in this chapter appeal to you most? Why?

Can you trace the gradual alteration in the main constructive scheme of these works? Note the dates of their first production given above.

How do the works differ in tonality? Which is the most advanced in this respect?

Which of the works mentioned in this chapter made the greatest impression on you at first hearing?

Compare the symphony of Shostakovich mentioned in this chapter with other of his works. Do you think, as do some people, that he was spasmodic in his writing? Do you think his personal life in Russia may have affected his writing? (You might also consider these points with regard to Prokofiev.)

CHAPTER 35

Pre-Bach

⊷≈⊶

CHRONOLOGICAL SEQUENCE

In the course of our study we have marked a number of definite movements, each coming to a climax in the works of outstanding composers. We found, for instance, that nineteenth-century Romanticism—that mighty period of artistic achievement—started with the symphonies of Beethoven and came to a close with the composers who followed Wagner. In spite of the wealth of music material found in the Wagnerian music-dramas, no one appeared capable of developing their style any further. Seemingly, Wagner exhausted the possibilities of his medium, and later developments had to take other directions—Impressionism and those later anti-Romantic revolts which so largely make up the world of modern artistic expression. It seems valuable now to show, in chronological sequence, the earlier developments which led to the achievements of the Romantic and post-Romantic composers.

The history of music is absurdly short, compared with that of most other arts. We know next to nothing of art music before 800 A.D. For some six of the nine pre-Bach centuries (800-1400) composition can scarcely be said to have existed, but the period from about 1400 to the time of Bach (1700) includes a wonderful amount of fine music; in fact, we call part of it music's "Golden Age."

THE EARLIEST ART MUSIC

Let us see briefly what was accomplished in music during the troubled ages that we call "medieval." We must remember how

442

filled with disturbances these times were, how plagues, famines, crusades, and wars wasted man's substance and confused his will. The background of these ages might be gained by reading an outline of history to realize what little chance the arts had. We must also remember music's youthfulness as an art. Where is the music to compare with the literature and sculpture of ancient Greece? We know very little about it, but it cannot have had anything like the same developed form.

We can deduce that present-day music had two principal origins: plainsong and folk song—sacred and secular sources. The developments from these followed concurrent paths, but it is much easier to trace those of ecclesiastical music, since its written records are much more plentiful. In the earliest days of the Christian Era, church music must have been influenced by contributions from ancient Hebrew and Greek sources. From such materials the Christian musicians composed unison melodies with small vocal compass (called plain chant or plainsong), set to the words of the liturgy used in the services of the Church. Each of these melodies was written according to one of the "modes" that had been used by the Greeks. These unisonal chants have come to be known as "Gregorians," from St. Gregory, who sorted and ordered them for practical use during the sixth century.

It was a long time before the idea of simultaneous singing in two parts occurred to the church musicians. The results were primitive, since they were achieved through melodies sung in two pitches at once—in fourths and fifths. This was the practice in 900 A.D., before modern notation was used. *Organum*, as this process was called, had its theorists, among whom we chiefly remember the monk Hucbald, one of those remarkable Flemings who later were to blaze the trail for the "Golden Age." Organum started as parallel movement between the two lines of melody and developed into the more elaborate oblique and contrary forms—one part at first going always in the same direction as the other; then, after all manner of experiments that must have seemed bold and exciting at the time, going a way of its own. Guido d'Arezzo, some time after 1000 A.D., wrote about it and showed how to write the music down surely and (as far as it went) scientifically. What we now call two-part counterpoint (two independent melodies combined) became the thing

INSTRUMENTAL BAND OF THE BAVARIAN HOFKAPELLA
Orlando di Lasso is shown at the clavier.

in church singing; but it must have been dull, for there was no
"time" as we understand it—no variety of rhythm in the parts. Experiments with the rhythm of *words* were fruitful, and there was
established the basic triple time that for so long held sway. Various
subtleties developed; there were rather wild shots at freedom of
parts, as when one part sang a simple bit of melody and another
"discanted" above it.

So composition was born with, probably, a great many happy accidents among the laborious fittings of words and notes. Not until about 1300 did musicians find how delightful a change it would be to have duple meter. About this period some of the variation experiments and queer combinations became rather scandalous—interpolations from secular and often frivolous sources were common. In 1322 Pope John XII ordained a simpler style of church music in which the tune was copied exactly by the singers at the octave and third, as well as the fifth above. This gave a richer type of music— in "common chords," we would say—but it was not enough for composers, who began to find charm outside the walls of the Church. One such little part-song is a marvel for its time—the round *Sumer is icumen in,* which belongs to 1280 or early in the fourteenth century. It sings of open-air springtime joys, and there probably was a great deal of other secular music like it. What a pity that this has disappeared, leaving us with only an inkling of the freer, more "human" music which developed outside the Church!

MADRIGALS AND CHURCH MUSIC

English-speakers like to hail John of Dunstable as one of the first really free composers who provided all his own parts, instead of taking a church theme and working on it. But though the English may have started it, the Flemings, energetic, inventive, exploratory, brought about the first glories of composed music in the way of madrigals and church works. Dufay, Josquin des Prés, Di Lasso, and others developed counterpoint into a lively art. Listen to one or two of their pieces (many have been recorded and, since the early works of these composers are rather infrequently played or sung, these recordings are the best means we have for becoming acquainted with them); they may sound a bit primitive to our ears, but who can deny them perfection of their own kind?

The new delight spread over France, Spain, Italy, and into England. The last had a magnificent group of composers of this type of music, from Tallis through the long-lived Byrd and Morley, Weelkes, Wilbye, to Orlando Gibbons. The Flemings carried their art to Italy, and the composers in residence in that land of beauty clarified and intensified it; up to the time the Italians made this music their own, there was still a great deal of dusty scholasticism in it. Perhaps it is not without significance that democracy was just beginning to work out its destiny, too; the Church still dominated, but life was flourishing outside its command.

Palestrina brought this music to a pinnacle, but always under the auspices and guiding hand of the fatherly Church. Palestrina felt, with the Church, that music's function was not only to cheer men's minds, "but also to guide and control them." In that sentence we have the key to the medieval view of music, but the key must not be thought of as too harshly turning in what we moderns may regard as the excessively massive lock of that time. The oil of mysticism entered to smooth its turning. (This aspect of the age has been admirably treated in Daniel Gregory Mason's chapter on Palestrina in his *Beethoven and His Forerunners*.)

A NEW STYLE EMERGES

The complexities of this woven choral music were many. Other, developing ways of thought demanded greater flexibility and humanity in music. Before the end of the sixteenth century, even while Palestrina was penning his masterpieces of contemplative devotion, composers were turning to the greater freedom of solo writing which led to the great new form of *opera*. (We consider its development, which dates, roughly, from 1600, in a later chapter.)

Turning to Germany, we find a strong influence for the simpler solo type of music in Luther and his ideas about reforming the Church. These made unison singing popular. Schütz, who was born exactly a century before Bach, was the first great man of music in Germany; he composed Passion music which was greatly strengthened by his feeling for drama and oratorios.

A SUMMARY OF HISTORICAL DEVELOPMENTS[1]

The following chart shows the development of music during the principal periods in history:

[1] The dates of the periods are only rough approximations, for there is much overlapping; and they are meant to refer to musical, not historical, developments.

Music of Antiquity	The practice of music in the ancient civilizations—Egyptian, Hebrew, Greek, and Roman.
Early Christian Era to about 800 A.D.	One-part vocal music; a single melody with no accompanying parts.
Medieval Age: 800-1450	Organum: Melodies running in parallel parts. Descant: Gradual substitution of more independent parts and greater freedom of rhythm. Counterpoint: The evolution of involved part writing, with much use of imitation between the parts. Polyphony: The perfection of the contrapuntal art in the fugue.
The Renaissance: 1450-1600	New ideas of homophony and instrumental style introduced; study of chords and "vertical" music. Evolution of opera and oratorio.
The Seventeenth Century: The Baroque Period	Gradual adapting of the older contrapuntal styles to the new medium of instruments and the development of instrumental forms (suite, and so on) climaxing in the works of Bach (1685-1750) and his perfecting of fugal art.
The Eighteenth Century: The Rococo Period Classic Style	The development of the instrumental forms of the sonata, symphony, quartet. Music essentially homophonic in style (one chief melodic line with a harmonic accompaniment). Works of Haydn and Mozart.
The Romantic Period: 1800-1900	Romantic composers: Beethoven through Wagner. Gradual evolution of program music. Nationalism. Impressionism as the last manifestation. Strauss and the tone poem. Songs.
Modern Era: 1900—	Realism, and so on. Polytonalities, polyrhythms, atonality, and so on. Smaller intervals than half tones. New instruments.

LIST OF SUGGESTED MUSIC

The only way to obtain an idea of the pre-Bach developments is by hearing good musical illustrations of the music of the various periods. Fortunately, this is now not difficult, for the publishing companies have provided a number of collections of examples of this early music, and the recording companies have issued records to parallel these examples.

Prominent among the books are two published by W. W. Norton Co., New York:

Parrish and Ohl (ed.), *Masterpieces of Music before 1750*

Carl Parrish (ed.), *A Treasury of Early Music* (Covering the Middle Ages, Renaissance and Baroque Periods.)
In addition, the following records are valuable:

MUSIC OF ANTIQUITY

History of Music in Sound, Vol. I. Ancient and Oriental Music
(RCA Victor)

EARLY CHRISTIAN ERA

History of Music in Sound, Vol. II. Early Medieval Music
(RCA Victor)

Gregorian Chant Records by Solesmes Choir (London)

MEDIEVAL AGE

History of Music in Sound, Vol. II. Early Medieval Music
(RCA Victor)

Music of Middle Ages   (Lyrichord)

English Polyphony 13th and Early 14th Centuries (*Expériences Anonymes*)

French Ars Antiqua 13th Century (*Expériences Anonymes*)

THE RENAISSANCE

History of Music in Sound, Vol. III. Ars Nova and Renaissance
(RCA Victor)

Music of the Renaissance   (Lyrichord)

Boulanger French Renaissance Vocal Music (Decca)

Brussels Pro Musica Antiqua—Renaissance (DDG Archive Series)

Greenberg Pro Musica Antiqua—Elizabethan Verse and Music (Columbia)

Greenberg Pro Musica Antiqua—Elizabethan and Jacobean Ayres (Decca)

Greenberg Pro Musica Antiqua—Spanish Renaissance Music (Decca)

THE BAROQUE PERIOD

Masterpieces of Italian Baroque (Bach Guild)

TOPICS FOR DISCUSSION

Some modern composers—for example, Boulez—have sought to evoke a spirit akin to that of the medieval mysticism. Is this spirit likely to appeal to all nations? Might it appeal as a relief from the non-Romantic and prosaic tendency in general life? What form do you think this mysticism might take in the United States? To whom would it appeal?

In recent years many groups have taken to singing music from Palestrina and others. What are the reasons for this? What conditions do you feel are suitable for this type of music? Would modern churches be the proper setting?

What do you think were the reasons for the decline of the madrigal?

Can music continue on present-day paths for very long? Is our contemporary way likely to lead us as far as the ancient music went?

What do you think are the reasons for changes in musical "styles"? Can you determine any permanent factors in musical expression?

CHAPTER 36

Back to Bach

❧ ❧

BACH'S PLACE IN HISTORY

If we examine the music produced from the beginning of the
Christian Era up to the time of Bach (early eighteenth century),
we will find that it divides itself naturally into two great categories.
The first is that of *monophonic* music. The second style, the *polyphonic*, was developed and elaborated in instrumental and choral
composition during the time between the twelfth and seventeenth
centuries and culminated in the music of Johann Sebastian Bach.
After Bach there came still a third type of music—the *homophonic*,
in which one voice or melody was prominent, supported by an
accompaniment mostly in chordal style. This principle underlies
practically all of nineteenth-century music, so that such music is by
far the most familiar to listeners.

It is difficult to imagine a more adequately prepared composer
genealogically or one more fortunately placed historically than J. S.
Bach. Born in the center of Protestant Germany in 1685, he was
descended from a long line of church and town musicians; it is a
matter of record that, out of thirty-two of his sixteenth-century
progenitors' descendants, seventeen were professional musicians.
Bach, as we have just said, completed the grandiose polyphonic
structure that stretched, through Palestrina, back to the Middle
Ages; he also foreshadowed the new harmonic style that was to take
complete possession of the musical world that followed him. He was
thus able, at an important turning point in music's history, to master

450

two fundamentally different styles of composition; he stands as a marvelous synthesis of the past and a symbol of things to come. Combine superb technical mastery, fortunate historical position, and outstanding strength of musical imagination with never-questioning religious faith, and you have the fundamental reasons for Bach's supremacy as a composer.

He wrote consistently from the days of his apprenticeship as a young teen-age organist, to the very last days of his life. "I worked hard," he said once to someone inquiring as to the secrets of his genius; "if you are as industrious as I was, you will be no less successful." His tremendous output divides itself into definite categories, which may be conveniently labeled as

The Baroque Bach
Bach the Church Musician
Bach the Instrumental Composer

THE BAROQUE BACH

The German historians like to say that Bach is the great man of the Baroque era, and they are certainly right insofar as one phase of his writing is concerned. The desire for the expression of a buoyant and rich vitality in art may be said to be one characteristic of the period which stretched roughly from the beginning of the seventeenth century to the latter part of the eighteenth. The Baroque period takes its character largely from grandiose Italian architectural constructions by which the Church, during the period of the Counter Reformation, endeavored to regain something of its lost prestige and power in the eyes of the world. It marks a period in European history strongly dominated by an upthrusting optimism never again equalled. No other period in man's existence has been more active in liberating his powers or in giving him the foundations on which he has built his life ever since. It was a time of great intellectual curiosity, of an amassing of wealth and prestige by the powerful individual; and it resulted in one of the richest and most vital outpourings of art of all kinds the world has ever seen.

Stimulated by the magnificence of the Italian ecclesiastical creations and catering to the rather satiated and cynical tastes of the time, architects and painters, landscape gardeners and sculptors over

RUBENS: MARY
WITH CHRIST AND
THE SAINTS

a good part of Europe worked in that grandiloquent manner of expression that we have come to know as the Baroque style. In all the
great capitals of Europe, especially those of the southern countries,
as well as in the numerous small principalities of Germany, building
flourished; animated by the example of the Sun King at Versailles,
the princely rulers sought to demonstrate their power of domain
through costly and elaborate architectural creation, just as the
Church had attempted to re-assert its glory and pomp through the
creation of fanciful and highly decorated structures, built in the
most eloquent and grand style imaginable.

It was a period of luxuriant strength, of colorful vitality, of
almost overpowering magnificence of creative thought which

This ceiling in an Austrian church shows the elaborate detail typical of Baroque art.

affected all phases of artistic activity. From his great predecessors—
men like Reinken and Buxtehude in the north of Germany and
Pachelbel in the south—Bach inherited this predilection for ponderous, flamboyant expression, and many of his great organ works unmistakably show its influence. Listen to a youthful organ composition such as his great *Toccata, Adagio and Fugue in C Major,* for
instance, and you will hear what we mean. In its constant upswirling
phrases, the grand balancing of its parts, and the soaring architectural design of its musical form, this work may be said to be
truly Baroque. Heard on an adequate and properly designed instrument, it is almost overpowering in its magnificence, as, indeed, are
the *Toccata and Fugue in D Minor* and the *Fantasia and Fugue in
G Minor.* Certainly there is a striking similarity of spirit between
such works and those architectural creations of his time and country,
the Residenz in Würzburg or the great abbey churches at Wein-
garten and Ottobeuren in southern Germany.

In comparing the forms of the different arts during the Baroque
period, our first impressions are those of the monumental magnil-
oquence and tremendous sweep of creative power to be found in
all. The architects of impressive structures were men possessed not
only of great imagination but also of superabundant technical
powers. Their superb craftsmanship was equal to their vision. If we
examine these Baroque architectural creations carefully, we shall
find that their imposing magnificence is made up of a wealth of
meticulously executed details; carefully balanced members, gracefully molded designs, and majestic rhythmic patterns give significance and purpose to the whole. In them all we find an inevitable
involvement of our spirits, powerful effects, and a sumptuous
ascent to a final and monumental climax which marks the real
essence of the Baroque. In this phase of his creation, Bach was as
truly a man of his epoch as were the great architects Fischer von
Erlach, Lukas von Hildebrandt, Jakob Prandtauer, or Balthasar
Neumann.

In addition to the twenty-six preludes and fugues which he wrote
for the organ, a number of other instrumental works should be included in this Baroque category. Prominent among these are the
Brandenburg Concertos, each written for a different combination

of instruments. With their tremendous vitality of expression and constant sustenance of creative energy, they are good examples of the decorated Baroque style, as are some of his clavier compositions, such as the *English* and *French Suites*, the *Goldberg Variations*, and the *Italian Concerto*.

Overlapping into this category may also be mentioned such choral works as the *St. Matthew Passion* and the *B Minor Mass*; their very length (each of them takes over three hours to perform) and their richly decorated, soaring architectural qualities make them monumentally impressive, as well as emotionally overwhelming. Charles Sanford Terry has called the *St. Matthew Passion* "the deepest and most moving expression of devotional feeling in the whole of musical literature"; certainly much of its emotional force is derived from the relentless Baroque intensification of the means used. The *B Minor Mass* is a more brilliant work, perhaps even more monumental, than the *St. Matthew Passion*, but its effect comes from the same underlying sublimity and structural grandeur.

BACH THE CHURCH MUSICIAN

The second phase of this composer's work will best be understood if we review briefly his career as a musical official in the service of the German Protestant Church. He was born in the Thuringian village of Eisenach, a little town deeply steeped in the traditions of the German Reformation; his father was town musician as well as *Hofmusicus* to the local duke, Johann Georg. This Bach musical tradition had been maintained for generations; in fact, the association of the two terms, Bach and musician, was so close throughout Thuringia that a musician was usually called Bach, no matter what his family name happened to be. The members of this great family were noted for their sturdy piety as well as for their musical ability, and so it is no wonder that much of Johann Sebastian Bach's greatest and most characteristic work was done during the rather prosaic discharge of his duties as church organist and choir director. As Schweitzer put it: "Music was an act of worship with Bach; his artistic activity and his personality were both based on his piety. If he is to be understood from any standpoint at all, it is from this. For him, art was religion, and so had no concern with the world or with worldly success. It was an end in itself . . . for him the tones do not perish, but ascend to God like praise too deep for utterance." All his music was the natural expression of a belief acquired through generations of God-fearing, simple-living ancestors, sheltered from the ways of the world, and it was heightened by an unusually fertile imagination and a superb expressive technic.

CHORALES

There is no better introduction to Bach than the chorales, for they were intimately associated with his career as a church composer and could have sprung from no other source. The Protestant Church had as one of its tenets the popularizing of its services, and so it encouraged the participation of the people in the liturgical part of worship. The chorale or hymn was developed so that large congregations could sing in unison with great effect; the services did not have to depend on the trained members of the choir, as had been the case in the older branch of the Church. The chorale goes back to the very beginnings of the Protestant faith, for Luther himself was a musician and poet of considerable ability and is supposed to have written some of the earliest examples of this type of worship music. By Bach's time, some two hundred years later, there had been produced a great number of these fine, sturdy tunes (about five hundred in all). One of Bach's most significant contributions to musical literature was the reharmonizing and re-arranging of some two hundred fifty of these so that they would be effective for congregational singing with the accompaniment of the organ.

These Bach chorales represent, in shortened form, the same technical mastery evident in his greater works, as well as the inherent strength of emotional expression peculiar to them. They were set largely in the harmonic style (in distinction to the polyphonic style, which he employed so largely) and have a tremendous appeal for all kinds of listeners, learned as well as inexperienced. "Nothing in music is more wonderful, perhaps more surprising, than the power and grip which these chorales have over all classes of musical listeners and over the singers themselves. In all choirs . . . these simple, four-part harmonie compositions hold singers and listeners probably more strongly than any other form of art. The Bach chorale has, in fact and in the supremest degree, a religious and mystic effect upon the hearer that cannot be explained or analyzed."[1]

At the end of this chapter will be found a short list of some of the best of these chorales. Many of them can be found in any good American or English hymnal, and complete editions with German and English texts are readily available. In case you are not familiar with them, listen carefully if you would penetrate to the soul of Bach's expression. Playing them on the piano gives a hint of their spiritual beauty; but to appreciate their mighty power, it is necessary to hear them sung by a large chorus or congregation.

CHORALE PRELUDES

One of the most common forms of organ composition in Bach's time was the chorale prelude, formed by taking a melody of one of the chorales and weaving other parts about it in such a way as to bring out its beauty in the highest degree. These chorale preludes were meant for practical use in the church service and are, in reality, small-scale tone poems embodying the spiritual character of the words of the chorale upon which they were based. Some of them are meditations uttered from the loneliness of the composer's soul; others are poems of praise, outbursts of joy, and thankful gratitude for blessings received. They are a musical world in miniature, containing a wonderful diversity of emotion and manifesting all the powers of expression of which Bach deemed the organ capable. They differ in the richness of their eloquence from everything else he wrote.

An instructive way to realize the difference between the harmonic and the polyphonic way of writing, as well as to get acquainted with the great beauties in Bach's more intimate music, is to select a chorale and compare it with the chorale prelude which Bach evolved from it.

BACH'S CHORAL WORKS

The best introduction for one not acquainted with the glories of the choral works which Bach wrote while fulfilling his duties as

[1] Hannam, *On the Church Cantatas of Bach*, by permission of Oxford University Press.

The Grand Stairway in the Castle at Würzburg.

organist and choirmaster is the study of one of the complete cantatas composed for performance at the Sunday morning services of the Thomaskirche, Leipzig. No better cantata for this purpose could be found than the one for the Twenty-seventh Sunday after Trinity: *Wachet auf* (Sleepers, Wake!) (No. 140 in the Gesellschaft Edition of Bach's complete works). As one ardent admirer of this work has said, we cannot help but feel that in it the highest art, the deepest feeling, and the most exalted expression are united into a single composition.

The general constructional plan of this cantata is easily followed. It is based entirely on one chorale, the words and music of which were written by a German pastor, Philip Nicolai, as the result of a deeply personal emotional experience. This chorale treats in a mystic way, very typical of its time (1599), the parable of the Wise and Foolish Virgins found in the Gospel of St. Matthew. Using the wedding scene of this story as a background, the hymn describes the coming of the Bridegroom, the Saviour, who invites the Bride, His Church, to her wedding. The text tells of their meeting, the Bridegroom comforting the Bride and promising her eternal bliss, with a final hymn of praise sung within the gates of the New Jerusalem.

Like many of the other texts which Bach set to music, this hymn of Nicolai's seems to the present-day listener unnecessarily confused and mysterious. Much of this religious poetry (some of it might better be called doggerel) came out of the period of Germany's greatest suffering, the Thirty Years' War (1618-1648), when the whole country was overrun by the armies of Europe and was in complete ruin; "the only thing of the soul that survived was religion, in whose bosom poetry took refuge." No wonder that this poetry was sometimes overemotional and overnaïve in its strained symbolism; we today are more interested in it as the basis for the expression of Bach's great musical communication than we are in its theological connotations or its high-flown poetic extravagances.

St. Matthew Passion

The custom of performing a Passion—that is, an epic, dramatic, and musical setting of the story of the sufferings and death of Christ —was an exceedingly ancient one in the Christian Church. In the Reformed Church, performances of such Passions in German may be said to have begun in the latter half of the sixteenth century. By Bach's time these had become exceedingly elaborate, embracing the best of the forms introduced from the musical drama (that is, the recitative and aria), as well as the traditional devices of the chorus and chorale. Salomon Deyling, the head of the spiritual affairs of Leipzig during Bach's tenure as organist there, thus addressed his talented Cantor on this subject:

> On each Palm Sunday and Good Friday the history of the Passion of our Lord is made known antiphonally, according to one or the other of the Evangelists, exactly in accordance with the sacred writer's words. Who could improve on this? They must be sung, how else are they to be understood by all? But they must be sung by someone who can sing, namely by you [meaning Bach!]. And so that everything may sound well and be impressive, they must be musically sung and accompanied.
>
> Your best singer, who can pronounce clearly and well, must sing the

words of the Evangelist in recitative, and, in order to produce more
impression of life and variety, the other persons of the story must be
represented by other singers, and the Jewish people by a chorus. At the
chief points of the story there will be pauses, during which, by means
of an aria, the congregation shall lay to heart what they have heard; and
that all of us shall be refreshed from time to time, there shall be well-
chosen verses from all the known hymns, in which the congregation
can join. Now, your business is to carry all this out in a connected and
artistic manner!

Which Bach proceeded to do. It is not known how many settings
of the Passion story he made; two of them have come down to us
complete, the Passions according to *St. John* (written for performance in the Thomaskirche, Leipzig, in 1723) and that according to
St. Matthew (first performed on Good Friday, 1729). Both follow
the same general scheme, but the latter is by far the more impressive
and effective work, employing all the resources of musical art: a
double, mixed-voice choir, a *ripieno* choir of sopranos, two complete orchestras, and a double organ part. The words of the evangelist are sung by the traditional tenor; the words of Jesus are given to
a bass, always accompanied by a string orchestra; the parts of the
other persons connected with this tremendous drama (Peter, Pilate,
Judas, and so on) are sung by solo voices. The words of the Jewish
turba or crowd are given to the two choirs and are set polyphoni-
cally. In addition to the Biblical words, Bach used a text by Picander,
especially written for him, for the accompanied recitatives, arias,
ensemble numbers, and gigantic choruses.

Typical of the Baroque spirit of magnificence and splendor is the
opening chorus, which Schweitzer feels to be a realistic description
of a crowd moving excitedly about, crying as Jesus is led through
the town to the Cross: "Come, ye daughters, help me mourn. . . .
See the Bridegroom, like a lamb"; part of the crowd cries from time
to time, "Whom? . . . How? . . . What?" while above the whole
surging mass soars the lovely line of the *ripieno* choir singing the
chorale: "O Lamb of God, Most Stainless."

The work should be heard, if possible, in its entirety (there are
now a number of recordings available), but an idea of its dramatic
impact is best gained from the section devoted to the description of
Christ's final sufferings and death on the cross, beginning with the
recitative.

ELIAS HAUSSMAN:
JOHANN SEBASTIAN
BACH

The Mass in B Minor

Nothing shows better the deep spiritual quality of so much of Bach's choral writing than some of the sections from the great *Mass in B Minor*. This is a work of tremendous proportions, set to the regular liturgical text in use in the Catholic Church, that Bach gradually composed during the maturest years of his life, from 1731 to 1737. Although many of its twenty-four sections were adapted from earlier works, it is difficult to imagine a more unified or more thoroughly inspired whole. It seems as though, as H. C. Colles has said, Bach in planning, composing, and adapting this work from the

treasures of his past experience and his present vision, resolved only to create a work which, though no temple made with hands should be large enough to contain it in its ritual, should rise "to the height of this great argument." We have to go outside music for the true parallel to the mystery of Bach's Mass, and we find it in Milton's composition of *Paradise Lost,* the writing of which, we must remember, also covered a long period of time.

To fully understand and appreciate the *Mass* takes a long time; the music must be placed against the background of Bach's great religious faith, as well as against the general Baroque ideals of the time. The great protagonist of this stirring piece is the choir; fourteen of its twenty-four numbers are choruses covering every phase of emotional expression, from the exaltation of the *Sanctus* to the gloom of the *Crucifixus*. These choruses are written for four to eight parts and constitute the most substantial contribution ever made to this phase of musical art. The contrasting solos and duets are of much less interest to modern ears; they were conceived in the pure Baroque decorated style and must be listened to with this constantly in mind. As was his custom, Bach loved to combine, in some of these numbers, the solo voice with a solo instrument—such as the violin in the *Laudamus te* or the oboe in *Et in spiritum sanctum*.

BACH THE INSTRUMENTAL COMPOSER

There is another aspect of Bach's life which we must consider: Bach, the servant of princes, producing music at a court of his period. His compositions belonging to this period have furnished the modern instrumental repertoire with some of its most significant numbers. In 1717 Bach entered the service of one of the many German princes of the time, Leopold of Anhalt-Cöthen, as master of the court music. He had no church duties at all but did have at his disposal a small orchestra; it was only natural that he began to experiment with it during his six-year term. At Cöthen he wrote for a number of small instrumental combinations, including a somewhat limited (from the modern viewpoint) orchestra consisting of strings, drums, oboes and bassoons, horns and trumpets, to which his experimental mind caused him to add, on occasion, other instruments.

It was this sort of experimenting that produced a different orchestration in each of the six concertos he wrote on commission from the Duke of Brandenburg. The experience he gained in this orchestral writing stood him in good stead later at Leipzig, when he was called on to furnish different kinds of orchestral accompaniments for his cantatas and Passions. To this Cöthen period belong also the English and French harpsichord suites—the distinctive titles of which point to slight differences in style between these sets of movements in dance form—as well as the four suites, or overtures, which he wrote for the orchestral combination mentioned above. The sequence of movements in these works follows the typical pattern of their time: an extended overture made up of a slow introduction and a fugue, plus a series of contrasted movements in idealized dance form. During the Cöthen period was also written the first part of that famous collection of preludes and fugues familiarly known as *The Well-Tempered Clavier*.

In all these instrumental works can be seen the particular aspect of Bach's manifold musical nature that was concerned with, and which superbly mastered, the forms of musical construction. Certainly no other composer has equaled him in this; he wrote freely and naturally in the difficult forms current in his day—the invention, the fugue, the partita—and we have no feeling that these gave him any trouble whatever, even if some of the music he produced in the process does not represent him at his greatest. He manipulated the texture of the fugue with an ease and fluency that is disarming, to say the least, for the fugue is probably the most abstract and difficult of all the types of construction developed during the long course of music's history. We find more than forty fugues scattered through his organ works alone, and there are many others used throughout his instrumental and vocal compositions. In his last work, left unfinished at his death in 1750, *The Art of Fugue*, this style of fugal and canonic writing may be said to have reached its climax. Although written as a sort of treatise, the series of fugal examples this work contains, based on one theme, seems fresh and exciting two hundred years after it was first put on paper.

The Well-Tempered Clavier

His best-known collection of fugues is in *The Well-Tempered Clavier*, a group of forty-eight preludes and fugues written to illustrate the advantages of a system of tuning which Bach favored, and which he wished to see generally adopted. Since the need for a free interchange of keys was being felt strongly by his time, he advocated dividing the octave into twelve equal semitones, each of them slightly false according to the scientific standards as established by experiment but giving a result that was entirely satisfactory musically in all keys. (We have discussed this in an earlier chapter.)

To establish this "well-tempered" or compromise system of tuning, Bach wrote a collection of two cycles of preludes and fugues, each set going through all the major and minor keys, twenty-four of each. The collection was designed to be played on any suitable keyboard instrument that happened to be available and not on the clavichord alone, as is often suggested by the rendering in careless translation of its German title as *The Well-Tempered Clavichord*. It is of great significance not only because of its qualities as music, but also because of its establishing, once and for all, the advantages of equal temperament as a basis for writing music.

BACH'S HEALTHY WHOLENESS

Perhaps any attempt such as we have made at classification of a composer's output is rather dangerous, for it presupposes that everything a man such as Bach wrote falls logically into one or another pocket, which can be definitely separated and labeled. This, of course, is not true, for many times the characteristics of one type are found in works which generally belong to another. When we say, for instance, that Bach was concerned largely with the problem of form in one broad type of music he wrote, we do not necessarily mean that these formal works are devoid of expressive feeling; many of the fugues in *The Well-Tempered Clavier* are full of emotional content. Nor should such a classification be construed to mean that the works which fall within the second of our groups are lacking in structural strength—they are carefully and superbly put together.

Nevertheless, some such grouping is a help in understanding the seeming contradictions of Bach's genius. Many a person has been somewhat repelled by what he has called the mathematical aspect of Bach, without knowing anything about the emotionally moving chorale-preludes or the Passions; others have been so fascinated by the supreme perfection of Bach's structural form that they have neglected or perhaps not understood what may rightly be called his romantic characteristics; and certainly some of the interpreters who have gloried in the grandiloquent, Baroque aspect of Bach's writing have never paid attention to the still, small voice of his more intimate works. Thus he is really the universal composer.

THE BAROQUE BACH

Organ

Toccata, Adagio and Fugue in C Major

Toccata and Fugue in d minor

Fugue in g minor (The Little g minor)

Passacaglia and Fugue in c minor

Orchestra

Brandenburg Concerto No. 5 (flute, violin, keyboard, and strings)

Harpsichord

Chromatic Fantasy and Fugue in d minor
    Nothing shows the advantage of the Equal Temperament in keyboard music better than this harpsichord work, written c. 1720.

BACH THE CHURCH MUSICIAN

Chorale Preludes for the Organ

Wachet auf, ruft uns die Stimme (Sleepers, Wake! A Voice is Calling)
    Taken from the cantata mentioned in the text, the chorale is given out on one manual of the organ against a dancing figure in the accompaniment and pedals. There is little doubt that Bach had in mind here illustrating the two lines of the chorale text:

> *Zion hears the watchmen calling*
> *And on her heart deep joy is falling.*

Christ lag in Todesbanden (Christ Lay in Bonds of Death)
    There is a sense of joy and freedom in this music, suggestive of the solemn jubilation of the Easter season. The chorale tune is in the

soprano, with accompaniment of triumph-motives in the other parts. A poetic interpreter thinks the fine pedal part was meant to symbolize the rolling away of the stone before the tomb. Bach's music is full of such rather naïve, imitative effects.

Herzlich tut mich verlangen (Passion Chorale)

Based on a tune originally secular in character, this wonderful tune is used many times in the St. Matthew Passion and is here given that sense of deep longing that Bach expressed so often:

> *Lord, hear my deepest longing*
> *To pass to Thee in peace,*
> *From earthly troubles thronging,*
> *From trials that never cease.*

CANTATAS

Wachet auf, ruft uns die Stimme (Sleepers, Wake!), No. 140

Christ lag in Todesbanden (Christ Lay in Bonds of Death), No. 4

Also based on a famous chorale, this is another of the more than two hundred surviving Bach cantatas now recorded and available for general listening.

Du Hirte Israel, höre (Shepherd of Israel, Hear), No. 104

A cantata for the Second Sunday after Easter, "the delicate lyricism, ravishing harmony, and perfect grace of this work have an immediate effect upon an audience and make this one of the most suitable works for overcoming the common fear of Bach."

Lobet Gott in seinen Reichen (Praise Our God), No. 11

MOTET

Singet dem Herrn ein neues Lied (Sing Ye to the Lord)

A motet was sung each Sunday at St. Thomas Church, Leipzig, at the beginning of the morning service. This is the best-known of the six of Bach's that have come down to us.

PASSIONS

St. Matthew Passion

St. John Passion

MASSES

Mass in b minor

Missa Brevis No. 2 in A Major

Missa Brevis No. 3 in g minor

Missa Brevis No. 4 in G Major

BACH THE INSTRUMENTAL COMPOSER

Suite No. 2 in b minor (flute and strings)
Overture
Rondo
Sarabande
Bourrée
Polonaise
Minuet
Badinerie (Playfulness)
Certainly one of Bach's happiest inspirations—graceful, gay, stately by turns.

Suite No. 3 in D Major (two oboes, three trumpets, drums, strings and cembalo)
Overture
Air
Gavottes
Bourrée
Gigue
Contains the world-popular *Air,* one of the most beautiful of Bach's lyric movements.

The Well-Tempered Clavier: Book One, First Eight Preludes and Fugues
The beginning of the so-called Old Testament of the musician's Bible.

The Art of Fugue
Bach's last work, this has been well called a titanic monument of all musical—and human—achievement. Bach himself gave no

specific performing directions for this music; it is available in several different instrumental arrangements.

TOPICS FOR DISCUSSION

Why is Bach so often called "the universal composer"?

What did the noted English critic Ernest Newman mean when he spoke of "sewing-machine Bach"?

The first performances of the *B Minor Mass* in the United States were given at the beginning of this century. Why do you think this work was so late in being presented here?

Compare Bach with some of his Baroque contemporaries.

CHAPTER 37

The German-English Handel

COMPARISON OF BACH AND HANDEL

Careers more different than those of Bach and his great Baroque contemporary, George Frideric Handel[1] (1685-1759), can hardly be imagined. Born in the same year, within a few miles of each other in Germany, these two giants never met. There are strong contrasts in their careers: Bach came from a long family line of musicians; Handel's father was a barber-surgeon, who did not wish his son to become a professional musician. Bach never became interested in the popular, courtly form of opera, and his vocal lines, when he did use them in his church works, have almost the character of instrumental music. Handel, however, was well trained in the field of operatic writing and achieved his first great successes with opera; it was natural that his writing should assume a lyric, vocal character that delighted the listeners of his day, as it has those of later times. He became a great operatic-oratorio composer and producer in London, known and revered everywhere; Bach hardly traveled beyond the borders of his native Thuringia in Germany and was known, if he was known at all, as an organ virtuoso rather than as a composer. Today it is Bach's music that is popular the world over, while Handel's is, outside of a very few works, much less often performed.

[1] This is the form of the name adopted by Handel himself after he settled in England.

HANDEL'S CAREER

After finally obtaining his father's permission to study music in Halle, his native town, Handel entered the university there as a law student. But after his eighteenth year he gave himself over to music, going to Hamburg in 1703 and playing in the opera orchestra there. He went to Italy in 1706, visiting all the principal cities and absorbing the Italianate ways of composing to such a degree that he was able to write an opera for Venice, in many ways the real home of Italian opera. Coming first to London in 1710, he settled there permanently a few years later and composed and produced several Italian operas a year with varying degrees of success, against a dangerous opposition on the part of the native musicians.

A man possessed of the utmost tenacity, great bravery, and an overwhelming fecundity of ideas, Handel pursued his exciting career in London through vicissitudes and misfortunes that would have broken a less determined spirit. After writing several dozen operas, he tried his luck with English oratorios when fashions and tastes changed. At first these oratorios were given only during the Lenten season, but they became so popular that Handel wrote and produced work after work in this style, nearly twenty in all. Between the parts of these oratorios, the composer would perform his organ concertos with great success. His later years beginning with the *réclame* of the first Dublin performance of *Messiah* in 1741, were triumphant ones, although darkened by ill health and final blindness.

Handel was a quick worker and gave most of his time and tremendous energy to the production of music, unbothered by social demands or family obligations. The result was a tremendous amount of vital, energetic, and thoroughly likable music. Much of it is in the fresh, open-air, forthright English style of his talented predecessor Purcell (1659-1695). Although on occasion Handel could penetrate as deeply as Bach, he does not consistently or even often do so. That is one reason his operas do not hold the stage today; another is their unusual, unreal librettos and the fact that they call for a type of singing no longer fashionable. Of his oratorios, few are sung today except the *Messiah*, which is still the standard war-horse of village choirs and metropolitan choral societies throughout the

English-speaking world. Handel's orchestral concertos are less heard than Bach's, though in their lighter way they can take a place by the side of his contemporary's *Brandenburg Concertos*.

THE *MESSIAH*

Messiah remains (and probably always will) Handel's best-loved work. In its massive choruses, beautiful solos, and fine orchestral background, it embodies an affectionate and intimate portrayal of the Christ story through its three phases—birth, death, and resurrection. It has its weaknesses as well as its moments of great strength; it is typically Baroque and fully Christian at the same time. To be convinced of this, one has only to listen to such a thoroughly graceful, beautifully decorated, and completely successful (vocally speaking) recitative and aria as the very first one, given to the tenor:

> Comfort ye, my people, saith your God; speak ye comfortably to Jerusalem and cry unto her that her warfare is accomplished, that her iniquity is pardoned. The voice of him that crieth in the wilderness: "Prepare ye the way of the Lord, make straight in the desert a highway for our God."
> Every valley shall be exalted and every mountain and hill made low: the crooked straight and the rough places plain.

Compare this with the terrific emotional intensity of such a chorus as the second one in the Second Part:

> Surely He hath borne our griefs and carried our sorrows! He was wounded for our transgressions: He was bruised for our iniquities; the chastisement of our peace was upon Him.
> And with His stripes we are healed.

Surpassing all in majestic dignity is the great *Hallelujah*, about which Handel himself said: "Whether I was in my body or out of my body when I wrote it, I know not. God knows."

> Hallelujah: for the Lord God Omnipotent reigneth.
> The kingdom of this world has become the kingdom of our Lord, and of His Christ; and He shall reign for ever and ever.
> King of Kings, and Lord of Lords, Hallelujah!

Though some of this music may have been in his mind before he began to write it, he composed *Messiah* in three weeks, utilizing here and there pieces he had written for other purposes. His orches-

LONDON IN HANDEL'S DAY

Painted by his contemporary, Canaletto (1697-1768). In the river may be seen two barges similar to those for which Handel wrote the Water Music.

tration did not take that long, for this art was not yet thought to be of equal importance to choral and vocal writing.

THE CONCERTI

The twelve *Concerti Grossi*, mentioned above, were written in 1739 in the incredibly short space of a month, less time than it would take for a good copyist to write them out. It is said that at the beginning of his compositions Handel would write out all the parts in full; as he proceeded, he would, in his impatient haste, drop first one part and then another, ending with the bass alone as a hint for what the other parts would be. Before he finished one piece he would begin another, sometimes working on two or three at the same time.

His instrumental style may be best observed in these *Concerti Grossi*, all of them written according to the accepted formulas of the time: an alternation (perhaps opposition is a better word) of a small solo group of instruments and a larger orchestra. These *concertino* solo parts were always performed in Handel's case by two violins and a cello; the *tutti* or full orchestra was a body of strings divided into first violins, second violins, violas, violoncellos reinforced by the double bass. This seven-part texture was enriched and tied together by a keyboard instrument (the harpsichord), from which the composer conducted the performance of the music.

Typical of the whole set, each one of which has its own organizational pattern, is the last, No. 12, in b minor, consisting of four main movements with a short *largo* introduction to the last. The first solemn, overture-like movement contains a constant alternation of the tutti and the concertino; the second is lively, with long stretches for the solo instruments; the third is a song-like aria, which, if compared with the air from Bach's *Third Orchestral Suite*, will show the difference between the lyric style of these two great composers. This aria is followed by the two decorated variations, called in the parlance of the time a *double*, in which concertino and the tutti play together. After a short, slow introduction comes the final movement, a four-part, light-hearted fugue, and again the concertino and the tutti play together.

All twelve of these concertos are different, filled with the utmost variety of material and means. All in all, they represent Handel at his very best: the grand master of Italianate song style, the skilled improvisator, the fertile mind teeming with ideas. They show, like the rest of this composer's works, that, generally speaking, Handel is easier to absorb than Bach, but that he hardly ever equals his contemporary in range or depth, in lasting power or in philosophical insight. This does not mean, however, that he has not written some magnificent music, typical of its time and teeming with forceful strength.

LIST OF SUGGESTED MUSIC

Messiah
Available in several good recordings, this should be studied in its entirety by those wishing to know Handel's varied characteristics.

Concerti Grossi, Op. 6, Numbers 1 to 12
These are available in a magnificent performance by a group of chamber-music players conducted by Adolf Busch.

Water Music

Royal Fireworks Music
Written by Handel for special occasions and now generally played in modernized orchestral versions, these are Baroque-styled in real *pomposo* vein.

Arias from Operas and Oratorios
"Sound an Alarm" (Tenor) from *Judas Maccabeus*
"O Sleep! Why Dost Thou Leave Me" (Soprano) from *Semele*
"Hear Me, Ye Winds and Waves" (Bass) from *Scipione*
"Ombra mai fu" (Tenor) from *Xerxes*
(Popularly known as Handel's *Largo;* see page 97.)

TOPICS FOR DISCUSSION

Why do you think fashions in music change?
What was the cause of John Byrom's famous epigram?

> *Some say, that Signor Bononcini,*
> *Compar'd to Handel's a mere ninny;*
> *Others aver, to him, that Handel*
> *Is scarcely fit to hold a candle.*
> *Strange! that such high dispute sho'd be*
> *'Twixt Tweedledum and Tweedledee!*

CHAPTER 38

The Rococo Age

❧ ❧

The Baroque was a period of brilliant activity, of intellectual, artistic and material achievement. During it Europe experienced the full power of the tremendous forces which had been set in motion by the Renaissance. The seventeenth century was a time of fierce and joyous pride in national life. Under Elizabeth, James I, Charles I, and Cromwell, and under Richelieu and Louis XIV, England and France became conscious of new powers and struggled towards new destinies. There were great discoveries in physical science; this was the time of Francis Bacon and his turning of the current of man's thought towards material things, of Galileo and his telescope, of Isaac Newton and the law of universal gravitation. New lands were discovered and opened up, England reached out towards India on the one hand and the New World on the other. There was a complete revaluation of literature and art; it was the time of Shakespeare and Milton, of Corneille and Molière, of Rubens, Rembrandt, Velásquez, and Van Dyck (these latter carrying on the traditions instituted by the sixteenth-century Renaissance painters). And last but by no means least, there developed new and rather unaccustomed ideas of religious tolerance and freedom. Music during this time came out from under the protection of the Church and developed an entirely new method of expression—the more personal instrumental style.

ROCOCO ART

After all this enthusiasm, these strong opinions, these great discoveries, this tremendous activity in the arts, and these many wars,

*A Composer of the Eight-
eenth Century.*

there came a period of natural and inevitable reaction. After an
epoch of great creative forces, it seems necessary for nature and
man to recoup their strength and regain their balance. And so in
this new century, the people, weary and disillusioned, no longer
pursued intense ideals of religious, political, and intellectual life.
"There could be no wars of religion now, for men had not much
faith in anything. The intellectual outlook was frank and tolerant,
but not serious. Life was an art, to be pursued gracefully by all who
had the means to live like educated people" (Mowat). The strong
feelings of nationalism had degenerated into political bickerings,
the earlier enthusiasm for scientific discovery into a period of research. Instead of the universal curiosity and burning enthusiasms of
the earlier time, artists of the eighteenth century reflect the grace
and intelligence of their period. It was an era of French domination.
Louis XIV, the Sun King (who lived well into the eighteenth
century), and his successor Louis XV became models for all

Probably the finest example of Rococo in Europe—the Amalienburg in Munich, built 1734-1739 after plans by Cuvilliès. Here are the molded curves and the facile ornaments of the eighteenth century at their best.

Europe; their luxurious court at Versailles was the envy and pattern of every king, prince, and courtier. The society of this century was, as Strachey observes, the most civilized that history has ever known. Art, religion, intellectual activities, economic conditions—everything was organized and disciplined for the advantage of the absolute monarchs who ruled in the different European countries.

All the arts catered to the manifest desire of the times for the enjoyment of life in the most aristocratic manner possible; the century has come to be known as the Rococo period. In reality, the art of the Rococo period, derived from that of the earlier Baroque, was a graceful refinement and an aristocratic adaptation of its rich strength and buoyant vitality. Rococo architecture had harmonious, gracefully flowing lines; the interior decorations, dainty in style, made use of gay draperies and formal furniture. These provided an ideal setting for the gorgeous dresses, formal wigs, and lace jabots affected by the *haute monde.*

Against this gleaming background, the polished and stilted manners, the carefully stylized diversions, and the witty, malicious conversations of the period are easily understandable. Writers and composers paid less attention to spontaneous and inspired creation and more to the development of craftsmanship and skill for the delectation of their princely patrons. Painters filled their pictures with distinguished figures in ravishing colors, ladies and gentlemen in glistening silks, or lovers ensconced in Fairy Islands of the Blest— dainty fantasies of luxurious idleness as well as of tender love. Sculptors, jewelers, wood carvers, iron workers, even chinaware makers catered to this passion for decorative grace. Everything and everybody, insofar as the creative world was concerned, combined to form a fit setting for the existence of superlative luxury. In this ostentatious setting there was little tolerance for the bold expression of emotion in art.

Although this Rococo art was created to frame the social graces of the period, and so possesses a stylized, formal aspect, it should not be thought of as being only artificially conventional and pleasingly correct. The artists of the time used mediums of expression that were natural and logical for their purpose, and explored these mediums with an almost unbelievable ease and fluency. But underneath all this seeming ease and natural complexity there exists a profound art; the effects attained were the results of the most skillful manipulation of materials. Accent, quantity, and proper stressing of syllables; ornaments, scrolls, and harmoniously curving lines; gilded scale passages, lovely in their thin airiness, lightly curving melodies, and exquisite harmonies—all were molded by the artist of the century into real significance, and if we learn to know the achievements of one type of artist in this luxurious period, we can better understand the others. The writings of Pope and Thomson will help us appreciate the paintings of Watteau, Boucher, and Chardin; the creations of Cuvilliès and Neumann are the architectural counterparts of some of the music of the younger Scarlatti, Haydn, and Mozart.

A MIRROR OF THE EIGHTEENTH CENTURY

It is in the works of Haydn and Mozart (especially the latter), that we find a musical incarnation of this eighteenth-century

FRANÇOIS CUVILLIÈS:
INTERIOR OF THE
RESIDENZTHEATER,
MUNICH
*This eighteenth-century
theater is a perfect setting
for Mozart's operas.*

Rococo spirit. Naturally these composers were affected by the intellectual and spiritual characteristics of the period, and to a degree
their music suggests the airs and graces, the molded curves and facile
ornaments of the eighteenth century. Yet we are coming to realize
that there is much more than the mere suggestion of the elegance of
this age in their works; otherwise they would have passed into obliv-
ion long ago. Haydn is not merely the individual who wrote jolly,
conventional, light-hearted but not very significant music; and
Mozart's hold on posterity is the result of far more than the limpid
clarity and perfection of his style. Both these men were composers
who were able to feel deeply as well as to write clearly, they were
not merely periwigged courtiers buried under the patronage of
dukes and bishops; they were living, sensitive individuals. Haydn,
for all his simplicity and spontaneity, has a depth of feeling, in some
of his slow movements, that anticipates Beethoven. Underneath
much of the intuitive grace, the melodic charm, and the refined perfection of Mozart's music we can surely feel a peculiar sadness
which suggests that he, like Beethoven and Brahms, realized the

tragic futility of all human activity—that he could feel the taste of death on his tongue, as he himself phrased it.

Mozart's compositions group themselves naturally into two great divisions: first, the "galant" works, strongly Rococo in spirit; and second, the greater compositions, which transcend time, place, and circumstance. Part of his chamber music, his sonatas and concertos, his church music (strangely enough), his serenades, and some of his earlier operas belong in the first group. His great symphonies, notably those in E minor, E flat Major, and C Major, the six quartets that he dedicated to Haydn, his *G Minor Quintet*, the operas *Don Giovanni* and *The Magic Flute*, can be classed together in the second group. No better introduction to the beauties of his Rococo style can be found than the charming serenade *Eine Kleine Nacht-musik*, written for performance at some courtly, outdoor occasion. Holmes, one of the early Mozart biographers, has this to say of these Mozart serenades:

> Sunday garden fêtes in the spring and early summer were peculiarly characteristic of life in Vienna, where the pleasure of the promenade and the enjoyment of the air and sunshine regularly succeed the observances of religion. In such a scene, where all the beauty, rank, and talent of the capital are assembled, the spirit of the season is irresistible. And there is the music. An orchestra is erected in some green walk among the trees; and the first sound is the signal to suspend conversation, to sit quietly, or to cluster round the musicians. . . . A style of instrumental music at once light and ariose—somewhat between the symphony and the dance, but calculated to give elegance and tenderness of sentiment to the promenaders—was at any time attractive to Mozart and among his easiest work. His serenades were not such as the starved lover sings, but imbued with all the genius of the South; in fact, when we consider the emotions aroused by his instrumental music, and by the adagios of his symphonies in particular, the imagination of the author may be compared to a Mohammedan paradise; for in no other element can such refined voluptuousness and elegance be conceived to originate.

The four short movements of this work well suggest the Rococo backgrounds of Mozart's life. Born in Salzburg in 1756, the son of a court musician to the Prince-Archbishop's household, his early life was that of a child virtuoso touring the courts of Europe.

Settling down as one of the Archbishop's retainers, he later went to Vienna, where he was received by the emperor, supported by the nobility, and made his reputation as a composer of operas. A number of these, including *The Marriage of Figaro*, are typically Rococo in

WOLFGANG AMADEUS
MOZART

spirit and form. Another fine example of this galant (see Glossary) style is the *Symphony in D Major* (often called the Haffner Symphony), K. 385, written in the almost incredible time of two weeks, at the request of his father, for the Haffner family of Salzburg. Six months afterwards, when Wolfgang was arranging for its rehearsal and first performance, he had so completely forgotten the contents of the score that he wrote to his father: "the new Haffner symphony has quite astonished me, for I do not remember a note of it. It must be very effective."

And very effective it is, especially if we can listen to it interpreted by a Mozart specialist. The slow movement again suggests the serenade style of "refined voluptuousness and elegant repose." The last movement, in rondo form, is full of high spirits and keen wit but there is none of the vigorous boisterousness that we so often find in the last movements of Haydn symphonies.

MOZART'S *G MINOR SYMPHONY*

To turn to Mozart's *G Minor Symphony* from some of his earlier works is to realize the depth and range of his mind. His ultimate richness was far above the somewhat superficial Rococo graces of his time, as expressed in the galant works. It is amazing to consider what must have been his mental concentration and illumination in the summer of 1788, when within a couple of months he produced three of his greatest symphonies, each of them as different from the other emotionally as it could possibly be, works happy, noble, and troubled. Truly that "heart of fire and brain of ice" that Wagner speaks of as vital necessities for a composer were Mozart's.

There is a breath of foreboding in the *G Minor Symphony*, a more somber feeling than that of the other two works in this group. It is music peculiarly for study in the waning days of the year, when the face of nature has changed from summer pride to autumn brooding. The dignity and power of nature are in the music, too, it suggests the unchanging processes of life, which in right contemplation are noble, however sad.

The orchestration suits the work's mood—strings, wood wind, and horns only. The blare of the heavier brass would be out of place; the gravity of the horns alone is required. It may be noted that, although no clarinets are found in the first version of this work, they are used in the second which Mozart prepared.

First Movement

Over a soft, impassioned pulsating viola figure is given out the first theme, *Allegro molto:*

In the second theme (44), we may feel sweetness and a faint sadness, in a gliding chromatic movement:

The magnificent dramatic life of the whole movement is lived in the spirit of the first theme only, with the interweaving of parts suggesting the complexity of life. A wistful dialogue for wind and strings (138) leads back to the recapitulation (164). Here the first theme is extended, and there is an urgent coda (281), mounting toward and ending on the heights of dramatic tension.

SECOND MOVEMENT

This is in regular "first-movement form," like the first and the finale. It may be that Mozart felt this form, with its possibilities of conflict and tension in the development, to be peculiarly fitted as the stage for his drama in music. The first theme of the *Andante* seeks comfort and finds it within. Soon after the second subject has begun (37), there is a poignant chord (44) that hints at much behind the self-control of the opening. Throughout the movement the modulations and the calling and answering of the themes are emotionally suggestive and artistically masterly.

MINUET

Is there spiritual conflict here also? In the first part, its firmness is curiously austere. The trio (43) brings a softer mood as strings and wind graciously bow to each other. The return of the first section, with its earnest, almost stern, urgency emphasizes the feeling that Mozart has departed from the usual minuet spirit because he so strongly felt the work as an organic whole. Among its four movements there is a rare consonance in moods and power.

FINALE

In this section we hear restlessness, anxiety, a going to and fro in the mind, and a searching of the spirit. Here is something of the first movement's imperiousness in the sweeps of the strings and the chordal interjections of the wind. The first theme enters at once:

the second at 71:

Here again is the chromatic hint of noble melancholy that we found in the earlier movements. At 125 Mozart begins to work out his thoughts by declaiming the first in interrupted sentences; before settling down to tear the heart out of it in impassioned exhortation and the weaving of argument, he moves masterfully from key to key and leaves the issue uncertain when he turns to the recapitulation (207). The change in the latter portion of the second theme (twice, at 251 and following) will not escape attention. It is as if at the last the composer sought to make the poignancy of his thought even more urgent.

PIANO CONCERTO IN D MINOR

Nowhere is Mozart shown to better advantage than in his piano concertos; they were written, for his own use as soloist, during the busiest years of his short life, and are excellent examples of his characteristic mature style. Perhaps the most popular of the twenty-five works in this form is the *Concerto in D Minor*, K.466. It belongs to a wonderful year of productivity, 1785, when its writer was twenty-nine; about this time Haydn assured Mozart's father that Wolfgang was the greatest composer he knew. The key is a rather rare one with Mozart, and when used in his other works it seemed to signify drama to him.

First Movement

Here is Romance, of a dark brooding type, felt in the very first measures; the opening seems to suggest something menacing, and we think of the world of the *G Minor Symphony*. Just before the solo instrument enters, another mood is suggested, that of pathos. The pianist's theme, when it does come in, contrasts sharply with what the orchestra has foreshadowed passionately. It is as if (as Einstein puts it) "the orchestra represents an anonymous threatening power, and the solo instrument voices an eloquent lament." Much of the dramatic sense of conflict felt throughout this movement develops from the opposition of the orchestra and the solo parts. The end is quiet, but not peaceful.

Here are the principal themes:

2) **Allegro**
(Wood Wind)

3) **Allegro**
(Piano)

Second Movement

Mozart entitles this, unusually, a "Romanze." There is something sweet, almost fragile, in it; and we find, for a time at least, amid the suave orchestration—strings, wood winds, and horns—the peace that seemed so unsure when the first movement's conflict ruled. But in the course of this Romanze, which is in rondo form (the gentle theme appearing at measures 1, 68, and 119), there is a return of the fierce romantic spirit of the first movement in the strange middle section (90-119). Here there are brief, tense, repeated passages in which the orchestration, instead of being extended, is concentrated into the wildness of a few instruments; remarkable craftsmanship is shown in displaying the cutting, driving power of the reeds. In the last section peace reigns, the piano uttering a parting sigh.

Third Movement

The finale is again in rondo form, with the trumpets and drums, omitted in the Romanze, restored. Its principal theme begins:

Allegro assai
(Piano)

Thus is recalled the intensity of spirit, and something of the passion, of the *G Minor Symphony*. The first contrasting theme is also in the minor, beginning:

The second of the contrasting themes sings happily in the major:

On its return this theme appears in the minor, and the sky is clouded. After the cadenza, the first idea is momentarily recalled before the clouds finally roll away; then the wood winds echo the cheerful three-octave tune in sunny cordiality.

BERNARD SHAW ON MOZART

In one of the best descriptions of the Mozart style ever written, Bernard Shaw says that nothing but the finest execution—beautiful, expressive, and intelligent—will serve for this music. The phrases look straightforward and clear, but a deviation of a hair's breadth from perfection shows up immediately, though the music sounds so obvious that it seems as if anyone could do it.

It is impossible to make an effect with Mozart, to work up an audience by playing on their hysterical susceptibilities. It is still as true as it was before the *Eroica Symphony* existed that there is nothing better in art than Mozart's best. We have had Beethoven, Schubert, Mendelssohn, Schumann, and Brahms since his time . . . but the more they have left the Mozart quartet or quintet behind, the further it comes out ahead in its perfection of temper and refinement of consciousness. In the ardent regions where all the rest are excited and vehement, Mozart alone is completely self-possessed: where they are clutching their bars with a grip of iron and forging them with Cyclopean blows, his gentleness of touch never deserts him: he is considerate, economical, practical, under the same pressure that throws your Titan into convulsions. We all in our barbarism have a relish for the strenuous: your tenor whose B flat is like the bursting of a boiler always brings down the house, even when the note brutally effaces the song; and the composer who can artistically express in music a transport of vigor and passion of the more muscular kind, such as the Finale to the *Seventh Symphony* of Beethoven, or the *Ride of the Valkyrie* of Wagner, is always a hero with the interpreter in music. . . . With Mozart you are safe from inebriety. Hurry, excitement, eagerness, loss of consideration are to him purely comic or vicious states of mind. . . . Give me the artist who breathes the true Parnassian air like a native and goes about his work in it as quietly as a common man goes about his ordinary business. Mozart did so; and that is why I like him. Even if I did not, I should pretend to; for a taste for his music is a mark of caste among musicians, and should be worn, like a tall hat, by the amateur who wishes to pass for a true Brahmin.[1]

While it is hardly necessary to follow Shaw's whimsical suggestion and feign a liking and understanding of Mozart's music, this will gradually assume its proper place in the repertory of the listening amateur if we give it a chance. Acquiring a taste for Mozart is an invaluable experience, if for no other reason than the sensing of the value of a consummate perfection of workmanship in art.

HAYDN THE PATHFINDER

It was Haydn who gave Mozart the form of the quartet and symphony that he was so quickly to make his own. We cannot remind ourselves too often that Haydn was the composer who first used the orchestra in its modern sense and who developed the general type of music which it was to play. Basing his work on the experiments carried out by earlier men (notably Carl Philipp Emanuel Bach, a son of the great Johann Sebastian, and the various conductors of the orchestra at the ducal court at Mannheim), Haydn laid out a plan for the symphony which we still use today—that of writing it in four movements, each with a different form. Particularly important was his scheme for working out a plan for the first movement—the sonata form, as we have come to call it. It was Haydn who introduced the minuet, a dance in great favor with court circles at the time, into the symphony as its third movement.

[1] Shaw, *Music in London—1890-1894*. London: Constable.

FRANZ JOSEF HAYDN

Instead of arranging his orchestra as a general unit and giving parts rather indiscriminately to all the instruments, no matter what their individual tone might be, Haydn separated his band into groups (we call them "choirs"), each of them having a special significance in the make-up of the whole. He uses these "choirs" according to their significance: strings alternate with wood winds for special dialogue effects, for instance, instead of always combining with them as they did in the orchestra of Johann Sebastian Bach; contrasts of timbre and tone are frequent, with many sudden changes and rather whimsical turns throughout the music. It was this general scheme which Mozart adopted, adding some instruments to it and polishing it up as to style and finish; Beethoven took it up in turn and passed it on to the later composers—Liszt, Berlioz, Wagner, and Strauss—for their further development. We could also call Haydn the father of the string quartet, for he chose the four instruments that are used in this combination and marked out for them a type of music well suited to the display of their essential traits.

Naturally, when compared to the heaven-storming work of his followers, Beethoven and Brahms, or even the more perfect compositions of his friend and contemporary, Mozart, Haydn's writing sounds a bit uneven and experimental, especially in those passages which we call "bridge passages." He had not learned how to lead gradually and almost imperceptibly from one theme to another, as Beethoven knew so well to do. Some of Haydn's phrases lack the concentrated perfection of Mozart's writing, but there is always a fresh, spontaneous quality about Haydn's work that makes it most acceptable to us today.

Of Teutonic stock, Haydn was born at Rohrau in 1732 and brought up in a humble atmosphere abounding in Croatian and Hungarian folk-songs, full of rhythm and gracious melody. Thus, it was natural that he should introduce the idiom of these songs into his music. He was a choirboy in the cathedral at Vienna and later taught music in an attic. Later he entered the service of a Hungarian nobleman and after that became musical director to the famous Esterhazy family, long influential in European politics and art. At the various Esterhazy establishments Haydn had a full force of musicians at his command, and he wrote a great deal of experimental music for them. Typical of this early *galant* style is his series of three symphonies—*Le Matin, Le Midi, Le Soir*—the first of the many works he composed for Prince Esterhazy.

THE SURPRISE SYMPHONY

After long years of courtly service, Haydn finally resigned and travelled to Paris and London, where he was feted and honored as the leading musician of the time. In the works which he wrote for performance in these great metropolitan centers there is a sincerity and feeling suggestive of his great Romantic successor Beethoven. Perhaps the most popular of them is the *Surprise Symphony*, to which the Germans gave the name *Paukenschlag* and the French, *Battement de timbales*. The "surprise" is not, to modern ears, much of a shock; it is just a loud chord suddenly introduced in a soft part of the slow movement. Although it is supposed to wake up sleepy listeners, in reality it is just a bit of showmanship. We must remember that this symphony was designed for Haydn's London season of 1792, when he had to do everything possible to direct attention to his concerts.

First Movement

The symphony, scored for flutes, oboes, bassoons, horns, trumpets, drums in pairs, and the usual string parts, begins with his favorite slow introduction, a device he used so often and Mozart so rarely. The tone is grave, and the climbing chromaticism foreshadows the Romantic age. The *vivace* movement, to which this is the preface, has a first theme closely allied to that of the slow introduction's opening:

Its easygoing gaiety echoes some figuration from the introduction. Haydn has fun joining together his two themes; indeed, he is already developing ideas before the expected development section is due. He seems to play a "false alarm" trick at measure 54, but it is just his way of leading out the second theme, which waltzes in at 69:

Very soon a third theme follows, restful, *dolce*:

And so he goes on to the development (109), which, although it consists of less than fifty measures, has the usual delicious diversity of keys and contains some quite strenuous, even fierce, music. In the recapitulation we find Haydn reaching his waltz theme earlier than before, in order to bring in some new developments—a device characteristic of his methods of composing; changed figurations in the accompaniment will be noticed: a new combination of thematic material (196-200) and a feeling of his being about to work this into a long final coda. The third theme duly makes its reappearance, to crown all with a benevolent farewell. The actual coda comprises but a few measures of definitive ending.

SECOND MOVEMENT

The slow movement consists of a set of variations on a tune that was then well known; the version now familiar is set to the words *"Ah, vous dirai-je, maman"* (the plowman whistles this tune in Haydn's oratorio *The Seasons*):

The surprise comes at the sixteenth measure. In the first variation the decorative elements are simple, sufficient, and perfectly obvious. In the second comes a typical Haydn outburst, in the minor key, with the two halves of the tune treated quite differently. This, a frequent device in variations, makes what is called a "double." The variation ends with a tiny cadenza. In the third the strings and wood wind duet and the flute sings a new melody.

In the fourth there is more diversity: large chords and a broad swing mark its outer features, and a much milder tone its inner ones. The coda artistically carries on for a short time in the swashbuckling style; then there is a pull-up, as if a new section were to begin or (if this had been a concerto) as if a cadenza were to be inserted. But it is only one of Haydn's genial false alarms. Some sweet, new, forward-looking romantic harmonies delicately put the theme to rest.

THIRD MOVEMENT

The swinging, countrified *Ländler* spirit of the minuet reminds us that Haydn was a man of the people. He neatly avoids squaretoedness in phrase lengths and shows a delightful amount of variety in his keys. The two sections of the minuet (before the trio comes) make a hearty little piece, complete in itself.

The trio uses the same sort of running figure that we heard as the second part of the minuet began, but it is now reversed—upside down. Bassoon and flute get their turn. This trio is so shaped that it, too, is by itself complete, forming a short, three-part piece (which could be lettered A—B—A, the B bit being briefly developed into eleven measures, against the A's eight).

FINALE

This is in what we know as sonata-rondo form, partaking of the nature of both these forms; this is a very common structure for symphonic finales in the eighteenth century. Haydn begins lightly:

Allegro di molto

The orchestra comes in gradually as he develops this first idea immediately. This development takes the place of what might usually be expected, some kind of bridge to the second theme, which enters at measure 75, demurely, accompanied by the twinkling figure from the start of the main theme:

Very quickly the first is back again for an extremely short visit; in the middle part of the movement there is a development along the lines of the first theme, in which string ejaculations are uttered in various keys while the wind instruments leap about. At measure 140 Haydn feigns a recapitulation, but the chase is still afoot with new hedges to jump, the real recapitulation coming in at measure 182. In this the first theme is cut short by ten measures; the second gets short shrift, too. The coda comes at measure 226 with deceptive quietness; in it there is one final scurry over hill and dale with a few final "Hollos!" before the wild chase comes to its end.

HAYDN'S HUMANISM

In the slow introduction to the *Clock Symphony* (also written for his London concerts) we have an opportunity to observe the depth of feeling that has been suggested as characteristic of Haydn. Full of grave beauty, it is an excellent foil to the graceful theme which immediately follows it. The rest of the movement is in the usual sonata form. The second movement gives the work its popular name, for the repeated chords of the accompaniment are very suggestive of the slow ticking of a clock. Over this is heard a sedately shaped melody of great charm, typically Rococo music. After the usual minuet we come to the rapid last movement; here it will be interesting to try to determine the formal scheme used—is it sonata or rondo?

Two of the works of his old age are among the great favorites of choral literature—*The Creation* (1798) and *The Seasons* (1801), oratorios somewhat in the Handelian tradition. The latter is particularly charming in a Rococo way, with its occasional naïve suggestions of country sights and scenes. *The Creation*, on the other hand, foreshadows the intense Romanticism which was to permeate the music of the next century.

HAYDN AND MOZART COMPARED

Sacheverell Sitwell in his little book on Mozart, a book that contains some strange inconsistencies as well as much that is good, has a neat word to say as to the differences between the music of Haydn and Mozart—differences easier to feel than to describe. He says:

> If music is loved for its simple and pure qualities, unmixed with introspection and self-analysis, the best of Haydn's symphonies are as beautiful as anything that the civilization of Europe has given us. Their clean, neat workmanship; the manner in which the simplest things of life are taken up and charged with humor and poetry; the grace and liveliness of his minuets; the speed and brilliance of the finales. Mozart is more delicate, less earthly; his perfection of beauty is to be found in the *andante* (the slow movement). There he has an angelic, a seraphic tranquillity; a peace in which, as it were, you could hear Haydn breathe. In the Minuet and Trio Haydn is always predominant; in the hands of Mozart the Minuet is very often the subject of a courtly and aristocratic sadness; with Haydn it is a true dance which touches the blood. The Trio grows out of it, not merely stands in contrast with it, and it sometimes has the character and force of a Landler or Viennese waltz; when the Minuet comes back again after the Trio, it is with the grateful comfort of music heard once more that might have gone forever.[2]

Sitwell thinks, and with good reason, that the physical contrasts of the two men have a great deal to do with these differences: Haydn was a strong, peasant sort of man, robust, straightforward, with an unspoiled childhood back of him and the good chance of a strong maturity before him; Mozart's childhood had been spent

[2] Sacheverell Sitwell, *Mozart*. Quoted here by permission of Appleton-Century-Crofts, publishers.

playing at all the courts of Europe. His hectic life, the fact that he was always pressed for money, that he must have realized that his earthly course was to be soon run, give a nervousness and a sadness to much of his music, even as they add an aristocratic distinction and polish to it. The richness, quickness, and facility of his invention are inevitably felt in everything Mozart wrote; they are the hallmarks of his inimitable style. Haydn went more slowly and for that reason was very often more deeply and emotionally convincing.

HAYDN AND MOZART, CLASSIC COMPOSERS

After having had the music of Haydn and Mozart classified as *Rococo*, the listener may be somewhat confused upon seeing it characterized as *Classic*—a distinction which sets it off from the kind of *Romantic* music written by Beethoven and his nineteenth-century followers. The difficulty here is one of semantics. Baroque and Rococo are period terms descriptive of the kind of art produced during a certain definite era in the cultural history of man. Classic and romantic, on the other hand, are style terms which define certain qualities of the art to which they are applied. It has become customary to designate as classic those tendencies in any age which make for regularity, control, and rationality of expression; which tend to produce art works in accordance with some coherent system, with parts that are well coordinated and carefully proportioned so as to secure the best aesthetic results. In time these works assume the characteristics given by Sainte-Beuve in his definition of classic —"that which is very good and made to last"—and they become criteria by which other works are judged. By romantic, on the other hand, we usually mean art which is characterized by freedom of fancy, both in conception and treatment, which emphasizes personal expression rather than perfection of structure, and which claims relationships with events outside the world of art.

Up until the nineteenth century the various periods which constitute the development of European art seem to have been characterized by either one or the other of these two stylistic qualities, the two alternating in a sort of continuous cultural cycle. Greco-Roman art, of course, was classic in spirit, a spirit which spread over all of Romanized Europe (and so, called Romanesque) between the close of the classical period and the rise of Gothic art—roughly from

600-1200 A.D. The Gothic spirit, which prevailed in Western Europe from the thirteenth to the fifteenth centuries, was entirely romantic in its tendencies. The Renaissance is known for its revival of classical traditions. During the Baroque period romantic tendencies were again predominant, and during the ensuing Rococo era the classic ideals came once more to the fore. During the eighteenth century occurred the great Classic revolt, manifested in all the arts. This in turn produced the intensity and vigor of nineteenth century Romanticism, which was able to fuse all tendencies into one overwhelming art style.

Perhaps the following table may clear up these seeming conflicting tendencies:

600	1200	1450	1600	1750	1800
Romanesque	*Gothic*	*Renaissance*	*Baroque*	*Rococo*	
					ROMANTICISM
classic	romantic	classic	romantic	classic	

In all of his larger works—symphonies, concertos and string quartets—Mozart accepted the solution of the problems of musical form worked out by his great contemporary Haydn. The question of how to put together a musical composition of considerable length, written for the instruments then available, in order to sustain interest, provide contrast, and achieve climax, was one of great concern to both composers. It may be said that this was one of the phases of the general problems of ordered expression so characteristic of the "rational" thinking of their time. That it was successfully solved by these two men and their lesser contemporaries, working in the congenial atmosphere of the Austro-German music world, is evidenced by the fact that they are so generally referred to as Viennese Classical Composers, that their type of musical composition became the model for later composers. The work of Haydn and Mozart, founded on earlier experiments by such men as Carl Philipp Emanuel Bach, the Stamitz family in Mannheim, and Francis Joseph Gossec in Paris, established for all time the classical principles underlying musical construction and led directly to the later developments of Beethoven.

In addition, the general aesthetic climate of this period favored a style that cleared the composer's emotion of circumstances, cleansed it of personalities, and generalized it from human experience. This can be clearly felt in all the works of Haydn and Mozart which we have discussed in this chapter, their *galant* compositions as well as those which lay more stress on soul and sentiment. These are in strong contrast with such works as Beethoven's *Fifth* and *Ninth Symphonies*, for example, in which the composer is largely concerned with expressing his individual experiences.

In general, this may be said to be the great difference between Classical and Romantic art: the one delights us because of its beautiful molding of its material and the olympic serenity of its expression; the other because of its communication of emotions to which we can readily and fully respond.

LIST OF SUGGESTED MUSIC

C Major Symphony, K.34	MOZART
Eine kleine Nachtmusik, K.525	MOZART
Symphony in D Major, K.133	MOZART
Symphony in g minor, K.183	MOZART
Piano Concerto in d minor, K.466	MOZART
Surprise Symphony in G Major	HAYDN
Clock Symphony in D Major	HAYDN
Le Matin, Le Midi, Le Soir Symphonies	HAYDN

TOPICS FOR DISCUSSION

Following on the section "Haydn and Mozart Compared," can you add some impressions of your own as to the clear distinctions between (a) the aims and (b) the styles of these composers? How far were their aims determined by the differing circumstances of their life and work? This point, about the influence of a composer's circumstances on his work, might be discussed in relation to others, both earlier and later than Haydn and Mozart.

What do you consider one of the strongest formal elements in Haydn's finales—one that is rarer in Mozart's?

By referring to the scores, compare the orchestration of the following: Wagner's *Götterdämmerung*, Beethoven's *Fifth Symphony*, Mozart's *G Minor Symphony*, Haydn's *Surprise Symphony*.

Supplement

The following chapters contain material which, while not an essential part of the course covered by the text, will enlarge the reader's understanding of the music. They may be used at any point in the book where they seem relevant. They may also prove helpful in increasing the reader's information about topics in which he may be particularly interested.

CHAPTER 39

The Piano

ঙ১১৯

    Let us begin with a brief resumé of the history of this most popular of all solo instruments, the one surviving representative of the keyboard type of stringed instrument so prevalent in all phases of the development of European music. From the time of the Renaissance, keyboard instruments have always been fairly accessible and are, fortunately, fairly easy to play. The accuracy of ear so necessary for the players of instruments like the violin, the cello, and the trombone is not an important factor in the case of the keyboard instruments. Players of the organ, the piano, and the harpsichord find their tones already formed for them, and their ability as players depends on their powers of co-ordination and manual dexterity.

ANCESTORS

    Our present-day piano is a logical descendant of two types of earlier keyboard instruments, the clavichord and the harpsichord. These forerunners of the piano were themselves the result of the attempt, somewhere about the fifteenth century, to produce tone from the existing stringed instruments by means of a keyboard or clavier, each key of which would set in vibration one string. In the clavichord type, the tone was produced by means of metal tangents fixed to one end of a long lever, on the other end of which was the key. The tangents were forced up against the string when the key was depressed, making a delicate, metallic sort of tone, well suited to a small room but quite lost in a large one. Since the tone could

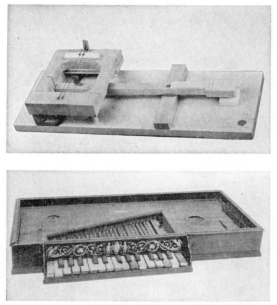

Courtesy, Steinway and Sons, New York

CLAVICHORD
(GERMANY, CIRCA
1533)

*This direct descendant of
the Monochord had a range
of four octaves and pro-
duced a soft, hesitant tone.
Blades of brass, called tangents, were fitted to the
keys. When the tangents
struck the string, tone and
pitch were produced simultaneously.*

be varied in volume (for the harder one hit the key, the firmer was the tangent forced against the string) and had a sympathetic quality, this instrument was a favorite of musicians for several centuries. The harpsichord (in its smaller forms it was called *spinet* or *virginal*) tone was louder and more definite, but it was incapable of direct control of volume. It was produced by mechanically plucking the string with a plectrum made of quill or leather inserted in the action; this gave a twangy, guitar-like tone that had considerable power, especially when the instrument was of concert size. The incapability of direct variation in tonal power of this instrument led the makers to seek a new type, one that would give a brilliant tone and yet would be able to play both softly and loudly. In the early part of the eighteenth century Cristofori, an Italian clavier maker, an-nounced that he had perfected such an instrument, a *gravicembalo col piano e forte*—a harpsichord that could play both soft and loud. Cristofori's instrument was not actually a harpsichord, for the tone was produced by means of small hammers which struck the strings; it did what Cristofori claimed, however, and the name stuck. The century following the announcement of this invention was given over to improving the action of the instrument, largely by German

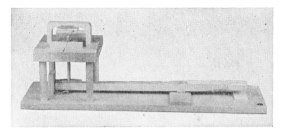

SPINET (ITALY,
CIRCA 1700)

*Quills fitted into jacks set
the strings of this instrument into vibration by
plucking them. Since there
was only one string for
each note, the volume was
small and tone modifica-
tion, difficult.*

and English makers. In the first part of the nineteenth century
Broadwood, an English maker, supplied pedals which made it possible to sustain the tones generated by the strings, as well as to soften
them. The problem of stringing the piano to produce maximum richness and depth of tone was one of the most important that the later
makers had to solve. In the early years of the nineteenth century
American manufacturers invented a complete iron frame capable
of withstanding a tension of thirty tons, and in 1853 steel wire instead of iron wire began to be used, allowing a much greater string
tension and thus improving the tone immeasurably. The development of our modern gargantuan instrument has been a gradual one,
but it seems now to have reached the stage where further improvement seems improbable.

THE PIANO—BOON AND BANE

The piano—its full and formal title is the pianoforte—may rightly
be called the universal musical instrument. Although, as we have

already suggested, it was the typical instrument of the nineteenth century, its popularity has lasted well into our own time and programs of piano music are greeted with enthusiasm during every modern concert season. There is good reason for this popularity, for not only has the piano one of the richest repertoires of any instrument, but it can on occasion assume that of other instruments, be they voice, violin, orchestra, or organ. It is one of the few instruments capable of furnishing not only a solo part but a harmonic accompaniment also, one that is sometimes of great complexity; in this way it functions as the violin, clarinet, or trombone never can. It is as well suited to the demands of the virtuoso as to those of the modest amateur—both find in it a satisfying medium for the conveyance of their ideas and the display of their abilities. It is, as Fox-Strangways has said, the boon as well as the bane of present-day music, for with all its ingratiating qualities, the piano lacks a soul of its own, a fact we realize only gradually and upon long acquaintance. The piano is like a brilliant friend who seems master of every situation in which he finds himself, attractive in personality, versatile in conversation, brilliant in wit, and yet when we really get to know him, one who reveals himself as having no personality of his own. "The piano is a first-rate actor: it can assume any part and make a good thing of it—sing, dance, prattle, argue, storm, wail, and do all these things in different voices," but all the time its percussive tone is incapable of being modified or prolonged to any appreciable extent. Once the piano tone has been produced by the hammers which set its string vibrating, there is no way of prolonging, shading, or otherwise altering the tone. The only thing that can be done is to produce another tone having the desired change. This is a serious handicap, for certainly long-drawn melody is the soul of music. In order to have that sense of continuity—of going on— which is the very essence of its life, music must consist of more than short, choppy phrases such as are suggested by the quickly fading tones of the piano. A composer for the orchestra can make use of its power for sustaining tone, its immense range of different degrees of power, its infinite possibilities of combining different tone colors; but a writer for the piano must recognize the incapacities of his instrument in these respects. He must find means to overcome them and to suggest to the hearer more than is actually trans-

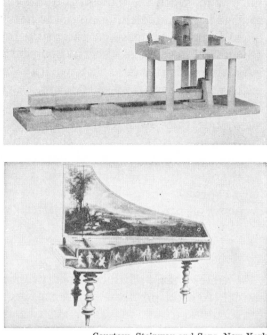

HARPSICHORD (ITALY, CIRCA 1680)

Resembling a grand piano in form and arrangement, the harpsichord was the outstanding keyboard instrument of the eighteenth century. Although the jack and quill action gave it individual tone and some power, it lacked the ability to produce any expressive character through touch.

Courtesy, Steinway and Sons, New York

mitted to the ear by inferring things of which the instrument is not actually capable. In other words, the writer of music for the piano has had to evolve a style of writing which takes advantage of the instrument's peculiar characteristics—ease and facility of handling. There must be plenty of fast and brilliant passages in piano writing; the attaining of great elasticity in accent through the ability of the player directly to emphasize any note or group of notes he plays means that piano music must have plenty of rhythmic appeal. But these are not enough in themselves. Music written to exploit these rather crude possibilities alone would make the pianoforte one of the most objectionable instruments ever invented and one of the most potent depravers of human taste imaginable. The piano, Jekyll and Hyde among instruments, can also sing angelically—fit interpreter for a Chopin or a Franck.

Indeed, the attempt to remedy these natural handicaps of piano tone has resulted in the only individual contributions the piano has made to the world's great musical literature. In spite of the fact that

since 1850, when the modern form of the instrument may be said
to have been perfected, piano music has been one of the most frequent forms of composition, there have been only a few great composers who have made essential contributions to piano literature—
who have written music that would be unthinkable on any other
instrument. These few—Schumann, Liszt, Chopin, Debussy, and
Ravel—have not only recognized the shortcomings of the instrument, but they have done more: they have used these shortcomings to the advantage of their own piano style. The other great
composers, with very few exceptions, have written voluminously
for the piano, but in so doing they have convinced us that they could
have expressed themselves better through other instruments—the
orchestra or, perhaps, the string quartet.

THE RESOURCES OF THE PIANO

What are these characteristics peculiarly indigenous to piano
music? A little practical experimenting will help answer such a
question. Go to a good piano and strike a full chord, holding down
the keys after the hammers have produced the tone; the notes will
sound with gradually diminishing tone until the strings have entirely
ceased to vibrate. Now strike the same chord again, at the same time
holding down the damper pedal (the one to the right) and remove
your fingers from the keys as soon as the hammers have struck.
Exactly the same result will follow, for the pedal locks the dampers
of the strings belonging to the keys that have been struck, thus
allowing them to vibrate until they cease of their own inanition.
The natural function of these dampers is to clamp down on the
string as soon as the player removes his finger from the key, and
thus stop further vibration and consequent mixing of tones. Now,
holding down the damper pedal, play the same chord in varying
parts of the keyboard—low, medium, and high—or better still,
break it up into an arpeggio. Notice how this sustains the tone, giving it a semblance of the same notes being prolonged; it is this plan
of playing scales, arpeggios, and ornamental passages to give the
idea of sustained utterance that is one of the cardinal principles of
good writing for the piano. Liszt and his followers developed this
idea to such an extent and with such virtuosity of technic, massing

CRISTOFORI'S
"PIANO E FORTE"

A perfected hammer action, invented by Cristofori in 1710, gave this instrument greater power and wider range than its predecessors.

Courtesy, Steinway and Sons, New York

chord upon chord in such reckless profusion and producing such climaxes of cascading tone that the piano seems almost like a sonant instrument.

Now try another experiment: while sounding the arpeggio of any common chord on the piano with the damper pedal down, introduce a few notes that do not belong to this chord; notice what such a procedure does to the *color* of the result (provided the added notes are not too discordant). There seems to be a new richness of *timbre*. By the ingenious inclusion of just the right notes in his runs and arpeggios Chopin made a great contribution to piano writing. Listening to his romantic Preludes or Nocturnes, we are almost persuaded that the piano is not a monochromatic instrument. Robert Schumann was the great Romanticist of piano music; he loved to dream "with the pedal down," and came nearer than anyone else ever has to finding a soul in the piano. He seized upon its peculiar capacities and gave it what others would have given to the orchestra, and not entirely unsuccessfully—far more successfully than when he gave to the orchestra what he should have given to the piano. His short

LISZT AT THE
PIANO
(CARTOON)

pieces *Aufschwung* (Soaring), *Warum?* (Why?), or the *Romance*, Opus 28, No. 2, will give the hearer an idea of this composer's love for blended chords and poetic thought. The evanescent quality of the piano and its capacity for blending and mixing tone by the use of the damper pedal make it the ideal instrument for playing Impressionistic music. Men like Debussy and Ravel were able to wash in their colors with broad sweeps and blur their outlines without making them so indistinct as to lose character. Debussy's *Poissons d'or*, his *Jardins sous la pluie*, or any of his *Préludes*, as well as Ravel's *Pavane pour une infante défunte* or *Jux d'eau*, illustrates the adaptability of the piano for this type of music. There are many who think that this kind of writing shows the piano at its best. (For further treatment of this style of piano music, see the chapters on Impressionism.)

THE PIANO AS PERCUSSION

In line with the almost universal trend of contemporary developments in art, composition for the piano in the recent century has enormously altered its character. In place of romantic persuasiveness and generous communication of feeling which, beginning in the nineteenth century music of Liszt, Schumann, and Chopin, seems to have ended in the sunset glow of Rachmaninoff, we find the instrument being treated in a hard, mechanistic, percussive style. Illustrations of this will be found below.

A LIST OF SUGGESTED MUSIC

1721 *Prelude and Fugue in C Major*, No. 1 of
    The Well-Tempered Clavier   BACH

Bach wrote these compositions so that they could be played on any keyboard instrument, although he preferred to use the clavichord. They sound well on the modern piano if not overemotionalized with the use of the damper pedal.

1778 *Rondo alla Turca* from *Sonata in A Major*, K.331   MOZART

While Mozart's piano was a less powerful instrument than our modern one, it was capable of some very characteristic effects. It will be interesting to compare a piano rendition of this lively *Rondo* in the Turkish style (an affectation of the Rococo period) with one played on the harpsichord, which was still largely used in Mozart's day. Such a comparison would show clearly the differences between the style demanded of the two instruments.

c. 1797 First Movement of *Sonata in C Major*, Op. 13
    (Pathétique)   BEETHOVEN

This strong, dramatic, sonata-form movement shows Beethoven's almost orchestral treatment of the piano. His set of thirty-two sonatas is one of the most important contributions to the literature of the instrument.

1837 *Aufschwung* (Soaring) from the *Fantasiestücke*   SCHUMANN

Here is the eager Romantic poet, dreaming at the piano "with the pedal down."

(Revised 1848) *Fantasia quasi sonata—D'après une*
    lecture de Dante (Fantasy Sonata—After Reading Dante)   LISZT

Franz Liszt was the first of the great modern virtuoso pianists to travel over Europe giving "recitals." He wrote a great deal of piano music to show off his prodigious technical ability. His style, like the man himself, was a peculiar combination of affecting sincerity and rhetorical bombast, but it suits the instrument, which by Liszt's time had developed into the elephantine instrument we know today.

Polonaise No. 6 in A flat Major, Op. 53   CHOPIN

Although this is one of the compositions of this master of the piano unfortunate enough to be maltreated by the abominable adaptations of adolescent arrangers, it does show Chopin at his best and fits the style of the instrument perfectly. Note what we have said above about his style.

1926-1937 *Microcosm*   BARTÓK

These one hundred fifty-three pieces are progressively arranged.

1911 *Allegro Barbaro*   BARTÓK

1909-1910 *Rumanian Dances*   BARTÓK

1929 *Capriccio for Piano and Orchestra*   STRAVINSKY

1943 *Amores for Prepared Piano and Percussion*   CAGE

Examples of Impressionistic piano music are mentioned in Chapter 24 on impressionism.

TOPICS FOR DISCUSSION

Compare your personal impressions of the qualities and beauties of piano tone with those received from the tone of the harpsichord and other instruments of its type.

What is your opinion on the vexing question as to whether Bach's *Well-Tempered Clavier* sounds better on the harpsichord-type or the piano-type instrument?

Why did the fully developed piano so handsomely serve the interests of the Romantic composers?

The modern electronic development of the piano makes it capable of sustaining and even swelling its initial sound. Discuss the advantage and disadvantage of this new resource.

What do you consider to be the best and the worst qualities of modern piano virtuosity? Can you name individual players to illustrate your points?

CHAPTER 40

The Organ

❦❧

Lovers of the organ and organ music are apt to lament the fact that present-day players of this instrument are not regarded by critics and concert-goers as in the same artistic class as pianists, violinists, or cellists. Lists of virtuosi in various branches of music invariably omit mention of the organist, just as the music critic demurs from listening to his playing or treating his instrument seriously. The musical amateur trying to familiarize himself with all types of music may well wonder why this is true. The organ, one of the most ancient of instruments, has always been held in esteem by many music lovers; grand, sublime, impressive, inspiring—these are the adjectives that have been used in characterizing the tone of this King of Instruments. As an ancient writer put it: "When its tones swell forth, there is no denying it, it is like the fiat of the Omnipotent." A more modern organ lover has thus apostrophized it:

> *Temple of Tone art thou! The shrine supreme*
> *Of sound's mysterious powers and richest gifts,*
> *God-given thought alone could have inspired*
> *The human mind to frame so grand a work!*
> *Great Organ—Monarch of all Instruments.*
> George Ashdown Audsley[1]

Why then the musical public's lack of interest? The writer quoted above suggests that the low standard of playing in vogue among organists until recently has been largely responsible; but there are

[1] By permission of J. Fischer & Bro.

other and remediable causes for the lack of general interest in the organ and its music.

The impressive, soul-satisfying dignity of the organ's tone is a result of the manner in which it is produced, not by means of beating reed or vibrating string, but by metal and wooden pipes blown, as Emperor Julian described it in the fourth century, "by a blast that rushes up from a leathern cavern beneath their roots, while a mortal running with swift fingers over the keys that are their concordant rulers makes them give forth melodious sounds." In principle the organ is nothing more than a mechanical means for playing a Pan's Pipe or syrinx—one of the earliest of all instruments, consisting of tubes of varying lengths bound together in such a way that they could be blown upon by the player's breath. In the organ the air is supplied mechanically and its admittance to the pipes is controlled by means of keys, one of them for each pitch produced. In order to produce varied qualities of tone, the pipes are made in different ways and whole sets of them, one for each note on the keyboard, are used for certain qualities of tone desired. To build up a suitable ensemble the various sets of pipes are used together, so that often when a single key is depressed in a large organ it gives breath to as many as fifty or sixty pipes of different sorts all sounding the same note, its octaves, or other ratio notes.

A VARIED HISTORY

The broadly elevated character inherent in organ tone was early recognized by the Christians as being ideal for providing music in their services—in spite of its unfortunate associations, for it had been used by the Romans for theatrical and gladiatorial spectacles. Ever since the fourth century its most natural and fitting place has been in the church, especially since the magnificent interiors supplied by the early church builders were ideal for the proper hearing of organ tone. As ecclesiastical architecture grew more and more magnificent and the church interiors vaster and vaster, those responsible for providing organs for these buildings experimented with various means for flooding their great churches with tone, and the organ's mechanism became more and more elaborate in order to provide adequate tonal resources. It was not until the seventeenth and early eighteenth centuries that the development of the mechanics of organ

SILBERMANN ORGAN
(CATHEDRAL OF
FREIBERG)
The sound-producing mechanism of Bach's day.

building allowed the builders to attain their ideal in producing an ensemble completely suitable for their purpose. The organs of these years, in spite of crudities of mechanical control compared to our modern instruments, were able to provide a rich, satisfying, thrilling tone which sounded to wonderful advantage in the resonant interiors available. And, as has always been the case in similar circumstances, composers were inspired to achieve suitable music, once the instrument became capable of playing it. The organ of those days was an important, living, vital instrument in the sense that it hardly is today. Johann Sebastian Bach was providing it with a repertoire which in extent and quality has never been equaled. It had arrived at a point of perfection in its tonal development that has not been greatly improved upon in the years since. It had the advantage of adequate and proper surroundings into which to project its glorious voice.

Since then the organ has fallen on rather evil days, especially as

far as many instruments in America are concerned. Although most
European builders have followed more or less closely the ideals of
the eighteenth century in developing their instruments and have had
the incalculable advantage of proper auditoriums for their organs,
those following what has come to be known as the "modern trend"
have forsaken the sunny fields of adequate, dignified tone and
wandered into ear-tickling and sensation-mongering paths. This has
been partly due to the small, stuffy, "parlor" churches which many
societies have seen fit to provide in order to secure homey, social
surroundings for their services. Organ tone, because of its peculiar
quality, demands a certain amount of reverberation—echo, to use
an everyday term—to make it completely effective. Because this
enlivening influence has been impossible in churches of wood and
plaster, it is natural that the organ builders and players should turn
their attention to effects that could come off in these unresonant
surroundings. Soft, enervated tones, effects borrowed from the
orchestra, string, wood-wind, and brass imitations, percussive, harp,
and chime tones, all of them justifiable in themselves but only as
subsidiary to essential organ tone, became the rule. Many of our
present-day instruments are built from a rather miscellaneous collection of these pleasing effects, and the glorious richness and dignified strength which should be provided above all things is likely to
be forgotten. And, as was inevitable, a school of organ composition
suitable to these conditions arose, and we have had the rather pitiable
spectacle of the King of Instruments being called on to discourse
sobbing accompaniments or to produce orchestra-like imitations un-
suited to its natural dignity.

The Auditorium an Important Factor

The importance of the character of the auditorium into which an
organ sounds cannot be overestimated. Technically speaking, the
auditorium is an acoustical device of great importance to any instrument—orchestra, piano, voice, as well as organ. Its chief purpose,
insofar as music is concerned, is to enable persons assembled to hear
what occurs in it to best advantage. Ignorance or perhaps neglect of
sound phenomena within confined spaces has given us many very
bad auditoriums. If these are not properly constructed, an echo

caused by the reflection of the sound pulsations from the various wall surfaces will so confuse the music being produced as to make it an unpleasant jangle of discordant elements, and thereby destroy its beauty. On the other hand, if every bit of reverberation is removed (as is usual in a broadcasting studio), the music will sound lifeless to the auditors who are somewhat removed from its source. This period of reverberation is more important for organ tone than for that of any other instrument; a certain amount of echo, even an amount that would somewhat confuse other types of musical tone, is necessary if we are to get the power and thrill of the full organ as well as the beautiful floating quality possible from some of the softer tones. Those who have heard a properly designed organ speaking into a fine, large, resonant interior, playing the type of music really suited to the character of the instrument, know what organ tone should sound like. Unfortunately, the coincidence of these necessary factors in the production of good tone is rare; and many of us, critics as well as laymen, have never heard great organ music as it can sound, although we are surrounded on every side by instruments that are supposed to produce it. Practically every church in the country possesses an organ, they have been placed in many auditoriums in all the large cities, and the wailing tones of a certain species greet our ears almost continuously on the radio.

Fortunately architects, organ builders, and players all have seen the light, and in recent years we have had some interiors that are almost ideal for sound; there has been a gradual but certain swing away from the rather theatrical ideals of tonal appointments that prevailed in recent years back to those of the classical period. Young players are coming to the fore, equipped with splendid technic and possessing high musical ideals, ready to take advantage of the changes which impend. Perhaps we are on the verge of a renaissance in organ music.

RHYTHM AND REPERTOIRE

There are two factors, however, that militate against the organ's becoming a popular instrument in the sense that the piano or the orchestra is. The first is its essentially unrhythmic character. Organ tone by nature is broad, thick, rather unsuitable for any change in pulse; there is an added difficulty for the organist who strives to maintain a good rhythmic flow in his playing—mechanical obstacles must be overcome to obtain accent, the chief means by which rhythm is attained. When a pianist wishes to accentuate a particular note, he does so by extra pressure on the key; the violinist obtains the same effect by a stronger pressure on his bow. No such direct means are available to the organist. He has to resort to subterfuge, for the only ways he can produce accent are by suddenly increasing his tone by the addition of extra stops (an awkward mechanical feat), by opening the shutters which enclose a group of pipes in a "swell box," thus swelling the tone at the particular place desired, or by breaking the flow of the music to give at least a suggestion of pulse. The continuously flowing, largely unaccented tone of the organ, lacking definite percussive quality, becomes confusing to those who are more familiar with orchestral or chamber music.

The other serious handicap of the organ is its lack of repertoire. Whereas instruments such as the piano, the string quartet, and the orchestra have had compositions written for them by such masters as Beethoven, Haydn, Brahms, Chopin, Schubert, Schumann, and so on—in prodigious amounts—the organ has to fall back on the works of two writers for its really *great* music: Johann Sebastian Bach and César Franck (and even in the case of these two men, the amount of music available is limited). Practically all the other great masters, through a combination of circumstances, left the organ severely alone. To be sure, Handel gave us some organ music, but like much of his other work, it seems outmoded today; Brahms wrote a few lovely things; Mendelssohn and Rheinberger (neither of whom by any stretch of the imagination could be called great) wrote their best music for the organ. The more recent German composers for the organ include Max Reger, who left behind a plethora of involved works interesting largely from the viewpoint of construction, and Karg-Elert, who has given us some well-written program music. We also have the rather pretentious works of the modern French writers, men like Widor, Vierne, and Tournemire, who surround a few interesting pages with stretches of rather disappointing wastes. More recent French composers of organ music include Dupré, Duruflé, Langlais, and Messiaen; their works exploit complex rhythmic patterns and dissonant harmonic schemes with effective results. Some of the younger English and American composers have paid attention to the organ, but so far they have not produced very important music. So the repertoire of the organist is rather limited unless he falls back upon transcriptions of music originally written for other instruments.

This situation is one which would seem to preclude the organ from becoming a concert instrument in the full sense of that term, unless we come upon an unexpected period of fecundity on the part of writers of organ music. Since so much of the best which has been written for the organ is suggestive of its religious associations, its place for many years to come will probably be in the church.

MECHANICAL PROBLEMS

The problems involved in the development of our modern organ have been three: (1) securing a satisfactory composite tone from a large number of pipes sounding together; (2) obtaining a satisfactory means of controlling the admittance of the air to the pipes by the mechanism of the keys; and (3) perfecting a satisfactory wind supply. All these problems were present in the organ of the Alexandrian Ctesibius, which was built about 250 B.C. and had rows of bronze pipes controlled by slides connected to iron keys by ropes. They are still with us today. Our tonal ideas, as has been suggested, are in a state of flux, and the elaborate electrical mechanisms which have been devised for connecting key and valve controlling the admittance of air to the pipe are not satisfactory in every respect. The early organs in the cathedrals had large keys which were connected by ropes and shafts to slides or valves under the pipes; these slides or valves had metal springs to pull them shut when the pressure was removed from the key. This crude mechanism is the essence of our modern organs. It was very difficult to manipulate because it had to work against the wind pressure ready to enter the pipes, and the only way the keys could be depressed was by striking them; the organ players came to be known as organ beaters, a name they have not entirely lived down today. When more than one note at a time was to be played, a second beater was brought into action, and as can be readily imagined, harmony as we consider it today was quite impossible. The providing of wind for these early instruments was a formidable task; a Winchester chronicler thus describes the organ—an instrument of some four hundred pipes—in his cathedral: there were "ten pipes to one of forty slides, for which the wind supply come from twenty-six bellows in two rows at which seventy strong men did labor with their arms and covered with the effects of their efforts, yet did each incite his fellows to drive up the wind with all their might." Playing, blowing, and listening to the organ must have been strenuous!

In these medieval instruments, there was no way to prevent all the pipes grouped on the slide and controlled by a single key from sounding when that key was depressed; one had to have all or nothing. Then in the sixteenth century a Dutch builder invented the "stop," a mechanism which controls the air supply to each set of pipes. If the player pulls out the little lever placed at the side or above the keyboard, the particular set of pipes governed by that lever will sound; if the lever is pushed in, the air supply to that set of pipes is shut off and they remain silent. The same mechanism, called by the same name, is in use today.

Various divisions in the big cathedral organs developed according to the demands upon them; each division was played by its own keyboard. Hence we have the two, three, four, or five keyboards or "manuals" in the present-day instrument. We still call one manual the *great*, meaning that the loud stops representing the old medieval organ are largely grouped on this manual. The *swell* division derives its name from the device, already mentioned, invented in the early eighteenth century by which the pipes are placed in a box fitted with shutters that can be opened or closed by a pedal, thus giving the organist a means for swelling or diminishing the tone. The *choir* organ suggests the days when this group of pipes was placed at the back of the player (the Germans still call this division the *rückpositiv*) and used to accompany the choir; it consists of the softer stops and provides a pleasant contrast to the tone of the other manuals. The stops which are used in *solo* (having some particular quality of tone standing out from a softer accompaniment) are grouped on a fourth manual called the *solo* organ. The *pedal*, probably first developed in the fifteenth century, provides a sustained bass to the whole ensemble; this device was later supplemented by the development of an independent pedal organ with pipes of its own, most of them of large size and providing the deep bass which we always associate with organ tone.

For centuries the mechanism of this complex instrument consisted of delicately adjusted levers between the keys and the pipe valves (once the crude early slides and ropes were done away with). Later, because it required too much physical strength from the player's fingers to actuate this mechanism, engineers devised small pneumatic bellows for doing the actual work of pulling down the pipe valves. Today the whole mechanism is controlled electrically, so that the organist's touch on the keys actually completes an electric circuit which actuates a small pneumatic motor regulating the wind supply to the pipe. All this has been so perfected that the response is practically instantaneous once the key is depressed. The troublesome problem of wind supply has also been satisfactorily solved: the modern organ is blown by large rotary fans actuated by electric motors, giving an absolutely steady, dependable supply of air.

THE ORGAN'S TRUE GLORY

The quality of tone emitted by the pipes depends on how they are constructed, their size, the proportion of length to diameter, the materials used, and so forth. This is where art enters the organ industry, for the designing and constructing of the various sets of pipes condition the tonal result of the whole instrument. Music lovers are apt to think of the organ builder as a sort of glorified mechanic; in reality he should be a consummate artist as well as a thorough craftsman. Until recently modern builders concentrated on the mechanical and electrical side of the organ's development and neglected its tonal improvement. They became so fascinated with the means that they almost forgot the end for which all the mechanism exists—the production of a glorious blend of tone, brilliant without being harsh, thrilling without being overpowering, masterful and compelling, soothing and appealing in turn, the sort of tone which rightfully belongs to the organ and which cannot be obtained from any other instrument; the sort of tone which not only causes the thrills up and down the spine, but which leads closer to the Infinite. Rolland describes such an effect on Jean Christophe when he hears his first organ music. He is in church with his grandfather; suddenly there is a deluge of sound from the organ. He does not understand or know the meaning of it; it is dazzling, bewildering, and he can hear nothing clearly; but it is good. It is as though he were suspended in mid-air like a bird. When the flood of sound rushes from one end of the church to the other, filling the arches, reverberating from wall to wall, he is carried with it, flying and skimming hither and thither with nothing to do but abandon himself to it. This is the real glory of the organ, a glory that is *sui generis*, but obtainable only through the necessary coincidence of instrument, auditorium, and player.

In spite of the fact that the days of its greatest glory have apparently departed, the organ has a definite place in the present scheme of the musical universe if we give it an opportunity for being treated as it should be. If we place it where it sounds at its best, if we design it so that its full beauty becomes apparent and do not make it merely a collection of pretty-sounding devices, and if we play on it music that suits its real character, then, in spite of its evident weaknesses and its limited repertory, the organ will maintain its place as an instrument worthy of the serious consideration of critics and music lovers.

THE BAROQUE ORGAN OF THE TWENTIETH CENTURY

There has been a recent revival of interest in the type of organ used at the time of Bach, the instrument for which he wrote his grandiose organ works. Organ builders have devoted a great deal of time and energy to studying the instruments that survive in Europe from the seventeenth and eighteenth centuries, with a view to imitating their tonal qualities in modern organs. The results have been most interesting and, in some cases, very effective. The distinctive feature of these new-old organs (they are called Baroque because they imitate the instruments of that period) is not the massive, diffuse, romantic tone to which many present-day listeners are accustomed, but a brilliant, sparkling, light clarity hitherto unassociated with the organ. The music of Bach and his predecessors takes on a new quality when played on these instruments; it seems more alive, if less impressive; more rhythmic and lyric, if less colorful. These Baroque organs lend themselves to recording, and a number of Bach and pre-Bach recordings have been made by different companies.

THE ELECTRONIC "ORGAN"

In recent years various electronic tone-producing systems, inaccurately called "electric organs," have come into being. In these, the tones are produced by generating frequencies corresponding to the vibrations of notes and then amplifying them through speakers. By controls which select and regulate the intensity of certain overtones, the players of these instruments are able to reproduce, more or less faithfully, the qualities of organ stops. In addition, electronic devices can produce indigenous sounds different from those of any other instrument. Their flexibility and comparative cheapness have resulted in their wide use in churches, as well as in places of public amusement and in homes.

LIST OF SUGGESTED MUSIC

Much of the recorded organ music will be found in the catalogues under the name of the various composers, Buxtehude, Bach, Handel, Franck, Brahms (*Chorale Preludes*), and Mendelssohn. In addition there are collections of interest to be found under the general heading of organ music in the *Schwann Catalogue*.

Fiori Musicali	FRESCOBALDI (1583-1643)
Chorale Preludes	FRESCOBALDI
Preludes and Fugues	BUXTEHUDE (c. 1637-1707)
Chorale Preludes and *Toccatas*	PACHELBEL (1653-1706)
Messe a l'Usage des Couvents	COUPERIN (1668-1733)
Toccata and Fugue in d minor	J. S. BACH (1685-1750)
Toccata, Adagio and Fugue in C Major	BACH
Fantasia and Fugue in g minor	BACH
Toccata and Fugue in F Major	BACH
Passacaglia and Fugue in c minor	BACH
Orgelbüchlein	BACH
Organ Concertos, Op. 4 and 7	HANDEL (1685-1759)

Concerto in E flat Major for Organ and Orchestra	C. P. E. BACH (1714-1788)
Sonatas for Organ and Strings	MOZART (1756-1791)
Sonatas for Organ Nos 1, 3, 4, 6	MENDELSSOHN (1809-1847)
Fantasia and Fugue on B.A.C.H.	LISZT (1811-1886)
Three Chorales for Organ	FRANCK (1822-1890)
Pièce Heroïque	FRANCK
Chorale Preludes, Op. 122	BRAHMS (1833-1897)
Sonata on 94th Psalm	REUBKE (1834-1858)
Symphony No. 3 in c minor, Op. 78	SAINT-SAËNS (1835-1921)
Sonata No. 7, in f minor for Organ	RHEINGERGER (1839-1901)
Carillon de Westminster	VIERNE (1870-1937)
Symphonie concertante	JONGEN (1873-1953)
Variations on Recitative, Op. 40	SCHÖNBERG (1874-1951)
Chorale Preludes, Op. 67	REGER (1873-1916)
Chemin de la Croix	DUPRÉ (1886-)
Preludes and Fugues, Op. 36	DUPRÉ
Concerto for Organ and Chamber Orchestra, Op. 46, No. 2	HINDEMITH (1895-)
Concerto in g minor for Organ, Strings, Timpani	POULENC (1899-)
Suite Brève	LANGLAIS (1907-)
L'Ascension	MESSIAEN (1908-)
Le Nativité du Seigneur	MESSIAEN
Classic Concerto for Organ and Orchestra	SOWERBY (1895-)

TOPICS FOR DISCUSSION

Taking the part of the person who "hates the organ," give reasons for your point of view. Then, taking the part of the organ lover, defend the instrument.

Describe the Baroque organ as you understand it and discuss any advantages and defects it possesses. Argue its suitability for modern organ music.

Why do you think so few modern composers have written for the organ?

Compare the qualities of the older pipe-organs with those of the newer electronic instruments. To which type would you first introduce a potential music-lover?

Why has the organ so slight a repertoire as compared with the piano? How could writing for the organ be encouraged?

CHAPTER 41

Opera: Its Various Styles

᠊ᢟᢖ᠊

THE BEGINNINGS

The art form we know as opera—a peculiar hybrid born of the union of music and the drama—may be traced to the type of musical declamation used by the Greeks in reciting their poetry and producing their great dramas. The modern opera came into being during the exciting days of the Renaissance through the endeavors of a group of Florentine noblemen. These musical amateurs, possessing the characteristic enthusiasm of the period for the culture of the Greeks, tried to write music in imitation of the Greek declamation; the result was a work that may be called the first opera—*Eurydice* by Peri and Caccini, produced in 1600. Long before that, however, the eternal human passion for dressing up and enacting dramas (many of them containing bits of music) began to show the way towards a final union of the two forms. The medieval miracle and mystery plays contained music, and they must have turned the attention of composers toward a possible music-drama union. Italian soil was particularly fruitful, and when the madrigal had reached the great heights of its development and no more could be done in that direction, the influence of songs inserted into stage comedies and of the *dramma pastorale* permeated Italian thought about the stage in the sixteenth century. The intricate weavings of the music of the madrigals made their poetry of little account, and people wanted fresh emotional interest in their music. Drama took hold of the imagination, and the solo voice, always beloved by the Italians,

THE OPÉRA IN PARIS

began to seek mastery. The solo song with lute accompaniment was very popular as a form of musical expression during the late sixteenth and early seventeenth centuries. (Dowland's "Awake, Sweet Love" is a fine example of this new interest in music for the single voice.) Harmony instead of counterpoint (that is, thinking of music in the vertical rather than the horizontal) had its chance, and the orchestra came into being. Instead of thought and song en masse there was more and more interest in individual thought and performance. The date 1600 is easy to remember, but the gradual growth of the idea of what we call opera during the whole sixteenth century must be kept in mind. There was no sudden birth.

Nearly all composers of vocal music up to that time had been singers. Monteverdi, the first extensive prober of the possibilities of the new form, was probably the first composer who was not a singer. Some of his harmonies were wonderfully fresh, and he experimented valiantly with orchestration, using the heterogeneous collection of instruments that came to his hand. The form of the opera was of no

importance at first; almost the entire work was written as a sort
of recitative. Only gradually were the mechanics of this new union
of drama and speech worked out. The *recitative*, a tonal declamation in imitation of dramatic speech, with a very spare instrumental
accompaniment, was found to be the best means for carrying on the
dramatic action; while the *aria*, a set song with richer orchestral
accompaniment, was used for displaying reflective emotion. The
various solo voices were grouped into different combinations—
duets, trios, quartets—and the chorus took a subordinate part. Characteristic themes were employed, and the orchestration devised to
introduce dramatic effects.

THE EARLY DEVELOPMENTS

We can realize how greatly advanced Monteverdi's work is over
the original ideas of Peri and Caccini by comparing such an aria as
Funeste piaggie from the setting they made of *Eurydice* ("Ye dismal
hillsides, how lonely and sad you are without Eurydice") with
Monteverdi's *Ecco purch' a voi ritorno* from his setting of the same
story, called *Orfeo*. In this latter, which is sung as Orpheus realizes
that Eurydice will never return to him, we recognize a much greater
freedom of melody and sense of dramatic strength. The great era of
dramatic music begins with Monteverdi.

The vanity of singers, fanned by popular applause, before long
carried the vocal floriations which composers had introduced into
their arias to great excesses. The singers were not content to sing
what the composers had given them but had to enrich and embroider
it with all sorts of vocal gymnastics and ornaments. The composers
raged, but in vain; they had to give the public what it demanded,
and the form of the opera became exceedingly popular. Opera
houses were opened in Venice in 1637, in London in 1656, and in
Paris in 1669. From a recreation of the nobility, opera became the
joy of the masses. Names we may remember in this Italian development of the early opera are, besides Peri and Caccini and Monteverdi, Cavalli, Cesti, Caldara, Stradella.

EARLY DEVELOPMENTS OUTSIDE ITALY

Lully carried the new ideas to France, and started opera there
under royal patronage. The French loved the ballet, and that soon

played a strong part in their adaptation of the opera. Early French operatic writers were not so brilliant as those of Italy, and there are fewer really distinctive names to remember; Destouches and Campra are among the more important.

Germany got the operatic taste from Italy, too, and opera houses were built in Hamburg and Vienna; native composers provided music for them. England developed her operatic ideas from the masque, that aristocratic entertainment of poetry, dancing, music, and scenic display which was cultivated before the Civil War. After the Restoration of Charles II (1660) we note, as an operatic landmark, Purcell's *Dido and Aeneas*. Handel, a German composer living in England and writing Italian operas, composed a whole series of works for London, beginning with *Rodrigo* in 1706. Although he largely swamped English effort, he was not the man to realize the need for reform in the artificial, singer-dominated form he used.

Gluck was the one who attempted the Herculean task of making the opera a truer, more dramatic unity. Like Wagner, Gluck learned as he went along. Beginning in the Italian style, he sought to leaven its artificiality with finer art. He began to compose in Vienna in 1746, when he was just past thirty. For sixteen years he developed mastery of his medium in such works as *Alcestis*, *Orpheus*, *Paris and Helen*, *Iphigenia in Aulis*, and *Iphigenia in Tauris*. The overture, from being a movement dramatically unimportant and even unrelated, became something to "prepare the audience for the action of the opera, and serve as a sort of argument to it," as Gluck puts it. Old habits were too strong, however, and after his death, Gluck's reforms did not endure. No finer example of this composer's success in achieving dramatic feeling in his music could be found than the great aria *Che faro senza Euridice* ("I Have Lost My Eurydice") from *Orpheus*. (It is interesting to compare this with versions by earlier composers.)

Mozart wrote his first Italian *opera buffa*, *La finta semplice*, at the age of twelve in Vienna, but it was during his three journeys to Italy from 1769 to 1772 that his style came to fruition in three operas commissioned for performance in Milan. Later works followed for production in Munich, Vienna, and Prague (for which music-loving city the greatest of his works, *Don Giovanni*, was written in 1787). No better representative of the Italian school at

INTERIOR OF THE THEATER OF THE MARGRAVE OF BAYREUTH

its best can be found than this opera, called by some critics the world's greatest work of art.

Mozart's *Don Giovanni*

It deals with the more-or-less traditional story of Don Giovanni (Don Juan), a dissolute Spanish nobleman whose insatiable pursuit of women induces a life of crime, for which he pays with an untimely death at the ghostly hand of a man whom he has murdered. What makes Mozart's treatment of this not-too-subtle story the towering achievement it is, is the wonderful psychological portrayal of the various characters involved in the drama and his profound wisdom as to the forces which seem to motivate man's actions. All commentators agree that this unique work of genius combines the powers of drama and music to "depict the most fundamental and subtle relationships of life, religion, and morals."

It is a standard work, perhaps more than any other opera, in the world's great opera houses; fortunately it has been wonderfully recorded by an ensemble that could be heard in few places today, carefully directed for musical and technical perfection. A fine idea of this work can be gained by following this excellent recording in its entirety.

DEVELOPMENTS OF THE 18th AND 19th CENTURIES

Working in Vienna a little after Mozart was Cimarosa, whose sense of perfection in comedy, as well as his similarity to Mozart may be heard in the popular overture to his opera *The Secret Marriage*, produced in Vienna in 1792. In Italy, Rossini was the grand figure of the early nineteenth century, with Donizetti and Bellini as popular second and third strings. This style of writing culminates in the operas of Verdi, who was born in 1813, the same year as his great contemporary Richard Wagner. Verdi's works divide naturally into two groups: the earlier, more popular operas, such as *Rigoletto, Il Trovatore, La Traviata, La forza del destino;* and the mature *Aïda, Otello* and *Falstaff.* A close student of Wagner's work, Verdi changed his style in his later works (the last two were written after he was seventy-five) employing a richer instrumentation and more dramatic treatment than in the earlier operas, with their "salt-box-and-tongs" accompaniment and excessive insistence on vocal display. Someone has rightly said that Verdi began his career as a composer of operas appealing to the taste of the period and ended it as a writer of works that will live for all time. Even in the mature works, however, it will be noticed that Verdi always keeps the voice supreme, with the orchestra furnishing a subordinate accompaniment—in complete contrast to Wagner. It is not difficult to hear the Verdi operas; they are popular in every opera house in the world, and most of them have been recorded in full, so that the inquiring student may easily compare the various styles. Selections characteristic of his mature style include:

> *Credo; Ave Maria; Salce, Salce* (Willow Song) from *Otello*
> *Sul fil d'un soffio etesio* (From Secret Caves) from *Falstaff*

After Verdi the Italian traditions were taken up by Puccini, probably the most popular of all the Italian composers today. His many works—the best known are *Manon Lescaut, La Bohème, Tosca,* and *Madam Butterfly*—abound in technical resource, dramatic invention, and power of emotional expression. They are tremendously effective works when seen on the stage; whether or not we like them depends on our taste for the Italian operatic conventions. In *Turandot*, which he left unfinished, he seemed to be moving towards new strength.

Mozart's *The Magic Flute* is generally considered the first real German opera—that is, a work treated in the more dramatic, romantic style loved by the Germans. Wagner, the greatest of all German writers of opera, said that *The Magic Flute* laid the foundations and exhausted the possibilities of German opera—rather an overstatement in view of what Wagner himself was to write later. Beethoven's one opera, *Fidelio*, has a noble theme (something rare in opera), and he made fine drama of it, human and tender. It was not until Weber that pure German opera found its prophet; and he, with his fine feeling for the German hearth and its affections in legendary heroism and romance, led directly on to Wagner. Weber's operas, *Der Freischütz*, *Euryanthe*, and *Oberon* (even though the last was written to an English text), may be said to be the first great German operas; Agatha's aria from *Der Freischütz*, *Wie nahte mir der Schlummer*, is a typical Weber aria.

THE OPERAS OF RICHARD WAGNER

It is impossible to write adequately of Wagner's contributions to operatic literature in a few paragraphs; his greatest works, *Tristan und Isolde*, *Götterdämmerung*, and *Die Meistersinger*, transcend the limiting borders of operatic style and must be included among the greatest treasures of all music. Put briefly, Wagner was the great reformer of opera; his ideal was to do away with those operatic traditions which he considered too artificial for real dramatic expression. In place of the accepted forms, he devised a new one called the "music drama." In its dramatic elements it was founded on the plays of Shakespeare and Schiller, and in its musical elements on the works of Bach and Beethoven. Theoretically the music, the drama, and the staging were of equal importance to his scheme, but in reality the music overshadowed everything else. To guard against the over-importance of the voice, so disturbing an element in the older scheme, Wagner made the orchestra the chief exponent of his dramatic action, weaving its score out of the short and character-

Photo by Hansa Luftbild

THE OPERA HOUSE AT BAYREUTH

Built by Wagner for the production of his operas.

istic "leading motives" (*leitmotifs*) definitely associated with various dramatic situations. In fact, these motives in such works as *Götterdämmerung* and *Tristan und Isolde* are woven into such a poignant and expressive musical fabric and form such an eloquent commentary on the ever-changing dramatic situation as to make the staging and singing almost superfluous.

The actors in these great works of Wagner's use a sort of declamation (*Sprechstimme*, he called it) which has striking dramatic power, though comparatively little musical interest. Consequently, most of the operagoers of Wagner's day (as well as some today) were at a loss to comprehend the new form, listening, as they did, to the voice for their chief interest. It is the orchestra that tells Wagner's story, and in richness, variety, and impressiveness his scores have never been equaled. He wrote his own librettos, using as subjects various Germanic legends, which he manipulated to suit his dramatic needs. These librettos leave something to be desired from the dramatic point of view, for they are full of strange and unnecessary inconsistencies and are often couched in phraseology that is anything but clear. As drama, for instance, the four operas that constitute the cycle of *The Nibelung Ring* (*Das Rheingold, Die Walküre, Siegfried, Götterdämmerung*) are something of monstrosities, built on dramatic motives which are not consistent and which have to be laboriously "explained" at length time and time again. They provide an excess of dramatic action that sometimes becomes unmanageable and demand cumbersome, spectacular development that is difficult to make convincing. *Tristan und Isolde*, on the other hand, suffers from the absence of varied dramatic motives; it is only in *Die Meistersinger* that Wagner achieved a balance between dramatic impulse and consequent action. But the more one hears these Wagner operas, the more he realizes that the only function of the libretto is to stimulate musical development and to provide a sustained musico-dramatic element never thought possible before Wagner's time and never equaled since.

Beginning with Wagner's early works—*Rienzi, The Flying Dutchman, Tannhäuser,* and *Lohengrin*—we can trace his gradual evolution from a devotee of the grandiose traditions of the German-Italian schools, through various experiments that gave more variety and refinement to his style, to the final achievements of his musical personality. His mature period begins with the first of the Ring cycle, *Das Rheingold*, and continues through the rest of that monumental series to *Tristan und Isolde, Die Meistersinger,* and *Parsifal,* his last work. In all these, as he himself put it, he tried to get rid of the mistakes in the earlier form of opera, in which the means of expression (the music) was the end and the end to be expressed (the drama) was made the means. In spite of these intentions, the music became so much more important than any of the other elements in his fusion that today we go to the mature operas of Wagner to revel in their music and not because of their dramatic power. As time passes, we see Wagner more and more in correct perspective—as a musical figure of colossal proportions. "He is one of those masterminds that belong to no time and no nation, whose work lives as one of the vital forces of civilization."

Since his death no one has arisen to carry on his work; there have been attempts to write in his style, but the results have been mostly unimportant. Humperdinck, in his two charming operas *Hänsel und Gretel* and *Königskinder*, uses the Wagner idiom with taste. Richard Strauss has written a number of works in a style peculiarly his own, achieving powerful effects without directly imitating the Wagnerian technique. The most important of these are *Salome*, *Elktra*, *Ariadne auf Naxos*, *Die Frau ohne Schatten* and *Arabella*. In *Der Rosenkavalier* Strauss, working more in the spirit of Mozart, achieved his greatest success.

THE DIFFERENCES OF OPERATIC STYLE

A brief word may well be given as to the essential differences between the several operatic styles, differences which should be taken into account when one listens to the various works. We should not expect Wagnerian profundity of thought or greatness of inspiration in the Italian works; nor do we look for Italian simplicity and melodious grace in the German operas. From the very beginnings of the opera, Italians have loved melodic flow and provided opportunities for vocal display and sonority in their works, often at the sacrifice of dramatic sincerity and musical worth. The Germans on the other hand, are much more introspective people dramatically and have demanded sincerity and musical truth above everything else in their operas. Gluck summarized the requirements of opera in this fashion, a summary that has influenced all German writers in this genre—Beethoven, Weber, Wagner, and Strauss: "The true mission of the music is to second the poetry, by strengthening the expression of the sentiments and increasing the interest of the situations, without weakening or interrupting the action by superfluous means for tickling the ear or displaying the agility of fine voices." These requirements have been met in various ways, perhaps most successfully in Wagner's *Die Meistersinger*, an almost perfect equation between dramatic impulse and musical action.

FRENCH OPERA

The French taste in opera was originally borrowed from the Italians: early works stressed the importance of the spectacle and the ballet, but gradually there evolved a definite national operatic style. Lully realized the possibilities of the *recitative* as a dramatic factor and made it an essential part in the development of the plot and not just a conventional link between arias and choruses. Rameau's works are now considered by the French to be the foun-

Cartoon by E. Simms Campbell
© King Syndicate, Inc.

"HERE COMES THE PART I LIKE BEST . . .

WHERE THEY MURDER THE SOPRANO."

*Despite what this cartoonist considers a typical American reaction
to opera—opera is more popular in the United States today than
ever before.*

dation stones of their operatic style; these contain more feeling
and show much more constructive skill than the operas of Lully.
Gluck's reforms were carried out mostly in Paris and were the chief
means by which French opera was rescued from Italian influences.
The writers of opera during the Romantic period in France were
men who were important enough in their own day, but most of their
works have disappeared from the present operatic repertory. Meyerbeer, a German possessed of real genius, lived most of his creative

life in Paris; he was clever enough to give the people what they liked, paying little attention to anything but his own immediate success. The lighter forms of opera writing chiefly engaged native talent at this time; men like Monsigny, Grétry, Gossec, Méhul, Boieldieu, Auber, Hérold, and Halévy developed the special characteristics of the *opéra comique*—comic, light opera that was not, as time went on, very different from *grand opera*.

Later important names in the development of French opera include Gounod, whose fame is largely the result of *Faust*, with its languorous love music and sweet, cloying harmonies which have made it one of the most popular operas ever written; Bizet, the genius who wrote *Carmen*, to many people an almost perfect opera; Saint-Saëns, who was equally at home in all forms, and whose *Samson et Dalila* has contributed two important arias to the repertoire of the operatic singer; Massenet, who has achieved great popularity in both Europe and America for his heavily scented romantic style; Charpentier, composer of the realistic *Louise*, based on a story of life in Bohemian Paris; and, greatest of all, Debussy, whose *Pelléas et Mélisande* is a work that is absolutely *sui generis*, standing alone in its difficult, reserved beauty as the one great modern French opera.

OPERAS OF OTHER COUNTRIES

The Russians have produced some very powerful works written in a most distinctive style, such as Moussorgsky's *Boris Godunov*, Borodin's *Prince Igor*, and Rimsky-Korsakov's *Le Coq d'or*. Smetana's *Bartered Bride* with Weinberger's *Schwanda* and Janaček's *Jenufa* and *Káta Kabanová* are representative of the Czech opera, which is characterized by works that are colorful and rhythmic without being very important. Hindemith, with his *Mathis der Maler* and his not very successful *Die Harmonie der Welt*, has further enlarged the German repertory, while Berg's *Wozzeck* and Schönberg's *Moses und Aron* (left unfinished at his death) are the most significant modern operas. The English-speaking nations have never seemed fitted for the rather exacting demands of operatic thought and have not yet produced any outstanding serious works in their various experiments with this form. Ballad opera was once very popular in England—for example, *The Beggar's Opera*. Vaughan Williams' *Hugh the Drover* is a modern production of this type. The most popular English operatic style is still "Gilbert and Sullivan"—comic opera.

LATER OPERAS

In England Benjamin Britten has been the oustanding figure of this century, with his *Peter Grimes*, a real "grand" opera; *The Rape of Lucretia* and *Albert Herring*, which he calls chamber-operas; his expressionistic and effective *The Turn of the Screw;* and his controversial setting of Shakespeare's *Midsummer Night's Dream*. In the United States Stravinsky collaborated with W. H. Auden to produce an opera based on Hogarth's pictures, *The Rake's Progress*. Native American composers have turned their attention to national themes with considerable success: Virgil Thomson's *Mother of Us All* and Douglas Moore's *Ballad of Baby Doe* are representative. Kurt Weill's *Street Scene* and *Lost in the Stars* are essentially opera in a popular form, although perhaps not quite as vivid and pointed as his earlier setting of Brecht's version of *The Beggar's Opera (Die Dreigroschenoper)*, produced in Berlin in 1928. Menotti's little opera buffas, *Amelia Goes to the Ball* and *The Telephone*, as well as his more serious *The Medium, The Consul*, and *The Saint of Bleecker Street* show how it is possible to fuse the more traditional characteristics of Italian opera with the demands of the popular Broadway stage.

SELECTIONS FROM OPERAS AVAILABLE ON RECORDS

"Hymn to Apollo"　　　　　　　　　　　Transcribed by Reinach

Very probably this transcription of one of the few authentic examples of Greek declamation-chant sung in translation does not sound to us the way it did to the Greeks of the first century B.C. It is impossible to reproduce these historical examples without such reproduction being affected by modern ideas and tastes. Nevertheless, this Greek fragment suggests the general character of the means which the Greeks used for the musical projection of their poetry and drama.

Recitative: *Tu se' morta* from *Orfeo*	MONTEVERDI
Solo: *Qual honor*	
Aria: *E dove l'aggini* from *Il Pomo d'oro*	CESTI
Aria: *"When I am Laid in Earth"* from *Dido and Aeneas*	PURCELL
Air: *O jour affreux* from *Dardanus*	RAMEAU
Aria and Recitative: *V'adoro, pupille* from *Julius Cesar*	HANDEL
Recitative and Aria: *Cara sposa* from *Rinaldo*	HANDEL
Recitative and Aria: *Misero* from *Livietta e Tracollo*	PERGOLESI
Che faro senza Euridice from *Orpheus*	GLUCK
Overture to *The Secret Marriage*[1]	CIMAROSA
Overture to *The Marriage of Figaro*[1]	MOZART
Una voce poco fa from *The Barber of Seville*	ROSSINI
Una furtiva lagrima from *The Elixir of Love*	DONIZETTI
Komm, O Hoffnung from *Fidelio*	BEETHOVEN
Agatha's aria from *Der Freischütz* (*Leise, leise*)	WEBER
Caro nome from *Rigoletto*	VERDI
Ah, fors' è lui from *La Traviata*	VERDI
The Final Duet, Act III, *Aïda*	VERDI
"Willow Song" from *Otello*	VERDI
"Credo" from *Otello*	VERDI

These different Verdi selections give an excellent opportunity for comparing the characteristics of his early, middle, and late styles.

Addio di Mimi from *La Bohème*	PUCCINI
Un bel di vedremo from *Madam Butterfly*	PUCCINI
Overture to *Rienzi*[1]	WAGNER
"Spinning Chorus" and "Senta's Aria" from *The Flying Dutchman*	WAGNER
Overture to *Tannhäuser*[1]	WAGNER

[1] Orchestral selection.

Dich, teure Halle from *Tannhäuser*	WAGNER
Prelude to *Lohengrin*[1]	WAGNER
"Elsa's Dream" from *Lohengrin*	WAGNER

This group of selections represents the earlier Wagner style.

Prelude to *Tristan und Isolde*[1]	WAGNER
Prelude to *Die Meistersinger*[1]	WAGNER
Prelude to *Parsifal*[1]	WAGNER
Funeral March from *Götterdämmerung*[1]	WAGNER
Wotans Abschied from *Die Walküre*	WAGNER
"Waldtraute's Narrative" from *Götterdämmerung*	WAGNER
Isolde's "Love Death" from *Tristan und Isolde*	WAGNER
Was duftet doch der Flieder from *Die Meistersinger*	WAGNER
Wahn! Wahn! from *Die Meistersinger*	WAGNER
Good Friday Music from *Parsifal*	WAGNER

No better means for understanding the method employed in the later Wagner works of building up the score from a multitude of leading motives can be found than in such excerpts as these.

Monologue of the Marschallin and Presentation of the Silver Rose from *Der Rosenkavalier*	R. STRAUSS
"Salome's Dance" from *Salome*[1]	R. STRAUSS
Finale from *Elektra*	R. STRAUSS
Final Scene from *Capriccio*	R. STRAUSS
Trinke, Liebchen from *Die Fledermaus*	J. STRAUSS
Overture and Pantomime from *Hänsel und Gretel*[1]	HUMPERDINCK
Coronation Scene and Death of Boris from *Boris Godunov*	MOUSSORGSKY
"Hymn to the Sun" from *Le Coq d'or*	RIMSKY-KORSAKOV
"Aria of Khan Kontchak" from *Prince Igor*	BORODIN
Polovotsian Dances from *Prince Igor*	BORODIN

[1] Orchestral selection.

Habanera, Seguidilla, and "Toreador's Song" from *Carmen*   BIZET

"Flower Song," "Jewel Song," and "Even Bravest
    Heart" from *Faust*   GOUNOD

Il sogno from *Manon*   MASSENET

Il est doux from *Hérodiade*   MASSENET

Depuis le jour from *Louise*   CHARPENTIER

"Marie's Lullaby" from *Wozzeck*   BERG

Four Sea Interludes from *Peter Grimes*[1]   BRITTEN

Ballad of "Jack the Knife": "Polly's Farewell Song"
    from *The Three Penny Opera*   WEILL

Overture to *Amelia Goes to the Ball*[1]   MENOTTI

"Monica, Monica" from *The Medium*   MENOTTI

TOPICS FOR DISCUSSION

Do you consider the invention of the opera something of a marvel, or was it simply inevitable?

The term *opera* covers a wide range of style. Which of them (dramatic opera, comic opera, and so on) appeals most to you and which least? Why?

Why was Wagner such a great power in opera? Were there any important reforms before his time? If so, who inaugurated them and how far did they go?

Do you think opera is likely to be increasingly cultivated by composers or will it decline? Which elements in present public interest do you see as contributing to the one trend or the other?

Why are performances of opera on television so unsuccessful in conveying the real nature of this art form? Can anything be done to improve this condition?

State the distinctive charms of light opera, using the works of Offenbach and Gilbert and Sullivan as a basis.

Similarly, make note of the distinctions between the Russian operas based on fairy tales and those based on history.

What do you think will be the sources of late twentieth-century opera? Can you see any of these emerging in the works of Menotti?

[1] Orchestral selection.

Discuss the various reforms and developments of Gluck, Weber, and Wagner. Why wasn't Wagner able to work out his ideal of complete union of all the elements in the production of an opera?

Can you think why composers like Bach and Brahms were not tempted to write in the operatic form? What are the special qualities needed for the composition of an opera? Do English-speaking composers possess these qualities?

How did Russians succeed in writing exciting operas so early in their composing lives?

CHAPTER 42

The Ballet

۶ و

We can define a dance as *movement guided by music*. Dancing
may be said to be the most universal of all the arts; at some time
and in some phase of his activities everyone has danced. A study of
the life of any primitive human society shows clearly that music
and dancing have been associated since their very beginnings. In
its primitive form, dancing was connected with the tribe and the
temple—with social, ceremonial, and religious rituals. In the more
"civilized" societies it has been used to express the personal pleasure of the performers or to entertain a public. It is in this last sense
of a highly complex activity, confined to specialists for the pleasure
of an audience, that we are interested; for this is what the ballet is.

EARLY HISTORY

Dancing existed in a highly developed state among the Greeks
and Romans; during the seventeenth and eighteenth centuries the
scene of its activity was transferred from Italy to France, where it
was further developed and completed in the form we know today.
It was exported into Russia, and from there spread throughout the
European world as "Russian Ballet." Today the ballet enjoys a
greater and more widespread popularity than ever before in history.
There are as many balletomanes (a word used first in Russia to
describe ballet fans) in New York as in London, Paris, or even
Moscow; and the influence this combined art has had and is having
on music is considerable.

DEGAS:
BALLERINA ON STAGE

Louvre, Paris

One man, the eighteenth-century *maître de ballet* M. Noverre, may be said to have been responsible for influencing the development of modern ballet, for he changed the elegant pastimes of the French court of that time, imported from Italy for the delectation and flattery of the king, into the sensitive art we know today. It was Noverre who, in his teaching and writings, insisted that the ballet be used not merely as an excuse for putting on a huge spectacle containing dance movements, but as *a means for expressing a dramatic idea.* Arnold Haskell sums up Noverre's aesthetic principles (upon which all our modern concepts of ballet are based): the well-composed ballet must be a living painting of the drama, character, and customs of mankind; it must be acted, as moving in its effect as a declamation, so that it can speak through the eyes to the soul, just as music speaks through the ears. And Haskell adds, ballet has flourished as an art when these precepts of Noverre's have been followed and has declined when they were forgotten.

Music, as well as the scenic background (technically called the *décor*) against which the ballet's action develops, is an important

DEGAS: BALLERINA
WITH BOUQUET

Louvre, Paris

part of the concept of the founder of the modern ballet. It must guide the spirit and suggest the tempo for the interpretative dancing that develops the ballet's theme or tells its story, just as the *choreography* (the arrangement of the movements of the dancers) and the *décor* suggest its atmosphere. It may be laid down as a fundamental precept that in good ballet, music, movement, and *décor* are of equal importance and parallel in idea.

Naturally, it is the personality and technical ability of the dancers (particularly the females) which have interested the public most in ballet; the careful planning of the choreographer who arranges their movements, or the inspiration of the composer who gives them rhythms to interpret, are less evident and less personal factors in the final result on the stage. Many a great dancer has arisen, flourished, and passed from the scene since Louis XIV started the modern ballet on its course with the founding in 1661 of *L'Académie Nationale de Musique et de la Danse*. During the time of the early nineteenth-century Romantics, ballet was used to exploit the new enthusiasm for the individual. Such great ballerinas as Taglioni, Elssler, and Grisi were among the most popular figures of the day in Paris and London, and there was great rivalry among them, much as there is today among baseball stars or professional prize-fighters.

Two of the ballets still in the repertories today, *Les Sylphides* and *Giselle*, have come to us, directly or indirectly, from the rivalries of this active nineteenth-century scene.

With the decline of these great figures and the substitution, towards the latter part of the century, of the ideals of realism, the art of the ballet in France waned and finally disappeared. The principles of Noverre were forgotten, and ballet was no longer looked on as an art but as a spectacle for the eye of the tired businessman, who evolved in Paris and London as a by-product of the Industrial Revolution. It became a popular feature of music-hall programs, such as those given today in the Radio City Music Hall in New York. It was rescued from this sad state by the invasion of the Russians (1909 in Paris and 1911 in London) under the leadership and direction of one of the most dynamic personalities in the whole history of the art—Serge Diaghilev.

THE RUSSIAN REIGN

This is not meant to be even an outline of the history of ballet, and so we make no attempt to explain why the Russians, following the example of the court of Peter the Great (1672-1725), became so enamored of the ballet during the eighteenth and nineteenth centuries. It will be sufficient to state that, under the direction of foreign masters, the Russians developed their ballet to such a high state of interpretative perfection that when Diaghilev, after reforming some of its artificialities and impressing his own artistic personality on it, took his company to Paris, the whole course of the art was changed. Nothing like it had been seen there before. It was Diaghilev, an impresario who had good sense and taste enough to employ anyone who could carry out his ideas, who was personally responsible for this triumph of the Russian Ballet style as we know it today.

This is particularly true of the music; before his time, ballet music had been either adapted from other sources or composed by men of inferior ability. Diaghilev commissioned Stravinsky to write the music for a whole series of ballets which he produced: *The Firebird* in 1909-10; *Petrouchka* in 1910-11; *The Rite of Spring* in 1912-13; *Renard* in 1916-17; *Pulcinella* in 1919; *Les Noces* in 1917-23. It was these works that made Stravinky's name as a composer and that

MARC CHAGALL: COSTUME SKETCHES FOR THE BALLET THE FIREBIRD

interested other serious musicians in the ballet. Among these were Ravel, who wrote *Daphnis and Chloe* for Diaghilev; Richard Strauss, who was commissioned for *Joseph's Legend;* and Falla, who did *The Three-Cornered Hat*. In addition, Diaghilev presented a number of ballets to music written by other composers for other purposes: *Les Sylphides* to music by Chopin; *Carnaval* to an orchestration of Schumann's famous piano piece; *Scheherazade* to Rimsky-Korsakov's tone poem; *Prince Igor*, to the Polovotsian Dances from Borodin's opera; *La Boutique fantasque* to music by Rossini adapted by Respighi; and *Le Spectre de la rose* to music by Weber.

Diaghilev also revived, recreated, and repopularized some of the ballets from an earlier day: *Giselle*, the famous Romantic ballet with music by Adolphe Adam, *Swan Lake*, and an abbreviation of *The Sleeping Princess*. These last two were Tchaikovsky's original ballet scores and contain some of his finest music. Most of Diaghilev's productions and revivals are, in one form or another, in every ballet repertoire today. No wonder audiences called him *ce prodigieux animateur*—that prodigious animator!

PERSONALITIES

There have been others, of course, who have contributed to the present popularity of ballet in Europe and America: De Basil, under whom for the first time ballet became self-supporting by barnstorming tours all over Europe and in many parts of the American continent; Massine, a choreographer of unusual ability originally discovered by Diaghilev in 1914 and the inventor of the choreography of many popular works; Ninette de Valois, the "animator, organizer, and teacher" of the excellent English Sadler's Wells Company, which has become the internationally famous Royal Ballet; Sol Hurok, the daring impresario who risked his money to make the ballet popular in the United States; Lucia Chase, a leading spirit and financial angel of the American Ballet Theatre; George Balanchine who has developed a wonderful ballet company in New York City; and Agnes de Mille, the choreographer of many of the best Broadway productions, such as *Oklahoma* and *South Pacific*.

Of necessity good ballet music is program music, with a real story to unfold, a definite plot to develop, or a distinct mood to create. It should possess obvious rhythmic qualities, and should inspire the dancer so that he can interpret it for the audience. It is, or should be, action rather than contemplative music, the controlling factor for the choreography and not simply a means for furnishing the right beat for action on the stage. Although most ballet music makes good concert music, and the average listener hears it in this form, in doing so he loses much of its significance. In seeing a ballet for the first time, we are usually surprised to perceive how much the effectiveness of the music is increased by the simultaneous paralleling of action, *décor*, and music. Since ballet is, as Haskell says, the result of the collaboration of a musician, painter, and choreographer in interpreting a common subject, each in his own medium, the closer the collaboration, the better the result. Remember this in listening to ballet music on the radio, in concert, or on records.

RECORDED BALLET MUSIC

Giselle Suite   ADAM

This Romantic ballet of the middle of the nineteenth century is rather tinkly and not very exciting musically apart from the ballet; yet it is interesting as characteristic of that period.

Swan Lake   TCHAIKOVSKY

First produced in 1877, this music was then considered too symphonic in style for good ballet; we have changed our mind and now realize that the score contains some of this composer's finest dance music.

Aurora's Wedding   TCHAIKOVSKY

This one-act abbreviation of *The Sleeping Beauty* was originally given in Russia in 1890 and became very popular in Paris and London.

Les Sylphides   CHOPIN

Based on a re-creation of the spirit of Taglioni's famous work, this white ballet (a term which suggests that it is largely for the *corps de ballet*, with their lovely white costumes) was set to Chopin's music by Fokine, the choreographer who was the father of contemporary ballet. A variety of instrumentation has been made of this music, although the piano pieces chosen remain the same.

Spectre de la Rose   WEBER

A choreographic poem after a poem by Gautier set to the music of the famous *Invitation to the Dance*.

Carnaval, Op. 9   SCHUMANN

A one-act ballet by Fokine to Schumann's well-known piano music, this is in every ballet company's repertoire.

Beau Danube   J. STRAUSS

Delightful Strauss waltz melodies are woven into a charming ballet, a refreshing reminder of the real musical quality of the Strauss waltzes.

Scheherazade   RIMSKY-KORSAKOV

Fokine did the choreography for this one-act ballet.

Prince Igor   BORODIN

The Polovotsian Dances from Borodin's opera have been choreo-
graphed by Fokine.

The Firebird   STRAVINSKY

Petrouchka   STRAVINSKY

The Rite of Spring   STRAVINSKY

The latter two are discussed in other places in this book. *The
Firebird*, written in 1910, is a magnificent composite of iridescent
Rimsky-Korsakov, Debussian impressionism, and neo-primitive
Stravinsky.

L'Histoire du Soldat (The Soldier's Tale)   STRAVINSKY

Calling for actors and a reader in addition to the dancers and a
small orchestra, this is an interesting experiment in "chamber ballet"
which can be produced with minimum stage equipment. Lively
dance tunes, tango-waltz-ragtime, some marches, and a chorale indicate the scrappy, rather flip nature of this score, imitative of the
French mannerisms of the time.

Les Noces   STRAVINSKY

Angular, percussive, dissonant, this is written for soprano, con-
tralto, tenor, baritone, four pianists, and a percussion ensemble. The
last of Stravinsky's purely Russian ballets, it is suggestive of the
informality and ruggedness of folk music.

Apollon Musagète   STRAVINSKY

Agon   STRAVINSKY

These are characteristic of Stravinsky's neoclassic style.

Miraculous Mandarin   BARTÓK

This expressionistic pantomime-ballet is characteristic of Bartók.

Création du Monde   MILHAUD

A ballet depicting the African Negro's concept of the creation of
the world, this is interesting because it shows the composer's use of
the jazz idiom in serious music. Someone has well said that the music

sounds like a combination of Duke Ellington and Bach, with an occasional polytonal procedure to enliven the whole.

Façade WALTON

Walton wrote this most amusing *suite de dances* when he was one of the brash young men of the 1920's.

The Three Cornered Hat FALLA

The choreography of this translation of Spanish folk dancing is by Massine.

Cinderella PROKOFIEV

One of this composer's best scores, the music is interesting in itself, quite apart from its connection with the old fairy story of the ballet.

Seven Deadly Sins WEILL

The suite is a most interesting expressionistic combination of ballet and song.

Billy the Kid COPLAND

The earliest ballet score of this outstanding American composer, this music is as fresh as its name would indicate; it is far from either the classic or the modern Russian idiom.

Appalachian Spring COPLAND

A beautiful ballet based on a very simple theme: a newly-wed couple build their home in the Pennsylvania hills in the early part of the last century and settle down to a pioneer life of hardship, love, joy, and prayer. Full of folksy feeling, tender passion, and rhythmic dances, it is American in a quite different way from the other ballet scores mentioned here.

Fancy Free BERNSTEIN

A lively, typically American score dealing with the story of three sailors on the town, this is excellent music, rather on the popular side.

West Side Story BERNSTEIN

This is a fierce, bitter delineation of the spirit which set off the juvenile gang wars in New York during the 1950's. The score is striking and very effective.

TOPICS FOR DISCUSSION

Compare the varying importance of the musician, choreographer, and scenic artist in the production of ballet.

Why do you think Stravinsky was so successful with his early ballets? Can you compare these and his later ones?

Taking the part of a ballet-lover, defend the artificialities of the classical ballet.

In which direction do you think modern ballet can best develop with regard to plot, freedom of interpretation, and style?

Do you think that abstract ballet is the highest form of choreographic expression? If not, defend your view.

CHAPTER 43

Film, Radio, and Television Music

❧ §∂❧

One of the outstanding influences that have shaped music in recent times is the (largely American-developed) music for film, radio, and television. Just as the demands and fashions of former times produced such widely employed forms of music as the Passion, the opera, the string quartet, and the symphony, so today's demand for background and running-commentary music for film, radio, and television productions has influenced the style of contemporary writing. Moreover, the kind and quality of music composed and produced for these media depend to a surprising degree on the intricate technical procedures involved.

EARLY FILM MUSIC

The earliest moving pictures were merely transcriptions from actual life—train rides, circuses, and so on—with little attempt at artistic arrangement. As soon as films began to be produced for their own sake, as a form of dramatic entertainment, music (literally speaking) entered the picture, if for no other reason than to cover up the mechanical noises incident to the showing of images on the screen. The early silent photo-dramatizations carried their thought and developed their action largely by pantomime, with printed matter thrown on the screen to explain otherwise unintelligible situa-

549

tions. Music was expected to help overcome the limitations of these silent films by emphasizing the dramatic situations and heightening the emotional moods. Initially, the music was provided by a pianist or organist placed in a pit in front of the screen, where he could watch the picture's development and, drawing on his own "inspiration" and the memory of other people's music, piece together an improvised musical accompaniment; the quality of the music depended entirely on his powers of invention, the effectiveness of his memory, and the resources of his musical technic. In most cases, especially in small theaters, these were not likely to be at a very high level.

Gradually the single musicians were replaced by orchestras, whose leaders arranged music so that it was a suitable accompaniment for each picture. "Cue sheets," prepared by the producers of the picture, specified the music to be used and supplied, in addition to suggestions from the standard and popular repertoire, quantities of specially concocted mood backgrounds—hurries, agitatos, love themes, mysteriosos, and the like, which were used over and over again. A few especially written scores were made for some of the most important films, but until the advent of the sound film this rather haphazard treatment was all that was given film music.

SOUND AND THE CINEMA

When, after years of experiment, the sound film arrived in 1927, an entirely new vista was opened to composers and arrangers. Now all the preparation of the music, the cutting and fitting it to meet the different dramatic needs, could be done beforehand at the studio where the picture was taken; then it could be recorded on and reproduced from the same film as the picture itself. Thus the same musical effects were available to the small, formerly poorly equipped theater as to the grand cinema palace which boasted a symphony orchestra. The whole structure of the motion picture was changed to gear speech and music to ideas and emotions, rather than merely suggesting them. This resulted in all sorts of improvements, especially in the type and quality of the music used. The directors of the new sound films did not hesitate to call on better composers. Such well-known writers as Weill, Toch, Shostakovich, Prokofiev,

Arturo Toscanini Conducting the NBC Symphony Orchestra

Walton, Vaughan Williams, Copland, and Thomson have provided music for the movies.

Unfortunately, because he must cater to mass audiences who have little sympathy for or experience with good music, the movie composer is limited in what he can write. The unique technical problems which must be solved so that his music will fit the constantly changing rhythms of the story do not help him either. Suppose, as one writer puts it, that a "composer of screen music is asked to provide 72 seconds of music for a love scene. He invents a melodic theme and sets to work on its development. Just as he gets into the middle of some really interesting composition, the action shifts to the sea, and his tender music is rudely interrupted by a foghorn or a ship's whistle. Then he must return to the beginning and shape and trim his material according to the time pattern. He is fortunate indeed if the length of the scene is not changed several times during the production, thus requiring his music to have rubber-band flexibility." In spite of the fact that Aaron Copland has said that this kind of timing does not straight-jacket his imagination, it is doubtful whether music composed under such circumstances will command any great amount of serious attention and interest when performed apart from the theater.

A factor which favors the production of movie music rather than concert works is that movie work pays the composer very much better. It is impossible to make a living from large-scale composition *per se*, and so it is inevitable that the good composer should turn to a medium in which he is well paid and can do reasonably good work. However, the artistic possibilities are necessarily limited by the time-needs of the film and the listening capacity of the audience. When attention is divided between the film and the music, neither is fully comprehended.

THE RECORDING PROCESS

Sound usually is recorded on a number of separate sound tracks. The dialogue of the actors is put on one. If the piece is musical and the actors are called on to sing, they only mouth the words; actual singing is furnished later from another sound track (often made by entirely different artists). The orchestral background, usually well played and interpreted, is put on a different track, the sound effects on still another. These are all blended together on one master sound track in the "dubbing room" by sound engineers, who manipulate a series of dials regulating the volume of the various components of this mixed mechanical brew. No wonder a well-known Hollywood musician has observed sarcastically that a movie composer's immortality "lasts from the recording stage to the dubbing room." Often parts of the score over which the composer has labored so carefully are cut out entirely so that these men must then feel, as one of them has put it, like nothing but a face on the cutting-room floor. Whatever effectiveness the music may have finally has to survive all these technical hurdles; the wonder is that anything worth while musically comes through it all.

In view of the trials and tribulations of producing music for use in films, it is only natural that the movie composer hopes to be able to use what he has written as a separate concert score for orchestral performance. If movie music has enough individuality to attract attention to itself to the detriment of what is projected upon the screen, it automatically destroys its own effectiveness. This fact would seem to militate against any great success when good movie music is made into concert music. But no hard and fast conclusion is possible here, for a number of very successful orchestral suites, in which the composer is no longer limited by the technical demands of his medium, have been developed from movie sources. A short list of them will be found at the end of this chapter.

THE ROLE OF RADIO

The role of radio in American life has been an extremely significant, if not very inspiring, one. Some time around 1910, when experiments proved that programs of speech and music could be successfully transmitted over a wireless, the radio industry as we know it today may be said to have started.[1] On November 2, 1920, broadcasting began as a regular service to the public from Station KDKA in Pittsburgh. What potentialities in the way of dispersing music and literature and of cultivating taste the new medium possessed!

These have to a degree been realized, for certainly a fair share of the credit for increasing interest in good music must go to the broadcasters. But that many opportunities have been missed is evident from the disappointment expressed in a letter sent to the National Association of Broadcasters by Lee DeForest, called the "Father of the Radio" because of his inventions which made this device possible:

> What have you gentlemen done with my child? He was conceived as a potent instrumentality for culture, fine music, the uplifting of America's mass intelligence. You have debased this child, you have sent him out on the streets in rags of ragtime, tatters of jive and boogie-woogie, to collect money from all and sundry for hubba hubba and audio jitterbug.
>
> You have made him a laughing stock of intelligence, surely a stench in the nostrils of the gods of the ionosphere; you have cut time into tiny cubelets, called shorts (more rightly stains), wherewith the occasional fine program is periodically smeared with impudent insistence to buy or try.
>
> The nation may have no soap, but soap opera without end or sense floods each household daily. Murder mysteries rule the waves by night and children are rendered psychopathic by your bedtime stories.
>
> This child of mine has been religiously kept to the average intelligence of thirteen years. Its national intelligence is maintained moronic, as

[1] Some claim that these experiments took place as early as 1906. See *History of Radio* to 1926 by Gleason L. Archer. New York: The American Historical Society.

though you and the sponsor believe the majority of listeners have only moron minds. The curse of his commercials has grown consistently more cursed, year by year.

Radio Music

As with the movies, music has been a concurrent part of radio production from its earliest days. Beginning with the scripts prepared in 1922, when advertising began to assume the necessary role of the angel that supports the American radio show business, music has been used as the "come-on" for all sorts of programs. The best talent in all fields, from crooners (who were a creation of the radio), through name bands, to the Metropolitan Opera and the New York Philharmonic has been attracted to the microphone; and all sorts of new talents, policies, and production procedures have been developed to exploit to the full the advantage of the radio advertiser.

Today radio scripts of every kind, commercial as well as educational, are unthinkable without music. Some of them contain especially prepared scores written by highly talented and salaried composers, who, in a workmanlike and thoroughly competent manner, bring together custom-built scraps to suit the dramatic needs of the script. Some of the scores consist of entirely original music composed for the occasion, often exploiting the new effects of sonority and color made possible by the radio medium. The composers have evolved a radio style of underscoring words and situations which, when used as skillfully as in the *Lincoln Portrait* of Copland, is really effective.

In the main, however, commercial "plugs" on the radio have the same importance as symphonic themes; as a matter of actual record, the plugs outnumber the themes a hundred to one. And so musicians bemoan the fact that, which much talent and energy go into the production of programs on the radio, there is very little real achievement. Radio music has been too largely associated with the tricks of the market place to have much significance as art, but like that of the movies, it is an important and significant part of the American scene. If it can be improved and if it develops better content, the taste and appreciation of the American public will also grow and improve. If not, any beneficial effect it may have will be, in the dis-

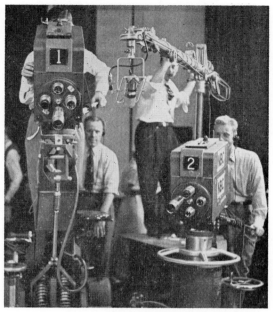

*Behind the Scenes in a
Television Studio.*

Courtesy, National Broadcasting Co.

consolate words of a former Director of Education to a big broadcasting concern, little but a "waif in the mounting radio storm."

One thing is certain, however: with the advent of all this radionic cacophony pouring out increasingly from loud speakers and television receivers in homes, hotels, trains, busses, any real contemplative activities on the part of the individual, such as reading, listening to music, or just plain thinking, becomes impossible. The two things which above all else seem characteristic of modern life are motion and noise. The American novelist William Faulkner thus describes the joys of a growing American town today:

> . . . But mostly and above all the radios and the automobiles, the juke boxes in the drugstore and the poolhall and the café and the bellowing amplifiers on the outside walls, not only of the sheet-music store but the army-and-navy supply store and both feed stores (that they might falter) somebody standing on a bench in the courthouse yard making a speech into one with a muzzle like a siege gun bolted to the top of an automobile, not to mention the ones which would be running in the apartments in the homes where the housewives and the maids made up the beds and swept and prepared to cook dinner so that nowhere inside the town's uttermost ultimate corporate rim should man, woman or

child, citizen or guest or stranger be threatened with one second of silence. . . .

TELEVISION

Although television is primarily a diversion for the eye, so much music, in one way or another, is inevitably a part of its production that the viewers are bound to have their listening habits and, probably, their tastes affected. The television presentation of solo or instrumental performances of opera are bound to differ in effect from performances in concert hall or theatre. In order to sustain the viewer's interest, the television cameras must constantly change focus from one artist or group to another; this disturbs the general impression received by a member of the audience and emphasizes the importance of viewing rather than of listening. In addition, what should be a broad, unified impression becomes a series of detached, often distorted, glimpses that do not make a coherent whole. Another abuse of music in television lies in its employment as what might be called a very inferior handmaiden—for instance, when it is used as a background for a picture accompanied by commentary. It is impossible to *attend* at the same time to all three—picture, talk, music. In such cases there is physical hearing, but no real listening.

LIST OF SUGGESTED MUSIC

Warsaw Concerto from the film *Suicide Squadron*   ADDINSELL

This music by an English composer shows how widespread is the traditional style of movie music; in every respect this out-Hollywoods Hollywood. Containing little but outworn clichés and stale repetitions of ideas that have been better expressed by others, it may be cited as an unfortunate example of bad music, the sort that passes as significant but really contains nothing of importance.

It may be asked in this connection just what the difference is between good and bad music. Simply this: good music has a significance that makes a deep impression on the hearer; it is original, well-wrought, shows evidence of skilled craftsmanship; it is ordered and unified to impress its message clearly and distinctively. Bad music, on the other hand, overstresses cheap and emotional material, often emphasizing the sex aspect; it is usually inartistically put together and simply a copy of other styles and mannerisms.

Music from the film *Alexander Nevsky* PROKOFIEV

This, on the other hand, is of a type that will probably remain a model of its kind for many years; excellently written, it is effective and exciting, especially in conjunction with the Eisenstein historical film for which it was composed.

A Lincoln Portrait COPLAND

This is a fine example of what may be done in the way of underscoring words to increase their significance in radio scripts.

TOPICS FOR DISCUSSION

Do you think that writing for the movies tends to weaken a composer's quality? Discuss the attitude that movies are made for the lower intelligence, and therefore, that movie music must be for lower intelligence.

Does radio music tend to be consistently poor? If so can you mention exceptions?

Is it possible that writing for films, since it must be for an exact duration of time, might stimulate the ingenuity of some composers?

Discuss the ultimate weakness of all film music—that it induces its hearers to be background-listeners rather than real listeners.

Composers

❧ ❧

PRONUNCIATION

Markings: ā in lāte, å in châotic, â in câre, ă in făt, ä in fär, à in làst, å in sofà; ē in mē, ê in rêturn, ĕ in mĕt, ĕ̃ in quiĕt, ẽ in uppẽr; g in get; ī in fīne, ĭ in tĭn; ĸ = ch in German *ach*; ṇ = ng, ɴ = ng in its effect (nasal) on the preceding vowel, but is not itself sounded; ō in nōte, ô in ōbey, ô in fôr (same sound as aw in saw), ŏ in nŏt, o̊ in so̊ft, ö (set lips as if to say oh, but then say ĕ as in mĕt, keeping the lips fixed in the first position); o͞o in scho͞ol, o͝o in wo͝ol; ᵵɦ in ᵵɦine; ū in tūne, ŭ in nŭt, û in bûrn, u̇ in su̇bmit, ü (set lips as if to say oo as in boot, but then say ee as in beet, keeping the lips in the first position); (′) indicates the heavily accented syllable, (′) indicates the syllable with secondary accent.

Adam de la Halle (ă·daɴ′ dü lä äl), *b.* Arras, 1240; *d.* 1287. A prominent trouvère; master of the chanson.

Albéniz (äl·bā′nēth), Issac, *b.* Camprodon, Spain, 1860; *d.* 1909. A Composer who reproduced the rhythms and other characteristics of Spanish popular music.

Arensky (à·rĕn′skē), Anton, *b.* Novgorod, Russia, 1861; *d.* 1906. A prominent composer-pianist of the Tchaikovskyian school.

Auric (ŏ′rĕck), Georges, *b.* Lodeve, France, 1899. A member of *Les Six,* who is best known for his film music.

Bach (bäĸ), Carl Philipp Emanuel, *b.* Weimar, Germany, 1714; *d.* 1750. Son of J. S. Bach; a pioneer of the sonata form and symphonic orchestration.

Bach, Johann Sebastian, *b.* Eisenach, Germany, 1685; *d.* 1750. The greatest composer of the polyphonic period and one of the greatest of all time.

Balakirev (bä'lä·kē'rĕf), Mily, *b.* Novgorod, Russia, 1837; *d.* 1910. A pianist and composer; a member of the Russian "Five."

Bartók (bär'tŏk'), Béla, *b.* Transylvania, 1881; *d.* 1945. Modern Hungarian nationalist composer and pianist.

Bax (băks), Arnold, *b.* London, 1883; *d.* 1953. English neo-Romantic composer who had Celtic sympathies.

Beethoven (bā'tō·vĕn), Ludwig van, *b.* Bonn, Germany, 1770; *d.* 1827. One of the greatest of all composers, especially of symphonic and chamber music. He welded the Classical and Romantic periods.

Bellini (bĕl·lē'nĕ), Vincenzo, *b.* Catania, Sicily, 1801; *d.* 1835. Opera composer.

Berg (bârg), Alban, *b.* Vienna, 1885; *d.* 1935. Modern atonal theorist and composer; pupil and follower of Schönberg.

Berlioz (bĕr'lē·ôs'), Hector, *b.* Cote St. Andre, France, 1803; *d.* 1869. A pioneer in program music.

Bernstein (bern'stīne), Leonard, *b.* Lawrence, Mass., 1918. A prominent figure in present-day American musical life; well-known as a conductor, lecturer, and composer.

Bizet (bē'ze'), Georges, *b.* Paris, 1838; *d.* 1875. Opera composer.

Bloch (blŏк), Ernest, *b.* Geneva, Switzerland, 1888; *d.* 1959. Composer whose music epitomizes the history and aspirations of the Jews.

Boccherini (bŏk'kä·rē'nĕ), Luigi, *b.* Lucca, Italy, 1743; *d.* 1805. Prolific composer, especially of chamber music.

Borodin (bŏr'ŏdĭn'), Alexander, *b.* St. Petersburg, 1833; *d.* 1887. One of the Russian "Five"; utilized folk music in his scores.

Boulez (boo·lāy), Pierre, *b.* Montbrison, France, 1925. A leading figure in the revolt against Schönberg's doctrines; advocated a return to a more constructive era in music.

Brahms (brämz), Johannes, *b.* Hamburg, Germany, 1833; *d.* 1897. One of the greatest composers of all time; combined romantic expression with classical form.

Britten (Brĭ'tĕn), Benjamin, *b.* Lowestoft, 1913. One of the most prolific of present-day English composers.

Bruch (brō͝oκ), Max, *b.* Cologne, Germany, 1838; *d.* 1920. A talented composer who excelled in choral music.

Bruckner (brō͝oκ′nēr), Anton, *b.* Ausfeden, Upper Austria, 1824; *d.* 1896. Symphonic composer of great facility.

Busoni (bōo·zō′nē), Ferruccio, *b.* Empoli, Italy, 1866; *d.* 1924. Pianist and composer of great influence on modern music; transcribed many of Bach's organ works for the piano.

Buxtehude (bō͝oks′tĕ hoo dĕ), Dietrich, *b.* Helsingborg, Sweden, 1637; *d.* 1707. Eminent organist and composer who influenced Bach's early career.

Byrd (bûrd), William, *b.* London, 1542; *d.* 1623. One of the greatest composers of Elizabethan madrigals.

Caccini (kă·chē′nē), Guilio, *b.* Rome, 1558; *d.* 1615. One of the pioneer opera composers. Collaborated with Peri to write *Dafne,* the first opera.

Carpenter (kär′pĕn·tēr), John Alden, *b.* Park Ridge, Ill., 1876; *d.* 1951. American composer successful in many forms.

Casella (kä·sĕl′lä), Alfredo, *b.* Turin, Italy, 1883; *d.* 1947. Prominent modern composer.

Chabrier (shăb·ryȧy), Alexis Emmanuel, *b.* Ambert, France, 1841; *d.* 1894. Active during the last quarter of the nineteenth century, this composer's works show great vivacity.

Chadwick (chăd′wĭk), George Whitefield, *b.* Lowell, Mass., 1854; *d.* 1931. American composer of the classical style.

Chaminade (shȧ′mē′nȧd′), Cecile, *b.* Paris, 1857; *d.* 1944. Composed in the lighter forms.

Charpentier (shȧr′pän tyā′), Gustave, *b.* Dieuzem Lorraine, 1860; *d.* 1956. Composer of the opera, *Louise.*

Chausson (shō′sôn′), Ernest, *b.* Paris, 1855; *d.* 1899. Pupil of César Franck; composer of great individuality.

Cherubini (kā′rōo·bē′nĕ), Luigi, *b.* Florence, Italy, 1760; *d.* 1842. A composer of the contrapuntal period, who was successful in both the operatic and sacred forms.

Chopin (shō′pän′), Frederic, *b.* Warsaw, Poland, 1810; *d.* 1849. The most individual and popular composer for the piano.

Copland (kŏp·länd'), Aaron, *b.* Brooklyn, N. Y., 1900. Composer and lecturer.

Corelli (kŏ·rĕl'lĕ), Arcangelo, *b.* Imola, Italy, 1653; *d.* 1713. Violinist and composer; founded violin style and technic.

Couperin (koō'pē·ràɴ'), François, *b.* Paris, 1668; *d.* 1733. Most eminent of a famous family of composers; his music is full of Baroque grace and charm.

Cui (kü·ē), César, *b.* Vilna, Russia, 1835; *d.* 1918. One of the Russian "Five," who is best known for his vocal compositions.

Czerny (chĕr'nĕ), Karl, *b.* Vienna, 1791; *d.* 1857. A pupil of Beethoven; eminent pianist and pedagogue.

Debussy (dē·bü'sē'), Claude, *b.* Paris, 1862; *d.* 1918. Founder of the Impressionist school and one of the most individualistic composers.

Delibes (dē lēb'), Leo, *b.* St. Germain-du-Val, France, 1836; *d.* 1891. Popular ballet composer.

Delius (dē'lĭ·ŭs), Frederick, *b.* Bradford, England, 1863; *d.* 1934. Outstanding English composer.

Des Prez (dē·prā'), Josquin, *b.* Burgundy, 1450?; *d.* 1521. A pioneer in vocal polyphonic style.

Daighliev (dyä·gē'lĕf), Sergei Pavlovich, *b.* Novgorod, Russia, 1872; *d.* 1929. Founder of the ballet which bore his name; commissioned the writing of many modern ballets, including many of Stravinsky's best works.

Dohnányi (dŏĸ·nän'yĕ), Ernst von, *b.* Pressburg, Hungary, 1877; *d.* 1960. Hungarian pianist, conductor, and composer. His compositions are conservative and individual in style and carry on the Romantic traditions of the nineteenth century, not the least attractive element being a tincture of Brahms's spirit.

Donizetti (dō'nĕ·dzĕt'tĕ), Gaetano, *b.* Bergamo, Italy, 1797; *d.* 1848. Popular opera composer.

Dukas (dü'käh'), Paul, *b.* Paris, 1865; *d.* 1935. French composer of considerable attainment, especially successful in the larger symphonic forms.

Dvořák (dvôr'zhäk), Anton, *b.* Mühlhausen, Bohemia, 1841; *d.* 1904. Leading Bohemian composer; lived several years in America.

Elgar (ĕl'gär), Edward, *b.* Worcester, England, 1857; *d.* 1934. The leading composer of modern England.

Falla (fä'yä), Manuel de, *b.* Cadiz, 1876; *d.* 1946. Spanish composer of opera and ballet; shows folk and nationalistic influences.

Foster (fŏs'tẽr), Stephen Collins, *b.* Pittsburgh, Pa., 1826; *d.* 1864. Creator of the American Negro popular song.

Franck (frängk), César, *b.* Liége, Belgium, 1822; *d.* 1890. Leading French composer.

Franz (fränts), Robert, *b.* Halle, Prussia, 1815; *d.* 1892. Master of German *lied*.

Gershwin (gûrsh'wĭn), George, *b.* Brooklyn, N. Y., 1898; *d.* 1937. A leading composer of American music, who never ever fully realized his aspirations to large-scale compositions.

Gibbons (gĭb'ŭnz), Orlando, *b.* Cambridge, 1583; *d.* 1625. A composer of madrigals.

Gilbert, William F., *b.* London, 1836; *d.* 1911. Part of the light opera team of Gilbert and Sullivan.

Glazunov (glä'zōō·nôf'), Alexander, *b.* St. Petersburg, 1865; *d.* 1936. Popular Russian composer.

Glinka (glĭng'kä), Michael, *b.* Smolensk, Russia, 1804; *d.* 1857. Pioneer Russian nationalistic composer.

Gluck (glōōk), Christoph Willibald von, *b.* Weidenwang, Upper Palatinate, 1714; *d.* 1787. An important operatic reformer.

Goldmark (gôlt'märk'), Karl, *b.* Keszthely, Hungary, 1830; *d.* 1915. Popular composer of many forms.

Gounod (gōō'nō'), Charles, *b.* Paris, 1818; *d.* 1893. Popular opera composer.

Grétry (grä'trẽ'), André Ernest, *b.* Liége, 1741; *d.* 1813. Important French opera composer.

Grieg (grēg), Edvard, *b.* Bergen, Norway, 1843; *d.* 1907. Outstanding Scandinavian composer.

Handel (hăn'd'l), George Frederic, *b.* Halle, Prussia, 1685; *d.* 1759. Well-known for his classical forms and styles, especially his oratorios.

Harris (hăr′ĭs), Roy, *b*. Oklahoma, 1898. Important American composer.

Haydn (hī′d′n), Franz Josef, *b*. Rohrau, Austria, 1732; *d*. 1809. Innovator of classical form; father of the symphony and sonata form.

Hindemith (hĭn′dĕ·mĭt), Paul, *b*. Hanau, Germany, 1895. Facile, modern composer.

Holst (hōlst), Gustav, *b*. Cheltenham, England, 1874; *d*. 1934. Modern British composer.

Honegger (hôn′ĕg′ēr), Arthur, *b*. Havre, 1892, of Swiss parentage; *d*. 1955. Lively exponent of advanced, piquant tastes. Enjoyed using counterpoint.

Humperdinck (hŏŏm′pēr·dĭngk), Engelbert, *b*. Bonn, Germany, 1854; *d*. 1921. A talented composer and follower of Wagner; famous for his opera *Hänsel und Gretel*.

Ippolitov-Ivanov (ēep·pŏ·lēet′·ŏff ēev·ŭn′·yŏff), Michael Michaelovich, *b*. Gatchina, 1859; *d*. 1935. Russian composer noted for his nationalistic operas and tone-poems.

Janáček (yän′·àh·chĕk), Leos, *b*. Hukvaldy, Moravia, 1854; *d*. 1928. Czech nationalist known for his operas on native themes.

Kodály (kō·dä′ē), Zoltán, *b*. Kecskemét, Hungary, 1882. Modern Hungarian composer and arranger of folk music.

Lassus (läs′sŏ), Roland De, *b*. Mons, Belgium, 1534?; *d*. 1594. Great master of sacred as well as secular polyphony.

Leoncavallo (lā′ŏn·kä·väl′lŏ), Ruggiero, *b*. Naples, 1858; *d*. 1919. Popular Italian opera composer.

Liszt (lĭst), Franz, *b*. Raiding, Hungary, 1811; *d*. 1886. World's greatest piano virtuoso and a composer successful in many forms, especially the symphonic poem.

Loeffler (lĕf′lēr), Charles Martin, *b*. Mühlhausen, Alsace, 1861; *d*. 1935. Alsatian-American composer in the modern style.

Lully (lü′lē′), Jean Baptiste, *b*. Florence, 1632; *d*. 1687. Important pioneer in opera; developed the overture and introduced the brass into the orchestra.

MacDowell (măk·dou'ĕl), Edward A., *b.* New York, 1861; *d.* 1908. Well-known American composer.

Mahler (mä'lēr), Gustav, *b.* Bohemia, 1860; *d.* 1911. Conductor and composer of symphonies, many of which are fantastic in conception.

Malipiero (mäl·ê·p'yā'rô), Francesco, *b.* Venice, 1882. Distinguished modern Italian composer.

Mascagni (mäs·kän'yê), Pietro, *b.* Leghorn, Italy, 1863; *d.* 1945. Popular composer of Italian opera.

Mason (mā's'n), Daniel Gregory, *b.* Brookline, Mass., 1873; *d.* 1953. Grandson of Lowell Mason and distinguished teacher and composer.

Mason, Lowell, *b.* Medfield, Mass., 1792; *d.* 1872. Pioneer American teacher and composer.

Massenet (mä's'nĕ'), Jules, *b.* Montaud, France, 1842; *d.* 1912. Popular composer of French opera.

Mendelssohn (mĕn'dĕl·sōn), Felix, *b.* Hamburg, 1809; *d.* 1847. Talented composer of many forms.

Meyerbeer (mī'ēr·bār), Giacomo, *b.* Berlin, 1791; *d.* 1864. Creator of spectacular and popular operas.

Milhaud (mēl'ō), Darius, *b.* Aix-en-Provence, France, 1892. One of the French group known as *Les Six.*

Monteverdi (mŏn'tä·vâr'dĭ), Claudio, *b.* Cremona, 1567; *d.* 1643. Pioneer of modern harmony and homophonic style.

Morley (môr'lĭ), Thomas, *b.* England, 1557; *d.* 1602. Well-known Elizabethan madrigalist.

Moussorgsky (mōō·sôrg'skê), Modest, *b.* Karev, Russia, 1839; *d.* 1881. Extremely nationalistic Russian composer.

Mozart (mō'tsärt), Wolfgang Amadeus, *b.* Salzburg, 1756; *d.* 1791. Perhaps the greatest natural genius music has ever known; a prolific composer throughout his short life.

Nicolai (nē'kô·lī), Otto, *b.* Königsberg, Germany, 1810; *d.* 1849. Gifted operatic composer.

Offenbach (ôf'ĕn·bäк), Jacques, *b.* Cologne, 1819; *d.* 1880. Popular composer of light operas.

Paderewski (pȧ'dĕ·rĕf'skĕ), Ignace Jan, *b.* Podolia, Poland, 1860; *d.* 1941. Renowned Polish pianist, composer, and statesman.

Paganini (pä'gä·nē'nĕ), Nicoló, *b.* Genoa, Italy, 1782; *d.* 1840. One of the greatest violinists in history; composer of many melodies which were later transcribed by others.

Palestrina (pä'lȧs·trē'nä), Giovanni Pierluigi da, *b.* Palestrina near Rome, 1525; *d.* 1594. The greatest and most important composer of the vocal polyphonic period.

Pergolesi (pēēr·gō·lĕh'zēē), Giovanni Battista, *b.* Jesi, Italy, 1710; *d.* 1736. Italian composer whose works became the prototypes of the later *opera buffa.*

Peri (pā'rĕ), Jacopo, *b.* Florence, 1561; *d.* 1633. The composer of *Dafne,* the first opera, in collaboration with Caccini.

Piston, Walter, *b.* Rockland, Me., 1894; *d.* 1953. Harvard professor of music; the composer of many orchestral works.

Poulenc (pōō'·länk), Francis, *b.* Paris, 1899. Prominent member of *Les Six,* whose style combines classical and caricatural elements.

Prokofiev (prō·kō'fē·ĕf), Serge, *b.* Russia, 1891; *d.* 1953. Prominent Russian modernistic composer.

Puccini (pōō·chē'nĕ), Giacomo, *b.* Lucca, Italy, 1858; *d.* 1924. Popular Italian operatic composer.

Purcell (pûr'sĕl), Henry, *b.* London, 1659; *d.* 1695. One of England's greatest composers.

Rachmaninoff (räк·mä'nĕ·nôf), Sergei, *b.* Onega, Russia, 1873; *d.* 1943. Outstanding composer-pianist.

Rameau (rȧ'mō'), Jean Philippe, *b.* Dijon, France, 1683; *d.* 1764. One of the important men in the development of French opera; wrote more than twenty operas.

Ravel (rȧ'vĕl'), Maurice, *b.* Ciboure, France, 1875; *d.* 1937. Modern composer of many works in the manner of Debussy.

Reger (rāy·gĕr), Max, *b.* Brand, Germany, 1873; *d.* 1916. German composer of late Romantic period; used massive effects which, unfortunately, often become turgid and tiresome.

Reigger (rĕg·ger), Wallingford, *b.* Albany, Ga., 1885; *d.* 1961. For many years before his death the acknowledged "dean" of American composers.

Respighi (rĕs·pē'gê), Ottorino, *b.* Bologna, Italy, 1879; *d.* 1936. Accomplished modern Italian composer.

Rheinberger (rīn'bĕrg'ēr), Josef, *b.* Liechtenstein, Germany, 1839; *d.* 1901. Eminent organist, teacher, and composer.

Rimsky-Korsakov (rĭm'skê·kôr'sà·kŏf), Nikolai, *b.* Novgorod, Russia, 1844; *d.* 1908. A leading Russian composer with a distinct feeling for the Oriental style.

Rossini (rôs·sē'nê), Gioacchino, *b.* Pesaro, Italy, 1792; *d.* 1868. Popular Italian opera composer.

Rubinstein (rōō'bĭn·shtīn), Anton, *b.* Bessarabia, 1829; *d.* 1894. Brilliant pianist and popular composer.

Saint-Saëns (săN'säNs'), Camille, *b.* Paris, 1835; *d.* 1921. Distinguished French composer.

Sarasate (sä'rä·sä'tâ), Pablo de, *b.* Pamplona, Spain, 1844; *d.* 1908. Great violinist and minor composer.

Scarlatti (skär·lät'tê), Alessandro, *b.* Trapani, Sicily, 1660; *d.* 1725. Pioneer in opera; advanced monodic composition.

Scarlatti, Domenico, *b.* Naples, 1685; *d.* 1757. Son of Alessandro; developed harpsichord style and technique.

Schmitt (shmĭt), Florent, *b.* Blamont, France, 1870; *d.* 1958. Modern and original French composer, trained in the impressionistic school.

Schönberg (shön'bĕrκ), Arnold, *b.* Vienna, 1874; *d.* 1951. One of the outstanding representatives of extreme modernism in music; founder and leading exponent of atonalism.

Schubert (shōō'bĕrt), Franz, *b.* Vienna, 1797; *d.* 1828. One of the great natural geniuses of music; had a prodigious output throughout his tragically short life.

Schumann (shōō'män), Robert, *b.* Zwickau, Saxony, 1810; *d.* 1856. Important early romanticist; possessed novel ideas as creator, interpreter, and critic of music.

Scriabin (skryà·bĭn'), Alexander, *b.* Moscow, 1872; *d.* 1915. Important Russian composer with unusual and often fantastic ideas.

Shostakovich (shŏs·tă·kō'vĭch), Dmitri, *b.* 1906. Russian composer—

neo-Romantic, original—who was one of the Leningrad group which followed Rimsky-Korsakov. He has written both symphonies and operas.

Sibelius (sĭ·bā′lĭ·o͞os), Jean, *b.* Tavastehus, Finland, 1865; *d.* 1957. Well-known and extremely talented nationalistic Finnish composer.

Sinding (sĭn′dĭng), Christian, *b.* Kongsberg, Norway, 1856; *d.* 1941. Well-known Scandinavian composer.

Smetana (smĕ′tä·nä), Bedrich, *b.* Leitomischl, Bohemia, 1824; *d.* 1884. Distinguished Bohemian composer.

Sousa (so͞o·sȧ), John Philip, *b.* Washington, D. C., 1854; *d.* 1932. The great American bandmaster and composer was best known for marches.

Spohr (shpōr), Louis, *b.* Brunswick, Germany, 1784; *d.* 1859. Violinist, teacher, composer.

Strauss (shtrous), Johann, Jr., *b.* Vienna, 1825; *d.* 1899. The "waltz king" who wrote over 400 waltzes.

Strauss, Richard, *b.* Munich, 1864; *d.* 1949. Distinguished in many forms, especially eminent as a song and symphonic composer.

Stravinsky (strȧ·vĭn′skė), Igor, *b.* near Petrograd, 1882. One of the leading modernists, especially significant as a composer of ballets and symphonic works.

Taylor (tā′lēr), Deems, *b.* New York, 1885. Distinguished American composer of operas and symphonic works.

Tchaikovsky (chī·kôf′skė), Peter Ilich, *b.* Votkinsk, Russia, 1840; *d.* 1893. Eminent Romantic Russian composer.

Thomas (tô′mä′), Ambroise, *b.* Metz, 1811; *d.* 1896. Successful composer of popular French operas.

Vaughan Williams (vôn wĭl′yȧmz), Ralph, *b.* Gloucestershire, England, 1872; *d.* 1958. Individual and talented leading British composer.

Verdi (vâr′dē), Giuseppe, *b.* LeRoncole, Parma, 1813; *d.* 1901. Greatest Italian opera composer, master of vocal melodic writing.

Vivaldi (vē·väl′dē), Antonio, *b.* Venice, 1669; *d.* 1741. Violinist and composer of distinction.

Wagner (väg′nẽr), Richard, *b*. Leipzig, 1813; *d*. 1883. The greatest dramatic composer of all time, replacing the old-fashioned opera with music drama.

Walton (wall′ton), William, *b*. Oldenham, 1902. A leading English composer.

Weber (vä′bẽr), Carl Maria von, *b*. Oldenburg, Germany, 1786; *d*. 1826. German composer, especially important in the field of opera; influenced Wagner's early career.

Webern (veb′ern), Anton, *b*. Mittersill, 1883; *d*. 1945. Important pupil of Schönberg; composed in twelve-note system.

Weill (vïel), Kurt, *b*. Dessau, Germany, 1900; *d*. 1950. Best known for his combination of modern and jazz idioms; famous for a number of theatrical works.

Weinberger (vīn′bĕrк·ẽr), Jaromir, *b*. Prague, 1896. Writer of picturesque operas, the most famous of which is *Schwanda*.

Widor (vē′dôr′), Charles Marie, *b*. Lyons, France, 1844; *d*. 1937. Distinguished French organist, teacher, and composer.

Wieniawski (vyĕ′nyäf·skẽ), Henri, *b*. Lubin, Poland, 1835; *d*. 1880. Brilliant violinist and composer for the violin.

Wolf (vȯlf), Hugo, *b*. Styria, 1860; *d*. 1903. One of the immortal masters of German *lied*.

Wolf-Ferrari (vȯlf′-fĕr·rä′rẽ), Ermanno, *b*. Venice, 1876; *d*. 1948. Popular opera and song composer.

Glossary

❧ ❦

This glossary is not meant to be a detailed dictionary, but a list of terms that music-lovers are likely to encounter.

Absolute music. Music which is sufficient in itself and does not depend on literary or other associations. (*See* Chapter 12.)

A capella (It. in church style). Music written for unaccompanied singing.

Accelerando (It.). Accelerate, to quicken gradually. Its opposite is *ritardando* or *rallentando*.

Accidental. A chromatic sign not found in the signature but introduced in the course of a piece.

Accompaniment. A part added to the leading melody or part to support or enrich it.

Acoustics. The branch of physics which studies the phenomena and laws of sound; the sound-affecting properties of an auditorium.

Adagio (It. slow, leisurely). A slow rate of movement. (*See* Scale of Speeds at end of Glossary.)

Ad libitum (L. at will). The performer may employ a tempo or an expression that suits his pleasure; sometimes used to signify that a passage may be omitted if desired.

Air. A melody of sufficient interest to stand alone without accompaniment; a self-contained solo movement from a larger work.

Alla breve (It.). An expression which indicates that the music is to be performed twice as fast as its notation would suggest.

571

Allargando (It.). Gradually growing slower and broader in time.

Allegretto (It.). Moderately fast; diminution of *allegro*. (*See* Scale of Speeds at end of Glossary.)

Allegro (It. merry, quick). A brisk rate of movement sometimes qualified by *non troppo* (not too much), *assai* (very), or *molto* (much). (*See* Scale of Speeds at end of Glossary.)

Andante (It. going, moving). A moderately slow rate of movement which implies moving along or flowing; sometimes qualified by *sostenuto* (sustained) or *con moto* (faster). Commonly applied to the slow movement of a sonata or symphony. (*See* Scale of Speeds at end of Glossary.)

Animato (It.). Spirited, with animation.

Anthem. A sacred choral composition of moderate length.

Antiphonal. Music in which groups of performers answer each other; most often applied to choral music.

Appogiatura (It. leaning). Usually, a note of varying length foreign to the harmony it introduces and into which it subsequently resolves.

Arco (L. bow). A direction for bowed instruments to resume bowing after a *pizzicato* (plucked) passage.

Aria (It. air). A composition for solo voice and instrumental accompaniment, often taken from an opera or oratorio.

Arpa (It.). Harp.

Arpeggio (It.). A chord in which the notes are played one after the other instead of all together.

Art Music. "Created" music.

A tempo (It. in time). At the original rate of speed; used after a change of pace.

Atonal. Having no fixed key; not centering on any single key.

Ayre. Normal seventeenth-century spelling of "air"; a song for one voice with instrumental accompaniment.

Ballet. A dance composition performed as an artistic unit employing a dramatic thread or story. (*See* Chapter 42.)

Bar. A vertical line dividing measures on the staff and indicating that the strong accent falls on the note or notes immediately following. The proper accent on the strong beat creates the rhythmic pulse in music.

Baroque. Generally used to signify the style of art which prevailed during the seventeenth and part of the eighteenth centuries, characterized by the use of grandiose and magniloquent forms. By association it is applied to music of the same time, especially to Bach. (*See* Chapter 36.)

Bass. The lowest register in voice or instruments; the lowest part of a musical composition.

Batterie (Fr.) or Battery. The group of percussion instruments in the orchestra.

Beat. In acoustics: the sudden reinforcement of sound, occurring at regular intervals and produced by the interference of sound waves of slightly different periods of vibration. In music: the regularly recurring and periodically accented pulse which constitutes a unit of measurement; in practical use, the term refers to the time value of the basic unit within a measure (such as the quarter note in 4/4 time) or the motion of the hand, baton, and so on, used in marking such units.

Ben, bene (It.). Well.

Benmarcato (It.). Well marked.

Berceuse (Fr.). A cradle song or lullaby.

Binary. A two-part form. A-B. (*See* Chapter 15.)

Bouree. A dance, French or Spanish in origin, in rapid tempo (2/4 or 4/4) frequently employed as a movement of the suite.

Brass Winds. The section of the orchestra which includes instruments made of brass or other metals.

Cacophony. The dissonant effect produced by sounds which are combined in such a way that they are displeasing to the ear.

Cadence. The series of notes or chords through which a melody or harmony is brought to a temporary or final close. Various types of cadences have varying degrees of finality; the greatest is the authentic or perfect cadence—a progression of the chord on the dominant to the chord on the tonic (V-I).

Cadenza. An extended ornamental section in a free, improvisatory style usually inserted near the end of a work to give the player an opportunity for displaying his virtuosity.

Canon. A form in which a melody begins in one part and is exactly copied by one or more parts, each at a given distance.

Cantibile (It.). Singable; in a singing style.

Canata. Originally a sung work, it now means a secular or sacred work for soloist(s) and chorus, usually with orchestral accompaniment.

Cantilena (It. a little song). A tuneful, songlike flowing passage.

Cantus firmus (L. fixed song). A given melody or plainsong tune to which other parts are to be set according to rule.

Caprice (It.). Name given to short piano pieces of a capricious nature by nineteenth-century composers.

Cembalo (It.). The Italian and German name for the harpsichord.

Chaconne. An instrumental piece consisting of a series of variations over a ground bass. Differs from the traditional *passaglia* in that the bass theme may occur in an upper voice.

Chamber music. Compositions written for a concert room, to be played by a small musical organization. (*See* Chapter 21.)

Chorale. A hymn tune of the German Protestant Church, slow and dignified; sometimes the name is applied to a choral group.

Chord. A simultaneously sounding of three or more notes of different pitch.

Chorus. A body of singers or a composition for them.

Chromatic. Largely including, or moving by, half tones. Opposite of diatonic. Also used to mean passages containing notes foreign to a given key.

Classicism. The style of composition in which the strongest emphasis is laid on formal beauty and feeling.

Clavichord. A precursor of the piano; a keyboard instrument in which the strings are struck by small brass tangents operated by the keys.

Clavier. A word used colloquially for whatever keyboard instrument was fashionable; at one time it meant the harpsichord.

Clef. A sign (formerly, a letter) put at the start of a line of music to fix the name and pitch of one note from which all others are reckoned.

Coda. A concluding phrase or section ending a piece.

Concert overture. A separate orchestral piece which is usually in sonata form and frequently programmatic.

Concerto. A work for one or more soloists and orchestra.

Concord. Sounds which by themselves give a sense of completion and repose.

Continuo (sometimes called Thorough Bass). The accepted manner of accompanying nearly all music during the seventeenth and eighteenth centuries. The composer wrote his bass part with figures which showed the harmonies to be employed, in a sort of musical shorthand. These were carried out by a cembalo, usually a harpsichord or organ, which provided a gentle harmonic background to the whole. To insure a good foundation, the bass line was usually strengthened by a violoncello, viola da gamba, or other suitable instrument.

Counterpoint. Refers to a type of composition with various simultaneously sounding musical lines. It is also known as polyphony.

Countersubject. In a fugue, the counterpoint is stated in continuation of the subject, while the answer is being given in another voice. (*See* Chapter 17.)

Courante. Early French dance in triple measure and lively tempo. Frequently found in the classical suite, as the second of its four cornerstone movements.

Crescendo. *See* Dynamics.

Czardas. A popular Hungarian dance consisting of the contrasting *lassu* (slow and impassioned) and *friss* (lively).

Da capo, D.C. (It. from the head). Repeat from the beginning.
Da capo al fine. Repeat from beginning to end.
Da capo al segno. Repeat to the sign (:S:).

Decrescendo. *See* Dynamics.

Descant. The first attempts at polyphony with contrary motion in the parts. The opposite of *organum* in which parallel motion was the rule. Now used to mean a free part added to a principal melody.

Development. The building up of the thematic material in a work after the theme has been expounded. (*See* Sonata form.)

Diatonic. Pertaining to, or designating, the standard major and minor scales made up of tones and semitones.

Diminuendo. *See* Dynamics.

Dissonance. A term used to describe the incomplete effect produced by certain intervals as against the completed effects of others.

Dominant. The fifth tone of the major or minor scale.

Dominant chord. A chord which has the dominant note as its root (dominant triad, dominant seventh, dominant ninth).

Duet, duo. Composition for two performers.

Dynamics. Of, or pertaining to, the scheme of tonal power used in interpreting music. The following abbreviations are in common use for designating various volumes of tone.

fff	*fortissimo assai*	As loud as possible
ff	*fortissimo*	Very loud
f	*forte*	Loud
mf	*mezzoforte*	Moderately loud
mp	*mezzopiano*	Moderately soft
p	*piano*	Soft
pp	*pianissimo*	Very soft
ppp	*pianissimo assai*	As soft as possible
fp } *pf* }	*forte piano* or *piano forte*	A quick transition from loud to soft or soft to loud
sfz	*sforzando*	A sudden increase of tone applied to single notes
rfz } *rf* }	*rinforzando*	A sudden increase of tone, applied to musical phrases
cresc	*crescendo*	A gradual increase of tone
dim *decresc*	*dimuendo* } *decrescendo* }	A gradual decrease of tone

Enharmonic chords. Chords differing in notation but alike in sound.

Ensemble. A term applied to any group of executants and to the art or effect of their playing or singing together.

Entr'acte. Interval between acts; hence, a light instrumental composition or short ballet interpolated between acts of a theatrical performance.

Episode. Generally applied to those portions of a musical work which connect sections of greater significance. In the fugue, it represents a digression from the principal theme interpolated between the statements of the theme. In large works such as symphonies and quartets, episodes may be said to be synonymous with bridge passages, that is, perform the functions of furnishing musical continuity between main theme sections.

Etude (Fr. study). Frequently designed for overcoming particular technical difficulties; many are intended for concert performance.

Euphony. The acoustical effect produced by sounds combined so that they please the ear.

Exposition. The first section of a movement in sonata form in which the themes are exposed for the first time; synonymous with Statement. (*See* Sonata Form.)

Fantasia. A composition free in form and feeling.

Figure. An easily recognizable form with a short pattern of notes. Synonymous with motive.

Finale. The last movement of an extended work; sometimes given the title of a separate piece; also the concluding portion of an operatic act.

Flat. The character (♭) which lowers the pitch of a note before which is placed by a semitone.

Folk Music. Music which comes from the people and becomes traditional with them. (*See* Chapter 15.)

Form. The element in music which is concerned with its scheme or architectural design.

Fugue (flight). A contrapuntal composition which is made of a characteristic sectional treatment, which is an imitation of at least one main subject or phrase.

Fuoco. (It. Con fuoco: with fire). Forcefully and fast.

Galant (Fr.). The elegantly light style of the Rococo as distinguished from the more elaborate style of the Baroque.

Galliard. An early dance in triple meter with elaborate and rapid steps.

Gavotte. An early French dance in strongly marked quadruple

time, beginning on the third beat; frequently employed as a
movement of the classical suite.

Gigue. Developed and idealized from the sixteenth-century Irish
or English jig; an early dance in rapid tempo and in triple or
compound time. In the classical suite, it is usually the last movement.

Glee. An English invention of the eighteenth century; an unaccompanied piece for (usually) four males.

Glissando (Fr. to slide). The performance of very rapid scales by
a sliding movement.

Grace note. A non-essential, ornamental note used as an embellish-
ment, generally designated in small notation.

Grave (It.). Slowly and solemnly.

Gregorian. The form of liturgical chanting codified during the time
of Pope Gregory the Great (590-604) and widely used ever
since, notably in the Roman Catholic Church. (See Chapter 35.)

Harmonics (Harmonic overtones). Additional notes produced
when a fundamental sound is generated; gives the note its characteristic sound. Flutelike tones produced on a stringed instrument by touching the string lightly with the finger.

Harmonization. The arrangement of tones to create chordal harmony.

Harmony. The science of manipulating chords; applied to music
produced by such manipulation.

Harpsichord. The chief keyboard instrument of the seventeenth
and eighteenth centuries.

Homophony. Music in which one part stands out and the others
accompany in chord effects. The music is formed vertically, as
opposed to polyphony where the parts move horizontally.

Imitation. The contrapuntal device of employing in one voice, a
melodic or rhythmic figure which has been stated in another.

Incidental music. Music played during the incidents and intervals
of a dramatic work.

Instrumentation. The choice of instruments for a composition.

Intermezzo. A short piece intended or suitable for an interlude.

Interval. The pitch distance between two tones.

Intonation. Truth of pitch; the beginning of chanting in plainsong.

Introduction. A preliminary section.

Kapellmeister (Ger. chapel music). Generally applied to the director of music in eighteenth-century choirs; used in Germany
to mean a conductor at the theatre or concert hall. (Sometimes
called *Capellmeister*.)

Key. The particular system of tones and semitones constituting a
scale and built on a selected tone (the *tonic*). The keynote or
tonic thus formed becomes the first note of the scale and becomes the name of the key. The term is also used for the black
and white digitals of the piano.

Larghetto (It.). Slightly faster than *largo*.

Largo (It.). Slowly and with dignity.

Ledger Line. A short line for scoring notes above or below the
staff.

Legato (It. bound). Applied to the smooth joining of notes; opposite of *staccato*.

Leitmotiv (Ger. leading theme). In dramatic music, an identifying
theme associated with a particular character, mood, or situation,
and usually accompanying its reappearance.

Lento (It.). Slow. (*See* Scale of Speeds at end of Glossary.)

Libretto (It. booklet). The book of words of an extended choral
composition, such as an opera, cantata, or oratorio.

Lied (Ger. song). Strictly used for the great number of art songs
by German composers.

Madrigal. A secular, contrapuntal vocal work. (*See* Chapter 15.)

Major. As applied to scales, a pattern of seven steps (eight sounds),
consisting of tones and semitones, the latter occurring between
the third and fourth and seventh and eighth steps. A major interval is greater than a minor interval. A major key is based on a
major scale.

Marcato (It.). Marked, that is, each note is to be played with emphasis.

Mass. Musical setting of the Roman Catholic Eucharistic service.

Master singer. German member of a medieval music guild; successor to the Minnesinger.

Mazurka. A Polish national dance in triple meter and moderate tempo. Frequently it has strong accents on the second beat.

Measure. A rhythmical unit of two or more beats.

Melody. Any agreeable and familiar series of notes.

Meter. Any specific scheme of rhythm, which is determined by the number and length of the notes it contains.

Mezzoforte (It.). Moderately loud. (*See* Dynamics.)

Mezzopiano (It.) Moderately soft. (*See* Dynamics.)

Minnesinger (Ger. love singer). The German counterpart of the troubadour—an aristocratic poet-musician of the Middle Ages.

Minor. As applied to scales, the pattern of seven steps consisting of tones and semitones, the latter either between the second and third, fifth and sixth, and seventh and eighth steps (harmonic form), or between the second and third and seventh and eighth steps ascending, and the second and third and fifth and sixth steps descending (melodic form).

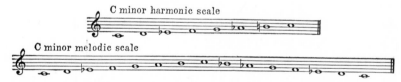

C minor harmonic scale

C minor melodic scale

Minuet. An old French dance in dignified 3/4 rhythm. It is conventionally found as the third movement of the classical symphony. As an art form it is usually a double minuet with contrasted sections, the first section repeated after the second (trio).

Mode. Strictly, any mode or manner of arranging tones and semitones to form a scale. Generally refers to the ancient scales used for both religious and folk music.

Modulation. The process of going from one key to another.

Motet. An unaccompanied choral composition based on a sacred Latin text; originally used in the liturgy of the Roman Catholic Church.

Motive. A brief theme or figure, either an integral part of a larger theme or the germinal idea from which the theme develops.

Movement. A division complete in itself, forming part of an extended work.

Music drama. Wagner's name for his operas.

Mute. A mechanical means for damping tone resonance.

Natural. The character (♮) which contradicts a sharp or flat.

Nocturne. Usually a piece with subdued or poetic feeling.

Note. The written or printed symbol for a tone.

Nuance. A shade of difference in tone color, tempo, or a degree of force.

Obligato (It.). An accessory part written for a particular instrument—for example, a violin part added to the piano accompaniment of a song.

Octave. A series of eight consecutive diatonic tones; also the interval between the first and eighth of such a series.

Opera. A musical drama sung to the accompaniment of an orchestra.

Opus. A word conventionally used by composers to number their works.

Oratorio. The sacred counterpart of an opera, usually not presented in the form of a theatrical production.

Orchestration. *See* Instrumentation.

Organ point. A tone sustained in one part (usually the bass) while harmonics are executed in the other parts.

Organum. The earliest attempts at harmonic or polyphonic music in which two or more parts progressed in paralleled motion (fifths, fourths, and octaves).

Overtones. *See* Harmonics.

Overture. An instrumental prelude to a choral work. *See also* Concert Overture.

Passacaglia. An early Italian dance in triple time and stately movement—with a ground bass, also describes an instrumental composition in this form.

Pavan. A slow, stately dance of Spanish or Italian origin.

Phrase. A musical clause composed of two or more measures.

Piano (It.). Softly. *See* Dynamics.

Pianissimo. Very softly.

Pizzicato (It.). Plucked.

Plainsong. The music of the early Christian church based on modal scales. Rhythm and tempo were governed by word accent and they were sung in unison; often used as a synonym for Gregorian Chant.

Polka. A lively round dance in 2/4 meter; originally a nineteenth-century Bohemian peasant dance.

Polonaise. A dance of Polish origin in 3/4 meter and moderate, animated tempo.

Polyphony. *See* Counterpoint.

Portamento. A smooth gliding from one tone to another, more deliberate than *legato*, since intermediate tones are actually sounded.

Prelude. An introductory section or movement. A choral prelude is a polyphonic instrumental treatment of a chorale. The prelude to an opera is usually called the overture.

Prestissimo (It.). Very fast.

Program Music. Music based on some scheme of literary or associative values, evoked by means of sound.

Quartet. Group of four executants or the music they perform.

Quintet. Group of five executants or the music they perform.

Rallentando (It.). Synonymous with *ritard*.

Recapitulation. The third section of a movement in sonata form, which presents the themes again.

Register. Section of an instrument's compass, characterized by a distinctive tonal quality.

Requiem. Mass or service for the dead; a memorial choral work.

Resolution. The process of discord progressing to concordance.

Rhapsody. A declamatory piece in free form.

Rhythm. The regular recurrence of like features in a composition; the organization of time elements of music.

Ripeno (It.). The full parts played in concert by the whole orchestra.

Ritard, ritardando (It.). Gradual slowing of tempo.

Rococo. The florid, ornamental style which characterized the eighteenth century.

Romanticism. A style of composition which places strong emphasis on the personal expression of poetic sentiment.

Round. A short, unaccompanied vocal canon.

Rubato (It.). Time borrowed in one part of a phrase is replaced in another part; a characteristic element of most romantic music.

Saraband. A stately dance of Spanish or Oriental origin which has two sections, slow tempo, and triple meter. It is the slowest movement of the suite.

Scale. A succession of tones which is used as the basic material for writing a piece; developed from the modes.

Scherzo. A type of third-movement form; introduced into the symphony by Beethoven.

Score. The parts of the various voices or instruments laid out beneath each other.

Semitone. A half-tone.

Sequence. The successive repetition of a melodic figure at different pitch levels.

Serenade. Applied to music suitable for performance in the open air.

Sextet. A composition for six executants or the music they perform.

Sharp. The character (♯) which raises the pitch of a note by a semitone.

Signature. The signs set at the head of the staff at the beginning of a piece of music.

Signs. Certain symbols are commonly used by composers for conveying performing directions. Those most frequently used are:

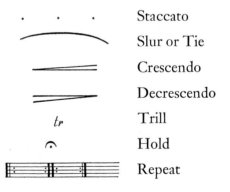

. . .	Staccato
⌢	Slur or Tie
⟨	Crescendo
⟩	Decrescendo
tr	Trill
⌢	Hold
𝄇 𝄆	Repeat

Sonata form. The first-movement form. A sonata is a whole work for one or more soloists, in several movements, each with its own form. (*See* Chapter 17.)

Sostenuto (It.). Sustained.

Staccato (It.). Detached or separated; in performance, the notes or chords are abruptly disconnected.

Staff or Stave. The five parallel lines used in modern notation.

Statement. *See* Exposition.

String Quartet. Two violins, viola, and cello or the music for these four instruments.

Style. A characteristic manner of expressing ideas.

Subject. A tune or theme.

Suite. A set of pieces either centering on some general subject or made up of contrasting or associated ideas.

Symphony. A sonata for orchestra.

Syncopation. A displacement or shifting of the normal beat, accent, or rhythm of a piece of music.

Technic, technique. Mechanical training, skill, dexterity.

Temperament. Systems of tuning in which the intervals deviate from the acoustically correct intervals derived from physics.

Tempo. Time; commonly used to mean pace.

Ternary. Three sections; A—B—A form.

Tessitura (It.). The position of a passage in the compass of the instrument or voice.

Theme. A tune or subject.

Timbre. Characteristic tonal color.

Timpani. Kettledrums.

Toccata. A piece designed to display brilliance of execution.

Tonic. The keynote of a scale.

Tonic Chord. A chord with the tonic note as its root.

Transition. Passages which lead from one principal idea to another.

Transpose. To put into a different pitch.

Tremolo (It.). The quick reiteration of the same tone on stringed instruments; imitated on the piano by rapid alternation of a tone and its octave.

Triad. A three-note chord—root, third, fifth.

Trill. An ornament consisting of the rapid alternation of a given
note with the major or minor above it.

Trio. Three performers or the music they perform. The middle,
contrasting section of a minuet or scherzo.

Troubadour. Aristocratic minstrel in medieval France, *circa* 1100-
1300.

Trouvere. The northern French counterpart of the troubadour.

Unison. A tone of the same pitch as a given tone; a higher or lower
octave of the same tone.

Variation. A new presentation of a musical idea.

Vibrato (It.). Slight fluctuation of pitch produced on stringed instruments or in the voice to increase the emotional effect of the
sounds produced.

Virtuoso. A superlatively equipped executant.

Vivace. Vivaciously.

Whole-tone Scale. A scale moving by full tones.

Wood wind. A generic term for the wind instruments of the orchestra.

A SCALE OF SPEEDS

Largo ⎱   Lento ⎱ —Andante—Allegretto—Moderato—Allegro ⎱ —Presto—Prestissimo
Grave ⎰ —Adagio ⎰   Vivace ⎰

Slow   Fast

Index